AFTER THE
MIRACLE

Also by Max Wallace

In the Name of Humanity

The American Axis

Muhammad Ali's Greatest Fight

AFTER THE MIRACLE

THE POLITICAL CRUSADES OF HELEN KELLER

⠁⠋⠞⠑⠗ ⠞⠓⠑
⠍⠊⠗⠁⠉⠇⠑

MAX WALLACE

GRAND CENTRAL

New York   Boston

Grand Central Publishing
Hachette Book Group
1290 Avenue of the Americas, New York, NY 10104
grandcentralpublishing.com
twitter.com/grandcentralpub

First Edition: April 2023

Grand Central Publishing is a division of Hachette Book Group, Inc. The Grand Central Publishing name and logo is a trademark of Hachette Book Group, Inc.

The publisher is not responsible for websites (or their content) that are not owned by the publisher.

The Hachette Speakers Bureau provides a wide range of authors for speaking events. To find out more, go to hachettespeakersbureau.com or email HachetteSpeakers@hbgusa.com.

Library of Congress Cataloging-in-Publication Data
Names: Wallace, Max, author.
Title: After the miracle : the political crusades of Helen Keller / Max Wallace.
Description: First edition. | New York : Grand Central Publishing, 2023. | Includes bibliographical references and index.
Identifiers: LCCN 2022053111 | ISBN 9781538707685 (hardcover) | ISBN 9781538707708 (ebook)
Subjects: LCSH: Keller, Helen, 1880-1968. | Deafblind people—United States—Biography. | Deafblind women—United States—Biography. | Political activists—United States—Biography. | Women political activists—United States—Biography. | Deafblind women—Political activity—United States. | Keller, Helen, 1880-1968—Political and social views. | Keller, Helen, 1880-1968—Political activity.
Classification: LCC HV1624.K4 W36 2023 | DDC 362.4/1092 [B]—dc23/eng/20221107
LC record available at https://lccn.loc.gov/2022053111

ISBNs: 9781538707685 (hardcover), 9781538707708 (ebook)

Printed in the United States of America

LSC-C

Printing 1, 2023

In memory of
my mother, Phyllis Bailey, who always fought the good fight
and
my niece, Hannah Wallace, whose spirit lives on

Contents

Part Three
HELEN AND THE REDS

Part Four
REWRITING HISTORY

Prologue

In February 1959, four months shy of her seventy-ninth birthday, Helen Keller received a letter from a civil rights activist named George Houser. He was writing to enlist her support for a cause that he knew she held dear. During a predawn raid three years earlier, South African authorities had rounded up scores of dissidents organizing against the brutal apartheid regime that saw millions of non-white citizens oppressed by a dominant white minority. Among the figures charged with high treason—and now facing the death penalty—was an activist named Nelson Mandela, a man still largely unknown even in his own country.

Years later, the fight against apartheid would emerge as a liberal cause célèbre, which saw an array of high-profile figures speak out against the racist system. But in 1959, much of the world was still firmly mired in the Cold War, and the South Africa Treason Trial was inextricably tied to an ideology that had served as a political bogeyman for most of the past decade. Mandela and the other defendants had been charged under the Suppression of Communism Act, and many Americans were still afraid to associate themselves with any progressive cause—let alone one that carried the explicit taint of Communism.

In fact, Helen herself had publicly stood up to the Red-baiting tactics of Joseph McCarthy a few years earlier and subsequently faced intense pressure from her longtime employer, the American Foundation for the Blind, who suggested that her outspoken political beliefs were jeopardizing her reputation and endangering the cause that she had worked for all her life.

Now, the South African legal defense committee was running out of the funds it desperately needed to fight the case, and Houser believed an endorsement from one of the world's most admired women could provide a much-needed boost. She was still haunted by the nearly three months she had spent in South Africa eight years earlier, where she had been horrified at the squalor and segregation that painfully reminded her of the Jim Crow system that was still very much alive in her home state of Alabama.

By this time, most Americans had forgotten that Helen was once a radical socialist firebrand who had used her celebrity to crusade against the oppression of women, the exploitation of workers, the crimes of Nazi Germany, and the indignities of Jim Crow while extolling the merits of revolution. Many preferred to think of her as the "inspirational" six-year-old deafblind girl who had learned to communicate thanks to a miraculous teacher. If Helen acceded to the committee's request and agreed to lend her name to a cause explicitly linked with Communism, there was a very real risk that the saintly image those around her had worked so hard to cultivate could be shattered. It could perhaps even derail the ongoing negotiations around a dramatization of her life called *The Miracle Worker.*

But Helen had once before chosen pragmatism over principle in an episode involving racial discrimination, and she had regretted it ever since. When the *Defense Trial Bulletin* appeared a month later, it carried an appeal for funds and a poignant statement from one of the world's most beloved icons:

> Freedom-loving, law-abiding men and women should unite throughout the world to uphold those who are denied their rights to advancement and education and shall never cease until all lands are purged from the poison of racism and oppression.

It was one more chapter of her extraordinary life destined to be ignored or forgotten in favor of a more familiar narrative.

Part One

. . . .

MIRACLE VS. MYTH

Chapter One

Before the Miracle

S he was among the most celebrated women of her generation. Newspapers and magazines throughout the world heralded the accomplishments of the remarkable girl who—afflicted by a terrible disease as an infant—was said to have been trapped in a void of darkness and despair before an extraordinary teacher single-handedly accomplished the impossible: taught the girl to communicate by spelling into her hand. Soon, she was reading and writing and, before long, had even mastered philosophy, history, literature, and mathematics. After the world's most famous writer publicized her story, she was inundated with letters from around the globe thanking her for humanizing people with disabilities. Until then, many assumed that people with her condition—"deaf, dumb, and blind"—were barely human. Now, celebrities flocked to meet her, and children everywhere knew her name.

But this was not Helen Keller. A half century *before* Helen came along, there was Laura Bridgman. And before Helen's teacher, Annie Sullivan, there was Samuel Gridley Howe. Bridgman and Howe are now mostly forgotten, but without their achievements, Helen's "miracle" would never have happened.

⠏⠜⠞ ⠕⠝⠑
⠉⠓⠁⠏ ⠞⠻

By the time Samuel Gridley Howe embarked on his first crusade in 1824, he was convinced he had been chosen by God for a noble calling.

From his upbringing in an undistinguished Boston family, Howe had coasted through his early life with few expectations placed upon him. Yet, unlike the city's Brahmin elite who claimed leadership of New England commerce and politics as their birthright, Howe was determined to make his mark based on his own merits.

Perhaps because of their diminished social status, the Howes were always a little out of step with Boston society. The family notably rejected the conservative politics usually associated with the rigidly Federalist city, embracing instead the liberal ideas of Jeffersonian Democratic Republicans. It often left Howe a pariah at Boston Latin—the school he attended as a boy—where Howe was frequently bullied for his family's unconventional views. This almost certainly influenced his decision to attend the liberal Baptist college, Brown, instead of the Federalist bastion, Harvard. Attending Harvard would have given him a leg up in society but would have forced him to coexist with his secondary school tormentors.

Following graduation, he remained directionless, leaving many of his circle surprised at his decision to attend Harvard Medical School, especially since he shunned Harvard years earlier and had always scoffed at the practice of medicine.[1] At the august institution, then considered America's finest university, he once again failed to distinguish himself, which confounded many who saw such promise in the bright young man. While his fellow students pored over anatomy charts and medical jargon, Howe could often be found reading his favorite poet, Lord Byron, long into the night. Byron's romantic epics had long inspired Howe's unquenched sense of adventure, but it was the English poet's real-life escapades that would finally spur the young student to leave his old life behind in favor of a heroic calling.

Across the sea in Greece, a revolution was underway between the philhellenes, the partisans for independence, and the Ottoman Empire, which had ruled Greece for more than four centuries. The Turks were portrayed as barbaric oppressors in a ceaseless Christian propaganda campaign designed to summon young men to the Greek cause. It was a war of the "crescent against the cross," trumpeted Harvard professor Edward Everett during Howe's time there.[2] After devoting much of his personal fortune to refitting the rebel fleet, Byron mustered his own brigade, which he was determined to lead into battle, but in the end, he contracted fever and succumbed before ever seeing the battlefield. Byron's demise came only weeks before Howe's Harvard graduation in 1824 and was very likely the impetus for the young man's sudden declaration that he planned to wade into the cause of Grecian liberty. Throwing himself into the Greek struggle, he fought in the siege of Athens and served as a ship's surgeon for a time, eventually rising to chief surgeon of the armed forces while periodically traveling back to the United States to raise funds for refugees displaced by the war.[3]

By the time he returned home for good seven years later, his accolades had received widespread attention from the media back home and Howe had earned the moniker "Lafayette of the Greek Revolution." Boston seemed his for the taking—a far cry from the undistinguished laggard who set sail fresh out of school. And yet, the young man returned disillusioned—unimpressed by his own heroics and the success of the revolution, which resulted in the Treaty of Constantinople, establishing Greek independence in 1832.

No closer to deciding on a vocation, his life's work came about through a fortuitous encounter with an old medical school classmate, Dr. John Dix Fisher, who had been a year ahead of Howe at Harvard. On a journey to Paris a few years earlier, Fisher had visited the Institut National des Jeunes Aveugles, the world's first formal school for the blind, founded in 1784 by Valentin Haüy.[4] By showcasing the art and music of blind children, the French educator had aimed to impress the public with the children's abilities rather than inspire pity for their condition. The school had also experimented with a new technique called raised type using embossed letters to teach its students to read, though this system would later be replaced by a tactile system of raised dots developed by one of its teachers, Louis Braille. Upon his return to America, Fisher resolved to establish a similar school in the United States. Appealing to the Massachusetts legislature, he had already received a state charter for his proposed school but had made no progress in finding the right person to head the institution until he ran into Howe on a stroll with two fellow trustees in 1831 and decided on the spot that he was their man.

In colonial America, the care of people with disabilities had often been considered a local responsibility. Many towns established "poor farms" and almshouses to support citizens whose families could not cope with their care. Under this system, however, people with disabilities were often associated with criminals and paupers, collectively considered undesirable populations who could acceptably be segregated from "polite society" in overcrowded and unsanitary conditions with a minimum of care.[5] Eventually, people with physical or cognitive disabilities were often sent to "lunatic asylums" to be contained, rather than cared for. By the beginning of the nineteenth century, the concept of "moral treatment" had been imported from Europe and more humane practices were employed to "treat" people with disabilities, who had come to be known as the "woefully afflicted."[6]

Until Samuel Howe took the reins of the New England school, the education of blind children was often restricted to wealthy families who could afford to hire tutors. Howe was determined to change that. Drawing from his considerable experience on behalf of Greek independence, he devoted his days to soliciting funds to ensure that blind people would no longer be treated as a "pauper class." "Blindness," he wrote in his first report, is "one of those instruments by which a mysterious Providence has chosen to afflict man...Much can be done for them...you may light the lamp of knowledge within them, you may enable them to read the Scripture themselves."[7] The latter sentiment was especially characteristic of the arguments that reformers of his era used to extol the virtues of educating blind people—the idea that such an education would enable them to "receive" Christianity.

Having secured permission from the trustees to travel abroad for several months to investigate European practices in the field, Howe returned to Boston in July 1832 unimpressed by what he had discovered. He was especially distressed to learn that fewer than 5 percent of the graduates of these schools could earn a living upon graduation. Many ended up begging or were institutionalized in asylums for the indigent.[8] Instead of receiving the tools to function in society, he lamented, blind people were treated as "mere objects of pity."[9] He was determined that his school would enable them to integrate into society free from the stigma of dependence.

Still lacking a building, the fledgling school commenced operations in July 1832 with an inaugural class of six pupils, ranging in age from six to twenty-one, in the sitting room of his father's house. He had recruited some of the students off street corners, others through appeals to the politicians of neighboring towns. Inspired by the methods of Valentin Haüy's work in France, he eventually staged a public demonstration at Boston's Masonic Hall to showcase his students' newly acquired skills. The children would sing hymns, read Scripture, and recite poetry while spectators marveled at their abilities, often in tears.[10] After a newspaper described the exhibition as "one of the most delightful and gratifying spectacles we ever beheld,"[11] society ladies throughout New England began competing with each other to stage fairs and exhibitions to raise funds for Howe's much-talked-about endeavor.[12] Before long, he was parading his students before the Massachusetts legislature, which dutifully appropriated the sum of $6,000 per year to cover the tuition of twenty students.[13] In 1833, a trustee named Thomas Perkins donated his home and estate on the outskirts of Boston to establish a permanent facility, which would be known as the Perkins School for the Blind.[14]

Despite its rapid success, Howe was soon bored with the mundane administrative tasks involved in running a school. Complaining to a friend that he was finding the job too "narrow," he confessed that he was craving new challenges. "If I am good for anything, it is as a pioneer in a rough untrodden path. I want the stimulus of difficulty." He soon found just the challenge.

More than a decade before Perkins came into existence, America's first school for deaf children had been established in Hartford, Connecticut, in 1817 by a Frenchman named Laurent Clerc. Similar to the early attitudes about the education of blind people, early advocates argued that teaching deaf children to read would help guide them to Christianity. By the 1830s, thousands benefited from the efforts of Howe and Clerc, both of whom succeeded in bringing the education of people with disabilities into the mainstream. Yet there was another category of disability—a condition little known by most Americans, but one that had captured the imagination of Howe, whose mission was to demonstrate society's obligation to educate all its citizens, regardless of their circumstances. If he was seeking a grand social experiment to prove his hypothesis, there would be no better example, he believed, than the challenge of educating someone who was both deaf and blind.

In future years, Howe was fond of quoting a passage from *Blackstone Commentaries*, an eighteenth-century British treatise that helped shape the early US legal system:

> A man is not an idiot, if he hath any glimmering of reason, for that he can tell his parents, his age, or the like matters. But a man who is born deaf, dumb, and blind, is looked upon by the law as in the same state with an idiot; he being supposed incapable of understanding, as wanting those senses which furnish the human mind with ideas.[15]

In fact, it was generally believed that someone who was blind and deaf—as well as "dumb," the commonly used expression for a person unable to speak—could not possibly possess the capacity for learning and understanding that had already been demonstrated by those restricted by the individual conditions. On a visit to the Asylum for the Deaf and Dumb in Hartford some years earlier, Howe met a resident named Julia Brace, who had already achieved a degree of fame as the only widely known deafblind person in America. Julia had contracted typhus at the age of four and lost both her sight and hearing. Arriving at the Hartford school as the only blind resident in 1825, shortly before her eighteenth birthday, Julia's education had been limited. She knew some rudimentary signs and learned to sew and knit, but there had been no attempt to formally educate her. During her time at the Asylum, she had reportedly shown little aptitude for learning to read or write.[16] In 1831, the famed French philosopher Alexis de Tocqueville visited the Hartford school and wrote about his observations after Julia was pointed out to him. "From time to time she smiled at her thoughts," he observed. "It was a strange sight. How could anything funny or pleasant take place in a soul so walled in, what form does it take? The director told me she was very gentle and easy to handle."[17] Julia also captured the attention of Lydia Huntley Sigourney, one of America's best-known poets, who had championed her story in verse and in a popular children's anthology.[18] These lyrical accounts had gained Julia a measure of celebrity and eventually inspired Howe to pay a visit to Hartford to meet her for himself. However, he concluded that at twenty-seven years old, her advanced age made her an unfit prospect for his goal of proving that a deafblind person could be educated.[19] His search resumed in earnest until the spring of 1837, when he read a report about the case of a seven-year-old child in a neighboring state.

Laura Dewey Bridgman was born in Hanover, New Hampshire, on December 21, 1829—the third child of farmer Daniel Bridgman and his wife, Harmony. Laura had been prone to seizures as an infant and her parents feared she would not survive. But by the age of twenty months, she appeared to regain her health and proved to be a lively, intelligent child. She was already beginning to speak in short sentences when, at the age of twenty-four months, scarlet fever ripped through the household. Both her sisters died, and Laura also nearly succumbed to the ailment, which infected countless children before the development of antibiotics made it a manageable illness. By the time the fever dissipated, the inflammation had taken a terrible toll. Laura lost her sight, hearing, and sense of smell. Her eyes were so sensitive to light that she had to be kept in a darkened room for five months.[20]

After Howe read an account about Laura written by the head of the Dartmouth College medical department, he immediately arranged to visit Hanover with a group of friends to seize the "rare opportunity" to determine whether this was the prospective pupil he had been searching for. Among the party that accompanied him on the outing was Henry Wadsworth Longfellow, who at the time was a young Harvard professor of modern languages but who would soon emerge as one of America's best-known poets. Upon meeting Laura, Howe knew his search was over. "I found her with a well-formed figure; a strongly marked, nervous sanguine temperament; a large, beautifully shaped head; and the whole system in healthy action," he later recalled.[21]

Three months later, in October 1837, the seven-year-old girl arrived at Perkins to begin her education. Laura was at first "much bewildered" by her strange new surroundings until she became acquainted with her fellow "inmates," as Howe described his students.[22] Once she settled down, he began his experiment in earnest, using everyday objects such as a spoon, a fork, and a key, and pasted labels with their name embossed in raised letters. Before long, she learned to place the labels on the correct objects, but Howe sensed that these skills merely demonstrated an aptitude for "imitation and memory" rather than an integration of language.

After weeks had passed, he resolved to try a new approach. Rather than simply assigning a label to an object, he cut it into separate components to introduce the concept of letters. Cutting up the word "book" into four pieces, he placed them in the correct order while guiding Laura's hand to a book. He then scrambled the letters and let her try to piece them together as if to let her solve the next step in the strange puzzle.[23] When this proved successful, he did the same with the word "key."

Once again, she placed the letters in the correct order with little effort. Describing her progress, Howe would later describe this break-through as the "supreme moment" when Laura grasped the idea that his efforts and that of the other teachers who had worked with her for weeks had established communication between "her thoughts and ours":

> Hitherto, the process had been mechanical... The poor child had sat in mute amazement, and patiently imitated everything her teacher did; but now the truth began to flash upon her, her intellect began to work, she perceived that here was a way by which she could herself make up a sign of anything that was in her own mind and show it to another mind... I could almost fix upon the moment when this truth dawned upon her mind and spread its beams upon her countenance. I saw that the great obstacle was overcome.[24]

Laura's biographer Ernest Freeberg would note that Howe's description of this eureka moment was missing from his earliest accounts of her progress and didn't appear until his annual report of 1841, three years later.[25] Nevertheless, it was evident that Laura had acquired the basic principles of language. Once she learned the twenty-six letters of the alphabet, she quickly mastered the concept of forming the letters into words.[26] From the moment she understood that objects have names, Laura eagerly demanded to be taught the name of everything she encountered.

Next, Howe directed Lydia Drew—one of many female teachers who worked closely with Laura—to teach her the manual alphabet, a method that he had first observed while visiting Julia Brace at the Hartford Asylum. The relatively simple technique involved presenting Laura with an object and then spelling its name into the palm of her hand. The speed at which she picked up finger spelling was astonishing to Howe and her teachers. "She signs words and sentences so fast and dexterously that only those accustomed to this manual language can follow with the eye the rapid motions of her fingers," he noted. The teachers often noticed her sitting alone entertaining herself by conducting imaginary dialogues or practicing her spelling.[27]

Watching her practice the manual alphabet for hours on end, he soon noticed a peculiar habit that illustrated the diligence she applied to her learning. "If she spells a word wrong with her right hand," he observed, "she instantly strikes it with her left, as her teacher does, in a mark of disapprobation."[28]

Howe would later admit that the process of building on each learning success was "slow and tedious," not least because there were no precedents from which to draw.[29] He confided his disappointment that, by the age of nine, after two years of instruction, Laura had only acquired the language skills of the average three-year-old. From the promise she had shown early on, he had clearly expected her to develop at a quicker pace. Still, by age eleven, her progress had reached the point that she was able to take her place in a classroom with the other blind students, while a specially assigned teacher spelled the lessons into her hand. Eventually, she would master a number of complex subjects, including math and philosophy. Long before that, however, Laura Bridgman had already become a household name and her achievements heralded as a "miracle" thanks to the breathless media coverage engineered by her mentor, whose reputation became inextricably tied to the "deaf, dumb, and blind girl from New Hampshire."

Within a year of Laura's arrival, Howe used the Perkins annual reports to trumpet her progress and paint an exaggerated and somewhat idealized portrait, despite his aforementioned disappointment about the pace of her development. In charting the trajectory of Laura's fame, Ernest Freeberg compares Howe's publicity skills to the legendary nineteenth-century huckster P. T. Barnum, who famously shaped the narrative to make stars of his attractions. "No less than Barnum," he wrote, "Howe mastered the art of manipulating the public's interest in her story…in order to advance his career and his institution."[30] Describing her as a very "pretty, sprightly and intelligent" girl deprived of her senses since infancy, Howe likened her mind to a "closed tomb at midnight" before he opened it up with his noble experiment.[31]

For readers who had previously assumed that deafblind people were uneducable, his inflated description of her rapid progress and mastery of the manual alphabet in a short four months caused an immediate sensation.[32] The popular press reprinted his accounts and, before long, Laura Bridgman had become a household name in America.

Eager to take advantage of her newfound celebrity, Howe revived a technique he had used to great effect during the earliest days of his school. He placed her on public exhibit to showcase her astonishing progress—arguing that such displays would increase interest in the education of blind children and "loosen the public and private purse strings."[33] Every month, hundreds of visitors flocked to Perkins desperate to get a glimpse of the prodigy. With a green ribbon wrapped around her eyes to cover her "deformity," Laura sat at a desk on full display on the lawn of the institute while the ever-expanding crowds watched her reading books with raised type, knitting, and finger spelling into a teacher's hand. Many poured forward demanding her autograph or pieces of her needlework. Some even asked for locks of her hair.

Describing the increasingly unruly crowds, one of Laura's teachers, Mary Swift Lamson, lamented in her diary, "The crowd has become so great...and presses so closely about Laura that we are obliged to surround her desk by settees, thus making a little enclosure and protecting her."[34] We have little record of how Laura felt about being exhibited like a zoo animal, but Lamson recalled the bemused girl's reaction when she realized they had enclosed her off from the crowd. "Are ladies afraid of me?" she asked her teacher.[35]

Howe's accounts of Laura's progress were careful to emphasize the qualities that he knew would capture the admiration of the adoring masses. Thus, he waxed eloquent about her strong moral character and impeccable table manners, along with her sewing skills and her delight in dressing and undressing her dolls. Meanwhile, there was no mention of the other qualities that were already being noted by her teachers—not always for the good—including her passionate views about the immorality of capital punishment and slavery. Having long since taken her place in the classroom with the other students, Laura was exposed to the well-rounded curriculum developed by Howe, who believed that blind children should be exposed to a "new world of intellectual development" so that they could learn to live independently and support themselves in later life.[36] Laura took to the lessons in natural history, mathematics, and geography and read voraciously from volumes of raised type that were the forerunners of braille.

Observing that, as a teenager, Laura had become a supporter of the Free-Soil Movement, which was formed to oppose the expansion of the slave trade to the western states, her teacher Mary Swift Lamson noted in her diary, "It was with difficulty that I convinced her that a man might have some good qualities even though he were a slave-holder."[37]

Before long, reports emerged that little girls throughout America were poking their dolls' eyes out, tying them with green ribbon, and calling them "Laura."[38] Many chroniclers have tried to make sense of the phenomenon. What was it about the girl that had struck such a chord? "Laura Bridgman became what the public wanted," social historian Rosemary Mahoney explains. "An idealized, sentimentalized symbol of suffering tempered by goodness and hard work. She was an example of the power of the human spirit to overcome adversity."[39]

Howe was fond of boasting that Laura had become the second-most-famous female in the world, after only Queen Victoria—one of his few claims about the girl that may not have been exaggerated. Indeed, her fame had quickly spread beyond the United States and nowhere more so than England, where newspapers and magazines breathlessly repeated Howe's accounts.

Among the many visitors who flocked to meet Laura over the years were countless celebrities of the era, so the visit of Charles Dickens to Perkins in January 1842 may not have aroused the same level of excitement that it otherwise might. The celebrated British author had just arrived for his much-anticipated first visit to America. He was only thirty years old but was arguably the western world's most famous novelist of the time, thanks to the acclaim of books such as *Oliver Twist, Nicholas Nickleby*, and *The Pickwick Papers*. The stated purpose of his trip was to compare American democracy to the class divisions of Victorian England that he abhorred.[40] He could have logically chosen Washington or New York as the starting point for his explorations, but he had long since made up his mind about which of America's famous attractions would be first on his itinerary. At noon on January 29, he paid a visit to the Perkins School for the Blind to see the girl he would describe as a wonder on par with Niagara Falls, in a travelogue he later published about his trip called *American Notes*.

Most of the chapter recalling Dickens's visit to Perkins merely reprints Howe's description of Laura's education taken from the school's annual reports. He closes his account by sounding a somewhat mawkish clarion call—as if to dare the reader not to be moved by the profound significance of Laura's achievement:

> Ye who have eyes and see not, and have ears and hear not, ye who are as the hypocrites of sad countenances...learn healthy cheerfulness and mild contentment from the deaf and dumb and blind. Self-elected saints with gloomy brows, this sightless, earless, voiceless child may teach you lessons you will do well to follow. Let that poor hand of hers lie gently on your hearts.[41]

When *American Notes* was published in October of that year, it only served to heighten Laura's celebrity in America and abroad. Little could she know that his widely read account would one day play a role in relegating her story to obscurity, in favor of another deafblind girl who would replace her in the public imagination.

Chapter Two

Teacher

Although her most famous pupil came to be known by millions as the ultimate symbol of "overcoming adversity," scant attention has been devoted to how much Annie Sullivan had overcome in her own life.

In later years, accounts of Sullivan's upbringing would highlight her "escape" from the horrors of America's most notorious institution, the Tewksbury Almshouse, setting her on the path to her fateful destiny. But long before scholars had documented the effects of intergenerational trauma, Annie was acutely conscious of the scars she carried from events that took place across the sea years before she was born. Her mother, Alice Cloesy, was only two years old and her father, Thomas Sullivan, a little older when the Great Famine overtook Ireland in 1845. Seventeen years later, both would join the mass exodus of Irish Catholic emigrants fleeing their homeland—escaping the devastating effects of the potato blight and British neglect that would leave millions ravaged by hunger and disease. With $25 sent to him for passage by his older brother, Thomas arrived in Massachusetts with his wife, Alice, in 1862 virtually destitute.

Annie—christened Johanna Mansfield Sullivan—was born in the rural village of Feeding Hills, Massachusetts, on April 14, 1866, the first of five Sullivan children. Growing up, she was mostly unaware of the recently concluded Civil War that had torn apart the nation. Instead, she took from her parents a very different history lesson from across the ocean—one that had left scars on both her parents. Thomas and Alice recounted to their children stories of their own upbringing surrounded by "starving children clinging to mothers already dead, of men in their madness eating grass by the roadside, of cholera on transport ships and other horrors too lurid and horrible to set down in print."[1] On the rare occasions that Thomas wasn't drunk, Annie remembered him telling her stories of the little people and the fairy folk from the old country. It was one of her few happy memories of Thomas, who, like many unskilled Irish immigrants, could rarely find meaningful work. Whatever pittance he managed to earn reaping wheat on a nearby farm was often squandered on drink while Alice struggled to raise her growing family. Of the four children who followed Annie in quick succession, only her sister Mary was spared the devastating health toll wreaked by poverty. Her youngest brother and middle sister Nellie both died before she was six, while her brother Jimmie was born with a tubercular hip that left him with a severe limp.

When Annie was five, she contracted trachoma, an infectious eye disease caused by bacteria. Untreated, the condition produces recurring, painful infections, making the eyes red and swollen. The resulting scarring of the cornea can cause severe vision loss or blindness.[2] The first words that Annie could remember hearing was a neighbor telling her mother, "She would be so pretty if not for her eyes."[3] They never had enough money to afford a doctor, but Annie remembered her father telling her that a drop from the river Shannon—which he compared to holy water—would cure her condition.

Whether it was the misery caused by her deteriorating eyes or the disposition she had inherited from her father, young Annie remembers being "passionately rebellious"—difficult to manage and prone to frequent tantrums.[4] During one of these episodes, she rocked her little sister with such force that it resulted in a scar on her forehead. Another time, jealous of a friend's white mittens, Annie grabbed them and threw them into the fire. "What a terrible child!" she remembered a neighbor complaining.[5] Such behavior would inevitably result in whippings from her father so brutal that her mother would be forced to hide her for her protection until he sobered up.

Her mother—known from childhood as "Gentle Alice Cloesy" for her kind demeanor—had always been Annie's refuge and solace. But at the age of eight Annie's world shattered when she was awoken by a commotion in the next room and walked in to find her siblings crying, while their mother was laid out in a brown habit brought by the village priest. This "death robe" signified Alice had succumbed during the night to tuberculosis.

In the carriage on the way to the funeral, she remembers jostling with Jimmie when he wouldn't give her his seat by the window to watch the horses. When he began to cry, their father struck him across the face. "A fire of hatred blazed up in me which burned for many years," Annie recalled.[6]

While Mary and Jimmie were sent to live with relatives, it was determined that eight-year-old Annie would "keep house" for Thomas in a little cabin on his brother John's property. Unsurprisingly, the idea of a half-blind eight-year-old girl looking after her alcoholic father was doomed to fail. Annie began to regard him with increasing contempt— openly pouring scorn on his "incompetence, his intemperance and his illiterate brogue."[7]

Annie eventually moved in for a time with Thomas's brother John and his wife, Anastasia, but, with a growing family of their own, they found it difficult to deal with a girl who, as she would later admit, was "defiant and unmanageable."[8] Five-year-old Jimmie had also proven a burden to the family. His hip ailment had grown worse, and he could only walk with the help of crutches. "There was only one place where he and his sister could be sent to be looked after," Nella Henney writes, "and that was the place where all the people nobody wanted were sent."[9]

Driven by social reformers such as Samuel Gridley Howe and his friend Thomas Mann, the middle of the nineteenth century saw an explosion of institutions dedicated to addressing society's ills. Out of these movements came a number of positive developments, including universal public education, abolitionism, and a commitment to treat people with physical and mental disabilities humanely. "In the history of the world, the doctrine of Reform had never such scope as at the present hour," declared Ralph Waldo Emerson in his 1841 essay, "Man the Reformer."[10] In this treatise, the noted American poet/philosopher argued that history is shaped by the fortunes of the poor and that every man should have the opportunity to "conquer the world for himself."[11] Not everybody agreed.

At the same time, a parallel philosophy had begun to emerge arguing that poverty was not an opportunity for citizens to rise from their circumstances but a character flaw in need of eradication. Out of this belief came the increased prominence of the "poorhouse"—designed to instill a work ethic and cure the stigma of dependence that many reformers believed was a by-product of an era when relief and charity were administered on a local level, often by the churches.[12] Drawing on the tradition of the English almshouse—a centuries-old institution that provided charitable housing to widows and indigent workers—the first workhouses were established in colonial America as correctional institutions that equated poverty with criminality.[13]

"Between the 1820s and the late nineteenth century, there was a huge growth in the number of poorhouses in America," writes social historian David Wagner. "Some were small, even homey, and held ten or twelve people with a superintendent and a matron, usually his unpaid wife. Large cities and some states had more notorious concrete block institutions which held thousands. Among the most notorious was the Tewksbury Almshouse in Massachusetts."[14]

When Annie and Jimmie set off for Tewksbury on February 22, 1876, neither had any idea of their destination. Anastasia had informed them they were off to Springfield and would get to ride on a train, so both regarded the trip as an exciting adventure.[15] Mary, the only sibling without a disability, had stayed behind to live with her aunt Ellen.

Upon their arrival at the foreboding facility, the Sullivan children were herded onto a carriage and transported to the "house of derelicts" where their condition was recorded in a ledger. Annie was described as having "weak eyes" while the clerk documented five-year-old Jimmie's "hip complaint." Neither had ever gone to school, notes the handwritten admission form.[16] Residents of Tewksbury, including children, were separated by gender. But when Annie was informed that Jimmie was to be assigned to the men's section, she raised such a fuss that the officials gave in and permitted him to bunk among the women.

So, sister and brother were sent to the women's ward where the inmates included women who had both physical and mental health disabilities, labeled by the institution as the "pauper insane." The largest group were poor immigrants from Europe. The population—predominantly Irish Catholic like herself—was not strikingly different than the one she had known in Feeding Hills. Rather than feel shame about the grim surroundings, she felt "happier and freer" than she had ever felt before—perhaps a sense of liberation from the childhood privations and the whippings of her father.[17]

Only three months after they arrived at Tewksbury, however, Jimmie succumbed to tuberculosis, leaving Annie all alone among the inmates that she would later describe as "tramps, petty thieves, pickpockets, professional beggars, men out of work, drunkards, blind men, lame men, bedraggled and slovenly, with shamed furtive eyes."[18] The death of her six-year-old brother was one of the few incidents she would recall as profoundly upsetting during her time at Tewksbury. "I must have been sound asleep when Jimmie died, for I didn't hear them roll his bed into the dead house," she later recalled, describing her shock when she later visited the makeshift morgue and felt his dead body under a sheet. "Something in me broke. My screams waked everyone in the hospital. Someone rushed in and tried to pull me away; but I clutched the little body and held it with all my might."[19]

Among the lasting impacts of her brother's death was an increasing rejection of the Catholicism that had always played a profound role in the Sullivan household. Annie had befriended a woman with severe disabilities named Maggie Carroll. When Jimmie died, this deeply religious woman advised her to resign herself to a life at the institution, this being God's will.[20] But Annie would not accept that as her future. Nor would she agree to continue taking part in Catholic rituals such as confession. She grew increasingly skeptical of organized religion, while at the same time retaining a strong appreciation for her Irish Catholic heritage. A grim fatalism stalked her for much of her life.

One of Annie's biographers, Kim Nielsen, notes that in her often-disparaging description of the inmates, she fails to make a connection between her own disability and those of the other residents. As her vision steadily declined, Nielsen notes, her face likely resembled those she described as "having faces with inflamed, swollen eyelids... like animals, the blind bumping into the fence and each other."[21] Annie described her own condition as "bright colors dancing in a perpetual and bewildering procession" before her eyes.[22] Her complaints became so severe that she was sent to a nearby Catholic hospital for the first of the many operations she would undergo throughout her life. After two subsequent failed surgeries, her vision had deteriorated to the point that she was now classified as "blind in the public records."[23]

Later, as an adult, Annie would look back at her Tewksbury years and acknowledge that, in retrospect, the experience was "cruel, melancholy and indecent." At the time, however, she felt quite the contrary. "Everything interested me," she recalled. "I was not shocked, pained, grieved or troubled by what happened. Such things happened. People behaved like that—that was all that there was to it. It was all the life I knew. Things impressed themselves upon me because I had a receptive mind. Curiosity kept me alert and keen to know everything."[24] Like many of her fellow inmates, she was enamored with the Irish nationalist politician Charles Stewart Parnell, who had taken up the Fenian cause of home rule that advocated for Irish self-government. When he visited the United States in 1879 to seek assistance from "our fellow exiled countrymen," Annie followed news of his trip with great excitement at the thought that her people might finally throw off the shackles of English dominance that she remembered her father bitterly cursing when she was a child.[25]

Even as she took an interest in the plight of her compatriots across the ocean, however, she remained mostly unfazed by her own surroundings. Long before she arrived, Tewksbury had become infamous throughout the state of Massachusetts for its frightful conditions, including rumors of medical experimentation, cannibalism, sexual assault, and dead babies being dug up and sold to Harvard Medical School for dissection. While many of the reports proved to be apocryphal, they were enough to launch multiple investigations by the Massachusetts Board of State Charities, which had once been chaired by Samuel Gridley Howe. Shortly before his death, in fact, Howe had complained about the "mephitic" conditions of the almshouse and recommended installing a new ventilation system to alleviate the foul odors that the inmates had long complained about. After his successor Franklin Sanborn took over and launched his own investigation into excessive mortality, he produced a report revealing a systematic pattern of "cruelties, vices and crimes."[26] In the years following, Sanborn made periodic inspection visits to the almshouse. It was on one of these visits that Annie had planned her liberation from Tewksbury. A number of the girls she had befriended in the Almshouse had told her about the Perkins School where blind children could receive an education. When she heard that an inspection was imminent, she believed that Sanborn was the key to improving her situation. During that fateful visit, she followed the group of men touring the facilities, trying to find a moment to make her appeal, and ultimately, according to her biographer's account, "hurled herself into their midst without knowing which was he, crying, 'Mr. Sanborn, Mr. Sanborn, I want to go to school!' "[27]

Her plea was apparently successful. Sanborn himself would later recall his part in arranging her education. "It fell to my lot in the year

1880," he wrote, "to procure the admission to the Perkins Institution, at her own request, of a poor child Johanna (since known as Annie) Sullivan, originally of Agawam."[28]

When the day finally came to leave Tewksbury, October 7, 1880, Annie was accompanied on the train by a state charity official. Upon her arrival at the Perkins School, she recalled, she was unable to even spell her name. She remembered the students giggling when she told them her age. She would later describe to her biographer her embarrassment at arriving at the school as a fourteen-year-old unable to read or write. Her fellow students, most of whom had been there for years, had never heard of a girl so lacking in the basic necessities that she didn't even own a toothbrush, a hat, a coat, or a pair of gloves. "Certainly, they had never heard of a girl without a nightgown," wrote Nella Henney. "That night for the first time in her life Annie slept in one. A teacher borrowed it from one of the girls. And that night and many nights thereafter she cried herself to sleep, lonelier than she had ever been in Tewksbury, sick with longing for the familiar and uncritical companionship of her friends in the almshouse."[29]

By the time Annie arrived at Perkins in 1880, its most famous pupil had been largely forgotten by the general public. A year earlier, in fact, the school had thrown a fiftieth birthday celebration for Laura Bridgman, eliciting surprise from a Boston newspaper, which noted that the party would likely come as a surprise to many people "that have supposed that she was no longer among the living."[30]

In 1843, Samuel Gridley Howe had married a woman named Julia Ward and turned most of his attention to his new bride, who shared his passion for social reform. By the time they returned to Perkins following their honeymoon, Howe had shifted his philanthropic focus from his celebrated pupil Laura Bridgman to other causes, especially the abolitionist movement where he would later distinguish himself as a member of the "Secret Six," who funded the raid on Harpers Ferry by the radical abolitionist John Brown. "By the end of 1844, Laura had outlived her usefulness to Howe," notes her biographer Elisabeth Gitter. "The excitement—the miracle—was in the drama of her rescue. Howe had got from it, and Laura, nearly all that he could."[31] Samuel Gridley Howe died in 1876, four years before Annie's arrival, but years earlier he had raised money to permanently establish a cottage on the Perkins grounds where Laura still lived, occupying her days reading the Bible and knitting.

When Annie arrived, she lived for a time in this cottage, where she remembered Laura spending much of the day in her favorite position, "sitting beside her window quietly like Whistler's Mother as we know her in the picture, with her sightless eyes turned towards the sun, a frail woman with fine features and delicate hands which wove their way in and out through the intricacies of beautiful needlework."[32] It was while sharing the cottage with Laura that Annie learned a skill that would soon prove to be very useful: she mastered the manual alphabet in order to converse with the older woman. She later recalled spelling into Laura's hands the "gossip of the girls and the news of the day."[33]

Meanwhile, Annie had shown great aptitude for academics despite her lack of previous schooling. Her remarkable progress didn't escape the notice of the Perkins director, who became something of a surrogate father figure. Howe's successor at Perkins was a man named Michael Anagnos, a Greek patriot who had met the founder in 1867 during the Cretan insurrection when Howe returned to the scene of his previous glories to distribute relief supplies donated by Bostonians. Both Howe and his wife, Julia, were immediately taken by the charismatic young man, who had volunteered to serve as an unofficial secretary during their stay. When he returned to Boston, Howe invited the young Greek to join him and work at the Perkins School. It is here that he captured the eye of Howe's daughter, Julia Romana, whom he would marry two years later.

Anagnos took the new arrival under his wing and acted as a mentor to the girl, even as Annie's quick temper found her on the brink of expulsion on more than one occasion. "My mind was a question mark, my heart a frustration," Annie recalled. She struggled to find kinship with her fellow students, feeling her background set her apart, enabling her to better understand the world than her more cloistered peers. "All my experiences had unfitted me for living a normal life," Annie later asserted, recalling how she "learned quickly and thought [herself] superior to the other girls." She colorfully described her sense of how "the new ideas which flooded my mind were sown in the deep dark soil of my life at Tewksbury and grew rapidly, sending out wild shoots that spread and overshadowed the puny thoughts of my more delicately nourished schoolmates."[34]

A year after she arrived at Perkins, Annie underwent her first successful eye operation, the first of two surgeries that would finally restore her vision after "ten years of almost no usable sight."[35] Despite her late start, she graduated at the top of her class and was chosen to give the Perkins valedictory address in June 1886: "And now we are going out into the busy world, to take our share in life's burdens, and to do our little to make that world better, wiser and happier," she implored her fellow graduates."[36] Yet even as she delivered those words, she was terrified at the idea of facing the world outside Perkins—a world for which, despite her outward self-confidence, she believed herself thoroughly unsuited and life's burdens very much beyond her capabilities. Two months later, a letter arrived that would change her mind and her destiny.

Chapter Three

"The Second Laura Bridgman"

I n early 1888, the trustees of the Perkins School for the Blind received the school's fifty-sixth annual report, summarizing the highlights of the previous year. Carrying on the tradition of his late father-in-law, Michael Anagnos used his report to highlight the achievements of the school. As was his custom, he included a lengthy tribute to Samuel Gridley Howe, whom he credits with "purveying mental pabulum to the starving mind of Laura Bridgman."[1]

After noting some of the deafblind students in various American schools who owed their education to the path that Howe had forged with Laura's "deliverance," he includes a notable new addition. Of all the "blind and deaf-mute" children under instruction, he writes, "Helen Keller of Tuscumbia, Alabama is undoubtedly the most remarkable. It is no hyperbole to say that she is a phenomenon."[2]

The events that would catapult Helen to the attention of Anagnos and eventually the public imagination began with a series of letters from an Alabama man named Captain Arthur Keller seeking a teacher for his daughter. Helen had been born on June 27, 1880, to Captain Keller and his second wife, Kate. There are conflicting reports on what caused her condition, but as Captain Keller recalled in his initial correspondence, at the age of nineteen months, the girl experienced a "violent attack of congestion of the stomach," resulting in a total loss of sight and hearing. Before her illness, he noted, Helen had enjoyed "perfect health, and is said to have been an unusually bright and active child. She had learned to walk and was fast learning to talk."[3]

During the sickness, "her life hung in the balance for several days, and after recovery there was no evidence for some time of any injury to her eyes, except a red and inflamed appearance." The full extent of the damage soon dawned upon her parents, however. They tried every available avenue of relief, carrying her to the best specialists of the day, but none offered the slightest hope that their daughter's sight or hearing could be restored. For many months, little Helen's eyes were very painful, and she buried them in the bedclothes away from the light. Soon, she ceased to talk, "because she had ceased to hear any sound."[4]

For a number of years afterward, some members of the family considered her a hopeless case—a "mental defective" beyond redemption. Helen's uncle urged the family to place her in an institution. But her mother, Kate, was horrified at the prospect, and she had an ally in Arthur's sister, Ev, who had grown exceedingly fond of the young girl. "This child has more sense than all the Kellers if there is any way to reach her mind," she protested.[5] Kate Keller was a voracious reader and happened to have read Charles Dickens's account of Laura Bridgman's education, so she was already aware that a deafblind child could be educated. And while Samuel Gridley Howe had died years earlier, the Kellers were also familiar with the achievements of an educator even more illustrious.[6] And so Arthur Keller set off on a journey north to consult with Alexander Graham Bell.

Although Bell was best known for the invention of the telephone in 1876—four years before Helen was born—few knew that this soon-to-be-ubiquitous technology was influenced by his lifelong mission to improve the lives of the deaf community rather than as a means of universal telecommunications. Both his wife and his mother were deaf, which set the Scottish-born scientist on a decades-long path to experiment with hearing devices. To earn extra money to fund his research, Bell had established a private practice teaching deaf children using principles developed by his own father. Alexander Melville Bell had developed a learning technique called visible speech—a system of phonetic symbols designed to help deaf people learn to speak by illustrating the position of the mouth and the throat in the formation of different sounds.[7]

Arthur Keller was so convinced that Bell might have the answer to his daughter's condition that he made the journey by train to Washington to consult with the famed inventor. A letter from Bell to Thomas Gallaudet—founder of North America's first permanent school for the deaf—indicates that Bell thought Helen an interesting case even before he met her. "Mr. A. H. Keller of Tuscumbia, Alabama will dine with me this evening and bring with him his little daughter (age about 6½) who is deaf and blind and has been so from nearly infancy," he wrote. "He is in search of light regarding methods of education. The little girl is evidently an intelligent child and altogether this is such an interesting case that I thought you would like to know about it."[8]

Details are sparse about their meeting that evening. Although it is widely believed that Helen was incapable of communicating before Annie Sullivan came into her life, the truth was that she had created at least sixty signs on her own that she used to convey her basic needs and emotions. If she wanted bread, for example, she would imitate the act of cutting and buttering slices. If she desired ice cream, she would make a sign for working the freezer while shivering, indicating cold.[9] And while she later claimed that she remembered little from her early childhood, this initial meeting with Bell evidently made a lasting impression. "He understood my signs, and I knew it and loved him at once," Helen later wrote. "But I did not dream that that interview would be the door through which I should pass from darkness into light, from isolation to friendship, companionship, knowledge, love."[10]

Although Captain Keller may have been expecting Bell to offer his services as a private tutor for his daughter, the inventor appears to have immediately recognized Helen's potential. Rather than offer to instruct her, he recommended that Captain Keller write to Michael Anagnos at the Perkins School for the Blind and seek a teacher to work with her exclusively.[11] Having read about Laura Bridgman, Kate was already familiar with Perkins and so, with her blessing, Arthur dispatched his first letter to Anagnos. "The case of your little daughter is of some exceeding interest to me," the director responded. "Your brief description of her mental activity reminds me possibly of Laura Bridgman, and I would certainly go and see her if the distance which separates us were not so great."[12]

Anagnos later claimed that he knew immediately who was most suited for the challenge. "My thoughts were almost instinctively turned towards Miss Annie M. Sullivan," he recalled. "She had just graduated from our school, where she had stood at the head of her class, and her valedictory address—a beautiful original production, teeming with felicitous thoughts clothed in a graceful style—was a revelation even to those who were acquainted with her uncommon powers."[13]

Anagnos forwarded Arthur Keller's letter to Annie and asked her whether she would "be disposed to consider favourably an offer of a position in the family of Mr. Keller as the governess of his little deaf-mute and blind daughter." If she decided to be a candidate for the position, he offered to write back and ask for "further particulars."[14]

It would take almost five months for Anagnos to respond to Arthur Keller's request for a teacher. Although a number of theories have been offered to explain the long gap, contemporary records reveal that Annie was hesitant to accept for at least one significant reason—she didn't believe she was up to the task. Annie had grown up in the shadow of Samuel Gridley Howe. Almost from the day she arrived, she heard little else except the stories of Howe's achievements with Laura. Until six years ago, she couldn't even read or write. Now, she was being asked to embark on a challenge worthy of great men like Howe. The prospect must have been frightening and intimidating to the twenty-year-old. Rather than give a definitive response when Anagnos enlisted her for the mission, Annie simply replied that she would "try."

For the next five months, she threw herself into studying the path that Howe had followed four decades earlier to free Laura Bridgman

from her "entombment." According to Anagnos, she "perused voluminous books on mental development, read the reports of Dr. Howe with
assiduous care, mastered his methods and processes in their minutest
details, and drank copiously of his noble spirit and of the abundance
of his faith in the efficacy of human capacities and innate powers for
redemption and improvement."[15]

Finally, "having become convinced by actual observation that she
was well equipped for her work and absolutely competent to take charge
of the little girl," Anagnos wrote to Captain Keller in January 1887 rec-
ommending Annie for the job as governess "without reservation."[16]

By now, Annie's apprehension about the task before her may not have
yet subsided, but the director clearly believed she was up to the challenge. Receiving the recommendation, Captain Keller gave a qualified
commitment. He was about to embark on another journey to Washington with Helen to consult an "eminent oculist and aurist." Although
it was not yet official, he believed he would be ready upon her return
to employ Annie as her teacher. He offered what Anagnos would later
describe as "liberal terms"—$25 per month, plus board and washing,
considerably more generous than the $5 average weekly salary a female
teacher in Boston could expect to earn during the 1880s.[17]

Arthur Keller's Southern roots ran deep. He had served as a captain
in the Confederate army and his mother was a second cousin to Robert
E. Lee.[18] His second wife, Kate, Helen's mother, however, was descended
from the Adams family of Massachusetts, which had produced two US
presidents and was long associated with the abolitionist movement that
was anathema to most white Southerners. Kate's father, Charles Adams,
however, had severed this Northern lineage when he moved to Arkansas
before she was born, and later fought on the Confederate side in the
Civil War. Despite her Northern bloodline, Kate was raised in Memphis
and was very much a Southern belle by the time she married Arthur
at the age of twenty-three.[19] If Arthur Keller had any hesitation about
employing a Yankee to educate his daughter, it was nowhere evident in

his return letter to Anagnos, in which he assured the director that he would treat Annie as "one of our immediate family."[20]

Annie accepted the terms with great excitement. On the eve of her departure in early March 1887, the girls at Perkins presented her with a doll as a gift for her young charge. Fifty-seven-year-old Laura Bridgman, who spent most of her days sewing and reading the Bible, had made a dress for the doll along with a note for Helen addressed to "my sister in Christ."

When Annie arrived in Tuscumbia on March 3, she was still nervous about the adventure before her. After a train journey lasting two days, she arrived at the train station to be greeted by Kate Keller, who was thirty-one but, Annie noted, seemed not much older than herself. As they approached the Keller home—named Ivy Green for the English ivy that climbed its walls—she reflected on her emotions: "I became so excited and eager to see my little pupil that I could hardly wait to sit still in my seat. I felt like pushing the horse faster."[21] Helen would also later recall the moment of Annie's arrival, the moment she would describe as her "soul's birthday." "I felt approaching footsteps," she wrote. "I stretched out my hand as I supposed to my mother. Someone took it and I was caught up and held close in the arms of her who had come to reveal all things to me, and more than all things else, to love me."[22]

In a letter to Michael Anagnos a week after her arrival, Annie appeared optimistic about the task ahead of her. "I find Mr. and Mrs. Keller very kind people. Helen, my little pupil, is all that her father described her. It is really wonderful the knowledge the little thing has acquired by the sense of touch and sense of smell."[23]

Despite Annie's glowing report, she was a little more candid with her former Perkins housemother, Sophia Hopkins, in a letter she wrote her longtime confidante about the encounter:

When at last we reached the house, I ran up the porch-steps, and there stood Helen by the porch-door, one hand stretched out, as if she expected someone to come in . . . I remember how disappointed I was when the untamed little creature stubbornly refused to kiss me and struggled frantically to free herself from my embrace. I remember, too, how the eager, impetuous fingers felt my face and dress and my bag which she insisted on opening at once, showing by signs that she expected to find something good to eat in it. Mrs. Keller tried to make Helen understand by shaking her head and pointing to me that she was not to open the bag; but the child paid no attention to these signs, whereupon her mother forcibly took the bag out from her hands. Helen's face grew red to the roots of her hair, and she began to clutch at her mother's dress and kick violently.[24]

The description of Helen's tantrum and subsequent unruly behavior would eventually become a central theme of the narrative around Annie's role in Helen's education thanks, in part, to Anagnos's initial description in the 1887 Perkins annual report, drawn from Annie's accounts. "She inherited a quick temper and an obstinate will and owing to her deprivations, neither had ever been subdued or directed," he wrote. "She would often give way to violent paroxysms of anger when she had striven in vain to express intelligibly some idea."[25]

For Annie, whose experience with the care of young children had been limited to her time spent with her brother Jimmie before he succumbed at Tewksbury, Helen's behavior presented a significant obstacle even if it was not so different from the description she later provided about her own frequent tantrums and unruly behavior before she arrived at Perkins. "I find considerable trouble in controlling her," she complained to Anagnos. "She has always done just as her fancy inclined and it is next to impossible to make her obey. However, I think I shall succeed sometime. The greatest problem I shall have to solve is how to discipline and control her without breaking her spirit." Annie resolved to try a gradual approach, saying she would "go rather slowly at first and try to win her love. I shall not attempt to conquer her by force alone; but I shall insist on reasonable obedience from the start."[26]

Despite these difficulties, Annie appears to have wasted no time in throwing herself into a lesson on the very first day. Using the doll sent by the Perkins girls, she spelled D-O-L-L into Helen's hand. Later, she did the same thing with C-A-K-E. Before long, her pupil had learned six words. "She would manifest pleasure when she was told the name of a new object and was always delighted to receive a pat of approval." When given one of these objects, Annie recalled, she could spell its name, but it was a while before she understood that all things had their own names.[27]

In between lessons, she frequently engaged in a battle royal with the girl, especially at the dinner table, where Annie professed to be appalled by the six-year-old's poor table manners. Once, she stopped Helen from picking food from her plate with her fingers, which precipitated a tantrum. After the girl finally calmed down, Annie proceeded to finish her breakfast while Helen sat nearby determined to discover what was happening, not comprehending why she had been stopped from eating. Meanwhile, the family quietly left the room, unable to bear watching what they felt were Annie's harsh disciplinary methods. The family had always previously let her do whatever she pleased, Annie lamented.

A battle of wills ensued that shaped Annie's teaching philosophy. She complained to Mrs. Hopkins that her earliest efforts were beset with many difficulties. The girl wouldn't yield a point without "contesting it to the bitter end." To get her to do simple tasks, such as combing her hair or washing her hands, she explained, it was "necessary to use force." Whenever she did so, however, a "distressing scene followed." The lesson was clear, Annie believed. "I saw clearly that it was useless to try to teach her language or anything else until she learned to obey me. I have thought about it a great deal, and the more I think, the more certain I am that obedience is the gateway through which knowledge, yes, and love, too, enter the mind of the child."[28]

Annie soon became convinced that the biggest obstacle to getting her pupil under control was her family's constant vigilance. She also implied that much of the difficulty stemmed from the culture clash of having a Yankee in their midst.

"The Civil War had been fought and won," she later told her biographer, "but the issues that brought it forth were not settled. Futile arguments went on endlessly. With fiery Quixotism I took up the cudgels for the opponents of the South, hot with indignation when they attacked Sumner or were lukewarm towards Lincoln."[29]

If only she could separate Helen from her interfering family, she believed, she could fully devote herself to the task at hand. She recounted in a letter that she "told [Mrs. Keller] that in my opinion the child ought to be separated from the family for a few weeks at least—that she must learn to depend on and obey me before I could make any headway."[30] Finally, a solution was agreed upon. Kate suggested a nearby one-room annex occupied by one of the family's young Black servants.

So, on March 11, eight days after Annie's arrival, Helen and Annie went to live in the garden annex. Within two days, Annie wrote Mrs. Hopkins again, suggesting that the experiment appeared to be working: "Helen knows several words now, but has no idea how to use them, or that everything has a name. I think, however, she will learn quickly enough by and by. As I have said before, she is wonderfully bright and active and as quick as lightning in her movements."[31]

On March 20, she wrote another letter to Mrs. Hopkins signaling a breakthrough: "My heart is singing for joy this morning. A miracle has happened! The light of understanding has shone upon my little pupil's mind, and behold, all things are changed! The little savage has learned her first lesson in obedience and finds the yoke not too hard."[32] At least one biographer wondered about the nature of this miracle. "Did Annie subdue Helen by beating her into submission as her brutal, physically abusive father had tried unsuccessfully to break her wild spirit?" asked Dorothy Herrmann, noting that Annie later admitted to Nella Henney that she wasn't "averse" to whipping.[33]

In fact, there are indications that the conflicts between Annie and the Kellers may not have stemmed from a North-South cultural clash, as Annie asserted, after all. Instead, their misgivings about the young teacher appeared related to the discipline that Annie used to achieve her goals. "The family naturally felt inclined to interfere," Annie wrote Mrs. Hopkins, "especially her father, who cannot bear to see her cry."[34]

Recalling these methods years later, Helen herself downplayed any resentment she may have had about Annie's physical discipline, seeming convinced that it had been necessary. "Force was wasted on a child of [my] temperament," she wrote in her 1955 biography, *Teacher*, "but the obstinacy of the imp reached a stage when something had to be done to save her from the habits that make children repulsive."[35] One day, after Helen persisted in biting her nails against Annie's instructions, she recalled, "there descended upon [me] a human whirlwind who boxed [my] ears and tied [my] hands behind [my] back, thus shutting off all means of communication."[36]

Ironically, "boxing" was a Victorian punishment that involved a hard simultaneous blow to both ears—a practice that medical textbooks of the era warned often led to deafness through severe rupture of the eardrum.[37] Helen also recalled that Annie once slapped her cheek with a chunk of wet clay that she often used in her geography lessons to help Helen create three-dimensional maps. "However, there was an indescribable dearness about Teacher which caused her to repent easily her cross behavior and call herself the worst names she could think of," she wrote. "She came to me soon after the tempest and said, 'Do forgive me Helen! I can never imagine you as deafblind—I love you too much for that.'"[38]

Annie would later offer a candid assessment of her own personality. "By nature, I am as intolerant as Bismarck or a Mussolini, and if I had not met Helen, I should probably have remained a human porcupine all my life," she wrote shortly before her death.[39]

On April 5, two months shy of Helen's seventh birthday, Annie wrote Mrs. Hopkins a fateful letter describing another breakthrough. Considering its significance in the narrative of Helen Keller's life, it is interesting to note that this letter appears to display less enthusiasm than the one she had sent Mrs. Hopkins two weeks earlier describing Helen's new obedience, which she had described as a "miracle":

> Something very important has happened. Helen has taken the second great step in her education. She has learned that everything has a name, and that the manual alphabet is the key to everything she wants to know... This morning, while she was washing, she wanted to know the name for "water." When she wants to know the name of anything, she points to it and pats my hand. I spelled "w-a-t-e-r" and thought no more about it until after breakfast... We went out to the pump-house, and I made Helen hold her mug under the spout while I pumped. As the cold water gushed forth, filling the mug, I spelled "w-a-t-e-r" in Helen's free hand. The word coming so close upon the sensation of cold water rushing over her hand seemed to startle her. She dropped the mug and stood as one transfixed. A new light came into her face. She spelled "water" several times. Then she dropped on the ground and asked for its name and pointed to the pump and the trellis, and suddenly turning round she asked for my name. I spelled "Teacher."... All the way back to the house she was highly excited, and learned the name of every object she touched, so that in a few hours she had added thirty new words to her vocabulary.[40]

Annie's biographer Nella Henney aptly captured the magnitude of the incident at the water pump, which would play an outsize role in forming the narrative that persists today. "Religions have been founded on less," she wrote.[41] Helen herself would later describe the moment as her "soul's sudden awakening."[42]

Annie's description of Helen's breakthrough closely parallels Samuel Gridley Howe's description of Laura Bridgman's own awakening when she first made the connection between words and objects. Like Laura, it unleashed a torrent in Helen, and she was soon learning at a prodigious pace.

"I left the well-house eager to learn," Helen later wrote. "Everything had a name, and each name gave birth to a new thought. As we returned to the house every object which I touched seemed to quiver with life. That living word awakened my soul, gave it light, hope, joy, set it free! I did nothing but explore with my hands and learn the name of every object that I touched, and the more I handled things and learned their names and uses, the more joyous and confident grew my sense of kinship with the rest of the world."[43]

Chapter Four

· · · · · · · · · ·

"A Bold Plagiarism"

In the days and weeks after the breakthrough at the water pump, Annie couldn't contain her excitement. "She knows almost three hundred words and is learning five or six a day," Annie reported to Anagnos in May 1887. "Their length does not seem to make any difference to her. One day she pointed to the railing of the stairs and wanted me to give her the name for it. I spelled *balustrade* to her two or three times. Two days afterward I thought I would see if she remembered any of the letters, when, to my surprise, she spelled the word without a mistake; and such words as *ice-cream, strawberry, raspberry,* and *rocking-chair* she learns as readily as words of two letters."[1]

A month later, she wrote Mrs. Hopkins in apparent alarm: "She is restless at night and has no appetite. The doctor said her mind was too active, but how are we to keep her from thinking? She begins to spell the minute she wakes up in the morning and continues all day long. If I refuse to talk to her, she spells into her own hand, and apparently carries on the liveliest conversations with herself." She proposed a solution, presumably tongue-in-cheek: "So far, nobody seems to have thought of chloroforming her, which is, I think, the only effective way of stopping the natural exercise of her faculties."[2]

Although she continued to use many of the methods employed by Samuel Gridley Howe in the earliest stages of Laura Bridgman's education, she also took advantage of the natural surroundings of Ivy

Green—one of a number of creative methods that she used to instill a love of learning into her pupil. The forest and streams became an outdoor classroom to stir Helen's imagination and every "blade of grass" became a learning tool. "Long before I learned to do a sum of arithmetic or describe the shape of the earth, Miss Sullivan had taught me to find beauty in the fragrant woods," Helen wrote years later.[3] Describing Annie's creative teaching methods, she also noted that for much of the first months, she had no "regular lessons." Instead, her education seemed "more like play than work." Everything Annie taught her, she recalled, was "illustrated by a beautiful story or poem."[4]

The first accounts of the "second Laura Bridgman" began to emerge very early on. Before long, her story had spread as far as New York, where one newspaper described Helen's breakthrough at the water pump as if its reporter had witnessed it in person. "She became wild with joy and ambition, which were both pitiful and inspiring," declared the *New York Sun*.[5] The story had already begun to take on a life of its own. It is difficult to determine which of two figures was more responsible for Helen's early fame—Alexander Graham Bell or Michael Anagnos. Bell, who believed he had played a crucial role in developing the new prodigy when he recommended Perkins to Captain Keller, wasted no time in trumpeting Helen's achievements. He sent a photo of her and an account of her progress to a newspaper and even furnished a letter Helen had written him when she was seven demonstrating her rapid grasp of language, using distinctive block letters that Annie had taught her early on:[6]

Dear Dr. Bell. I am glad to write you a letter. Father will send you a picture...I can read stories in my book. I can write and spell and count, good girl. My sister can walk and run. We do have fun with Jumbo. Prince is not good dog. He cannot get birds. Rad did kill baby pigeons. I am sorry. Rad does not know wrong. Nancy will go with me. She is a good doll. Father will buy me lovely new watch.

Cousin Anna gave me a pretty doll. Her name is Allie. Good-by, Helen Keller.[7]

As word rapidly spread about Helen's achievements, Annie was not inclined to take credit—at least not at first. On the contrary, she repeatedly fretted about the increasingly laudatory coverage. Only a few weeks after she arrived in Tuscumbia to begin Helen's education, a friend sent her an article from the *Boston Herald* containing a wildly exaggerated account of Helen's progress. "How perfectly absurd to say that Helen is 'already talking fluently,'" she wrote Mrs. Hopkins. "Why, one might just as well say that a two-year-old child converses fluently when he says, 'apple give,' or 'baby walk go.' I suppose if you included his screaming, crowing, whimpering, grunting, squalling, with occasional kicks, in his conversation, it might be regarded as fluent—even eloquent."[8]

As the stories of Helen's triumph became increasingly widespread, Annie again lamented the attention. "I am heartily glad that I don't know all that is being said and written about Helen Keller and myself," she confided to Mrs. Hopkins. "Nearly every mail brings some absurd statement, printed or written. The truth is not wonderful enough to suit the newspapers, so they enlarge upon it and invent ridiculous embellishments." She cited a recent example: "One paper has Helen demonstrating problems in geometry by means of her playing blocks. I expect to hear next that she has written a treatise on the origin and future of the planets."[9]

By the summer, however, it was Michael Anagnos who was primarily responsible for the growing legend. In June 1887, shortly after Helen turned seven, an article in the *New York Sun*—widely picked up around the country—quoted Anagnos's claim that Helen had already mastered almost five hundred words. "She would spend all her time adding to her knowledge if permitted," the paper reported.[10]

Later the same year, Anagnos would give a more detailed account of Helen's progress in the Perkins annual report, which devoted a significant portion to her education while celebrating Annie's role as her instructor. "Miss Sullivan's talents are of the highest order," he wrote. "In breadth of intellect, in opulence of mental power, in fertility of resource, in originality of device and in practical sagacity she stands in the front rank... Miss Sullivan is truly an honor to the graduates of this institution. She undertook the task with becoming modesty and diffidence, and accomplished it alone, quietly and unostentatiously."[11]

Annie confided her bemusement to Mrs. Hopkins, revealing that the director's hyperbole about her motives "rubs me the wrong way." She also goes out of her way to dispute the idea perpetuated by Anagnos that she had accepted the job because of a noble calling. "I came here simply because circumstances made it necessary for me to earn my living, and I seized upon the first opportunity that offered itself, although I did not suspect nor did he, that I had any special fitness for the work."[12]

Nevertheless, it was becoming increasingly clear to Annie that Helen's prodigious pace was unprecedented. She was familiar enough with the evolution of Laura Bridgman's progress at the same stage in her education to know that Helen had far exceeded Laura's milestones and was leaping far ahead by the day, especially after Annie taught her braille a month after her seventh birthday. The tactile system—developed sixty years earlier by the blind French educator, Louis Braille—allowed Helen to read voraciously on her own.

But Annie remained unsure of herself, writing Anagnos asking "for any suggestions you may offer from your store of experience as to what and how she should be taught" and seeing her role as merely "laying a good foundation on which more accomplished teachers may build the superstructure."[13] And to her confidante she continued to display humility, dismissing the praise she received from Anagnos when she remarked that "'genius' and 'originality' are words that we should not use lightly. If, indeed, they apply to me even remotely, I do not see that I deserve any laudation on that account."[14]

And yet, while Anagnos had indeed lavished praise on Annie in his first report, it did not escape her notice that each subsequent account appeared to downplay her role in Helen's progress, suggesting that the teacher had simply adopted techniques that had been pioneered in the education of Laura Bridgman. Rather than acknowledge her strenuous work in teaching Helen, he asserted in his 1888 report that "Helen's darkened mind was reached through the sense of touch and was filled with rays of celestial light. The stupendous feat was accomplished instantaneously, as by the touch of a magic wand. The little prisoner was triumphantly rescued and became at once a citizen of the world."[15] These suggestions that Helen learned as if by magic, rather than by the deliberate and ongoing instruction of Annie Sullivan, also began to frustrate the young teacher.

Considering the narrative that would later emerge framing Annie as the central figure, it is instructive to examine the earliest media accounts around Helen's achievements. As Helen's fame spread, newspaper accounts always noted Annie's role, but spent few column inches attributing the accomplishments of the "wonderful deaf blind girl" to her "instructress." And, although the word "miracle" was frequently used in relation to her progress, it was more often than not attributed in those early years to the pupil rather than the teacher.

Reprinting one of Helen's letters written when she was seven years old, a Boston newspaper gushed, "This gifted author is endowed with extraordinary mental powers. The quickness of her perceptions is simply miraculous."[16]

Meanwhile, as Annie watched the increasingly hyperbolic coverage, there was a perceptible shift in her attitude. In contrast to her early protestations that she wanted no credit, her letters to Mrs. Hopkins indicated that she was becoming increasingly resentful of the way Helen's progress was being reported. Her letters to her mentor were no longer filled with the earlier insecurity or doubt. "I want to say something which is for your ears alone," she wrote the day after Helen turned seven. "Something within me tells me that I shall succeed beyond my dreams...I know that [Helen] has remarkable powers, and I believe that I shall be able to develop and mould them. I cannot tell how I know these things. I had no idea a short time ago how to go to work; I was feeling about in the dark; but somehow, I know now, and I know that I know. I cannot explain it; but when difficulties arise, I am not perplexed or doubtful. I know how to meet them; I seem to divine Helen's peculiar needs."[17]

In June 1887, Annie wrote Mrs. Hopkins, warning her that "no one can see her without being impressed. She is no ordinary child, and people's interest in her education will be no ordinary interest. Therefore, let us be exceedingly careful in what we say and write about her...My beautiful Helen shall not be transformed into a prodigy if I can help it."[18] It was as if she sensed that a narrative was already beginning to form that Helen's achievements were God-given and formed largely by her own genius.

Anagnos had been urging Annie for some time to bring Helen to Perkins, where she could access the "tools" to take the next giant steps in her education. Although the family had qualms about being separated from their daughter, Captain Keller understood that she couldn't reach her full potential within the narrow confines of Ivy Green, and he finally agreed in the spring of 1888 to allow Helen to travel north with her teacher.

On their way to Boston, Annie and Helen stopped in Washington, where Captain Keller had arranged for them to be received by President Grover Cleveland—the first of thirteen presidents Helen would visit during her lifetime. "We went to see Mr. Cleveland," Helen wrote about the visit. "He lives in a very large and beautiful white house, and there are lovely flowers and many trees and much fresh and green grass around. And broad smooth paths to walk on...Mr. Cleveland was very glad to see me."[19] A week later, seven-year-old Helen arrived at the Perkins School to begin the next phase of her education. She was "delighted to make friends with the little blind children" and to discover that many knew the manual alphabet. Until then, she recalled, "I had been like a foreigner speaking through an interpreter."[20]

Not long after her arrival, she was brought by Annie to meet Laura Bridgman, then fifty-eight years old, who had long since faded from public memory. The meeting did not go smoothly. "We found her sitting by the window crocheting lace," Helen recalled. "She refused to let me feel her needlework or touch her face."[21]

"You have not taught her to be very gentle," Laura chided Annie. At the conclusion of their visit, when Helen attempted to kiss Laura goodbye, she annoyed Laura by stepping on her toes, leaving Helen feeling like "the bad girl of the schoolbooks."[22]

Although Annie would later imply that she had continued to provide most of Helen's instruction even after they arrived at Perkins, contemporary records show that her pupil was being taught by a variety of different teachers. Despite Annie's determination that Helen not be labeled a prodigy, it was hard to come to any other conclusion—especially after Anagnos publicized a letter she wrote to him when she was eight with some passages written in nearly flawless French, along with a note to her aunt revealing that she was also in the process of learning to write and speak in three other languages. In her note, Helen showed off some of what she was learning and her excitement about the prospect of sharing her new knowledge with her younger sister:

> I am studying French and German and Latin and Greek. *Se agapo* is Greek, and it means I love thee. *J'ai une bonne petite soeur* is French, and it means I have a good little sister. *Nous avons un bon pere et une bonne mere* means, we have a good father and a good mother. *Puer* is boy in Latin, and *Mutter* is mother in German. I will teach Mildred many languages when I come home.[23]

She would eventually become fluent in each of these four languages along with Italian and Esperanto, the "universal language" created by Polish ophthalmologist L. L. Zamenhof in the 1870s, designed to bring the world together by eliminating language barriers.[24]

Annie's return to Perkins with her celebrated pupil in tow should have served as a triumphant homecoming, but it was marred by her increasing annoyance with Anagnos, which came to a head once more when he continued to imply that Samuel Howe's methods were primarily responsible for Helen's achievements. It prompted a passive-aggressive letter to the director in February 1889, which reveals Annie's mounting frustration: "I think you will understand me when I say that it puzzles me to know why I deserve especial congratulations for following a course which was clearly and definitely indicated by another."[25]

The director was less than conciliatory in his patronizing response, acknowledging her "annoyance" but counseling her to "make the best of the inconvenience."[26]

Meanwhile, Anagnos wasn't the only figure at Perkins with whom Annie found herself at odds. The founder's widow, Julia Ward Howe, appeared to see Annie's increasing fame as a threat to her husband's legacy. "One day when an admiring group were saying complimentary things about my success in teaching Helen," Annie recalled, "I turned to Mrs. Howe who had not joined in the conversation, and said, 'Can it be possible, Madam, that the almshouse has trained a teacher?' 'I would say,' she answered coldly, 'it has nurtured the vanity of an ill-mannered person.'"[27]

"It was not easy for a young woman of my humble origin and limited education to defend herself against people like the Howes," Annie later observed to her biographer.[28]

Even as the director continued to give short shrift to Annie's part in Helen's education, a number of distinguished Americans were beginning to take notice of Helen's teacher. "Your parents and friends must take great satisfaction in your progress," wrote the future Supreme Court justice Oliver Wendell Holmes to ten-year-old Helen in 1890.[29] "It [does] great credit not only to you but to your instructors." That same year, the distinguished poet and abolitionist John Whittier wrote, "God has been good to thee in giving thee such a teacher as Miss Sullivan."[30] But most people were willing to accept Helen as a miracle and let it go at that. Only one man appeared more interested in how Helen had been taught.

As one of the most respected figures in the field of deaf education, Alexander Graham Bell's words carried great weight with the deaf establishment. After *The Silent Educator* ran a profile of Annie's methods in 1892, Bell wrote a response singling out one factor above others that he believed carried "enormous importance" in teaching all deaf children:

> She adopted the principle of talking to Helen just as she would to a seeing and hearing child, spelling into her hands the words and sentences she would have spoken to her if she could have heard, in spite of the fact that at first much of the language was unintelligible to the child. She did not pick and choose her words, but by frequent repetition of complete sentences containing ordinary idiomatic expressions, she sought to impress the language upon the child's memory and thus lead her gradually to imitate it. The great principle that Miss Sullivan seems to have had in mind in the instruction of Helen is one that appears obvious enough when it is once formulated, and one with which we are all familiar as the principle involved in the acquisition of language by ordinary hearing and speaking children. It is simply this: *That language is acquired by imitation.* This means that language must be presented to deaf children before it is understood; the children must be familiarized with the model before they have anything to imitate.[31]

With Bell's ringing endorsement, Annie Sullivan's methods had been pronounced as the gold standard for teaching deaf children. How else to explain Helen's astonishing rapid command of language? It is an assessment that would remain largely unquestioned in the annals of special education until another explanation emerged decades later when linguists discovered evidence that humans are born with innate faculties for acquiring language. Led by MIT professor Noam Chomsky, a field of linguistic theory emerged in the 1960s arguing that babies' brains are wired with certain principles that guide them in developing the grammar they will eventually use when they begin to talk. "I know that there's considerable debate about Helen Keller's linguistic abilities, and Anne Sullivan's role," Professor Chomsky explains. "There is by now good evidence that basic rudiments of language are in place by two years old or less."[32]

In fact, by the time Helen lost her hearing, she was nineteen months old and had already learned a number of words, including—notably— "water."[33] The miraculous acquisition of language that Bell attributed to Annie's "methods," then, is more likely primarily explained by biological factors unrelated to her education (although the Harvard scholar Dr. Sanjay Gulati—who specializes in research around deafness—believes that Helen's development would have been significantly stunted if the Keller family had waited any longer to hire a teacher).[34] Moreover, Helen's rapid acquisition of idiomatic English that Bell always attributed to Annie may be explained in part by her prodigious reading. Still, it would be many decades before these concepts were widely understood. Bell's endorsement was the first important step in creating the narrative of an extraordinary teacher who had produced a miracle—shifting the narrative from a miraculous child to a miracle worker.

Almost from the time that Helen arrived at Perkins, Anagnos wasted no opportunity to exploit her fame for the benefit of the school—showing her off at countless fundraisers—even as Annie continued to fume at his failure to give her the credit she believed she was due. Although she had mostly kept her frustration in check for some time, she succeeded in stirring up a hornet's nest among the trustees when she gave an interview to a local newspaper in 1890 that appeared to dismiss the role Perkins had played in Helen's education. "Helen is not a regular pupil at the Perkins Institution being under the care of a private teacher there," she told a reporter for the *Boston Daily Journal*. "She is there simply to obtain the advantages of the apparatus which the Institution contains, and for those other advantages desirable for a child in her condition in the possession of which the City of Boston excels all others. I have the whole charge of her, and my salary is paid by her father; so, you can see that she is not a pupil of the Institution."[35]

The interview sent shock waves through the school. Summoned to explain herself, Annie told John A. Bennett—who was acting director while Anagnos toured Europe—that she was "sick and tired to death of having people speak of Helen as belonging to this institution" and that she wanted to put a stop to it. Bennett quickly laid down the law. "I told her that I would not tolerate that from any inmate, whether guest or not, and that so long as she remained, she would have to be at least outwardly civil," he later recalled.[36] Annie took the hint and sent a conciliatory letter apologizing for her indiscretion. "There it would appear that to me alone is due all the credit of Helen's education," she wrote the trustees in June 1890, "whereas the truth is that the advantages she had at the Institution during the past year have done more to develop and broaden her mind than any training that I could possibly have given her in years, alone."[37]

By the following year, all appeared to have been forgiven when Anagnos sat down to write his annual report. His account of eleven-year-old Helen's progress was, if anything, even more hyperbolic than in his previous reports, calling her "a phenomenal child...as fascinating as a fairy tale...like a new star, shining with its own light and differing from all others in glory, and seemingly independent of the rest of the host of heaven."[38]

Shortly before he dispatched this report to the printer, Anagnos received from Annie a copy of a short story Helen had written called "The Frost King" about a man called King Frost, who lived in "the land of perpetual snow" with a band of "merry little fairies" as his servants. "I think you will be pleased with this little story Helen wrote for your birthday," Annie wrote from Tuscumbia, where she and Helen were staying. "We thought it pretty and original."[39]

He was so taken by the story that he included it in the January 1892 issue of the Perkins alumni journal, *The Mentor*. Weeks later, it was reprinted in the *Goodson Gazette*, a weekly newspaper published by the Virginia Institution for the Education of the Deaf and Dumb and Blind. Announcing it as the "most extraordinary literary production" in its history, the paper billed the story as a "fantasy" written by Helen Keller. Not long afterward, a reader brought to the paper's attention the fact that Helen's story resembled a children's story called the "Frost Fairies," written seven years before she was born in a volume of short stories by an author named Margaret Canby under the title "Birdie and His Fairy Friends." The *Gazette* published extracts of the stories side by side—including large passages from Helen's story that borrowed word-for-word from Canby's version—and announced Helen's version a "bold plagiarism."[40]

On the shocking revelation, they wrote, "The *Goodson* does not blame little Helen Keller for this attempted fraud, far from it. She has done merely what she was told to do. The blame for the fraud rests not upon her, but upon whoever knowingly attempted to palm off the 'Frost King' as her composition, and there the blame will lie."[41]

This harsh assessment ignored the fact that, if Anagnos had not decided to publish it, Helen's story would have simply been taken for what it was—a fable that she loved and decided to share as a gift to a friend. The accusations of "plagiarism" that emerged repeatedly throughout the affair appeared to assume Helen had knowingly used Canby's words as her own even though there may very well have been another explanation. As early as 1888, Annie had written Anagnos noting that she had to be extremely careful when reading stories to Helen "because the little witch has such a wonderfully retentative (sic) memory that she can remember the thread of a tale after it has been read to her once."[42]

Still, the clear insinuation of the *Gazette*'s accusatory report was that it was Annie who was somehow responsible for Helen's transgression. Purportedly to "protect the reputation" of the Perkins School, Anagnos called an investigative committee made up of four blind and four sighted members. When Helen was summoned before the committee, she denied all knowledge of ever having read Margaret Canby's story before. Likewise, Annie denied ever reading it to her. At the conclusion of the hearing, the verdict was split with four voting for "acquittal" and four for "conviction." This left Anagnos to cast the deciding vote and he sided with Helen—seemingly removing the cloud that had hung over both Helen and Annie since the plagiarism allegations first went public.

Meanwhile, Annie conducted her own "investigation" into what might have happened. Claiming that she had never even heard of Canby's book, she first searched the Perkins library but failed to find a copy and expanded her pursuit. Before long, it appeared that the mystery had been solved. Her explanation, printed as a statement in the respected journal *American Annals of the Deaf*, traced the story to her former Perkins housemother and longtime mentor, Sophia Hopkins. After "making careful enquiry," she discovered that Mrs. Hopkins had a copy of the book, which had been received as a gift by her daughter years earlier. During a visit, Mrs. Hopkins had allegedly read to Helen from a number of different children's books, and Annie noted that "while Mrs. Hopkins does not remember this story of 'Frost Fairies,' she is confident that she read to Helen extracts, if not entire stories, from this volume."[43]

Annie's explanation appeared to put the controversy behind them. But although the two had been officially cleared, it wasn't long before Helen sensed that a cloud of suspicion remained. "I felt that there was something hostile and menacing in the very atmosphere," she later recalled.[44] At the end of the school year, she and Annie returned to Alabama to spend the summer with her family, the Frost King incident "forgotten." But Michael Anagnos had evidently not forgotten, as is evident from the tone of a letter that Helen sent him from Alabama in October 1892: "My dear Mr. Anagnos, I begin to fear you are not going to write to me anymore: it has been such a long time since we have heard from you. I thought I should have had an answer to my poor little letter long ago, but the weeks have grown to months; I have spent the summer at Fern Quarry; and now am home again in Tuscumbia, wondering what has become of my dearest friend."[45]

It was the first hint that there may have been more to the story than people had been led to believe. The stigma surrounding the affair caused great anxiety for Helen, who claimed she was long "tormented" by the fear that some of what she wrote "might not absolutely be my own."[46] But it clearly took a far greater toll on Annie, who knew that both Helen's family and Michael Anagnos blamed her for the incident. "Scarcely anyone held Helen responsible," she later told her biographer. "It was the perfidious teacher who had warped the child."[47]

A year after Annie first arrived in Tuscumbia to begin Helen's education, Anagnos had written her a heartfelt letter in which he declared, "I take as much success in you as if you were my daughter. In fact, I consider you as such."[48] In the aftermath of the Frost King affair, Annie did everything in her power to restore their bond. "I wish to be near you because I love you and I am happier near you than anywhere else in the world," she wrote him in August.[49] But she could sense that her efforts were in vain. Annie's biographer Kim Nielsen believes that the director assumed he could retain his hold over Helen while distancing the school from her teacher.[50] But Annie was not about to let that happen. Despite her entreaties, the chill between her and her one-time father figure would eventually become a permanent estrangement and Helen would never return to Perkins as a student.

In the years that followed, Helen's education took a rapid ascent through a series of private tutors, a stint at the Wright-Humason School for the Deaf in New York, and eventually enrollment at one of the country's most prestigious prep schools, the Cambridge School for Young Ladies in Boston. At each successive step, she had only one goal. "When I was a little girl," she later wrote, "I visited Wellesley and surprised my friends by the announcement, 'Someday, I shall go to college—but I shall go to Harvard.'" The dream of going to college, she recalled, "took root in my heart and became an earnest desire, which impelled me to enter into a competition with seeing and hearing girls, in the face of the strong opposition of many true and wise friends."[51]

Harvard would not admit women until 1920, so Helen eventually settled for its sister institution, Radcliffe—the most prestigious of the "seven sisters" group of elite women's colleges at the time. Against all odds, and the obstacles that Radcliffe threw her way at every turn, she would become the first deafblind person ever to earn a university degree when she graduated cum laude in 1904—with Annie interpreting for her, spelling into her palm every step of the way.

Chapter Five

· · · · · · · · · ·

The Story of My Life

A hush fell over the crowd at the Santa Monica Civic Auditorium as Maximilian Schell took the podium to announce the winner of the best actress Oscar at the 1963 Academy Awards ceremony. When he opened the envelope and announced Anne Bancroft's name, the result came as little surprise to the myriad of stars gathered that evening. Her powerful performance in *The Miracle Worker* had captivated audiences and critics around the world, and she was widely considered the odds-on favorite to win the coveted award. Earlier in the ceremony, Bancroft's sixteen-year-old costar, Patty Duke, had captured the less prestigious Oscar for best supporting actress. Few noted the irony of the fact that Bancroft had portrayed the teacher, Annie Sullivan—the film's titular character—while Duke had occupied the lesser role as her pupil, Helen Keller.

Indeed, in the seven decades since Keller had vaulted into the public imagination with her stirring story of overcoming multiple disabilities, her life story had conspicuously taken a back seat to the saga of the teacher who had been credited with her remarkable transformation. In life, like the movie, Helen Keller had been relegated to a subordinate role in her own story while Annie Sullivan was designated the heroine who had almost single-handedly achieved the astonishing "miracle." As it turned out, this was not entirely accidental.

⠠⠗⠑⠃⠏⠀⠀⠠⠋⠓⠄
⠗⠄⠏⠃⠀⠸⠑⠄

Shortly after passing the Radcliffe entrance exam in 1899, nineteen-year-old Helen shared her aspirations in an essay for *American Magazine*: "I have been so long nothing in the world. I have made up my mind that I must be something before I die. The question is what? I believe I should love to write. I have always had aspirations in that direction, but who knows if college life will not develop something else in me."[1]

As fate would have it, her sophomore year would see her enrolled in the English composition class of a man determined to cultivate that love of writing. Charles Copeland, or "Copey," as his students affectionately called him, had mentored some of America's greatest literary lights, including T. S. Eliot and John Dos Passos. His lectures, Helen later recalled, were filled with "original freshness and power" that helped her take her writing to new heights.[2] Copeland encouraged her to "dig into her own experience," and soon recognized that her deeply personal essays deserved a wider audience. He helped bring her story to the attention of the *Ladies' Home Journal*, which offered Helen a contract in 1901 to write the story of her life in five installments.

The prospect of assembling her compositions into a comprehensive narrative was daunting, especially at the same time as completing the grueling Radcliffe coursework. Helen considered passing on the project, but as she was deliberating, her friend Lenore Kinney introduced her to a young Harvard instructor named John Macy, who happened to be boarding at the same Cambridge house as Annie and Helen.

Macy, who was descended from a Nantucket whaling family with limited means, had established quite the reputation on campus as both a writer and a scholar during his Harvard undergraduate career, serving as editor in chief of the arts and literary magazine the *Advocate* as well as an editor on the famed *Lampoon*. Lenore was convinced the worldly young man would be the ideal candidate to assist Helen through the demanding process of assembling her life story. Macy had recently graduated with a master's and had assumed the position of editor for the *Youth's Companion* magazine. He also occasionally taught English at both Harvard and Radcliffe, for which he was poorly compensated, and so welcomed any work he could pick up on the side.[3] "Both Annie and Helen took to the tall young man in his early twenties," noted biographer Joseph Lash, "and when they wanted something, they were difficult to resist. Soon, Macy had learned the manual language and went to work with them."[4]

John Macy, however, was not as impressed with Helen as the coterie of distinguished admirers who had been singing her praises for years. "She is not a 'brilliant genius,'" he declared in an essay he wrote about her Radcliffe years for the *Youth's Companion*. "She is not even scholarly in her interests. Her mind is stout and energetic, of solid endurance. Many women have keener minds and deeper capacity for scholarship. I, for one, cannot see that she has the intellect of a genius, or much creative power, or great originality."[5] Macy's condescending assessment would eventually be widely disputed but, as it turned out, he had another reason for sticking with the project. Despite his somewhat lackluster opinion of Helen's abilities, it was soon clear that he had become enamored of Annie. Before long, the three were inseparable and Macy began to look on Helen's literary project as more than just a job.

By the time that Helen's memoir was complete, it had taken on a dramatically different form than she had first imagined. "It was Annie's first intention to have nothing in it about herself except what Helen wrote," Nella Henney claimed in her 1933 biography.[6] In Nella's telling, Annie reluctantly consented to include a section about her teaching methods only after she received a lengthy handwritten letter from *Journal* editor Edward Bok, who had commissioned the original magazine piece. "I know that the public wants to know more about you than Miss Keller will tell in her articles," he allegedly pleaded.[7]

But a letter that John Macy wrote to the New York publisher Charles Scribner's Sons in February 1902—even before Helen submitted her installments to the *Ladies' Home Journal*—reveals that he was already shopping the story around as a book, which he intended to sell to the highest bidder. Instead of simply reprinting Helen's autobiographical story, he proposed that the book would comprise three sections. The first part would be Helen's story, as first published in the *Journal*. The second section, he explained, would be "selections from journals and letters." The third part would be written by Macy himself, "in which I shall set forth all that has not been fully covered in the other two parts."[8] It's unclear whether he consulted with Helen about these ideas before shopping the project to publishers. Macy's letter, however, reveals that, whatever initial doubts Annie may have had about being included in the book, it was almost certainly his idea, rather than Edward Bok's, to turn the book into what it would become: a celebration of Annie Sullivan as the person primarily responsible for Helen's achievements. When *The Story of My Life* was published in 1903, it took almost exactly the form that Macy had laid out in his letters to publishers a year earlier—adding a "Supplementary Account of Helen's Life and Education" written by Macy, along with letters written by Helen, Annie, and others.

To the millions of children for whom *The Story of My Life* would one day be required reading, the section where Helen tells her own story—spanning the period from her infancy to her early Radcliffe years—would be widely heralded as an inspirational tale of overcoming insurmountable odds. But the supplementary section about Annie's role in the girl's education, written by John Macy, would serve to catapult Annie into the annals of history as a creator of miracles.

The book, when it appeared in 1903, was an instant worldwide sensation, billed as "the remarkable achievements of a deaf, dumb, and blind girl." The account of Helen's unruly behavior when Annie first arrived attracted particular attention and would provide the most dramatic scenes for *The Miracle Worker* decades later. Among those enraptured by the description of Annie's role in taming her "wild" pupil was a Nevada man who wrote the publisher expressing his admiration for her methods.

"I think she has done more for education and the people than Miss Frances Willard," he asserted, comparing Annie to the well-known, fiery American educator and temperance reformer. "I broke horses all my life and I think Miss Sullivan's theory is all rite on a colt...I think when she went to Alabama and took charge of that little Bronco, it proved it."[9]

Nearly every article highlighted the breakthrough moment at the water pump, which, according to the *San Francisco Call*, had unleashed "one of the most precocious intellects of the age."[10] Most reviews especially singled out the description of Annie's remarkable teaching methods, described by John Macy in the supplement. "Miss Sullivan asked herself, 'How does a normal child learn language?'" the *Brooklyn Citizen* wrote. Comparing her to Samuel Gridley Howe, the paper claimed that he taught deaf students each word separately while Miss Sullivan followed the "natural method"—the term that John Macy had coined to describe the idea of introducing the "endless repetition of language" before a child can fully understand the meaning of words.[11]

For the average reader, Annie's supposedly innovative methods appeared superhuman. But William Wade, a wealthy Pennsylvania landowner who was deeply familiar with deafblind education and the methods that Dr. Howe had employed in the education of Laura Bridgman more than fifty years earlier, considered the account to be "shocking rot and rubbish."[12]

Wade first encountered Helen at nine years old when he read a magazine profile that mentioned her "small dog." Convinced that a blind child should have a more substantial pet, he arranged to send her a mastiff, whom Helen named Lioness. Before long, he also sent her a donkey named Neddy and a pony she would call Black Beauty—presumably named after the beloved 1887 novel by Anna Sewell.

Thus began a long friendship between the young girl and the fifty-year-old philanthropist, whom historian Frances Koestler described as "the patron saint of every deafblind child he could find."[13] For reasons still unclear, Wade had decided that he would take the deafblind community—still very much on the fringes of disability education at the time—under his embrace. He became known for bestowing gifts such as braille typewriters, sewing machines, bicycles, dolls, vacations, and, most importantly, books, which he would pay to have transcribed in braille.[14] For decades, Wade traveled from school to school and befriended dozens of deafblind children throughout the country. He would eventually publish a monograph in 1901, *The Deaf-Blind*, which was the first concerted effort at constructing a roster of the seventy-two known deafblind persons in the United States at the time.

Having almost certainly encountered more deafblind children than anyone else in history to that point, Wade was dismissive of the idea that Helen's educational accomplishments had been the product of innovative methods. He believed that Helen was a prodigy who would have been "equally wonderful" in the hands of any teacher. In fact, he saw no difference between the way Helen was taught and the education of Laura Bridgman.[15] Shortly after *The Story of My Life* was published in 1903, he released an updated edition of his monograph to weigh in with his "emphatic dissent" about the claim that Helen's prowess had been accomplished by the "splinter new methods" devised by Annie Sullivan.[16]

"It is cruel, as well as absurd, to stick one's head in the sand to avoid seeing the proved fact that Helen is a prodigy," he wrote, "for it loads down other teachers of the blind-deaf with the weight of mistaken feeling that, if they could pursue such methods as Miss Sullivan's, they would make Helen Kellers of their pupils. I am quite certain that Miss Sullivan will go as far as I do in scouting such preposterous error."[17]

Wade argued that Annie's methods were not new or innovative at all. He credited her instead with "wise application" of existing methods while disputing the idea that she had conceived any original techniques. "If necessity had arisen," he wrote, "Miss Sullivan would have devised new methods to suit but that, as I see it, such necessity did not turn up."[18]

He took particular aim at John Macy's description of Annie's use of the "Natural Method" in the supplement. The book includes a letter from Annie to Mrs. Hopkins about her early success with Helen describing her thought process: "I have been observing Helen's little cousin lately. These observations have given me a clue to be followed in teaching Helen language. I shall talk into her hand as we talk into the baby's ears."[19]

Many reviewers had zeroed in on this in their effusive discussion of Annie's remarkable prowess as a teacher, but Wade would claim that these laudatory descriptions "poured numberless buckets of ice water down my spinal column."[20] In a letter to Macy, he refers to "the delusion in the public mind" that Helen's education was accomplished by "magical means." He takes particular aim at John's description of Annie as a "strikingly original and detached discoverer."[21]

"She may be to you, who know nothing of other teachers of the blind-deaf, or of other such pupils; To me, knowing more or less of all such teachers, and how they did their work, I know that all used the same methods as Miss Sullivan, and one of the ablest of them says that Miss S naturally and inevitably fell into those methods."[22]

Even while he dismissed the growing narrative of the miracle, however, Wade went to great lengths to stress his admiration for Annie and her "complete devotion" to Helen. He insisted: "While I cannot but resent such absurdity as that Helen was nothing much, and that the methods of her education were ninety-nine per cent of her development, I will not detract even one per cent from the credit justly due Miss Sullivan."[23]

For Helen herself, however, there was no doubt whatsoever about who should get credit for her achievements. "Obviously I am not the person to compare the methods of my own education with those employed in teaching Laura Bridgman and other deaf-blind children," she wrote in her subsequent 1929 memoir, *Midstream*. "I leave the task to those who are more detached. From what I have read of Laura, I am sure that she was bright and eager, and I believe that if she had my teacher, she would have outshone me."[24]

The section extolling Annie's teaching methods wasn't the only element of Helen's first memoir that attracted widespread public attention. When *The Story of My Life* was published in 1903, many readers were taken aback with the lengthy account of the largely forgotten Frost King plagiarism incident and naturally aghast at the unseemly inquisition launched against an eleven-year-old girl. A full ten pages were devoted to the affair, which Helen explained she had chosen to write about "because it was important in my life and education, and in order that there might be no misunderstanding."[25]

And yet, considering the crucial role of *The Story of My Life* in the deification of Annie Sullivan and in shaping the narrative that would persist for generations, the prominence of the account may have another explanation. John Macy, as editor, could not have been unaware that if Annie—whom he would later marry—was to emerge as the hero of the story, it was first necessary to convincingly erase the stain that hung over her role in the plagiarism affair. Helen was all too willing to absolve her teacher of any blame. Acknowledging her transgression, she takes full responsibility in her memoir while casting Annie as the unwitting victim.

"The two stories were so much alike in thought and language that it was evident Miss Canby's story had been read to me, and that mine was a plagiarism," she wrote. "It was difficult to make me understand this; but when I did understand I was astonished and grieved. No child ever drank deeper of the cup of bitterness than I did. I had disgraced myself; I had brought suspicion upon those I loved best."[26]

Shortly after publication, Mark Twain wrote Helen expressing his disdain for what she had been put through: "Oh, dear me, how unspeakably funny and owlishly idiotic and grotesque that 'plagiarism' farce! For substantially all ideas are second-hand, consciously and unconsciously draw from a million outside sources, and daily used by them garnered with a pride and satisfaction born of the superstition that he originated them."[27]

For anybody who had read Helen's version of the debacle, the case appeared to be settled. It seemed clear that she and Annie had been subjected to a grossly unfair stain on their reputations, resulting from a misunderstanding and mistake. And yet both continued to hint throughout their lives that there was more to the story. Annie would later acknowledge to Nella Henney that Helen had furnished "damaging information" during the initial enquiry, but she did not elaborate.

It was a mystery that was never satisfactorily answered—until decades later, when a typed manuscript, bound in leather, emerged in the archives of the Perkins School titled *Miss Sullivan's Methods*. Written approximately fifteen years after the Frost King incident, the unpublished manuscript takes the form of a report compiled by an investigator, believed to be David Prescott Hall, Julia Ward Howe's son-in-law, who was a lawyer.[28] The 171-page manuscript contains a detailed analysis of previously undisclosed notes taken during the plagiarism enquiry, as well as a comparison between reports that Annie had furnished to Perkins about Helen's education at the time and the claims later published in *The Story of My Life*. It is unclear why the report was commissioned and why it was never released, but its most damning content sheds light on an incident that was never made public.

It reveals that Helen had confided to one of her teachers, Fannie Marrett, that it was *Annie* who had read her "The Frost Fairies," the original Margaret Canby story at the heart of the plagiarism allegations, even though Annie had always claimed she had no knowledge of the story.

The anonymous investigator assiduously examined three years of letters and stories written by Helen—phrase by phrase—and discovered that, between 1888 and 1891, she had repeatedly "assimilated" from four other Margaret Canby stories published in the same volume as "The Frost Fairies." More significantly, he purports to show that Annie herself repeatedly used passages from Canby's stories in teaching Helen during this period and leaves little doubt that Annie was in fact very familiar with the Canby book after all despite her adamant denials at the time.

The implications of the damning unpublished revelations are clear. It suggests that it was Annie who had, in fact, read Helen the stories and, when the accusations of plagiarism surfaced, had almost certainly asked both Mrs. Hopkins and likely Helen herself to lie to cover up the truth. This startling revelation was enough to convince both of Helen's major biographers, Joseph Lash and Dorothy Herrmann, that Annie had fabricated the account about Mrs. Hopkins and lied when she had denied any knowledge of Canby's book. Both agreed that neither Helen nor Annie had set out to deceive Anagnos when Helen originally sent him the story, and that the plagiarism itself was likely inadvertent. Lash, in fact, was convinced that Annie did not understand the meaning of plagiarism, which was "why she allowed Helen to send the story to Anagnos and to present it as her own, and then, taking fright because of the uproar, denied she had read the Birdie stories."[29]

It appears that the Frost King incident may not have been the only time that Annie attempted to embellish her history. In 1933, Helen wrote her sister, Mildred, about the forthcoming biography of Teacher being written by Nella Henney. In this letter, she confides to Mildred that, while Nella was researching Annie's life, she had come across some letters from Kate Keller. These contradicted Annie's description of Helen's unruly behavior that furnished much of the most dramatic sections of *The Story of My Life*. Annie, it appeared, was now threatening to censor them.

"Teacher insists that two of the more unpleasant letters be destroyed— those written by mother in which she denied that I was a 'wild, uncouth creature' before Teacher came to me," Helen confided.[30] From the accounts of other family members, there seems to be no question that Helen was an obstinate child given to frequent tantrums before Annie arrived and taught her to communicate, so Mrs. Keller's protests may simply have been a mother protecting her daughter. But these letters certainly raise the possibility that Annie had, at the very least, exaggerated her young pupil's behavior to portray her role in the eventual "taming" as more significant. Helen herself would admit that she had little memory of the events portrayed in the account published under her name. In a telling passage from her first autobiography, she writes, "When I try to classify my earliest impression, I find that fact and fancy look alike across the years."[31]

Despite these seemingly damning revelations that call into question some of the hagiography that has emerged around the role of Annie Sullivan for more than a century, it is important to view both Helen's and Annie's actions in context. The rarely discussed truth about the Frost King incident certainly casts a shadow over Annie's legacy. And yet it is important to consider the circumstances. If Annie had admitted the truth, she would have faced the very real prospect of losing her livelihood. And perhaps, just as alarmingly for her, it may have caused her to be separated from Helen. Can anybody blame her for doing what she felt she must at the time to protect herself, and that bond?

Similarly, it is hard to fault Annie for exaggerating her accomplishments or perhaps taking undue credit for the "miracle" of Helen Keller—an achievement for which she was justifiably proud. It would be disingenuous to deny the role that Annie played in Helen's extraordinary development, notwithstanding the debate about whether more credit is due the pupil or the teacher. Despite his own unique perspective on deafblind education, it is hard to take seriously William Wade's assertion that any teacher could have achieved what Annie Sullivan had accomplished simply by employing the methods of Samuel Gridley Howe.

Although Annie may not have been a miracle worker, she was clearly a skilled teacher whose emphasis on child-centered education allowed Helen to thrive. Perhaps the most significant difference of all between Annie Sullivan and Samuel Gridley Howe was that, unlike Howe, Annie didn't abandon her pupil when she had "outlived her usefulness," as his biographer charged, describing how the Perkins founder had lost interest in Laura's education after he married.

And so, while it's important not to judge Annie's actions too harshly lest we discount her very real contributions, it is also important to consider one undeniable consequence of the miracle narrative that has remained largely intact for generations. No matter the significance of events that took place in Alabama when Helen was six, they have served to largely overshadow or erase the extraordinary eighty years of her life that followed.

Chapter Six

"Mr. Clemens"

When Charles Dickens wrote about Laura Bridgman in 1842, the attention of the world's most celebrated novelist helped make Laura a household name. By some quirk of historical fate, Helen Keller also owed much of her early fame to the most famous writer of his generation.

The first time Helen encountered Samuel Clemens—better known by his pen name, Mark Twain—was at a New York party given in her honor by Laurence Hutton, literary editor of *Harper's Magazine*, when she was fourteen years old. A number of distinguished guests had been invited to meet the girl, whose achievements had already begun to attract widespread attention. Twain, who attended the party with his friend Henry Huttleston Rogers, the Standard Oil tycoon, would later recall the encounter in his unpublished autobiography: "The wonderful child arrived now with her about equally wonderful teacher, Miss Sullivan. Without touching anything, and without seeing anything, obviously, and without hearing anything, she seemed to quite well recognize the character of her surroundings. She said, 'Oh, the books, the books, so many, many books. How lovely!'"[1] Helen would also record their first meeting, writing that "the instant I clasped his hand in mine, I knew that he was my friend."[2]

Their next encounter took place around the time that Helen was preparing to enter college and Hutton had once again assembled an eclectic array of distinguished guests to meet her at a gathering at his home in Princeton. Helen had recently announced her intention to attend Radcliffe but encountered significant obstacles when she discovered that officials at the famed institution were unwilling or reluctant to make the necessary accommodation to facilitate the instruction of a deafblind student in the classroom. Instead, it was proposed that she follow a "special" course developed to allow her to pursue her studies privately at her own pace. It was only after an impassioned plea by Helen and the lobbying efforts of Hutton's wife, Eleanor, that the university eventually agreed to admit her in the regular program.

At another gathering hosted by the Huttons, she met Woodrow Wilson, who was, at the time, a professor at Princeton, which, like Harvard, still did not admit women. Helen recalled that upon being introduced to the future US president, he asked her why she had chosen Radcliffe rather than another prominent women's college such as Wellesley or Bryn Mawr. "I said, 'Because they didn't want me at Radcliffe, and as I was stubborn by nature, I chose to override their objections.'"[3]

Although she had already overcome one significant obstacle when Radcliffe agreed to accommodate her disabilities by allowing Annie to attend classes with her to spell the lessons into her hand, it had appeared for a time that another might derail her plans. It had become increasingly likely that she would not be able to afford the hefty financial commitment that would be required to pay both her tuition and the significant Boston living expenses for herself and Annie. Although Helen had been born into comfortable circumstances, Captain Keller had long since fallen on hard financial times—so bleak that he had been unable even to muster Annie's $25 monthly salary beyond the first year after her arrival in Tuscumbia. Her subsequent expenses had instead been covered by various benefactors and later by Helen herself.[4]

Twain's own schooling had been interrupted at the age of twelve when the death of his father forced him to quit school to support his family. He was famously dubious about the merits of formal education and was fond of quoting an adage first expressed by the Canadian novelist Grant Allen: "Never let school interfere with your education." Despite these reservations, Twain was determined that nothing should stand in the way of Helen's educational goals. When he discovered that her promising academic career was in jeopardy, he summoned his extensive connections. Although he had squandered his own considerable fortune with failed financial ventures and poor investments, he was able to call on a wide assortment of wealthy friends.

"It won't do for America to allow this marvelous child to retire from her studies because of poverty," he wrote to Emelie Rogers, wife of the Standard Oil executive Henry Rogers. "If she can go on with them, she will make a fame that will endure in history for centuries. Along her special lines, she is the most extraordinary product of all the ages...So, I thought of this scheme. Beg you to lay siege to your husband and get him to interest himself and Messrs. John D. and William Rockefeller and the other Standard Oil chiefs in Helen's case."[5] In the end, Rogers became the largest contributor to a substantial trust set up to put Helen through Radcliffe—the beginning of a trend that would see a number of prominent society figures anxious to attach their names and financial largesse to the famous girl as an extension of their philanthropic endeavors. For Twain, however, there was clearly a deep bond of affection.

A number of theories have been offered to explain the unlikely friendship between the young deafblind girl and the aging author. For her part, Helen remarked on how candid and unabashed he was with her, recalling how his "talk was fragrant with tobacco and flamboyant with profanity. I adored him because he did not temper his conversation to any femininity...He treated me not as a freak but as a handicapped woman seeking a way to circumvent extraordinary difficulties."[6] As far as Twain's affection for Helen, it is worth noting that Twain's eldest daughter, Susy, had died tragically of spinal meningitis shortly before he took it upon himself to arrange for the sponsorship of Helen's education. Could he have seen Helen as something of a surrogate daughter?

Whatever the reason, their friendship burgeoned into increasing expressions of mutual admiration.

The first time that many Americans ever heard of Helen Keller, in fact, was from a report in which Twain allegedly described her and Napoleon as the two most interesting characters of the nineteenth century.[7] The quote was later prominently featured in the promotional campaign that Doubleday launched to promote *The Story of My Life* upon its release. Later, in what is almost certainly an apocryphal addition, his words were expanded to embellish the comparison: "Napoleon tried to conquer the world by physical force and failed. Helen Keller tried to conquer the world by power of mind and succeeded."[8]

He would eventually add to the superlatives, describing her in his autobiography as "the most marvellous person of her sex since Joan of Arc" and "fellow to Caesar, Alexander, Napoleon, Homer, Shakespeare and the rest of the immortals."[9] At a dinner honoring Helen in 1901, he would add another widely quoted aphorism to the growing list, but now her teacher was included in the hyperbole: "Helen Keller is the eighth wonder of the world. [Annie Sullivan] is the ninth."[10] By this time, he had also formed a deep attachment to Annie and declared that Helen was merely a "lump of clay" before Annie entered her life. Drawing on mythology to spin a larger-than-life story, he wrote that Helen was "deaf, dumb, blind, inert, dull, groping, almost insentient. Miss Sullivan blew the breath of intelligence into her and woke the clay to life."[11] And in keeping with his dubious views on the state of education, he wrote, "Has Miss Sullivan taught her by the methods of the American public school? No, oh, no; for then she would be deafer and dumber and blinder than she was before."[12]

For Helen, in fact, one of Twain's most endearing traits was his fondness for Annie. "He was interested in everything about me—my friends and little adventures and what I was writing. I loved him for his beautiful appreciation of my teacher's work," she wrote about their friendship years later. "Of all the people who have written about me, he is almost the only one who has realized the importance of Miss Sullivan in my life, who has appreciated her brilliancy, penetration, wisdom, character, and the fine literary competences of her pen."[13]

After a party Twain threw honoring Helen, his longtime friend and biographer Albert Bigelow Paine observed, "To see Mark Twain and Helen Keller together was not easily forgotten."[14] Despite the author's fondness for Annie, whom Helen usually relied on for interpretation, Twain could induce peals of laughter from Helen even when Annie was not present to spell his words into her palms. "He made me laugh and feel thoroughly happy by telling some good stories, which I read from his lips," Helen recalled, having learned as a teenager at the Wright-Humason School to "listen" by placing her hand over a person's larynx, throat, and lips.[15] By this time, she had also spent several years painstakingly learning to talk, so it's instructive here to find her recalling a full-fledged early conversation without Teacher's assistance.

Fittingly, their exchanges were often characterized by the wit that had long become associated with America's most famous humorist. "I must mention that beautiful creature, Helen Keller, whom I have known for these many years," Twain told members of the New York Woman's Press Club in 1900. "If I could have been deaf, dumb, and blind I also might have arrived at something."[16]

Helen was fond of telling the story about her friend's response when the journalist Peter Dunne lamented to him how dull Helen's life must be, "every day the same and every night the same as the day." Twain retorted, "You're damned wrong there; blindness is an exciting business, I tell you; if you don't believe it, get up some dark night on the wrong side of your bed when the house is on fire and try to find the door."[17]

One of the most frequently quoted anecdotes about their friendship described an incident that took place when Helen was visiting Twain's Connecticut estate. "He was passionately fond of billiards, and very proud of the billiard table with which Mrs. H. H. Rogers had presented him," she later wrote. "He said he would teach me to play. I answered,

'Oh, Mr. Clemens, it takes sight to play billiards.' 'Yes,' he teased, 'but not the variety of billiards that Paine and Dunne and Rogers play. The blind couldn't play worse.' "[18]

And while only Twain would have dared to tease Helen about her disability, such was the nature of their relationship that she had no compunction about making fun of his advanced years in a 1905 letter marking his birthday. "And you are seventy years old?" she wrote her longtime friend. "Or is the report exaggerated like that of your death? I remember, when I saw you last...you said, 'If a man is a pessimist before he is forty-eight, he knows too much. If he is an optimist after he is forty-eight, he knows too little.' Now, we know you are an optimist, and nobody would dare to accuse one on the 'seven-terraced summit' of knowing little. So probably you are not seventy after all, but only forty-seven!"[19]

Many chroniclers have documented Twain's famous friendship with Helen, usually highlighting these anecdotes reflecting their gentle banter, humor, and mutual admiration. What is usually missing from these accounts, however, are their frequent interactions on matters more serious. "To one hampered and circumscribed as I am it was a wonderful experience to have a friend like Mr. Clemens," Helen wrote. "I recall many talks with him about human affairs. He never made me feel that my opinions were worthless...He knew that we do not think with eyes and ears, and that our capacity for thought is not measured by five senses."[20]

She recalled especially his refusal to accept injustice: "He thought he was a cynic, but his cynicism did not make him indifferent to the sight of cruelty, unkindness, meanness, or pretentiousness. He would often say, 'Helen, the world is full of unseeing eyes, vacant, staring, soulless eyes.' He would work himself into a frenzy over dull acquiescence in any evil that could be remedied."[21]

Nor do most accounts mention that Mark Twain and Helen Keller shared a dark bond. They were both transplanted Southerners who believed their lineage was deeply stained by their families' connections to the evils of slavery. "My family all belonged to the master class, and were proud of their birth and social prestige, and they held slaves," Helen wrote long after she had moved away from Alabama for good.[22]

In his autobiography, Twain also wrote about "the fifteen or twenty Negroes" enslaved by his uncle John when he was growing up in Hannibal, Missouri: "In my schoolboy days I had no aversion to slavery. I was not aware that there was anything wrong about it...the local pulpit taught us that God approved it, that it was a holy thing, and that the doubter need only look in the Bible if he wished to settle his mind." Later, he would be deeply shaken when he witnessed an enslaved man killed by a rock-throwing white man for the crime of "merely doing something awkward."[23]

Race, and their Southern heritage, would eventually play a strong role in awakening the political consciousness of both figures. Only weeks before he met Helen for the first time, Twain had published a novel, *The Tragedy of Pudd'nhead Wilson*, using the literary device of babies switched at birth to expose the malignant evils of American racism—a more explicit indictment than his most celebrated novel, *The Adventures of Huckleberry Finn*, which had famously served to humanize Huck's formerly enslaved companion, Jim. Years after slavery was abolished, a series of mass lynchings in his home state of Missouri further inspired him to pen an impassioned essay, "The United States of Lyncherdom," decrying the crimes as an "epidemic of bloody insanities."[24]

Twain's growing disgust at racial intolerance almost certainly played a role in his increasingly political views around other causes that would later be deeply important to Helen, including support for women's suffrage and labor unions. And although he was never an avowed socialist, he publicly supported the first Russian Revolution of 1905, declaring, "I am always on the side of the revolutionists because there never was a revolution unless there were some oppressive and intolerable conditions against which to revolute."[25]

Although Helen had not yet spoken publicly about her own burgeoning political beliefs when she knew Twain, she later reflected how "all his life he fought injustice wherever he saw it in the relations between man and man—in politics, in wars, in outrages against the natives of the Philippines, the Congo, and Panama."[26] And in their discussions of the issues of the time, she recalled that "I loved his views on public affairs, they were so often the same as my own."[27] Unlike so many around her, he invited her to share her opinions on serious topics, building their deep mutual respect.

⠗⠗⠒⠓ ⠓⠓⠈
⠗⠔⠓⠈ ⠍⠑⠈

In 1909, a year before Twain's death, he invited Helen, Annie, and John Macy to visit Stormfield, his recently acquired mansion in Redding, Connecticut. Helen was thrilled to receive his invitation, which read, "I command you all three to come and spend a few days with me in Stormfield." It was indeed the "summons of a beloved king," she recalled.[28]

We only have fragments of what was discussed during the three days she spent at Stormfield, which Helen would later recall fondly, including a memorable anecdote about the first night of her visit: "When the time came to say good night, Mr. Clemens led me to my room himself and told me that I would find cigars and a thermos bottle with Scotch whiskey, or Bourbon if I preferred it, in the bathroom."[29] The rest of the stay, she recalled, was filled with lively discussion, including a spirited debate over the authorship of Shakespeare's plays—a topic that had captured the fancy of Helen and John Macy, who had recently embraced the possibility that the Bard's works had actually been written by Francis Bacon.

It was at the end of this visit that Twain bestowed on Annie the moniker by which she is still best known today when he inscribed these words on a photo:

To [Annie Sullivan] with warm regard and with limitless admiration of the wonders she has performed as a "miracle worker."[30]

This would be Helen's last visit with Twain, who died a year later, though there is no surviving record of her reaction to the demise of her friend. Booker T. Washington famously claimed that nobody could ever carry on his legacy. "As to Mark Twain's successor, he can have none," Washington wrote upon Twain's death in 1910.[31] And yet Twain scholar Brent Colley believes there may have been at least one natural successor—a woman who would also shed her conservative Southern upbringing and emerge as a radical firebrand determined to use her fame to transform America.[32] Some time after her visit to Stormfield, Helen took out a membership in the Socialist Party.

Part Two

THE LEFT-WING
JOAN OF ARC

Chapter Seven

Political Epiphany

As with much of Helen's life story, the roots of her conversion to socialism are still something of a mystery, caught up in contradictory accounts and a search for pat answers to fit a conventional narrative.

According to Helen, she first came to embrace the controversial political ideology when Annie recommended that she read H. G. Wells's book *New Worlds for Old: A Plain Account of Modern Socialism*. Teacher was "attracted by its imaginative quality and hoped that its electric style might stimulate and interest me," Helen recalled.[1] The book was published by the celebrated English author in 1908, a year before she reportedly took out an application to join the Socialist Party of Massachusetts. At the time, Wells was best known for futuristic science-fiction novels such as *The Time Machine, The Invisible Man*, and *The War of the Worlds*. But he was also a prominent social commentator who had written extensively about his hopes for a future socialist society while he was engaged in an effort to reform the Fabian Society, a British organization of intellectuals and freethinkers. The Fabians envisioned democratic socialism as a more moderate alternative to the revolutionary communist principles of Karl Marx, who believed that workers must throw off their chains and revolt against the industrialists and capitalists who controlled their lives. "Socialism lights up certain once hopeless evils in human affairs and shows the path by which escape is possible," Wells wrote in his influential treatise.[2]

Despite Helen's official explanation, many chroniclers—echoing Nella Henney's chronology—have assumed that it was John Macy who converted Helen to socialism. This has become a widely accepted truism. And yet there appears to be little evidence to back it up, especially since Macy's own conversion nearly coincided with Helen's.

Macy had married Annie in 1905, a year after Helen graduated from Radcliffe. The marriage followed a long courtship dating back to the days when he was editing *The Story of My Life*. Annie later claimed that she had long resisted John's proposals of marriage for many reasons, not the least of which was her devotion to Helen. "Helen must always come first," she told him. Their age difference may have also played a role. When they married, she was thirty-nine, a full eleven years older than Macy, who was closer to Helen's age than Annie's.[3] The age difference was so glaring, in fact, that during their courtship, some newspapers speculated that John intended to marry Helen rather than her teacher.[4] By the time they finally tied the knot in a small ceremony at home attended by twenty friends, Annie had vacillated so often, she joked, that John threatened to write, "Subject to change without notice" on the wedding invitations.[5]

At the time of his marriage to Annie, twenty-five-year-old Helen was decidedly fond of John, who had worked closely with her on her autobiography and a variety of other projects. After the honeymoon, the three of them settled into their home in Wrentham, Massachusetts, forty miles south of Boston. Helen and Annie had purchased the home ahead of Helen's attendance at Radcliffe, thanks to the proceeds of stock given to Helen by one of her many wealthy benefactors, John Spaulding, known as the "Sugar King" of Boston. Kim Nielsen has observed that there is little record of domestic life at Wrentham during the years after the marriage beyond the occasional fragment gleaned from letters. "On weekdays, Annie drove John to the train station for his commute to Boston and then did the daily shopping," she wrote.[6] Helen, meanwhile, stayed behind researching and writing or tending to an ever-increasing menagerie of animals, which included dogs, chickens, and horses. On weekends, they often hosted parties. Friends remembered Annie as a "consummate and vibrant host."[7] John would later imply that he resented Annie's constant attention to Helen during their marriage, but contemporary evidence shows that the trio each had their own separate routines and the household appeared to run smoothly for years with little conflict. Nielsen points out that Helen always described this Wrentham period "idyllically."[8]

In the years since he married Annie, Macy had emerged as an influential literary critic and wrote a well-received biography of Edgar Allan Poe.[9] He continued his work as an editor at the *Youth's Companion*, a Boston-based magazine for children and families, and he occasionally published his own poetry and literary criticism in leading magazines. While he would eventually distinguish himself in the sphere of left-wing politics and would count among his circle many of the leading radicals in America, at the time Helen picked up *New Worlds for Old*, there is no evidence that Macy had yet become a full-fledged socialist or that he had played any direct role in her political awakening. Helen herself never once credited Macy for her embrace of the ideology and, on at least one occasion, she appeared to deny his influence. While Helen never provided a convincing explanation to explain why the H. G. Wells book served as her socialist epiphany, there is a body of compelling evidence that suggests a number of other factors likely played a significant role in her ideological evolution.

⠠⠵⠑⠇⠁ ⠵⠑⠺⠄
⠎⠑⠇⠄ ⠍⠊⠄

Years before Helen encountered Macy, she had struck up a friendship with a man named Joseph Edgar Chamberlin—a longtime advocate for the Perkins School who wrote frequently about its endeavors in his weekly column, "The Listener," in the Boston *Evening Transcript*. In 1888—not long after she moved north to attend Perkins—Chamberlin invited eight-year-old Helen and her teacher to spend the weekend at his rented property in Wrentham.

Known as "Red Farm," this lively homestead was something of a bohemian enclave where Chamberlin often hosted an eclectic array of artists, intellectuals, and political activists. Drawing on her family archives, Chamberlin's great-great-granddaughter Elizabeth Emerson describes how her visits to Red Farm served as a "refuge" for young Helen—independent from her family for the first time. "For Helen, it was a family home in which she could play and enjoy a normal childhood away from her studies and the whirl of social events required of her," writes Emerson in her book *Letters from Red Farm* about Helen's friendship and lifelong correspondence with Chamberlin.[10] For more than forty years, Helen would call him "Uncle Ed" and Helen would describe her time at Red Farm with Annie as "the richest and brightest experience of our lives."[11] Their fondness for Red Farm, in fact, is what would eventually inspire Helen and Annie to buy their first house in Wrentham, not far from Chamberlin, where they would continue to live for a number of years following Annie's marriage to John Macy.

An assortment of writers have written superficially about Helen's frequent trips to Red Farm. Lorena Hickok described it as a "jolly place" where Helen played with horses and dogs and encountered snow for the first time.[12] But there is also evidence that Chamberlin's home may have been where Helen experienced her political coming-of-age—from sheltered Southerner to a revolutionary who would soon rattle American society.

Among the eclectic coterie of characters she encountered during her time there were two Indigenous women who had taken up residence at Red Farm. One of the women, Angel De Cora, was the granddaughter of a Winnebago chief and would become one of the best-known Indigenous artists in America during the early twentieth century. Chamberlin had also befriended a woman named Zitkála-Šá—a Lakota poet also known as Red Bird—who would later found the National Council of

American Indians to lobby for Native American interests.[13] Years later—perhaps in part inspired by her encounters with the women at Red Farm—Helen would become an outspoken champion of Indigenous rights.

In 1897, when Helen and Annie faced the greatest crisis of their relationship, it was Red Farm that served as their sanctuary. Some of Helen's circle had become concerned about Annie's rigorous instruction and were convinced that Teacher was driving Helen to the point of physical and mental exhaustion as she prepared her pupil for university. At the time, Helen was enrolled at the Cambridge School for Young Ladies, whose principal, Arthur Gilman, was one of Annie's primary antagonists in the drive to separate the women because of these growing concerns. Alarm bells were triggered when Annie's longtime confidante, her former Perkins housemother, Sophia Hopkins, visited Cambridge and reported to Gilman that she had found Helen "in what I might term a state of collapse."[14] It is unclear to this day whether he genuinely believed he was acting in Helen's best interest or whether the battle was part of an ongoing power struggle between himself and Annie, who had often clashed about the pace of Helen's study and the best strategy to prepare her for higher education. In a purported attempt to protect his student, Gilman enlisted the support of Mrs. Keller, who wrote a letter in December 1897 authorizing him to act as "guardian" for Helen, as well as for her younger sister, Mildred, who also attended the school.[15]

Not long afterward, Kate Keller wrote a letter informing Annie of the new arrangements, thanking her for her efforts on behalf of Helen "in the past." It suggested that Gilman's plan was a fait accompli. Helen would later claim that Annie was so "overcome with despair" by the effort to separate her from her pupil that, as she passed Boston's Charles River one evening during this period, "an almost overmastering impulse seized her to throw herself into the water."[16] If he had counted on the seventeen-year-old Helen to quietly acquiesce in the plan to separate her from her beloved Teacher, Gilman severely underestimated the unbreakable bond that had formed in the decade since Annie first arrived in

Tuscumbia. Turning to Chamberlin for support, Helen told him that if she had to choose between her mother and Annie, "I will go with Teacher. She has meant more to me than my mother has. She made me everything that I am."[17] Mrs. Keller would later claim that she had lost her temper and "didn't realize what a cruel thing I had been doing" when she assigned Gilman the guardianship.[18]

Helen withdrew from the school and absconded with Annie from Boston to Red Farm. Here, they lived with Chamberlin and his wife, Ida, for nearly a year while Helen received instruction from a private tutor in preparation for her Radcliffe entrance examinations.[19] A year later, Chamberlin wrote an article for the *Ladies' Home Journal* reflecting on their stay, which offers a valuable window into Helen's evolving political beliefs: "Helen is an unconquerable liberal in her ideas," he wrote. "She inclines to take the side of the people in all matters which they make their concern. She is instinctively philanthropical and benevolent. Her notions in sociological matters are pretty nearly the direct opposite of those of Miss Sullivan, who is extremely conservative."[20]

In many ways, in fact, Chamberlin would become more of a kindred political spirit to Helen than Annie herself. In 1912, Helen wrote an article for *American Magazine* that provides an important clue about his early influence:

> I understand that newspapers are not hospitable to radical and pro-gressive ideas. Mr. Chamberlin's thought, as he expresses it to his friends, is far in advance of his written work. His conscience is alive to the wrongs and perils of our social institutions. Long before I knew what it all meant, he talked with us about Socialism and William Morris's *News from Nowhere*.[21]

It is instructive to learn here that, years before Annie recommended the H. G. Wells work that Helen cited as the book that converted her to socialism, Chamberlin had introduced her to a work by another science-fiction writer whose left-wing political convictions predated Wells. In *News from Nowhere*, published in 1890, Morris describes a utopian vision of a socialist paradise in which capitalism, private property, and industry have been overthrown and where people live in equality.

Helen would also later credit Chamberlin—who had served as a correspondent for the *Saturday Evening Post* during the Spanish-American War—as having a profound impact on her view of war. "Another thing Uncle Ed has told me, that there are some kinds of success not admirable," she wrote in her journal in August 1898, at the height of the war. "He has talked about Caesar and Napoleon. I had supposed they were benefactors because they were praised and extolled to the skies in everything I read about them. But he said they became famous by killing great numbers of their fellow men, ruining their lands, and spreading misery and hatred everywhere. He went on to say that whatever good they accomplished was small compared with the evil they did and the suffering they caused."[22] Given that Helen would emerge as one of the country's most prominent anti-war activists two decades later, it is impossible to ignore this significant early influence.

As with Mark Twain, most biographers have focused on the superficial aspects of Helen's relationship with Chamberlin, but these long-ignored writings help fill in some important gaps that explain the process by which Helen transformed into one of the most prominent radicals in America—a transformation that evidently took root long before her much-discussed encounter with Wells's book.

Among the other overlooked factors that almost certainly played a role in Helen's political evolution was her religious faith. While she was growing up in Tuscumbia, the Keller household had practiced a blend of mainstream Christianity. Arthur Keller was a Presbyterian and a deacon in his church while Kate had been raised Episcopalian. Because of Helen's deafness, however, the family had made no attempt to provide her with religious instruction—at least not until after Annie arrived.[23] Annie herself had long ago rejected the Catholicism with which she had been raised and was, in all likelihood, an atheist by the time Helen came under her tutelage. "I am not religious," Annie later wrote. "When I am deeply troubled, divergent aspects of nature comfort me. I cannot conceive of God separate from nature. The idea of God as Father, friend, or consoler is unthinkable."[24] Despite her lack of religious conviction, she appeared to believe that she nonetheless had an obligation to provide theological instruction as part of Helen's education. By the time Helen was ten, Annie was already conflicted around how best to do so.

In a summary of Helen's progress that she submitted to the Perkins School annual report in 1891, Annie described Helen's earliest enquiries about theology: "She knew that the Greeks had many gods to whom they ascribed various powers, because they believed the sun, the lightning and a hundred other natural forces were independent and superhuman powers. But after a great deal of thought and study, men came to believe that all forces were manifestations of one power, and to that power they gave the name God. She was very still for a few minutes, evidently thinking earnestly. She then asked, 'Who made God?' I was compelled to evade her question, for I could not explain to her the mystery of a self-existent being."[25] Annie later revealed that she attempted to distract her from the discussion by talking to her about Mother Nature, but this merely led to awkward questions about Father Nature.[26] Eventually, Helen's questions became so persistent that Annie felt compelled to seek the kind of religious instruction that she was unable to provide.

Without consulting Anagnos, she took Helen to Father Phillips Brooks, an Episcopalian priest at Boston's Trinity Church—a decision that angered the Perkins director when he learned that she had disregarded his advice about Helen's religious instruction. Anagnos had previously suggested that Helen's religious beliefs should be allowed to develop without any outside interference to help answer the question about whether religious belief is "innate."[27] While Helen remained fond of Bishop Brooks for the rest of his life—so fond that she persuaded her parents to name her new baby brother Phillips Brooks Keller when she was eleven—his religious instruction never filled the spiritual void that she had been seeking or answered her persistent questions. She was especially troubled by the brand of religion he preached that condemned Jews and others who failed to embrace Christianity. "I had been told by narrow people that all who were not Christians would be punished," she later recalled, "and naturally my soul revolted, since I knew of wonderful men who lived and died for truth as they saw it in the pagan lands."[28]

Her true religious awakening would come several years later, courtesy of John Hitz, the head of Alexander Graham Bell's Volta Bureau, the headquarters established by Bell in 1887 to promote his ideas around deaf education. Hitz introduced her to the doctrine of an eighteenth-century Swedish mystic named Emanuel Swedenborg and his "New Church." Born in Stockholm in 1688, Swedenborg had led a full life as a scientist, an inventor, an engineer, an astronomer, and a mathematician until, at the age of fifty-five, he suddenly abandoned his scientific pursuits in favor of a spiritual path. He would eventually publish eighteen theological works outlining his vision as "a servant of the Lord Jesus Christ." His best-known work was titled *Heaven and Hell*, in which he describes the afterlife in vivid detail.[29] It is this work that Hitz presented to Helen when she was a teenager—published in raised type, a system of embossed letters that predated braille. She later described her joy at discovering Swedenborg's philosophy. "Here was a faith that I felt so keenly—the separateness between soul and body, between a realm I could picture as a whole and the chaos of fragmentary things and irrational contingencies that my limited physical senses met at every turn," she wrote.[30]

From the age of sixteen, Helen would become a devoted adherent of Swedenborg.[31] Later, she published an entire book, *My Religion*, about her deep attachment to the faith. She would even occasionally take to the pulpit of the New Church to preach a sermon.[32] Although she never explicitly linked her left-wing politics to her new religion, Swedenborgianism had long been associated with a movement known as Christian socialism, which applied Christ's teachings to principles of social justice.

As far back as the eighteenth century, Swedenborg's disciples, together with the Quakers, were at the forefront of the movement to end the slave trade in Europe.[33] In 1895, a year before Helen first encountered the teachings of Swedenborg, the New-Church Socialist Society was established in England "to study and promulgate the teachings and practice of our Lord Jesus Christ as applied to every human duty."[34] By the late nineteenth century, a sizable component of American Swedenborgians had linked the New Church with the philosophy of the French philosopher Charles Fourier, one of the founders of utopian socialism, which played a key role in American reform circles in the mid-nineteenth century. So while Helen never directly linked her socialist awakening to her faith, it is not inconceivable that her immersion in the sect had a powerful influence on her political consciousness, which would soon see her indicting capitalist society while referring to Jesus Christ as "Him who stood with the oppressed and the defrauded."[35] She would later describe socialism as the "new religion of humanity."[36]

Helen's embrace of Swedenborgianism stands in marked contrast to Laura Bridgman's own religious awakening, which appeared to drive a permanent wedge between her and Samuel Gridley Howe, especially when her born-again Christianity set her at odds with Howe the reformer. Annie, in fact, was determined that her pupil never fall prey to the pious evangelism that she remembered well from her Perkins years when she shared a cottage with Laura. Notorious for her support of abolitionism and other social reforms when she was a teenager, Laura had abandoned her once progressive political beliefs after one of her teachers took the opportunity to convert her to Calvinism during Howe's honeymoon years earlier. "I shall guard Helen very carefully against those notions and opinions which made Laura's religion so repulsive to all but the most narrow of Christians," Annie assured Anagnos when Helen was ten years old.[37]

Politics had long played a prominent role in the Keller household while Helen was growing up. Arthur Keller's fortunes, in fact, were very much tied to the Democratic Party, which in the postbellum South had very different associations than it does today. The Republican Party was the party of Abraham Lincoln, abolition, and Reconstruction, and was largely popular in the North. The Democrats, meanwhile, symbolized the Lost Cause of the Confederacy, and the Southern states stood very much as a bulwark of white supremacy for decades while the Dixiecrat wing of the party worked to preserve the odious Jim Crow system of racial segregation.

Following the failure of his business enterprises, Arthur had taken over a sleepy country weekly called the *North Alabamian* and transformed it into a pro-Democratic organ. Eventually, Democratic president Grover Cleveland would reward him for his loyalty with a plum patronage position as a US marshal. So, Helen was raised by an adamant Democrat. But when sixteen-year-old Helen told a reporter named Franklin Matthews in 1896 that she understood the concept of parties and politics, she was ambivalent in response to his attempt to ascertain her political affiliation.

"Well, which are you, a Democrat or Republican?" he demanded.

"Oh, I am on the fence," she said, laughing. "I used to be a Democrat but now I think I am inclined towards the Republicans."[38]

In the years after she graduated from college, Helen wasn't quite sure what she wanted to do with her life. While establishing her path, she wrote a number of magazine articles about the prevention of blindness. It became increasingly apparent that she was destined to help those who were visually impaired, though it is still unclear why she was more drawn to advocacy for the blind community rather than the deaf community— a question that would frequently emerge later on.

Following that conviction, she dipped her toes into the waters of political activism for the first time in March 1906, when she sent a letter to the Massachusetts committee of education urging the creation of a permanent state commission for the blind community. "Generous provision for the sightless must be a gain not only to them but also to the community and is in keeping with the fundamental declaration of America, which guarantees the right of all men to life, liberty, and the pursuit of happiness," she wrote.[39] Her efforts paid off when Governor Curtis Guild Jr. established the commission that she had requested, though she appeared to be taken aback a few months later when he also appointed her as a member of the commission in July of the same year. Annie was more qualified for the position, she protested.[40] Despite her misgivings, she would later credit the appointment as raising "the curtain on my life's work."[41]

Her tenure on the commission lasted less than a year, but her activities during this period reveal an increasing willingness to wade into controversial topics. In 1907, she wrote an article for the *Ladies' Home Journal* about "unnecessary blindness," drawing attention to a condition called ophthalmia neonatorum, which caused blindness in babies born to women with venereal disease. The condition was easily preventable simply by applying drops of silver nitrate into the infant's eyes but, to Helen's disgust, prudery was preventing discussion of the unseemly topic. Though she felt it was important to address this taboo issue, her first article was couched in medical jargon and innuendo while largely skirting the topic of sexually transmitted disease. She later admitted that she wrote "guardedly and with hesitation"—unsure how to approach the delicate subject, which she noted was a topic "forbidden in society."[42]

A year later, she wrote another article on the subject for the same publication. This time, she didn't mince words. "I cannot without accusing myself of cowardice, gloss over or ignore the fundamental evil," she wrote. "What is the cause of ophthalmia neonatorum? It is a specific germ communicated by the mother to the child at birth."

Here, she adds the salient point that she had refrained from including in her first essay for fear of upsetting the sensibilities of her readers. The germ, she notes, is usually passed on through "licentious relations before or since marriage."

"Must we leave young girls to meet the danger in the dark because we dare not turn the light upon our social wickedness?" she asked. "False delicacy and prudery must give place to precise information and common sense."[43]

It would not be the last time she took up matters that were rarely talked about in prurient society. Meanwhile, she still mostly found herself confined to tackling issues involving blindness, a source of growing frustration that surfaced publicly in 1908 when John Macy negotiated a contract for her to publish a book of essays called *The World I Live In* focusing on how she perceived the world. Upon publication, the book didn't receive a lot of attention, and its sales paled in comparison to *The Story of My Life*,[44] but its preface foreshadowed Helen's determination to speak on weightier matters, as well as her mounting frustration with the ableist attitudes that relegated her to her disability alone:

Every book is in a sense autobiographical. But while other self-recording creatures are permitted at least to seem to change the subject, apparently nobody cares what I think of the tariff, the conservation of our natural resources, or the conflicts which revolve about the name of Dreyfus. If I offer to reform the education system of the world, my editorial friends say, "That is interesting. But will you please tell us what idea you had of goodness and beauty when you were six years old?" . . . Until they give me opportunity to write about matters that are not-me, the world must go on uninstructed and unreformed, and I can only do my best with the one small subject upon which I am allowed to discourse.[45]

To this point, her opinions about the "affairs of the universe" had been confined to like-minded friends along with her "little circle" of classmates at Radcliffe, who, she recalled, "stripped everything to the naked skeleton" as they discussed literature and world affairs. "All of us were individualists, yet all of us responded to the altruistic movements of the time," she later wrote. "We believed in the rising tide of the masses, in peace, and brotherhood, and 'a square deal' for everybody. Each one of us had an idol around whom our theories revolved like planets around the sun. These idols had familiar names—Nietzsche, Schopenhauer, Karl Marx, Bergson, Lincoln, Tolstoi, and Max Stirner. The more we read and discussed, the more convinced we were that we belonged to that choice coterie who rise in each age and manage to attain freedom of thought."[46]

To the list of idols, Helen would eventually add a former Pullman engineer named Eugene Debs, who had emerged as the leader of the American socialist movement. She later revealed that she had been following his career since she was fourteen, "in connection with the Great Northern Strike in 1894," though it was only years later that she "began to understand the significance of the liberating movement for which he stood."[47] For Debs, who had headed the Socialist Party of America since 1901,[48] socialism meant the "emancipation of the working class from wage slavery and collective ownership of the means of production and distribution and the operation of all industry in the interest of all the people."[49] By 1909, his party counted more than forty thousand adherents including, allegedly, two new members—John Macy and Helen Keller.[50] But if this is the year that both Helen and Macy joined the Socialist Party, as labor historian Philip S. Foner, Joseph Lash, and others later claimed,[51] there is scant evidence of it from their activities or writing that year.[52] Little is known about Macy's own political evolution, other than what he later told Ernest Gruening when he was compiling a brief passage about him years later in the *Dictionary of American Biography*. Macy claimed that he had embraced the ideology "largely through observing the asininities of the present system," but didn't provide a date for his affiliation.[53] Nella Henney, who never met John Macy and wouldn't encounter Helen and Annie for another fourteen years, later wrote a dubious but oft-cited account of the evolution of their political conversion: "The Wrentham household went into socialism slowly, one by one, first Mr. Macy, then Helen, and one or two years later, Mrs. Macy."[54]

The first public hint of Helen's involvement in left-wing politics came in October 1910 when a Utah group calling itself the "Marxian Club Socialists" published a newspaper column praising Helen for her recent indictment of charitable institutions as "monuments of our ignorance, stupidity and folly." In a sign that she had already begun to embrace a Marxist analysis, the column quoted her complaining that all the energy of the charity worker "merely goes to prolong a system which ceaselessly grinds out the very results he is seeking to overcome."[55]

Soon after, she waded into a long-standing controversy involving Fred Warren, editor of the country's largest socialist newspaper, *Appeal to Reason*. Warren had been convicted the year before on federal charges for offering a reward for the capture of a Republican politician who fled the state of Kentucky after allegedly assassinating his Democratic opponent before he could be seated as governor. After a lengthy appeals process, the sentence was upheld by a higher court, prompting the socialist press to declare that "the six months Warren serves in jail will be the hottest six months that capitalism has yet seen in the United States"—a warning that turned out to be more bluff than bluster.[56]

In December 1910, on the eve of Warren reporting to federal prison to serve his sentence, the *Appeal to Reason* announced that it had recently received a letter and a check from an unlikely source. "I am prompted to this by indignation at the unrighteous conviction of the editor, Mr. Fred Warren," Helen wrote. "What surgery of politics, what antiseptic of common sense and right thinking, shall be applied to cure the blindness of our judges and to prevent the blindness of the people who are the court of last resort?"[57]

Despite her support for Warren, Helen had not yet come out publicly as a socialist. Indeed, even the socialist press didn't quite know what to make of her foray into the Warren case. A month later, in an editorial headlined "The Dumb Girl Speaks," *Appeal to Reason* lauded her involvement: "Helen Keller, who is very advanced in her views, was deeply aroused by the incident. She is blind, deaf and dumb, yet in her blindness she sees oppression, in her deafness she hears the cry of her outrage, and in her speechlessness, she voices the demand for justice."[58]

In an essay about her involvement in the case, written two years later, Helen noted that a reporter from the mainstream *Boston Evening Transcript* had written an article about her support for Warren at the time, but his editor cut it out. "The money power behind the newspapers is against Socialism," Helen wrote. "I find the editors obedient to the hand that feeds them will go to any length to put down Socialism and undermine the influence of the Socialist."[59] This would appear to suggest that she already considered herself a socialist when she weighed in about Warren's conviction in 1910.

If her support for Warren still left room for doubt about her political leanings, a speech she delivered two months later revealed that she already had undergone an epiphany that would have as profound an effect on her as the moment that Annie held her hand under the pump and spelled "water"—the recognition of the links between disability and capitalism. She had recently discovered that industrial accidents caused by a lack of workplace safety were responsible for a significant amount of blindness and other disabilities in America. At a February 1911 meeting called to promote the "interests of the blind," she startled a Boston gathering who had likely come to hear her thoughts on the latest surgical treatments for blindness. Instead, she launched into an address that she would describe as a "battle cry"—declaring that blindness is caused by "ignorance, poverty, and the unconscious cruelty of commercial society." These are the "enemies" which destroy the sight of children and workmen and undermine the health of mankind," she told the crowd. "I do not believe that there is anyone in this city of kind hearts who would willingly receive dividends if he knew that they had been paid in part with blinded eyes and broken backs."[60]

Less than a year later, in November 1911, the city of Schenectady elected a socialist administration, headed by a former Democrat named George Lunn. The election came on the heels of a series of socialist victories in small municipalities throughout the country. As editor of the *Schenectady Gazette*, Lunn had distinguished himself as a reformer, intent on exposing municipal corruption and graft that had plagued the city. The campaigns he championed—including more playgrounds and free textbooks for schoolchildren—were hardly radical for the time, and when he decided to run for political office, Lunn appeared to ally himself with the socialists not out of ideological conviction but because it seemed his best chance for victory. It wasn't until September 1911 that he formally joined the Socialist Party when he accepted its nomination for mayor. That November, his ticket swept to victory—the first socialist administration ever elected in the state of New York.[61]

It was around this period that the first signs emerged that John Macy had become a socialist as well. Although he had sat as the water commissioner for Wrentham and a trustee for the local public library since 1909, he did not serve in either capacity as an avowed socialist. However, in November 1911, three weeks after George Lunn was elected mayor of Schenectady and a full year after Helen had come out in support of Fred Warren, a small notice appeared in a Boston newspaper about an upcoming lecture by Macy titled "Why a Harvard Man Should Be a Socialist."[62] A few months later, he would be recorded as a member of the Harvard Socialist Club and a member of the Intercollegiate Socialist Society.[63] These are the first known public records of his socialist affiliations—all dating from a period well after Helen herself had begun to embrace socialist politics, even if the exact date of her formal party affiliation is still uncertain.[64]

An additional clue about the chronology of Helen's ideological shift suggests that even if she hadn't yet formally declared herself a socialist in her own country, German socialists had already claimed her as their own. At a gathering of Germany's socialist party held the first week of January 1912, a letter from Helen was read out loud renewing her annual subscription to the German socialist journal, *Die Neue Zeit.*[65] "I can not sufficiently thank you for your noble work," Helen wrote. "Wherever possible, I recommend socialism to my friends. I wish somebody would come forward and start a periodical like the *Neue Zeit* for the American blind."[66]

Years later, when Helen's most prominent biographer, Joseph Lash, failed to find any evidence of her earlier socialist affiliations, he wrote a note to the Helen Keller Archives wondering if Annie and Helen had "fudged" the facts to bolster the picture of Helen as an "independent personality not manipulated by the people close to her."[67] Could it be that it was Helen who was a socialist before Macy, as this chronology would strongly suggest? Perhaps it was Macy who didn't want it known that he had followed Helen into socialism rather than the other way around. Lash also notably failed to cite any evidence backing up his assertion that Macy had joined the party in 1909.[68]

Four months after Lunn's election, the mayor's secretary, Walter Lippmann—who would later become one of America's best-known media critics—resigned his post, declaring that Lunn was a good man but that the playgrounds and dental clinics he championed were the domain of "progressives" rather than socialists.[69] Upon submitting his resignation, Lippmann recommended John Macy as his successor. "I am sure you will find him an asset to the city, a power to your administration, and a delightful person to have as a friend," he told Lunn.[70]

When Macy's appointment was announced in April 1912, the local media were far more excited about his wife's pupil than the appointment of the largely unknown Macy. "NOTED BLIND GIRL COMING WITH MACY," blared the headline of a local newspaper on April 12. "Retirement of Walter Lippmann Will Bring Famous Young Woman to Schenectady to live."[71] After the paper took note of John's wife and her famous student, it declared matter-of-factly, "Mr. and Mrs. Macy and Miss Keller are Socialists."[72] Although the reference turned out to be inaccurate in one regard, and it didn't get much attention at first, it was the first time most readers learned that "the wonderful blind girl" had embraced the anti-capitalist ideology.

Her political affiliations would cause a much greater stir six weeks later when Mayor Lunn announced that he planned to appoint Helen to his newly created Board of Public Welfare when she moved to Schenectady with Annie in the fall. "I will learn the sign language," declared the mayor, expressing his long admiration for Helen and his eagerness to work with her. "By Jove, now that I think of it, I believe I will anyway."[73]

For Helen, an eventful new chapter of her public life had begun.

Chapter Eight

"Industrial Blindness and Social Deafness"

Although Helen's political coming out had not yet attracted much attention among the wider public, the socialist press appeared excited at the allegiance of such a prominent figure—arguably the most famous woman in the western world since the death of Queen Victoria a decade earlier. This excitement was evidenced by an article in the *New York Call* published shortly after the announcement of her imminent appointment to the Schenectady welfare board. "For a long time, Miss Keller has been a Socialist in everything that the word implies," the party's organ declared. "This fact has long been known to most well-read Socialists who keep in touch with current events and will become still more widely known now that Miss Keller is to take an active part in the municipal administration of the City of Schenectady, which is now dominated by Socialists."[1]

Despite the fanfare, however, Helen never, in fact, received the personal invitation to join the Public Welfare Board that Lunn had promised. In July, she submitted an article to Albany's *Knickerbocker Press* about her priorities should she eventually be invited to serve. "I will first of all try in some way to improve conditions among the extremely poor," she wrote. "I would try to wipe out the slums."[2]

Poverty, she declared, is the fundamental cause of almost every evil. "Let us get rid of our money that is received from invested capital and give workingmen a chance to get a proper share of what rightfully belongs to them. I believe socialism is the only cure at present for existing conditions."[3]

Although this was the first time that she would publicly declare her lifelong belief that poverty was society's greatest plague, this conviction had long predated her entry into radical politics, as evidenced by an anecdote she shared in 1916 about a formative experience during her childhood:

> I was taught that God especially loves the poor and the weak. I remember vividly the first jolt to this idea that I had. It was Christmas—the first one that I recall with any distinctness. I was taken to a Christmas tree at the school in Tuscumbia. I received many pretty gifts, and all the children were loaded with presents, except one. My teacher said to me, "Helen, here is a little girl who has been forgotten"...For days afterwards I besieged my teacher with questions about [the little girl]. Why is she poor? Why did she not have any presents? If God loves the poor, why did he not give anything to that [little girl]. I was heart-wounded because I had everything while she had nothing.[4]

She described a feeling of resentment "burnt into my soul" against the God who had neglected the little girl while giving Helen so much. Although she didn't have the words to express these sentiments at the time, she would come to link her hatred for poverty and inequality to this incident. "I felt then, and I know now that there is no beauty in poverty. It is an abomination."[5]

In fact, as early as 1901, while she was still at Radcliffe, she had begun to publicly question the roots of the social ills that would later inspire her many future causes. In an article she wrote for the *Ladies' Home Journal*, headlined "I Must Speak," she wrote, "Once I believed that blindness, deafness, tuberculosis, and other causes of suffering were necessary, unpreventable. But gradually my reading extended, and I found that those evils are to be laid not at the door of Providence, but at the door of mankind; that they are, in large measure, due to ignorance, stupidity and sin."[6] When she later discovered socialism, then, its tenets appeared to confirm what she had already long believed and—more importantly—it offered a remedy.

Annie and Helen had originally planned to travel to Schenectady in the fall of 1912, at which point Helen still believed she would take up a post in the Lunn administration. In July, the *Cleveland Citizen* even reported that she had been appointed to Lunn's "cabinet," though Helen would later note that she never heard from the mayor himself.[7] Not long before her scheduled departure, she sat down at her Wrentham home for an interview with Alleyne Ireland, a prominent freelance reporter writing a profile for the *St. Louis Post-Dispatch*. Ireland begins the article by informing his readers that his conversation with Helen was one of the most interesting of his career. Perhaps already sensing the tide of public opinion that assumed others were responsible for influencing Helen's newfound political ideology, Ireland immediately lays any such assumption to rest. "This witty, adroit and well-informed woman is in no sense a mere reflection in the mental field of [Annie Sullivan] or of anyone else," he writes, "and that so far from being under the intellectual domination of her friends, she follows a highly independent tide of thought and takes the greatest pleasure in arguing against her friends in support of her convictions."[8] He goes on to explain that Helen's "adhesion to Socialism" continues despite the fact that her dearest friend Annie Sullivan, "whose influence must have been greater than that of any other with whom she has been brought in contact, is strongly opposed to the Socialist movement."[9]

When conversation turns to Helen's imminent departure to take up her post in Schenectady, she again emphasizes her determination to "study the laboring people and their lives" to improve the plight of the poor. When the reporter notes that poverty is "extolled and glorified" in the New Testament, it elicits an indignant response. "There! That just shows how blind people can be!" Helen interjects. "It's nothing but moral and intellectual blindness for people to think that Christ extolled poverty when he said, 'Blessed are the poor for they shall Inherit the kingdom of God.' That wasn't extolling poverty; what he meant was simply that the poor would have blessings in the future to compensate them for their sufferings." Here, she shares her Marxist impression about society's economic structure. "One of the things I want to write about is the social blindness from which so many people seem to suffer, inability to see and to understand the fundamental conditions underlying the relations between the workpeople and their employers. The keynote of the situation lies in the central fact of our present industrial situation, the ownership of everything by the few."[10]

At this point in the interview, the reporter notes that Annie comes over and says something to Helen using the manual alphabet. "Miss Keller laughed long and loud and clapped her hands, a sign of pleasure and amusement. Then turning to me she said, 'She says it's all very well to talk like that but my views don't prevent my collecting dividends on a few railroad shares that I own.'"[11]

And what did Helen have to say to that? the reporter wondered. "Oh, I don't set myself up to be perfect; and, anyhow, whatever you may think of my conduct, the instance certainly proves my point, for I know nothing whatever about railroads and I never worked for one, and yet I get my dividends just the same. That's exactly the point I've been trying to make."[12] Widely reprinted throughout the country, it is this article that could be considered her true political coming-out.

Though Helen seemed poised to take up a political position in Schenectady, not long after the story ran in mid-September, Mayor Lunn's office suddenly issued a statement announcing that Macy had resigned his position as executive secretary. His resignation was ostensibly because Annie was "ill"—suffering from what Nella Henney later described as an "obscure malady" that was sapping her strength and required an operation.[13] Although this was his official excuse, there had been hints for some time that John was already looking for a way out. Weeks earlier, Helen had written to her mother confiding that he was unhappy with the post. "We don't think that John wants to stay there much longer," she wrote Kate in August. "He seems to want almost any kind of work rather than that of a secretary."[14]

The ensuing newspaper coverage of Macy's resignation barely mentioned his name. Instead, most of the reports focused on the fact that Helen would not be traveling to Schenectady after all. "HELEN KELLER WILL NOT AID SOCIALISTS," blared the headline in the *Knickerbocker Press*.[15]

Despite the news of her withdrawal from the post that had never formally been offered to her, the cat was now out of the bag about her political conversion. Although some mainstream newspapers still treated her radical politics as something of a novelty, the conservative press reacted furiously to the news that the widely admired woman had resolved to lend her prestige to a movement that aimed to destroy capitalism. The backlash was so intense that Helen felt compelled to counter some of what was being said about her. In November, she chose the Socialist Party newspaper, the *New York Call*, to set the record straight—the first of many times she chose to go on the offensive to defend her political convictions.

Although she would employ a variety of rhetorical strategies throughout her life, her earliest tactics frequently took advantage of a trait that had long ago been discovered by her friends, most notably the celebrated humorist, Mark Twain—her biting wit. For much of the next decade, she would use a lethal combination of sarcasm and humorous wordplay to slay her critics and counter the patronizing and ableist narrative that often greeted her outspoken political opinions.

The opening volley came in an essay she composed in 1912 titled "How I Became a Socialist," carefully formulated to answer a wide range of attacks and innuendo that had surfaced since she had first declared her allegiance to the party earlier that year.[16] She begins by citing a recent article in the anti-socialist Jesuit periodical *Common Cause*, published under the headline: "SCHENECTADY REDS ARE ADVERTISING; USING HELEN KELLER, THE BLIND GIRL, TO RECEIVE PUBLICITY."[17]

The writer had declared that he couldn't "imagine anything more pathetic than the present exploitation of poor Helen Keller by the Socialists of Schenectady who had trumpeted her socialism to publicize their cause."[18] Helen had obviously been waiting some time to answer this charge. "There's a chance for satirical comment on the phrase, 'the exploitation of poor Helen Keller,'" she wrote. "But I will refrain, simply saying that I do not like the hypocritical sympathy of such a paper as the *Common Cause*, but I am glad if it knows what the word 'exploitation' means."[19]

She continues, "For several months, my name and socialism have appeared often together in the newspapers...Even notoriety may be turned to beneficent uses, and I rejoice if the disposition of the newspapers to record my activities results in bringing more often into their columns the word socialism."[20]

At this point, she takes the opportunity to explain for the first time how she had been converted to the cause while dispelling a persistent myth that had circulated widely since her political conversion was made public. She reveals that she had become a socialist by "reading," starting with the H. G. Wells book that had been recommended by Annie. "When she gave me the book, she was not a Socialist and she is not a Socialist now. Perhaps she will be one before Mr. Macy and I are done arguing with her."[21]

She explains that her reading had so far been limited and slow due to the lack of socialist literature available in braille and described the array of sources from where she had drawn her widespread knowledge of current events:

I take German bimonthly Socialist periodicals printed in braille for the blind...The other socialist literature that I have read has been spelled into my hand by a friend who comes three times a week to read to me whatever I choose to have read. She gives the titles of the articles and I tell her when to read on and when to omit. I have also had her read to me from the *International Socialist Review* articles the titles of which sounded promising. Manual spelling takes time. It is no easy and rapid thing to absorb through one's fingers a book of 50,000 words on economics. But it is a pleasure, and one which I shall enjoy repeatedly until I have made myself acquainted with all the classic socialist authors.

Although she had already dismissed the idea of Annie's influence on her radical beliefs, the idea naturally persisted that it must have been John Macy—unlike his wife, an avowed socialist—who was responsible. Responding to the allegation in *Common Cause* that "both Mr. and Mrs. Macy are enthusiastic Marxist propagandists," Helen took the opportunity again to correct a misconception that persists more than a century later. "Mr. Macy may be an enthusiastic Marxist propagandist, though I am sorry to say he has not shown much enthusiasm in propagating his Marxism through my fingers," she writes. "Mrs. Macy is not a Marxist, nor a socialist. Therefore, what the *Common Cause* says about her is not true. The editor must have invented that, made it out of whole cloth, and if that is the way his mind works, it is no wonder that he is opposed to socialism. He has not sufficient sense of fact to be a socialist or anything else intellectually worthwhile."[22]

Indeed, as Joseph Chamberlin had noted years earlier, Annie was still very much a conservative. Notwithstanding her one-time sympathy for the fiery Irish nationalist politician Charles Stewart Parnell and the Fenian cause of Irish independence when she was at Tewksbury, she made no secret of her disdain for the ideology shared by her husband and pupil.

Although much of Helen's vitriol was reserved for the conservative press, she doesn't spare the mainstream media in her essay. The previous September, the *New York Times* had published an editorial headlined,

"The Contemptible Red Flag," in which the paper had described the banner of the socialist movement as "detestable" and "the symbol of lawlessness and anarchy the world over...held in contempt by all right-minded persons." The bearer of such a flag, declared the paper, forfeits all right to "respect and sympathy," and should always be regarded with "suspicion."[23]

In her response to the piece, Helen reveals that, despite the fact that she is no worshipper of "cloth of any color," there is one that held a special place in her heart. "I love the red flag and what it symbolizes to me and other Socialists," she declares. "I have a red flag hanging in my study, and if I could, I should gladly march with it past the office of the *Times* and let all the reporters and photographers make the most of the spectacle."[24]

Here, she points out the irony that couldn't have been lost on anybody who remembered that only a short time ago—before her radical conversion—Helen was the darling of the American media, and newspaper readers couldn't get enough of her "inspirational" declarations and accomplishments.

"According to the inclusive condemnation of the *Times*, I have forfeited all right to respect and sympathy, and I am to be regarded with suspicion," she wrote. "Yet the editor of the *Times* wants me to write him an article! How can he trust me to write for him if I am a suspicious character? I hope you will enjoy as much as I do the bad ethics, bad logic, bad manners that a capitalist editor falls into when he tries to condemn the movement which is aimed at this plutocratic interest."[25]

It appeared that some newspapers were conflicted about how to approach the difficult balancing act of attacking one of America's most beloved figures. Predictably, some had chosen to blame Helen's politics on her disabilities. Nothing infuriated her more and she would often reserve her most withering criticism for these deeply offensive ableist attacks. Again, her biting sarcasm barely disguises her contempt:

The *Brooklyn Eagle* says, apropos of me, and socialism, that Helen Keller's "mistakes spring out of the manifest limitations of her

development." Some years ago, I met a gentleman who was introduced to me as Mr. McKelway, editor of the *Brooklyn Eagle*. It was
after a meeting that we had in New York on behalf of the blind. At
that time the compliments he paid me were so generous that I blush
to remember them. But now that I have come out for socialism, he
reminds me and the public that I am blind and deaf and especially
liable to error. I must have shrunk in intelligence during the years
since I met him. Surely it is his turn to blush. It may be that deafness and blindness incline one toward socialism. Marx was probably
stone deaf and William Morris was blind...Oh, ridiculous *Brooklyn
Eagle*. What an ungallant bird it is![26]

She challenged the paper to debate her on the merit of her ideas rather
than diminish her with ableist slights, admonishing, "Let it attack my
ideas and oppose the aims and arguments of Socialism. It is not fair
fighting or good argument to remind me and others that I cannot see or
hear." She also notably employed a tactic that would become an increasing feature of her rhetorical arsenal—the deft use of metaphors to suggest that her critics were "blind" and "deaf" to the ills of society. While
such language might be considered ableist today, the turns of phrase
were highly impactful coming from the famously deafblind figure. "If
I ever contribute to the Socialist movement, the book that I sometimes
dream of, I know what I shall name it: *Industrial Blindness and Social
Deafness*," she concluded the essay.[27]

⠏⠗⠝⠏⠀⠏⠞⠄
⠗⠄⠏⠄⠀⠍⠏⠄

Meanwhile, the socialist press continued to make hay of the affiliation of
such an illustrious figure. "Helen Keller is our Comrade, and her socialism is a living, vital thing to her," declared the *New York Call*. "All her
speeches are permeated with the spirit of socialism... If ever there was a
superwoman that woman is Helen Keller."[28]

With Annie still convalescing from her illness, Helen was reluctantly "packed off" to stay with her friend Lenore Smith (née Kinney), who had married a geologist in Washington, DC, since her Radcliffe days with Helen, where she had learned the manual alphabet and would sometimes substitute for Annie in the classroom.[29] Helen made no secret of the fact that she regarded the stay as a form of "exile."[30] Still, her old friend was a spirited companion and took her on a number of outings in the nation's capital.

In a letter to Annie written in October 1912, Helen provides a hint of her evolving attitudes around what she believes it will take to transform society. "No, I am not planning an article about Washington as the wicked capital of the United States," she assures her teacher. "I've no use for 'reform' work in that direction. It will always be hopeless until all the people unite and control the government for the benefit of all."[31]

In another letter sent during her monthlong stay, Helen wrote Annie excitedly about a planned outing: "I'm going with Lenore this morning to visit some of the worst alleys in the city. There are some active workers who are trying to induce the authorities to have these alleys cleaned up and give the people better dwellings."[32] Although such excursions helped to relieve the tedium, she confided to Annie that she felt like a "prisoner" at times, complaining that Lenore was a "bigoted plutocrat."[33] Her friend's views had not evolved much since the Radcliffe days and Helen was uncomfortable discussing politics with someone so clearly unreceptive to her newfound political leanings. "I don't feel free to talk about social questions obviously unwelcome in this atmosphere... I guess that's the experience of every crank, every heretic and every 'botherer of men,'" she wrote Annie.[34]

In a letter to John, she was even more forthright, describing a talk she gave to a group of Camp Fire girls. "They seemed earnest in their efforts to do something worthwhile," she told him, "but it is pathetic to see how many of those sweet, intelligent, helpless girls there are whose goodwill is going to waste because there is no one to direct it towards social service and social regeneration." Learning from Lenore about the economic beliefs of the so-called intellectuals in her neighborhood, Helen dismissed their "apparent stupidity and want of self-respect."[35]

In Washington, without access to the numerous subscriptions that regularly arrived in the mail to her Wrentham home, she was especially frustrated to be cut off from the socialist news sources that she relied on to keep abreast of political currents. "I am hungry for news that counts," she wrote Annie. "I hear nothing but newspaper gossip about Mr. Roosevelt and campaign fund disclosures. Is the Lawrence strike still on? What about the trial of Ettor and Giovannitti? Please, please don't throw me out of it all, it makes me too homesick."[36]

For months, reading the *New York Call* and other socialist periodicals, Helen had been following the Lawrence Textile Strike, a labor dispute involving mostly female Italian immigrant workers in Lawrence, Massachusetts—about seventy miles from her Wrentham home. The strike began in January 1912 after mill workers had been forced to accept a significant cut of pay and work hours. The battle would soon be given an enduring nickname—inspired by James Oppenheim's recent poem—the "Bread and Roses Strike."

> *As we come marching, marching, we battle, too, for men—*
> *For they are women's children and we mother them again.*
> *Our days shall not be sweated from birth until life closes—*
> *Hearts starve as well as bodies: Give us Bread but give us Roses.*[37]

Although Helen was a member of the Socialist Party, it was soon apparent that she had misgivings about the party's moderate stance of realizing gradual social change through the ballot box alone. As she followed the Lawrence strike from afar during 1912, she had become increasingly drawn to the militant tactics of Big Bill Haywood, a fellow socialist who had traveled throughout America for months to raise money for the defense of Arturo Giovannitti and Joseph Ettor. The two strike leaders had been charged with conspiracy to commit murder in the death of a thirty-four-year-old striker named Annie LoPizzo, even though witnesses claimed she had been shot to death by a police officer after the state militia cornered a group of peaceful marchers. On behalf of the Industrial Workers of the World (IWW)—the "One Big Union" whose members were nicknamed "Wobblies"—Haywood threatened a general strike unless the imprisoned leaders, who had clearly been framed, were released. "Open the jail gates or we will close the mill gates," demanded the charismatic labor leader. In the end, the workers achieved many of their demands, winning a 15 percent increase in pay along with overtime compensation. Enthralled by the successful battle, which eventually saw Ettor and Giovannitti cleared, Helen would later reach out to both men and would soon count the two strike leaders as close friends.

The dramatic success of the Lawrence strike convinced workers throughout the country that the tactics of the IWW—including mass marches, boycotts, even sabotage if necessary—could achieve meaningful results. Soon, mill workers throughout the East Coast were answering the Wobbly call to stand up for improved conditions. In November, John Macy traveled to Little Falls, New York, to assist Bill Haywood at a knitting mill strike involving mostly female workers who had seen their wages drastically reduced. Not long after John's arrival in November 1912, Haywood announced that he had received a check for $87.50 from Helen Keller—money she had recently earned from a Christmas card publisher for writing messages of "goodwill." The IWW leader shared Helen's message with the striking workers: "Their cause is my cause. If they are denied a living wage, I also am defrauded. While they are industrial slaves, I cannot be free...I want all the workers of the world to have sufficient money to provide the elements of a normal standard of living—a decent home, healthful surroundings, opportunity for education and recreation. I want them to have the same blessings that I have."[38]

While she was in DC, Helen yearned to visit the Bureau of Child Labor but was reluctant to ask Lenore to take her, she confided to Annie, "because there might be some embarrassment for her in the questions I wished to ask."[39] It was a reminder that her political awakening had come at the expense of alienating the circle of friends and patrons who had embraced her for years, many of whom had contributed to the fund that had sustained her education and living expenses during the Radcliffe years and beyond. The culture of the time allowed for great wealth but simultaneously encouraged philanthropy. Protestant ministers had taken to preaching the parable of Matthew 19:24 to their affluent parishioners— "And again I say to you: It is easier for a camel to pass through the eye of a needle, than for a rich man to enter into the kingdom of heaven." In response, society wives often took on charity as a form of noblesse oblige.

Among her financial supporters was Mary Thaw—widow of the coal and railroad baron William Thaw—whose relationship had survived Helen's radical conversion even as Helen appeared dedicated to waging war on her late husband's industrial interests. Unlike most of the other society wives who had convinced their husbands to support Helen as a feather in their philanthropic bonnets, Mrs. Thaw appears to have developed a genuine affection. "Even when she learned that I had become a Socialist, she did not withdraw her friendship and financial help," Helen later recalled. "She used to plead with me not to let fanatics preach their crazy theories through me; but the temper of her mind was such that while she abhorred my radicalism, she cherished me."[40]

Although she had gladly accepted the patronage of Mrs. Thaw and collected vast sums from the wives of Rogers, Spaulding, and Hutton, she initially drew the line (for reasons still unclear) at the patronage of one of America's wealthiest men—Andrew Carnegie, the notorious nineteenth-century steel tycoon who had famously devoted much of his vast fortune to philanthropic endeavors. In an 1889 treatise he called *The Gospel of Wealth*, Carnegie shared his belief that a wealthy man who fails to spend his money for the social good will die in disgrace "unwept, unhonored, and unsung."[41] In the years since, he had donated hundreds of millions of dollars to funding public libraries, schools, and cultural institutions. Carnegie first approached Helen in 1910 with the offer of an annual $5,000 annuity.[42] At that time, she politely refused his largesse, explaining that there were many deserving people for whom such a sum would increase "the joy in their lives." But Carnegie was not the sort of man who took no for an answer. She would later describe a memorable visit to his home:

> Mr. Carnegie asked me if I still refused his annuity. I said, "Yes, I haven't been beaten yet." He said he understood my attitude and sympathized with it. But he called my attention to the fact that fate had added my burden to that of those who were living with me, and that I must think of them as well as of myself... He told me again that the annuity was mine whenever I would take it and asked if it was true that I had become a Socialist. When I admitted that it was true, he found many disparaging things to say about Socialists, and even threatened to take me across his knees and spank me if I did not come to my senses. "But a great man like you should be consistent," I urged. "You believe in the brotherhood of man, in peace among nations, in education for everybody. All those are Socialist beliefs."[43]

Carnegie would never heed her appeal to embrace socialism, but by the end of 1912, Helen finally acquiesced and, with little fanfare, quietly accepted his pension.

Chapter Nine

Radical Shift

By 1913, Helen had thrown herself headlong into a new cause—the fight for women's suffrage.

For some time, she had closely followed the efforts of the radical British suffragette leader Emily Pankhurst, whose motto was "deeds not words." Her organization, the Women's Social and Political Union, had become notorious in the UK for its tactics of direct action and civil disobedience, including high-profile acts of vandalism, arson, and physical confrontation with police. These methods stood in marked contrast to the more genteel American suffragist movement, which was dominated by a coalition of liberals, women's temperance campaigners, religious leaders, and society women. The women who believed in gentle persuasion and constitutional tactics had come to be known as "suffragists" while the more militant campaigners often used the term "suffragette" as a way of reclaiming the word after a British newspaper used it to mock the movement in 1906.[1]

In October 1909, three years before she came out publicly as a socialist, Helen had received a letter from the British suffragette Rosa Grindon, inviting her to send along any writings that might appeal to women.[2] Two years later—inspired by an address Emily Pankhurst delivered during a recent tour of America—Helen wrote to Grindon revealing her skepticism about the potential for achieving suffrage through conventional means. "So long as the franchise is denied to a large number of those who serve and benefit the public, so long as those who vote are at the beck and call of party machines, the people are not free, and the day of women's freedom seems still to be in the far future," she wrote. "It makes no difference whether the Tories or the Liberals in Great Britain, the Democrats or the Republicans in the United States, or any party of the old model in any other country get the upper hand. To ask any such party for women's rights is like asking a czar for democracy... We choose between Tweedledum and Tweedledee. We elect expensive masters to do our work for us, and then blame them because they work for themselves and for their class."[3]

By the spring of 1913, Helen was no longer ambivalent about the movement, but her goals appeared markedly different from those of the growing chorus of respectable American suffragists. In May, she gave an interview to the *New York Times*, during which she expressed her solidarity with the tactics of Mrs. Pankhurst and declaring that the women of America should follow her example. Laying bare her increasingly radical politics, which would eventually find her at odds with the sizable moderate wing of the Socialist Party, she expressed support for the "smashing of windows, hunger strikes, anything that will bring publicity to the cause." Helen now considered herself a "militant suffragette" for one reason, she told the paper: "I believe suffrage will lead to socialism, and to me socialism is the ideal cause."[4]

Annie's biographer Nella Henney would later claim that Annie had followed John Macy and Helen into socialism shortly after the Lawrence Textile Strike, but the evidence is sketchy. If one of the cornerstones of socialism is equality for all people, Annie's views on suffragism well after the Lawrence strike are hard to countenance with somebody who had finally come to embrace the ideology shared by the rest of the Wrentham household. "She was not a woman suffragist and I was," Helen later recalled. "She was very conservative at that time."[5]

To earn money to renovate their Wrentham home, Annie and Helen had agreed to sign on for a nationwide lecture tour on the Chautauqua circuit—a popular social movement designed to expose Americans to culture and educational enlightenment, named for a lake in New York State where the first assembly was held in the 1870s. The tour launched in Boston in March 1913 and was an immediate success as crowds flocked to an old Baptist church that had been converted to a performance space—the same venue where Charles Dickens had performed his first reading of *The Christmas Carol* decades earlier and where Annie had delivered her Perkins valedictory address. "The great miracle of the 20th century was revealed to the 3000 people in Tremont Temple last evening," reported the *Boston Globe*. "It was the wonderful young woman's first appearance on the lecture platform, and she responded to the applause she felt but could not hear in a way that delighted everybody present. Her face was radiant. She trembled with delight—with the joy of the emotion she felt when the vast audience applauded... The crowning glory of a life that has struggled against such handicaps and obstacles, as no other human being in the world's history, for the light of knowledge."[6]

In the earliest days of the Chautauqua circuit, many of its most popular speakers were religious fundamentalists who used fire and brimstone to convert the crowds at tent assemblies throughout rural America. Helen likely believed her own brand of political evangelism would be equally effective. If it was difficult for the public to countenance the idea of the beloved Helen Keller as a socialist, her increasingly militant rhetoric about the perils of capitalism posed a new dilemma for the press, unsure how to report on her musings about society's ills during these appearances. Although Helen welcomed the opportunity to use her lecture tour as a vehicle to share her passionate political beliefs, many newspapers chose to ignore this aspect of her tour altogether or downplay its significance. The *Globe* review acknowledged her politics while ignoring most of what she had to say. "Helen Keller is a socialist and there were many Socialists present and many of her remarks were addressed to these friends," the paper reported. "She said, 'We are all bound together in a love for each other and the success of our movement and our lives depend on each other. Every one of us has the right to make the most of our lives—of the lives which God has given us.'"[7] Most of the article, however, described the lengthy presentation delivered by Annie about Helen's education.

Without mentioning the word socialism at all, the *Asheville Citizen-Times* simply alluded to it when the tour moved south. "With the particular political faith that Helen Keller professes we have nothing in common," sniffed the North Carolina daily, "but she does not obtrude that upon her audience. Her address is largely a song of triumph, a message of cheer; the gospel of hope to the hopeless and a note of optimism to the despairing."[8] Still, the acknowledgment of her political beliefs was nowhere to be found in some of the coverage while she and Annie crisscrossed the country delivering more than one hundred lectures. Some papers found a way to report on Helen's socialism without offending their conservative readers. When the *Nebraska State Journal* reported on the lecture, it focused on a humorous routine that Helen and Annie had worked out:

Annie: Are you a real socialist or a parlor socialist?
Helen: A real socialist.
Annie: What kind of socialist did you say you were?
Helen: A sure enough one. (audience laughs)
Annie: I know there is something wrong about socialism, if I could only find out what it was.
Helen: Please let me know when you find out what it is. The lazy ones won't get all the cake under socialism as they do now. (audience laughs)[9]

In 1913, Helen published her third book—the first since she had publicly embraced her new ideology—a collection of essays titled *Out of the Dark* that frankly discussed her socialist beliefs. With the exception of the radical press, most of the reviews were decidedly lukewarm or patronizing. "It must be acknowledged that if she were not Helen Keller, the 'wonderful blind and deaf girl,' her declarations of opinion might seem obvious and her judgments not original," opined one reviewer. "As a successor, however, of *The Story of My Life*, written by her, it is an intensely interesting document. It will be more interesting when its opinions may be compared with her more mature beliefs, which surely may be expected in future works."[10]

Despite her preoccupation with politics during this period, Helen often found time for socializing with her many society friends and was invited to many a glittering gathering, where she presumably held her tongue about her feelings around the source of the wealth that made possible the vast estates of the Thaws, the Carnegies, the Spauldings, and her other benefactors. But whenever she could, she also found time to escape to the country and take long walks through the woods with Annie. "My greatest enjoyment is nature," she later wrote. "The trees and the flowers, and the grass. When I feel wearied by the misery and ignorance which sometimes seem to be the only things in the world, I go out of doors and breathe the sweet fresh air and feel trees and flowers and grass and it strengthens me."[11] At night, she could be found playing checkers, chess, or dominoes with John or Annie. She also loved ballroom dancing, which she often practiced at home with Annie—a skill that she would frequently show off later on when she was comfortable enough to dance in public. After returning from a picnic one afternoon, she wrote her sister, Mildred, "We began dancing like mad, and waltzed between courses at dinner. I can't pride myself on a 'light, fantastic toe,' but I am slowly picking up the tango steps."[12]

Meanwhile, on the home front, John and Annie's marriage had shown signs of fraying for some time. It appeared to be over for good when John quietly moved out of the Wrentham house and rented an apartment in Boston while his wife toured the country with Helen on the Chautauqua circuit in late 1913. At the beginning of 1914, Kate

Keller read Helen a recent letter that John had sent about the breakdown of the marriage. His original correspondence has been lost, but a series of letters survive that Helen sent him between January and March of that year. They provide a picture of Helen's increasing frustration, as he appears to pour scorn on his estranged wife after nine years of marriage. Her responses provide telling clues as to some of John's grievances, although it is sometimes difficult to determine the context.

"It has amazed me and filled my heart with sorrow," Helen writes in January. "If you ever loved Teacher or me, I beseech you to be calm, fair, kind, to reconsider what you have said in that letter...You say, 'she has never been a wife to you, or done any of the things that a woman may be expected to do.'...You say you can never explain to me what your life with Teacher has been. Have you forgotten all the sunshine, all the laughter, all the long walks, drives, jolly adventures?"[13]

Among the long-standing issues in the marriage had been Annie's consistent refusal to embrace Macy's left-wing political beliefs. Despite Nella Henney's dubious claim that Annie had become a socialist following the 1912 Lawrence Textile Strike, John was evidently still frustrated by her conservative views. "The arguments between John and Teacher over socialism were carried on continuously, even on trains, where they went at it at the top of their voices," writes Joseph Lash.[14] Now, in an attempt at reconciliation, Helen appeared determined to persuade John that Annie had finally come around to his ideology. "I know that in the past year Teacher has changed in some essential respects," she wrote on January 25. "By talking with her daily, I have learned that you have helped her to see the world, the workers and economic, social and moral conditions as she never saw them before. Living so close to her as I do, I can prove, absolutely prove, that she has new aims, a new conviction, a new vision of life, a new ideal and a new inspiration to service, and you will know it too some day."[15] Not long afterward, Helen wrote John again informing him that she had recently joined the Los Angeles local of the Socialist Party. "They also asked Teacher to join, and she at once said she would, but they have not yet sent her a red card as they promised to."[16] Although she appeared to sympathize with some socialist tenets, including a strong concern for the plight of the working class, there is no evidence that Annie ever formally joined the party or embraced its goals, and this letter may have been a disingenuous and desperate attempt to convince John that she had finally come around.

Another of the letters Helen sent John during this period hints that the breakdown in the marriage may also have been influenced by Annie's temperament. "We realize how quick-tempered and changeable Teacher is," she wrote in February. "We know that when she gets angry, she blurts out things which she does not mean in the least."[17] In her 1955 biography of Annie, Helen would describe the "dark moods" that "continued to harass her every once in a while until her death."[18] Perhaps not coincidentally, she dates the worst of those moods to 1914, the height of her estrangement from John: "At that time, the melancholy which now and then seized Teacher became so dreadful and she was so overwhelmed with a constant fretfulness and a despair that made it a misery just to exist."[19] Annie's biographer Kim Nielsen believes that today she would have likely been diagnosed with clinical depression, though even at the time she appeared to understand that her moods were related to mental health issues. "She feared insanity for a while," Helen observed, "but that was due to a kink in her nervous system which she had no idea how to manage."[20] She was also increasingly plagued by physical ailments, including what Helen described as "the never-ceasing torment of her eyes" that would only get worse over the years when they deteriorated to the point that surgery could no longer repair the damage.[21] Annie also suffered from bouts of neuritis, rheumatism, and sciatica.[22]

Among John's apparent grievances, it appears that he had accused Annie of being less than generous with her money—an accusation for which Helen obviously had little patience. "You speak of her making 'a disgraceful row on two occasions' when you proposed to send some money to your mother," she wrote in February. "You say nothing about the many times that money was sent to your family when Teacher did not 'make a disgraceful row!' You know, John, and I know that she helped your family even before she was married. You should remember that during the years which followed it was often very difficult for us to pay our own bills...All this talk about money is very painful to me, and I hope I shall never have to refer to it again."[23]

His previous letter to Mrs. Keller had not apparently confined itself to a criticism of his wife. "What has happened to you to justify such cruel, suspicious language?" Helen wrote in February. "You had no business to call me a fool as you did in your last letter to mother."[24]

By March, it appears, John still had no desire to reconcile with Annie, but he offered to continue his collaboration with Helen, for whom he still acted as literary agent. "Every word of your two letters about Teacher is cruelly stamped upon my mind and will darken every day of my life as my physical blindness has never done," she responded to this entreaty. "As to your helping me in the future, how do you think we could work together with advantage when you keep saying that Teacher is dishonest, that you cannot be harassed by a woman whom you cannot trust, that she has lied and deceived you?"[25]

Despite this trail of vitriol, John would eventually move back for a time in the spring of 1914 after a carelessly discarded cigarette set his Boston apartment on fire, leaving him temporarily homeless.[26] It was clear, however, that the marriage was all but over and he would soon depart for good, leaving a grief-stricken Annie increasingly leaning on Helen for emotional support. "She kept demanding my love in a way that was heartbreaking," Helen recalled. "For days she would shut herself up almost stymied or trying to think of a plan that would bring John back or weeping as only women who are no longer cherished weep."[27]

To help fill the void created by John's departure, Helen and Annie hired a young woman from Scotland named Polly Thomson to take on some of the house management duties. "She had not heard of Helen and knew nothing of the manual alphabet or the needs of the blind and the deaf," wrote Nella Henney, "but she was eager and quick to learn...She could balance a bank account (no one at Wrentham had ever been able to do this) and she could read a time-table without the help of a ticket agent. She could manage a household, doing the cooking herself if it was necessary, and yet be the most gracious of hostesses. And she could stand a firm and uncompromising guard over a doorbell or a telephone, which was something else no one at Wrentham had ever been able to do."[28] For the next two decades, Polly would function mostly in the background, stepping in during the increasingly frequent periods when Annie was physically or mentally unwell. None of the trio could have imagined at the time that she would one day become known as the "second Annie Sullivan."

Meanwhile, as Helen increasingly focused her political crusades around women's issues, she had begun to advance a forward-thinking understanding of the links between gender and class—an analysis rarely heard within a suffragist movement largely dominated by white women of means. In a 1913 essay titled, "Why Men Need Woman Suffrage," she argued that democracy could not triumph until working men and women join together to solve their political, social, and economic problems:

> I realize that the vote is only one of many weapons in our fight for the freedom of all. Working men suffer from the helplessness of working women. They must compete in the same offices and factories with women who are unable to protect themselves with proper laws. They must compete with women who work in unsanitary rooms called homes, work by dim lamps in the night, rocking a cradle with one foot. It is to the interest of all workers to end this stupid, one-sided, one-power arrangement.[29]

It was one of a number of writings in which Helen explicitly argued the links between class and social issues. When a young Quaker woman from Alabama wrote on behalf of her group asking Helen what she would recommend they study if they wished to follow in her "altruistic" footsteps, her answer was unequivocal: "Study economics." Not until all women understand that "economic conditions underlie all altruistic work," she explained, will the world become a better place for all humanity.[30]

If her group wanted to understand the causes of poverty and misery, Helen advised, "I would urge them to study the people at their doors—the workers in the factories, mines and fields of Alabama." These are not mysteries hidden from our human eyes, she adds, but "practical human business" and it is necessary to understand why poverty dooms "little children to the horrors of child labor" and why thousands of useful men are "killed or maimed in the mills while their families are left without recompense."[31]

The fact that she should find herself counseling somebody to study economics, she continues, is something she never could have imagined a decade earlier when she was forced to study "the dismal science" at Radcliffe. "I thought it was a pathless wilderness of statistics and fruitless theories. Now I know that economics is life itself. It is the question of daily bread, of daily morals, of common justice and right thinking."[32]

In that spirit, she had recently read a German translation of *The People's Marx*—a popular distillation of Marx's classic economic critique, *Das Kapital*, which argues that the motivational force of capitalism is in the exploitation of labor. His class analysis would have a profound effect on her activism throughout her life and would deeply influence Helen's thinking around disability advocacy.

Even as she continued to make the case for suffrage, she embraced a number of other issues that again suggested her support for women's rights went much further than a superficial call for the vote. After the anarchist leader Emma Goldman was arrested in New York for distributing pamphlets advocating women's right to birth control, Helen weighed in, publicly offering her unconditional support in a 1913 letter to the *New York Call*:

The arrest of Emma Goldman for teaching effective methods of birth control seems to me to have raised the only important issue in the whole fight for family limitation...Many mothers already desire to limit the number of offspring. They live among families so large and so poor that hunger forces them to send their young children to labor...The law is offended only when someone takes direct action against the frightfulness of the industrial conflict. This is no mere fight to keep a woman out of prison; it is a battle for the freedom of all women. Anyone that refuses to take part in it because Emma Goldman happens to be an anarchist, is guilty of treason to the cause of the workers.[33]

Needless to say, the mainstream press was increasingly uneasy about her radical shift. "Helen Keller, as long as she played her part correctly, was one of the biggest platform successes," the *New York Herald* later wrote dismissively. "She was an inspiration to the world. America went wild over her. Then, in Boston, she became interested in radicalism and in a short time that ended her career. As a social revolutionist it was different, especially since she owed a great part of her success to the very capitalists she condemned."[34]

As usual, such criticism bothered Helen not at all. In the years since she had entered radical politics, she consistently fought the good fight—deftly taking on the press, the capitalist system, and her critics with a panache that still resonates a century later. Her next crusade, however, would leave a permanent stain on her legacy.

Chapter Ten

. . . .

"A Defective Race"

On the evening of November 12, 1915, Dr. Harry Haiselden, chief surgeon of Chicago's German American Hospital, was working late when he received an urgent summons to weigh in on a medical emergency. A woman named Anna Bollinger had just given birth to a baby boy with multiple medical issues. The infant was born paralyzed on the left side of his body and was missing his entire left ear as well as his right eardrum. His right cheek was connected to his shoulder and his intestinal tract was sealed.

Under ordinary circumstances, the decision about the baby's treatment would be strictly determined by established medical protocol that dictates doing whatever it takes to save a child. But Haiselden had long since stopped using science alone to guide his medical decisions. Instead of performing the surgery that would save his life, the doctor decreed that John Bollinger should be allowed to die. Otherwise, he claimed, the infant would grow up to be a "defective" who would become "a burden to society and pollute the human race with his impure genes."[1] His words were enough to convince Anna Bollinger to give her permission to withhold surgery. "I love the poor deformed little one as I love my three other healthy children," she told reporters. "But the doctor told me it would be a cripple all its life, that it would probably be an imbecile and possible criminal. With tears breaking in my heart, I gave consent to its death."[2]

At a hastily convened news conference, Haiselden defended his decision. "I have no doubt I shall be called a cold-blooded murderer for allowing this baby to die," he said. "I am prepared for bitter criticism. But its death is a question between me and my conscience. I would not kill the infant. I would not administer poison or take its life by any active surgical means. I shall merely stand by passively and let it die. I will let nature complete its bungled job."[3]

The case dominated headlines for days. As society reacted in horror to his decision to play God with the life of a baby, Haiselden would soon discover that he had a surprising and unlikely ally.

⠗⠏⠐⠏ ⠦⠁⠄⠐
⠏⠐⠏⠄ ⠛⠆⠄⠐

Many of the so-called "radical" causes that Helen supported during the first two decades of the twentieth century—including women's suffrage, workers' rights, and the abolition of child labor—would hardly be considered controversial today. One of her crusades, however, would cast a dark shadow over Helen's reputation—even if many writers have preferred to simply ignore her early entanglement with eugenics. It is one more chapter of her life that conflicts with the conventional narrative of Helen as a secular saint but offers rich evidence that she was all too human.

Other than Annie Sullivan herself, no figure likely had a greater early influence on Helen than Alexander Graham Bell, the man whose recommendation first brought Annie into her orbit. Bell was so influential in her life and education, in fact, that she dedicated *The Story of My Life* to him: "To Alexander Graham Bell, who has taught the deaf to speak and enabled the listening ear to hear speech from the Atlantic to the Rockies."[4]

By the time she wrote these words in 1903, Helen had become the poster child of oralism—the movement to teach deaf people to speak so that they could be better integrated into mainstream society, which Bell had championed almost since the time he had taken up the pursuit of deaf education. Two decades earlier, in 1883, he had published a paper, "Memoir Upon the Formation of a Deaf Variety of the Human Race," warning of a "great calamity" facing the world—the production of a "defective race" of human beings.[5]

Already, he warned, there were "societies of deaf mutes" in every city dedicated to "social intercourse" and even "public worship." If this trend is allowed to continue, he believed, their presence would pose a grave threat to society. Most worrisome of all, he declared, this "race" had adapted a "special language—a language as different from English as French or German or Russian."[6] This language was American Sign Language, a standardized system of communication using hand signs, developed by the deaf French educator Laurent Clerc, between 1814 and 1817, based on a similar system used in France. Although Bell had once taught sign language and occasionally used it to communicate with his deaf wife, Mabel, he was determined above all to eradicate ASL from the educational system because of his belief that it would lead to intermarriage among the deaf community. Bell's paper was just the latest salvo in a war that was already well underway in favor of his preferred method, oralism, which many believed would mitigate the "dangers" of a deaf subculture by ensuring deaf people could more easily interact with the general hearing population.

Advocates for ASL described it as the "natural language of the deaf" and argued that reliance on oralism alone would be educationally disastrous for most students, but the crusade against American Sign Language was remarkably successful. For decades to come, oralism would largely supplant sign language as the most commonly taught form of communication within the deaf community. Although ASL and other forms of sign language would eventually experience a resurgence of popularity, the battle caused deep divisions within the deaf community that persist to this day.

In the course of his research, Bell had embraced the pseudoscience of eugenics, which advocated the idea of improving the human species by selectively mating people with "desirable" hereditary traits. The term had been coined by the British social Darwinist Francis Galton in 1883, the same year that Bell presented his influential paper to the National Academy of Sciences describing the deaf community as a "defective race."

Later, Bell allied himself with the leader of the American eugenics movement, Charles Davenport, a former Harvard zoologist who believed that race influenced human behavior and who would help influence a wide range of scientists to embrace eugenics during the early years of the twentieth century. Davenport also believed strongly in strict immigration laws to keep "undesirable" elements out of the United States, influenced by his eugenic belief that people from western and northern Europe were genetically superior to those from southern and eastern Europe.[7] His racist theories were enormously influential throughout the US and directly influenced the passage of sterilization laws in several states along with virulently racist anti-immigration legislation. Bell embraced some of these xenophobic theories, emphasizing the need for legislation to prevent the entry of what he termed "undesirable ethnical elements" while encouraging the "evolution of a higher and nobler type of man in America."[8]

Unlike many of his contemporaries, however, Bell rejected the idea of so-called "negative eugenics," which sought to prevent "bad genes" being passed down to future generations by sterilizing "undesirable" populations. Bowing to the influence of the eugenics movement, a number of states passed laws allowing forced surgical sterilization of women with developmental disabilities. In the 1927 case *Buck v. Bell*, the United States Supreme Court would later overwhelmingly uphold the right of Virginia to forcibly sterilize a "feebleminded" woman named Carrie Buck. It was a practice that continued well into the 1950s, and eugenic attitudes would also witness many Black and Indigenous women sterilized against their will.[9] As an alternative to such barbaric methods, Bell supported instead the idea of encouraging procreation among those he considered "genetically fit."

Despite his opposition to sterilization, he did try to persuade deaf people not to intermarry because he feared that they would pass on their disability and create a "defective variety of the race." The evidence that Bell cited was faulty and hardly based on the science that he professed to follow. Although deafness can be hereditary, only a relatively small percentage of deaf couples produce deaf children.[10] "But the image of an insular, inbred, and proliferating deaf culture became a potent weapon for the oralist cause," notes Professor Douglas Baynton, a historian specializing in the history of disability in the United States. "Bell's claims were widely repeated for years to come."[11]

Through much of this period, many took notice of the protégé who was often by Bell's side. "When I was a little girl just learning to talk," Helen later recalled, "my teacher and I used to go with him to conventions to further the teaching of speech to the deaf."[12] Helen, in fact, had become one of Bell's most potent weapons in his crusade to promote oralism. By the time that she decided she wanted to speak, she could already communicate proficiently using a variety of methods. She had, of course, long ago mastered the manual alphabet, and was proficient in reading braille. As a teenager, she would learn to read lips by running her fingers over the speaker's face and larynx, which would eventually become her preferred method of conversing. As a child, she had even allegedly learned a unique form of Morse code that allowed Teacher to communicate by tapping her feet from across the room while Helen detected the vibrations. But when Helen wished to communicate with a hearing person, she was still often forced to rely on her companion to translate the words as she spelled them into Annie's palm.

Annie herself would later claim that she initially opposed the idea of teaching Helen to speak because she feared that it would interfere with her ability to use the manual alphabet, but "the impulse to utter audible sounds was strong within her, and the constant efforts which I made to repress this instinctive tendency, which I feared in time would become unpleasant, were of no avail."[13] As a great admirer of Bell, Annie readily adapted to his enthusiasm for the oral method. In an 1892 essay she penned called "How Helen Keller Acquired Language," she described her first lesson in what she called the "more natural and universal medium of human intercourse—oral language."[14] She cited the turning point as the day that Helen asked, "How do the blind girls know what to say with their mouths? Why do you not teach me to talk like them? Do deaf children ever learn to speak?" One of Laura Bridgman's former teachers had responded by telling Helen about a deafblind Norwegian child, Ragnhild Kaata, who had learned to talk. "Helen's joy over this good news can be better imagined than described," Annie wrote. "She at once resolved to learn to speak, and from that day to this she has never wavered in that resolution."[15]

Annie soon became as passionate a proponent of oralism as Bell himself and would often share with her audiences the first full sentence that her pupil had spoken as a nine-year-old after she began her oral education: "I am no longer dumb."[16]

Despite her own embrace of oralism, and years of painstaking lessons with voice teachers, however, Helen—to her lifelong frustration—never quite mastered speech. Although those who knew her well could make out her words, expressed in a guttural style that she would claim was not a "pleasant voice," she could often only make herself understood if she spoke very slowly, syllable by syllable. She lamented that she had only "partially conquered the hostile silence" and would frequently describe her failure to "speak normally" as one of her greatest disappointments.[17]

Bell would eventually distance himself from eugenics, as he witnessed the extreme iterations that resulted in compulsory sterilization laws passed in many states and later helped inspire the Nazis' euthanasia program—as described in historian Edwin Black's landmark 2003 work, *The War against the Weak*.[18] But, as Bell's biographer Katie Booth observed, "It also remains true that his work to promote oralism at all costs laid the groundwork for those eugenic ideas to flourish with the deaf in mind."[19]

Still, despite her role in promoting oralism, there is no direct evidence tying Helen's own embrace of the odious philosophy to her longtime mentor even if she was almost certainly aware of his troubling beliefs. It is just as likely that her own support for eugenics was influenced by a contemporary trend that saw an array of so-called progressive figures champion the movement during the period of her socialist zenith. Historian Diane Paul has documented the wide variety of prominent left-wing intellectuals and writers who advocated the "improvement of the genetic stock through selective breeding"—a group that included George Bernard Shaw, Julian Huxley, and the man that Helen credited with her conversion to socialism, H. G. Wells.[20] Wells was among its most enthusiastic proponents, hailing eugenics as the first step toward the removal "of detrimental types and characteristics" and the "fostering of desirable types" in their place.[21]

Regardless of where she had drawn her understanding of the purported benefits of a cause that hoped to eradicate people like her, Helen's entrance into a debate that gripped the nation in the autumn of 1915 came as a shock in many quarters.

Among the many prominent Americans who weighed in about the fate of the Bollinger baby was the celebrated suffragist Jane Addams. "A physician or hospital board has not the right to assume the prerogative that any person shall be killed but is required by the highest moral law to save every life that possibly can be saved," she argued in a widely printed newspaper essay at the height of the debate. Addams offered a list of "great defectives" who had emerged as among the greatest men and women of society in spite of their disabilities. She cited Helen Keller as the prime example: "She was not born with deformities, but they came afterward—blindness, deafness, loss of power of speech. Despite all these obstacles, she refused to be discouraged or thrown into discard. She is an accomplished woman today—a benefit to the world."[22]

As she was America's most famous person with disabilities at the time, one can assume that Americans were not surprised to watch Helen

Keller's name being summoned by Addams during the ongoing debate about the Bollinger baby. It almost certainly came as a jolt, however, when Helen herself weighed in with an article in the *Pittsburgh Press* two weeks later defending Haiselden's decision. Considering the compassion that she had always displayed for the most vulnerable members of society, her words were especially jarring:

> When Dr. HJ Haiselden permitted the Bollinger Baby to die in a Chicago hospital, he performed a service to society as well as to the hopeless being spared from a life of misery. No one cares about that pitiful, useless lump of flesh, but that baby has lived not in vain, because its death has brought us face to face with many questions of eugenics and control of the birth rate—questions we have been side-stepping because we are afraid of them. The hue and cry raised about the "murder" of this poor, mindless, crippled, half-dead little creature, indicates a deep-rooted error in American thinking... We have refused to listen to the Dr. Haiseldens when they have tried to rub into us the fact that the world is already flooded with unhappy, unhealthy, mentally unsound persons that should never have been born.[23]

Some of Haiselden's detractors argued that Helen herself might have been one of those discarded, though at least one paper pointed out that this was not a fitting argument since she had not actually been born deafblind. "The comparison of this breathing human flesh as has been made and Helen Keller and those of less deformities is odious," declared the *Washington Herald*—one of the few papers that defended Haiselden's actions at the time. "Such cases are not in the same class and are therefore not comparable. Dr. Haiselden conscientiously performed a merciful deed by not forcing life on this monstrosity."[24]

While it was Helen's defense of Haiselden that attracted the most attention, she also used the same article to weigh in on the case of William

Sanger, who had been arrested two months earlier for distributing a pamphlet advocating birth control written by his wife, the prominent activist Margaret Sanger. In this passage, Helen appears to explicitly link her eugenic beliefs to the misery caused by overpopulation—an argument that had also frequently been used by Margaret, a longtime proponent of eugenics. "Already countless mothers are obliged to work outside and leave their little ones without proper care," Helen wrote. "Unwatched, exposed to all the influences of evil, these children of the poor grow or waste away as they may, like plants in sandy soil, among rocks, weeds and rubbish, bereft of light and sunshine. Those who survive bring into the world, in spite of themselves, an ever-larger number of deformed, sickly, feeble-minded children, and the incalculable mischief of an uncontrolled birth-rate sucks up the vitality of the human race."[25] There is no record of Alexander Graham Bell's thoughts about the case of the Bollinger baby, but since he had long rejected "negative eugenics," he would have presumably disapproved of his protégé's shocking stand.

Meanwhile, an autopsy conducted five days after John Bollinger's death revealed that Harry Haiselden may have deliberately exaggerated the baby's health prognosis to further his own eugenic agenda. After the autopsy and hearing, a coroner's jury comprised of six prominent Chicago physicians and surgeons declared in a statement, "We find no evidence from the physical defects in the child that it would have become mentally or morally defective." Although the jury affirmed Haiselden's right not to operate, it concluded that a number of the baby's physical "defects" might have been corrected by plastic surgery and grafting.[26] One juror publicly disputed Haiselden's widely reported claim that John Bollinger would have ended up a "mental defective" if he had been allowed to live. "The brain was all right as far as we could tell," he said. "There was no physical evidence that the child would have ended up physically or morally oblique."[27] Although he was never charged for his role in the baby's death, Haiselden was later expelled from the Chicago Medical Society for his actions.[28]

A month later, writing in the *New Republic*, Helen appeared to soften her tone by proposing a science-based mechanism—a jury of expert physicians—to draw the line on a case-by-case basis and decide the fate of babies born with severe birth defects. Despite her more tempered approach, however, she uses the piece to simply double down on her eugenic arguments, asserting that a "mental defective...is almost sure to be a potential criminal."[29]

⠏⠬⠄⠃ ⠲⠓⠄⠒
⠒⠂⠃⠄ ⠐⠱⠄⠒

As near as can be determined, this is the last time she ever weighed in on the controversy. She never renounced her position on the Bollinger baby, nor did she address it again. Two decades later, however, she would take a very different course when the Nazis—very much inspired by the American and British eugenics movements—used similar arguments to justify their monstrous crimes. Then, Helen would use her role as a disability icon to place herself on the right side of history. But her brief flirtation with eugenics and her role as a poster child for Alexander Graham Bell's oralist crusade against American Sign Language would forever taint her legacy among some segments of the disability community.

Chapter Eleven

. . . .

Helen vs. Jim Crow

B orn only fifteen years after the abolition of slavery, Helen's earliest experiences with race were probably not much different than those of any other middle-class white child growing up in the postbellum South. A little more than 40 percent of the population of Tuscumbia in 1880 was African American, though most of the Black population lived in shanties far from the pristine confines of Ivy Green, the Keller household.[1]

Information is scant on what became of the Keller family's enslaved workers after abolition and whether any continued working for the household. In the 1830 federal census—at a time when Ivy Green was still a sprawling 640-acre cotton plantation—Arthur's father, David Keller, is recorded as enslaving 49 people, including 18 children under the age of ten.[2] By the time of the 1850 "slave census," his widow, Mary F. Keller, is recorded enslaving 16 people.[3] There is no existing record after that.

The first hint of the Keller family's relationship with the Black servants who worked for them during Helen's childhood comes from Helen herself, who wrote in *The Story of My Life* about a "little colored girl"—the child of the family cook—whom she referred to as "Martha Washington." Helen would later admit that she made that name up because she couldn't remember the girl's real name, which was eventually revealed to be Mary Hart.[4] Helen recounts bossing the young girl around under threat of violence when she was young: "Martha Washington understood my signs, and I seldom had any difficulty in making her do just as I wished," she wrote. "It pleased me to domineer over her, and she generally submitted to my tyranny rather than risk a hand-to-hand encounter."[5] It would appear, however, that Helen's treatment of the girl reflected how she had been taught to treat servants generally and may have predated her awareness of racial differences.

In a report to Michael Anagnos about Helen's progress shortly after arriving in Tuscumbia, Annie described the first time Helen became conscious of race: "On being told that she was white and that one of the servants was black, she concluded that all who occupied a similar menial position were of the same hue; and whenever I asked her the color of a servant, she would say 'black.' "[6]

The attitude of Captain Keller, who had served the Confederacy as an assistant quartermaster at the siege of Vicksburg,[7] likely set the tone for the family's attitudes toward race. "His view of the Civil War was that the South had been the innocent martyr, the North the mercenary aggressor," writes Joseph Lash. "He was kind to Negroes, providing they kept their place, were deferential and polite. 'We never think of them as human beings,' he told a shocked Northern visitor."[8] The visitor may have been more shocked by something Lash neglected to mention. Arthur Keller, in fact, was allegedly the first man in Alabama to "take the obligations of the Klan," as his former newspaper, the *North Alabamian*, reported after his death.[9] The earliest known Ku Klux Klan chapter in Tuscumbia dates to April 1868, and was implicated in the lynching of three Black men in September of that year.[10] There is no evidence, however, linking Arthur Keller to the incident, nor is there any indication that Helen ever knew of her father's purported Klan affiliations.

It wasn't until she embraced left-wing politics later on that she appears to have given any significant thought to racial matters. And, although her opinions on other contemporary issues were often very much influenced by a socialist analysis, the party's stand on the "Negro question" was anything but clear-cut by the time Helen stirred up a hornet's nest that would shake her world.

In a 1903 essay titled "The Negro in the Class Struggle," Socialist Party leader Eugene Debs set out his party's position on race. "The whole world is under obligation to the Negro, and that the white heel is still upon the black neck is simply proof that the world is not yet civilized," he wrote. "The history of the Negro in the United States is a history of crime without a parallel." Rather than using this observation to champion Black liberation, however, he employed somewhat equivocating language about the support the Socialist Party could provide, maintaining that "we have nothing special to offer the Negro, and we cannot make separate appeals to all the races... The Socialist Party is the party of the working class, regardless of color—the whole working class of the whole world."[11]

According to one biographer, Debs—although a lifelong opponent of racial discrimination—"refused to concede that poor Negroes were in a worse position than poor white people."[12] Still, his views on race were considerably more enlightened than some of his comrades', especially those of Victor Berger, who would become the first socialist ever elected to Congress in 1910. "There can be no doubt that the negroes and mulattoes constitute a lower race than the Caucasian and indeed even the Mongolian have the start of them in civilization by many thousand years—so that negroes will find it difficult ever to overtake them," Berger wrote in a 1902 editorial, concluding with a claim even more disturbing: "The many cases of rape which occur wherever negroes are settled in large numbers prove, moreover, that the free contact with the whites has led to the further degeneration of the negroes, as of all other inferior races. In the case of the negro all the savage instincts of his forefathers in Africa come to the surface."[13]

At successive party conventions between 1901 and 1919, members reaffirmed that the struggle for Negro equality was part of the larger economic question and therefore deserved no special consideration. Debs's declaration that "we have nothing special to offer the Negro" became the party line, though some have used these words out of context to falsely imply that the Socialist Party was indifferent to American racism.

Annie Sullivan also had a mixed record when it came to race. Her biographer Nella Henney claimed that she considered herself "vigorously pro-Negro and anti-Southern."[14] Such a position was not altogether surprising for somebody who had been educated at Perkins, whose co-founder, Samuel Gridley Howe, was a noted abolitionist. And yet despite her professed liberal beliefs, Annie's history also reveals a trail of casual and explicit racism. Shortly after she arrived in Tuscumbia, she wrote a disturbing letter to her former housemother, Sophia Hopkins, about Helen's progress: "After supper we go to my room and do all sorts of things until eight, when I undress the little woman and put her to bed. She sleeps with me now. Mrs. Keller wanted to get a nurse for her; but I concluded I'd rather be her nurse than look after a stupid, lazy negress."[15] In another letter, she wrote, "Helen plays with her dolls or frolics in the yard with the little darkies, who were her constant companions before I came."[16] Later, after a fact-finding mission with John Macy to study the "Negro question," she noted that she had come within "smelling distance" of the subject.[17] This sort of casual racism, of course, was hardly unusual for the time, even for an ostensibly racially enlightened New Englander. And yet it serves to make Helen's own evolution on racial issues all the more noteworthy, given the attitudes of those closest to her.

For Helen, it is difficult to pinpoint any specific epiphany that served as a touchstone for her own position on race, but the roots may be traced back to a visit from two men one afternoon in 1891 when she was eleven years old and studying at the Perkins School for the Blind. William James was one of America's preeminent philosophers at the time and a distinguished Harvard professor of scientific psychology. We have no record of what inspired his excursion to Perkins that day, but it is fair to assume that the outing was influenced by Helen's rising celebrity given how many others were attracted for similar visits. On this visit, James brought along one of his Harvard protégés, W. E. B. Du Bois, who would soon emerge as one of the most prominent civil rights activists in America, a brilliant scholar and an influential voice for African American equality. But on this occasion, he was still fresh from his undergraduate degree, years away from becoming a national figure. Du Bois would later recall the impression Helen made upon him during this visit. "When I was studying philosophy at Harvard under William James, we made an excursion one day out to Roxbury," he wrote. "We stopped at the Blind Asylum and saw a young girl who was blind and deaf and dumb and yet who, by infinite pains and loving sympathy, had been made to speak without words and to understand without sounds. She was Helen Keller. Perhaps because she was blind to color differences in this world, I became intensely interested in her, and all through my life I have followed her career."[18]

Helen would also keenly remember the visit, writing, "Most pleasantly I remember the day when Professor William James and [Du Bois] came to see me at Perkins in South Boston. I felt Mr. Du Bois's kindly interest in me, and the dynamic quality of his personality. As I grew older, I understood more fully his wonderful climb to manhood and the tireless zeal with which he has inspired and changed the lives of countless negro men and women, so that they maintain their struggle towards the equality of all human beings in opportunity, education, and self-fulfilment which is true civilization."[19]

Almost two decades after his visit to Perkins, Du Bois would play an instrumental role in founding a new movement following the Springfield race riots of 1908. The riot, sparked by the arrests of two Black men falsely accused of rape and murder, along with a number of other incidents of contemporaneous racial violence in America, galvanized a group of Black and white activists to come together on February 12, 1909. It was at this meeting—held on the centenary of Abraham Lincoln's birth—that they founded a national organization known as the

National Association for the Advancement of Colored People.[20] Du Bois would go on to serve as editor of the NAACP's monthly magazine, *The Crisis.*

In the years since he first encountered Helen, Du Bois, like herself, had emerged as a prominent socialist. Despite the movement's continuing vacillation on issues of race, he had no hesitation about defying the party line, and in 1913, he declared that the race question was "the great test of the American socialist."[21] Three years later, Helen received a direct appeal from Oswald Garrison Villard, cofounder and vice president of the NAACP. In contrast to Du Bois, Villard considered himself a syndicalist and rejected the "parliamentary socialism" of Eugene Debs, which he believed stood for "half measures, for palliatives, for concessions."[22] Recognizing that Helen, too, had shifted to a like-minded stance by 1916, Villard issued an appeal for her to endorse the NAACP. He knew well that the support of a prominent white Southerner could provide a tremendous boost for the fledgling organization. The deeply personal letter she wrote in response may have been one of Helen's finest and most poignant pieces of writing, free of the stale socialist rhetoric that characterized much of her other political writing from this period:

Dear Mr. Villard,

It has been my intention to write to you every day since I received your letter—an appeal which smote me to the depths of my soul... What a comment upon our social justice is the need of an association like yours! It should bring the blush of shame to the face of every true American to know that ten million of his countrymen are denied the equal protection of the laws. Truly no nation can live and not challenge such discrimination and violence against innocent members of society as your letter describes. Nay let me say it, this great republic of ours is a mockery when citizens in any section are denied the rights which the Constitution guarantees them, when they are openly evicted, terrorized and lynched by prejudiced mobs, and their

*persecutors and murderers are allowed to walk abroad unpunished.
The United States stands ashamed before the world whilst ten
million of its people remain victims of a most blind, stupid, inhuman
prejudice. How dare we call ourselves Christians? The outrages
against the colored people are a denial of Christ. The central fire
of his teaching is equality. Yet there are persons calling themselves
Christians who profit from the economic degradation of their colored
fellow-countrymen. Ashamed in my very soul I behold in my own
beloved southland the tears of those who are oppressed, those who
must bring up their sons and daughters in bondage to be servants,
because others have their fields and vineyards, and on the side of
the oppressor is power. I feel with those suffering, toiling millions, I
am thwarted with them... Let us hurl our strength against the iron
gates of prejudice until they fall, and their bars are sundered.[23]*

Accompanying Helen's message was a check for $100—a not inconsiderable sum in 1916. It's hard to imagine that she did not anticipate the maelstrom that would ensue from such a letter, which Du Bois published in *The Crisis* in February 1916. That same month, an anonymous benefactor who simply billed himself as "Alabamian" paid to have the *Crisis* piece reprinted in the *Selma Journal*—the daily newspaper of a city where a number of Helen's relatives resided, including her cousin Elizabeth Lassiter. The fallout was almost immediate. Helen had long become accustomed to the controversy surrounding her radical politics, even among members of her own family. Kate Keller had made no secret of the fact that she disapproved of Helen's maverick beliefs. "My mother talked intelligently, brilliantly about current events and she had a southerner's interest in politics," Helen later recalled. "But after my mind took a radical turn, she could never get over the feeling that we had drifted apart. It grieves me that I should have added to the sadness that weighed upon her."[24]

Now, wading into the explosive issue of racial equality, Helen had clearly crossed a line. More than any other state during this era, Alabama was firmly entrenched in its commitment to the dominance of the white race—so much so that the concept had been enshrined in the state's constitution in 1901 when Alabama Democrats convened a convention "to establish white supremacy in this State."[25]

Predictably, the anonymous Alabamian couldn't bring himself to believe that a "wonderful girl" like Helen was responsible for the blistering attack against racial segregation. In a piece printed alongside Helen's letter to the NAACP, he insisted that it could only have been the Northerners around her who had turned her "against" her native South. "The people who did such wonderful work in training Miss Keller must have belonged to the old Abolition Gang for they seem to have thoroughly poisoned her mind against her own people," he wrote.[26] The *Selma Journal* soon took up this theme and described Helen's letter as "full of untruths, full of fawning and boot-licking phrases directed toward Northern white and Negro fanatics."[27]

Susan Fillippeli, a professor at Alabama's Auburn University, provides a stark reminder about the potential consequences for Helen as she waded into the fraught territory of racial politics during this period. "You have to remember that if she were anybody but Helen Keller, she could very well have been lynched for expressing those views in 1916," Fillippeli explains. "She was an outspoken feminist and a socialist who came into Alabama and spoke out against Jim Crow. Those were dangerous views back then. There were white people killed in the South as late as the 1960s for preaching racial equality."[28] Fillippeli's alarming assessment is anything but hyperbole. Of the 347 people recorded as having been lynched in Alabama between 1882 and 1968, in fact, a sizable minority of at least 47 were white.[29]

In the midst of the storm, Kate begged her daughter to do something to preserve the family's honor. Within days, it appeared that Helen had acquiesced to her plea when the *Selma Times* announced that they had received a copy of a statement from Kate Keller, purportedly composed by Helen:

I have gone through my letter to Mr. Oswald Villard…printed as a paid advertisement in the *Selma Journal,* sentence by sentence and I do not find a phrase that justifies the editor's assertion that I advocate the social equality of white people and negroes, so repugnant to all. The equality I advocated in my letter is the equality of all men before the law, which the constitution of the United States is supposed to guarantee to every American citizen.[30]

One can imagine that it may have been Kate, not Helen, who included the uncharacteristic phrase about the repugnance of racial equality, but there is no question that Helen had dialed back her strongly held convictions to appease her family. Alas, her retreat would not be the last time she would backslide in the face of intense pressure from those around her.

Perhaps embarrassed by her insincere retraction, she soon had the opportunity to confront the issue once again when she appeared with Annie for a talk at Selma High School that same week. At this appearance, a man that Helen later described as a "Negro-baiter" asked her whether she had really given money "for the defence of Negroes." When she confirmed that she had done so, he asked her whether she believed in marriage between Blacks and whites. "No more than they do," she replied. She then conspicuously refused to shake hands with the man when he approached her. "I saw at once what he was," she told her friend Van Wyck Brooks.[31]

Likely unaware of Helen's retreat, Du Bois himself would later write about Helen's bold stand on behalf of his people: "Finally, there came the thing which I somehow sensed would come. Helen Keller was in her own state of Alabama, being feted and made much of by her fellow citizens. And yet courageously and frankly she spoke out on the iniquity and foolishness of the color line. And so, it was proven, as I knew it would be, that this woman who sits in darkness has a spiritual insight clearer than that of many wide-eyed people who stare uncomprehendingly at this prejudiced world."[32]

Eventually, she would once again publicly take up the battle against racial discrimination, but for now, she appeared to believe that her retraction was enough to mollify her chastened family. Little did she know that her brief foray into the minefield of Southern racial politics would soon play a profound role in the most tragic episode of her life.

. . . .

Chapter Twelve

"A Little Island of Joy"

When Helen was a teenager preparing to enter Radcliffe in the 1890s, Alexander Graham Bell, who had become something of a father figure, offered some words of counsel. Although he had famously waged a eugenic crusade devoted to the prevention of deaf people marrying each other, he held no such concerns about Helen since she had not been born deafblind and therefore could not pass on her disability. Bell sensed that it was only a matter of time before Annie, who had remained a constant presence in her life for more than a decade at that point, might marry. It was time for Helen to think about her future. Just because she couldn't see or hear, he argued, didn't mean she was precluded from the "supreme happiness" of marriage. "Heredity is not involved in your case, as it is in so many others," she recalled him telling her.[1]

"Oh, but I am happy, very happy!" Helen responded. "I have my teacher and my mother and you, and all kinds of interesting things to do. I really don't care a bit about being married."

"I know," he countered, "but life does strange things to us. You may not always have your mother, and in the nature of things Miss Sullivan will marry, and there may be a barren stretch in your life when you will be very lonely."

"I can't imagine a man wanting to marry me," she told him. "I should think it would seem like marrying a statue."[2]

It wasn't long after this conversation that John Macy entered their lives and Bell's words would appear prophetic. Helen later recalled a conversation with Bell shortly after John and Annie announced their engagement.

"I told you, Helen, she would marry," he said. "Are you going to take my advice now and build your own nest?"

"No," she replied, "I feel less inclined than ever to embark upon the great adventure. I have fully made up my mind that a man and a woman must be equally equipped to weather successfully the vicissitudes of life. It would be a severe handicap to any man, to saddle upon him the dead weight of my infirmities. I know I have nothing to give a man that would make up for such an unnatural burden."[3]

But by 1916, she appeared to have reevaluated that self-deprecating stance. Asked by an audience member during a lecture that year whether she would ever marry, she was unequivocal in her response: "Of course I shall marry if the right man comes along. Everyone is better married. I'll tell you what he must be like. First of all, he must be a socialist. Of course, he will be handsome, for eugenic reasons...for I shall see his face with my fingertips...He must have a sense of humor, for victory often turns on a laugh. He doesn't have to be rich. I am paying my own passage through the world and am proud of it."[4]

Unbeknownst to her audience at the time, she had already met the man who fit that description to a tee. Before he left Annie for good nearly two years earlier, John Macy had hired a friend from radical political circles named Peter Fagan to handle Helen's correspondence while she traveled the country on the Chautauqua lecture circuit.[5] After a brief stint as a reporter on the *Boston Herald*, Fagan—who had learned the manual alphabet to communicate with Helen—had recently been hired on again as her secretary while Polly Thomson left the country for an extended period to visit her family in Scotland. Relatively little is known about Fagan's background. His former newspaper described him as a "fair-haired, slender free-thinker" who liked to write on topics "allied to socialistic matters" and who, as a boy of fourteen, "preached in churches of the middle west."[6]

In her 1929 memoir, *Midstream*, Helen would later describe the fateful turning point in their relationship:

I was sitting alone in my study one evening, utterly despondent. The young man who was still acting as my secretary in the absence of Miss Thomson, came in and sat down beside me. For a long time, he held my hand in silence, then he began talking to me tenderly. I was surprised that he cared so much about me. There was sweet comfort in his loving words. I listened all a-tremble. He was full of plans for my happiness. He said if I would marry him, he would always be near to help me in the difficulties of life. He would be there to read to me, look up material for my books and do as much as he could of the work my teacher had done for me. His love was a bright sun that shone upon my helplessness and isolation. The sweetness of being loved enchanted me, and I yielded to an imperious longing to be part of a man's life.[7]

Helen, thirty-six at the time, never disclosed how long the romance had been going on with her twenty-nine-year-old secretary when he proposed marriage, though she had hinted to a Chicago reporter as early as June that year of a "possible heart affair," leading the reporter to write of a "certain young man who is attentive at this time."[8]

Despite some gaps in the history, one thing appears certain. The relationship had been carried on for some time without the knowledge of those around her. Helen had never before kept anything from Annie and the deception troubled her. "The thought of not sharing my happiness with my mother and her who had been all things to me for thirty years seemed abject, and little by little it destroyed the joy of being loved," she wrote years after the episode. "For a brief space, I danced in and out of the gates of Heaven, wrapped up in a web of bright imaginings."[9]

By the first week of November 1916, Helen had finally made up her mind to reveal her engagement to Teacher. Annie, suffering another bout of ill health, had been preparing to depart that same month to spend time at a Lake Placid sanatorium to treat what was believed to be tuberculosis. "Naturally, I wanted to tell my mother and my teacher about the wonderful thing that had happened to me," Helen recalled, "but the young man said, 'Better wait a bit, we must tell them together. We must try to realize what their feelings will be. Certainly, they will disapprove at first. Your mother does not like me, but I shall win her approval by my devotion to you. Let us keep our love secret a little while. Your teacher is too ill to be excited just now, and we must tell her first.' "[10]

Before they could reveal their secret, however, circumstances conspired to take the decision out of their hands. They had been spotted kissing in the study by the houseboy, Ian, who immediately alerted Annie about what he had witnessed. It would appear that Teacher attempted to put a stop to the relationship, and when that failed, she alerted Mrs. Keller in an attempt to persuade Helen's mother to intervene.[11] Annie had long claimed that her teaching methods were designed with the purpose of making Helen "independent." Now, with her pupil on the verge of achieving that goal, she may have sensed that marriage would threaten her own increasing emotional and financial dependence on Helen.

On November 18, the *Boston Globe* ran a front-page story revealing that Fagan had applied for a marriage license at the Boston registrar's office.[12] A week earlier, according to the paper, he had confided details about the relationship to a former colleague at the *Boston Herald*: "He told the editor that he and his employer were madly in love with each other and that they desired to be married in secret. They planned a literary career, and Miss Keller was to abandon the lecture field, in which Mrs. Macy was her necessary interpreter."[13] In fact, since Fagan knew the manual alphabet, he could have easily communicated Helen's words to audiences on her lecture tours, presumably making Annie's skills obsolete.

Boston registrar Edward McGlenen confirmed that the license was valid. "Fagan came to my office in city hall," he told the *Globe*. "He wanted to keep the matter quiet, and I replied, 'Absolutely no.' I said that in a case where a person of national prominence was involved it would not be safe. I felt it was a very serious matter he was undertaking. One part of the license was filled in with a peculiar print-like writing, resembling that of a blind person. Mr. Fagan's name was signed to the paper."[14]

When the registrar refused Fagan's request to keep the application a secret, he left the office, but not before he confided his reason for discretion. "It is understood that the secrecy requested is that Mrs. John Macy…seriously opposes the match," the *Boston Post* reported. Fagan himself told a *Post* reporter that he had an "awful argument" with Annie and that she had frequently reproached him for spelling to Helen in public.[15]

Although it was clear that Annie strongly disapproved of the relationship, Helen's later account of the episode mostly focused on the role of her mother, who was staying with her at the time, in coming between her and her fiancé:

Fate took matters into her own hands and tangled the web, as is her wont. I was dressing, full of the excitement of what I was going to communicate to my loved ones, when my mother entered my room in great distress. With a shaking hand, she demanded, "What have you been doing with that creature? The papers are full of a dreadful story about you and him. What does it mean? Tell me." I sensed such hostility towards my lover in her manner and words that in a panic I pretended not to know what she was talking about. "Are you engaged to him? Did you apply for a marriage license?" Terribly frightened, and not knowing just what had happened, but anxious to shield my lover, I denied everything. I even lied to Mrs. Macy, fearing the consequences that would result from the revelation coming to her in this shocking way. My mother ordered the young man out of the house that very day. She would not even let him speak to me.[16]

As newspapers throughout the country breathlessly reported on the imminent betrothal, all parties involved rushed to deny the news. Fagan himself insisted that the rumor was "unalloyed rot" and blamed it on a "disgruntled servant."[17] Meanwhile, Kate and Helen emerged from a meeting with a downtown Boston law firm and issued a statement. Helen denied "emphatically" that there had ever been an engagement between herself and Fagan. "Such a thing has never even been remotely contemplated by me," the statement read.[18]

Despite Helen's denial, the *Boston Globe* reported that Fagan still had every intention of going through with the marriage. "Fagan told me all of his troubles," a friend of his told the paper. "He told me the denials were necessary in order to soothe Mrs. Macy's feelings. Fagan told me he was going to marry Miss Keller, and I know that he consulted a lawyer about the marriage laws in the southern states, through which they were to travel."[19]

Annie also unequivocally denied the story, issuing her own statement describing it as an "abominable falsehood." But even if those closest to Helen believed the union was unthinkable, the public and the press appeared to have no such qualms. Responding to Annie's description of the engagement, the *Selma Times* weighed in: "Why shouldn't Miss Keller marry her secretary? What makes the idea of it abominable? It is abominable only in the sense that it would shatter an ideal. Miss Keller is idealized by the American people almost as a spiritual prodigy. If married, she would lose something of the hallowed association her name invokes."[20]

The *New York Tribune* was one of the few outlets that rushed to defend Annie, arguing, "Mrs. Macy's opposition to her pupil's marriage was not based on selfishness but on realization that it would hinder the further development of a marvellous girl, and so romance has been shattered."[21] Annie's biographer Kim Nielsen would later speculate that the opposition of Teacher and the Keller family to the union may have been due to "eugenic fears about her possible reproduction and sexuality."[22]

But Helen's great-grandniece Keller Johnson-Thompson, who grew up hearing the saga of Peter Fagan from her grandmother Katherine Tyson, has a different theory to explain Annie's vehement opposition. "I think Annie Sullivan may have been jealous or threatened by the idea of Helen marrying Fagan," says Johnson-Thompson, who still resides in Tuscumbia, not far from Ivy Green. "She needed to be needed. What would have happened to Annie if they had married?"[23]

Years earlier—when Helen found herself on the brink of physical and emotional exhaustion while she prepared for Radcliffe—Annie had indeed fought back desperately against the attempts by Helen's friends and family to separate her from her pupil. In relation to that episode, Joseph Lash posed a question that would appear to apply equally to the Fagan affair: "Had Annie thought in terms of what was best for Helen? She was as incapable of asking herself that question in relation to herself as any star-crossed lover. The friends that had rallied to help . . . had realized that these two, for better or worse, were married for life."[24]

Fagan's daughter, Ann Fagan Ginger, later recounted what her father had told her of what happened next and implied that the family's vehement opposition to the marriage may have been directly tied to the controversy around Helen's controversial support for the NAACP a few months earlier—a period in which she had been spending all her waking hours with Fagan. "As I have pieced it together, Helen's mother didn't like my father because he was a Socialist and believed in the equality of blacks and whites. Mrs. Keller was a Southerner," explained Fagan Ginger in 1984.[25]

Having received blanket denials from all the parties involved that a marriage was to take place, the *Boston Globe*—the paper that first reported the marriage rumors—declared the Keller-Fagan romance "finis." As it turned out, it was anything but.

While Annie departed for Lake Placid, Kate quickly spirited Helen back to Mildred's home in Montgomery, where she had moved in 1907 following her marriage to a man named Warren Tyson. But the family had very much underestimated Fagan's resilience, little knowing that he had already arranged to follow them back to Alabama. Fagan's daughter described a secretive plan devised by Helen and Fagan before they left Boston: "My father had written a message to Helen on the braille typewriter but in code saying that he would go to Alabama, drive in front of her house on a certain day, and he would stay there and if she wanted to come live with him and be his wife, all she had to do was walk out the door and he would be there." He was aware of the danger of this plan, she recalled, noting that "he didn't want the [brother-in-law] to shoot him in the process, which I guess there were stories in the paper that he would do."[26]

And indeed, when Helen's sister, Mildred, came out onto the porch one morning and saw a strange man spelling into Helen's hand, she immediately fetched her husband, Warren, who rushed out with a shotgun. Fagan stood his ground and declared his intention to marry Helen before retreating. "As I recall, Helen's mother was there, too, so I guess everybody made the decision for Helen," disclosed Helen's great-nephew Bill Johnson. "It was the notion that it was a bad idea for Helen and it's a good thing that they ran that rascal off."[27] Days later, Mildred woke in the middle of the night to the sound of someone on the porch. It was Helen, who had packed a suitcase and was waiting for Fagan to pick her up to elope. For reasons unknown, he never showed up.

⠗⠲⠄⠏ ⠏⠣⠄⠄
⠗⠄⠏⠄ ⠛⠾⠄

Helen continued to correspond with Fagan for a time until he married a woman named Sarah Robinson in 1917.[28] She would never find love again, though she would receive a number of marriage proposals from admirers she never met, including one from a life insurance salesman named Fred Elder six years after the thwarted elopement. In September 1922, she wrote Elder a poignant letter refusing his recent proposal of marriage:

As it is, we are like two boats signalling each other in a dense fog. I try vainly to visualise you in my thoughts as a real man. In spite of your very self-revealing letter, you seem remote, almost mythical. Through the wise, loving ministrations of my teacher, Mrs. Macy, who since my earliest childhood has been a light to me in all dark places, I faced consciously the strong sex-urge of my nature and turned that life-energy into channels of satisfying sympathy and work. I never dreamed of suppressing that God-given, creative impulse, I simply directed the whole force of my heart-energy to the accomplishment of difficult tasks and the service of others less fortunate than myself.[29]

Writing about the doomed romance in her 1929 memoir, *Midstream*, Helen claimed that she had acted "exactly opposite" to her nature and that the relationship with Fagan was destined to fail because of "the unhappiness I had caused my dear ones"—apparently resigned to a life that often prioritized others' happiness or feelings over her own.

"The brief love will remain in my life a little island of joy surrounded by dark waters," she wrote. "I am glad that I have had the experience of being loved and desired. The fault was not in the loving but in the circumstances. A lovely thing tried to express itself; but conditions were not right or adequate, and it never blossomed. Yet the failure, perhaps, only serves to set off the beauty of the intention. I see it all now with a heart that has grown sad in growing wiser."[30]

Well aware that Teacher herself had conspired with her family to thwart the engagement during its initial stages, Helen appeared to downplay Annie's role by alluding to the fact that she was far away in Lake Placid when the elopement eventually fizzled. "As time went on, the young man and I became involved in a net of falsehood and mis-understanding. I am sure that if Mrs. Macy had been there, she would have understood, and sympathized with us both," she wrote somewhat unconvincingly, perhaps unwilling to face the truth.[31]

Chapter Thirteen

Helen vs. Teddy Roosevelt

The dawn of 1917 saw Helen mired in a form of involuntary exile. Following doctor's orders, Annie had left Lake Placid to continue her convalescence in Puerto Rico while Helen remained with her mother and Mildred in Montgomery, where she had been spirited away months before in an effort to distance her from Peter Fagan. It was the longest she had ever been away from Teacher. Her correspondence with Annie provides biographers a valuable window into the mindset of both figures during this period.

In a letter Helen sent Annie in March 1917, she complains that she has been largely cut off from the lively circle of intellectuals and radicals who had been a fixture of their lives back home for most of the last decade. Stuck in Alabama, she lamented, her days were spent on trivialities. "So, you see what glorious entertainment mine is," she writes. "Parties, dresses, babies, weddings and obesity are the topics of conversation...I try to meet people and be interested in them, but I'm afraid it is mostly pretence."[1]

She was also cut off from the cause that had become something of an obsession. For much of the previous two years, Helen's political activities had centered on the movement to keep America from intervening in the Great War, which had raged in Europe since the summer of 1914. The United States was moving ever closer to joining the hostilities, and she had thrown herself into the battle to keep America out of the fray. Every day she could sense the drumbeats of war approaching. "A company of Alabama soldiers is back from the border, and the city streets are full of them," she wrote Annie that winter. "Mother says they are fine looking men, and I sicken at the thought of the South giving its new strength to another war."[2]

Annie, too, was alarmed at the thought of war but complained that she felt out of the loop from her vantage point in Puerto Rico. "The war, or rumors of war seem to have knocked the mail's galley West. I know very little of what is going on," she wrote. "We seldom see a paper; and when we do, it's two weeks old. So, I don't know this minute whether we are at war with Germany or not. And bless you, I don't seem to care greatly."[3]

But Helen cared a great deal. Her tireless crusade against "preparedness" for war had already caused deep divisions within her circles. Rather than preach pacifism or neutrality, her rhetoric had given the impression to some of her friends and comrades that she favored Germany over the Western Allies. This came to a head when she asked her German publisher to turn over the royalties from the sales of her books to all German soldiers blinded at the front until the end of the war. "I am neutral yes," she told a reporter, "but I consider my second country the land of Beethoven, Goethe, Kant and Karl Marx." Despite the fact that she had never visited the country, she was fluent in the language and frequently read Germanic books and periodicals. "My admiration for Germany has been heightened by their brilliant organization, their spirit and wild courage," she revealed.[4] In a letter to her mother, she implied that these sentiments had sparked something of a backlash: "I haven't taken sides, as you know; but I get hot because almost everybody is down upon Germany. Not a word is said about the centuries in which 'perfidious Albion' has pushed her conquests to the ends of the earth, strewing her path with blood, tears and untold crimes."[5]

Although women had not yet won the right to vote, and she still formally supported the Socialist Party ticket, Helen had given qualified support to Woodrow Wilson in the presidential election of 1916, reasoning that he was the best chance to keep America out of the war. She believed that Wilson had "kept the faith" by opposing the "preparedness insanity" for as long as possible. "He has announced to the world that America stands ready to join a league of nations to prevent war. If the nations are honest in their protestations that they are arming and fighting for peace and security, here is their opportunity to obtain peace and security without any more fighting," she told an audience in 1916.[6]

During her earliest Chautauqua talks, Helen had discussed a wide range of topics—from socialism and suffragism to the importance of love and understanding in bringing people together. By 1916, however, her lectures were primarily focused on one theme—keeping America out of the war. Though she lamented that pacifists are often "pelted with abuse," she framed her crusade as a patriotic duty. "If I were less an American, I should follow the brass band of preparedness or keep silent as a clam," she told her audience. "But this is my country, and I love it. I will not sit still and see a few excited leaders stampede it into war or preparedness for war."[7]

Although they were paid between $250 and $500 per lecture, the Chautauqua contract required Helen and Annie to cover their own expenses, and the tour wasn't as lucrative as they might have hoped. The constant travel was exhausting and took a physical toll on both women. But Helen was fast becoming one of the most influential anti-war voices in the country, and her booking agent, M. J. Stevenson, implored her to keep up the momentum, promising her a percentage of the gate if she embarked on a new tour of the Midwest. There is a "tremendous demand" for her preparedness lectures, he wrote in the spring of 1916. If she wished to serve "the cause," the tour would be a chance to reach "thousands of people."[8]

As she traveled the country warning against the forces pushing America toward war, there was a marked change in her goals. No longer was her rhetoric aimed at opinion makers and the White House. Now, she directed her warnings at the working class, who she warned were destined to be the cannon fodder in the inevitable coming war.

Although she remained an admirer of Eugene Debs, her disillusionment with the Socialist Party had been festering for years because of the party's increasingly moderate approach and appeared to have reached a breaking point by 1913 after the party voted to expel Big Bill Haywood, with whom she had become enamored during the Lawrence Textile Strike early on in her conversion to socialism.[9] If she had once attempted to remain neutral by urging conciliation within the party, any doubts about her sympathies were laid to rest in January 1916 when she granted an interview to Barbara Brindley of the *New-York Tribune* in which she announced that she had become a committed member of Haywood's Industrial Workers of the World (IWW). Brindley starts off by asking what had transformed Helen from the "sweet sentimentalist of women's magazine days" into an "uncompromising radical."[10] Here, Helen reveals the epiphany that she had been hinting at for some time, and that had become a consistent theme in her activism—the explicit links between disability and capitalism. Her awakening, she explained, came after she was appointed to the Massachusetts commission tasked with investigating conditions among the blind community: "For the first time I, who had thought blindness a misfortune beyond human control, found that too much of it was traceable to wrong industrial conditions, often caused by selfishness and greed of the employers."

The reporter was especially interested in the fact that Helen had come to these conclusions after she left college. Did she get any of this knowledge from her life at Radcliffe, Brindley wondered. "No!" came the emphatic reply. "College isn't the place to go for ideas. I thought I was going to college to be educated...Schools seem to love the dead past and live in it...Education taught me that it was a finer thing to be a Napoleon than to create a new potato."

Explaining that it was her "nature" to fight, she had concluded that she must join a "fighting party" to help with their propaganda. That's when she became a socialist. In the years since, however, she had come to identify more as a syndicalist. "I became an IWW because I found out the Socialist party was too slow. It is sinking in the political bog. It is almost impossible for the party to keep its revolutionary character so long as it occupies a place under government and seeks office under it."

It is the workers, she declared, who must declare freedom for themselves. "Nothing can be gained by political action. That is why I became an IWW." It was the Lawrence strike in 1912, she revealed, that convinced her that it was better to improve conditions for all people "at once" rather than incrementally. At this, the reporter asked whether she was committed to revolution or education. "Revolution!" came the swift reply. "We can't have education without revolution. We have tried peace education for 1900 years and it has failed. Let us try revolution and see what it will do now. I am not for peace at all hazards. I regret this war, but I have never regretted the blood of the thousands spilled during the French Revolution." The workers, she noted, are learning a lesson that will soon come in handy when they are mired in the trenches of the war that she knew was coming. "My cause will emerge from the trenches stronger than it ever was. Under the obvious battle waging there, there is an invisible battle for the freedom of man."

Here, she invokes the historical comparison that others, including Mark Twain, had long ago sensed from her passionate calling. "I feel like Joan of Arc at times. My whole being becomes uplifted. I, too, hear the voices that say, 'Come,' and I will follow, no matter what the trials I am placed under. Jail, poverty, calumny, they matter not. Truly he has said, 'Woe unto you that permits the least of mine to suffer.'"[11]

Although she publicly declared her membership in the IWW for the first time in 1916, her allegiance to the "Wobblies," as its members were known, was already apparent months earlier when she waged a very public crusade to free Joe Hill—the Swedish-born union organizer. Hill, born Joseph Hillstrom, was known as "Labor's Poet," and composed some of the IWW's best-known songs, including "There Is Power in a

Union." He had been arrested on a trumped-up charge of murder in January 1914, accused of killing a man and his son in a Utah grocery store. The subsequent trial attracted worldwide attention while thousands of supporters around the world appealed for his freedom, convinced that Hill had been framed because of his militant union activities.

Although Hill had countless prominent supporters calling for his freedom, only one had the ear of the president of the United States. Long aware that her celebrity status could be used effectively in support of her political goals, Helen wrote to Wilson pleading for him to "use your great power and influence to save one of the nation's helpless sons."[12] But the case had been tried under Utah state law, Wilson explained, and even he didn't have the power to grant clemency. "I was very much affected by your telegram and wish most sincerely it was in my power to do something, but unhappily there is nothing I can do," the president wrote back. "The matter lies entirely beyond my jurisdiction and power. I have been deeply interested in the case but am balked of all opportunity."[13]

Undeterred, she wrote Utah governor William Spry, who did have the power to spare Hill: "Thousands of intelligent people believe Hillstrom is innocent. I shall feel doubly deaf and blind if I learn tomorrow that this young singer has been taken from us."[14] But, to her dismay, Spry remained unmoved by her appeal and Hill was executed by firing squad in November 1915.

In January 1916, the same month that she declared herself an IWW, Helen delivered a speech at New York's Carnegie Hall calling for a general strike under the auspices of the recently formed Women's Peace Party. "The future of America rests on the backs of eighty million working men and women and their children," she told the packed gathering. "We are facing a grave crisis in our national life. The few who profit from the labor of the masses want to organize the workers into an army which will protect the interests of the capitalists...And we are whetting our sword to scare the victors into sharing the spoils with us. Now, the workers are not interested in the spoils; they will not get any of them anyway."[15]

Two weeks earlier, the *Outlook*—a weekly magazine prominently associated with former president Theodore Roosevelt—had written an editorial criticizing Helen's frequent assertion that the war in Europe was a "capitalistic war" and her recent declaration that the war was being pushed to serve the interests of the financier J. P. Morgan. It was a theme frequently trumpeted by the Socialist Party, but such claims were easier to ignore when they came from so-called wild-eyed radicals than the same claims from a widely beloved figure. Helen likely commanded enough respect in mainstream America that her high-profile crusade against US involvement had the potential to change hearts and minds, which may have been seen as a threat to the forces pushing America toward war. As much as it admired her "personality, character and spirit," the *Outlook* wrote, it regrets that it "must totally dissent" from her "unsubstantiated" charges. Such allegations weaken her influence, for "even the capitalist is entitled to justice."[16]

Fourteen years earlier, Helen had visited President Roosevelt at the White House and later gushed at his efforts to promote the "welfare of the nation."[17] But now Roosevelt, an editor of the *Outlook*, was one of the leaders of the preparedness movement, and Helen used her Carnegie Hall speech to describe him as "war mad," calling him the "most bloodthirsty man in the United States." Perhaps in response to his magazine's recent attack, she doubled down on her criticism in a newspaper interview after the speech, alluding to his widely publicized exploits as a hunter: "When he is not dreaming of plunging his country into war and shedding the blood of men, he is writing books about his own prowess in shedding the blood of animals."[18]

To her deep consternation, the Socialist Party failed to endorse the call for a general strike, arguing that such a tactic was "impractical." Eugene Debs declared that workingmen should undertake such a strike only if Congress declared war, knowing full well that this would be a nonstarter with the unions that stood to benefit from the influx of jobs a war would bring. Sure enough, only six days after Debs made this declaration, the American Federation of Labor and the railway unions pledged their "service to the country" should war come and revealed that they would call upon all workers to do the same.[19] Helen fumed at what she considered a betrayal of her ideals. In a letter to Annie, she later revealed that she had considered "breaking" with the party over its stand: "Teacher, I am going to remain faithful unto the death, with God's help, in my social beliefs; but I am thoroughly angry with the Socialist Party...It has turned traitor to the workers by saying that it opposes the class war. And the motion to call for a strike against war has been voted down! Shame upon those who wear the mask of Socialism."[20]

For a short period, she believed that she had found an unlikely ally when the industrialist Henry Ford suddenly announced that he planned to charter a Peace Ship and invite prominent activists aboard to sail for Europe to convene a peace conference and end the Great War before America could become involved. Helen was among a select group that he invited to join him on the mission, which would have seen Ford and a number of high-profile pacifists meet in Norway with representatives of the belligerent European nations to broker a peace agreement. The prospect of finding common cause with a prominent capitalist thrilled her at first. "The principle underlying Ford's plan is the General Strike which Gabriel Mirabeau proclaimed about one hundred and forty years ago and which the Industrial Workers of the World have gone to prison for," she declared. She was so excited at the prospect that she briefly equated Ford's plan with Karl Marx's exhortation "Workers, unite! You have nothing to lose but your chains."[21] But as she looked further into the auto magnate's planned mission—widely derided by the press as "the Ship of Fools"—she changed her mind in a hurry. She declined the invitation after she concluded that Ford "belongs to the same class as the diplomats and politicians that made the war" and that the only hope for peace lay in convincing the soldiers themselves to quit fighting.[22] A few weeks later, Helen told a reporter that she thought the Peace Ship was a "huge joke."[23] Eventually, Ford's mission fizzled and he returned to America at the end of December 1915, only five days after his ship, the *Oscar II*, arrived in Norway, having failed to enlist any of the warring nations in his plan.

Meanwhile, even as she soured on the Socialist Party, Helen's increasingly fiery approach and her frequent calls for a workers' revolution had endeared her to new allies in radical political circles. In February 1916, she received a letter from Emma Goldman, calling Helen's recent Carnegie Hall talk demanding a general strike "one of the most stirring events in my life." America's most famous anarchist praised her uncommonly "clear vision and such a deep grasp of the tremendous conflict going on in society today."[24]

Although Helen had long believed that Wilson was committed to keeping America out of the European war for as long as possible, Annie struck a more cynical tone. "You know I have never trusted President Wilson," she wrote from Puerto Rico in the winter of 1917. "He is an egotist, a tyrant at heart…When the bankers get nervous about their loans, they will force him to enter the war."[25] Weeks later, Annie wrote again shortly after Wilson went before a joint session of Congress on April 2 to request a declaration of war against Germany. "Didn't I tell you that entering the World War was one of the high purposes Providence had in store for America?" she wrote. "The Socialists—the intellectual variety—have behaved in all countries like the proverbial sheep. A few, a very few…have kept their heads. Hatred of Germany will soon transform their idealism into a hundred percent patriotism."[26]

Indeed, after America finally entered the war in 1917, Helen found herself forced at first to straddle a fine line between patriotism and sedition. She visited soldiers blinded at the front and announced her intention to raise $1 million in Liberty war bonds while dialing down her previous rhetoric about the folly of the Great War. Predictably, the newspapers resumed their fawning praise. "Here is a noble woman out of a world of darkness and silence, wanting an opportunity to help the cause of liberty and peace," heralded one Nebraska paper.[27]

Although she had mostly held her tongue since America's entry into the war months earlier—focusing instead on where she could ease suffering—her patience was finally exhausted when hundreds of IWW comrades and other radicals were arrested for sedition under the Espionage Act in September 1917. Among the high-profile figures incarcerated were Bill Haywood and Arturo Giovannitti, along with her new admirer, Emma Goldman. "The arrests have startled radical pacifist circles as they have not been stirred since the entrance of the United States into the war," declared the *Brooklyn Times Union*.[28]

Helen could not have been unaware of the reality that, if not for her iconic status, she would have almost certainly been among the first rounded up. No longer content to remain silent, she threw herself into the campaign of Morris Hillquit, one of the most prominent leaders of the Socialist Party of America, who was running for mayor of New York on an anti-war platform. Despite her previous discontent with the party over its failure to endorse a general strike, and severe misgivings about Hillquit—whose reformist ideas she rejected as ineffective—his campaign provided the ideal platform for her to express her continuing disgust over the ongoing war. It would be the first time she weighed in since America joined the hostilities.

Because of its large population of unionized workers and left-leaning immigrants, New York was likely the only city in the nation where a candidate like Hillquit could have found a receptive ear for his platform at the time, but it didn't stop the local press from likening him to a traitor. Days before the election, the *Herald Tribune* attacked Hillquit's admirers as "steeped in un-Americanism...Before this war is over the name of Benedict Arnold will have been displaced by some other name whose acts will have made those of Arnold seem patriotic in comparison."[29]

As usual, Helen wasn't dissuaded by the name-calling of the press. In an open letter to Hillquit the day before the election, she declared that if she were eligible to vote in New York, she would happily cast her vote for the socialist candidate "because a vote for you would be a blow at the militarism that is one of the chief bulwarks of capitalism, and the day that militarism is undermined, capitalism will fall."[30] Here, she took the opportunity to explain why she had waited so long after America entered the war to wade back into the battle:

> I have refrained from writing or giving utterance to the fierce protest in my heart against the war madness that is sweeping away the reason and common sense of our people, because I believed that President Wilson would defend our liberties and stay with his strong hand the forces that are invading them...I am not opposed to war for sentimental reasons. The blood of fighting ancestors flows in my veins. I would gladly see our young men go forth to battle if I thought it was a battle for true freedom. I would gladly participate in a war that would really make the world safe for democracy.[31]

She found no evidence, however, that her country was committed to true democracy. Instead, she charged, the United States had become a "democracy where Negroes may be massacred and their property burned, as was done in East St. Louis; a democracy where lynching and child labor are tolerated."[32]

"Though physically blind, she sees with her soul's vision the true issues of this campaign," declared the *New York Call* the following day.[33]

Despite the broadside she had launched against Woodrow Wilson during Hillquit's campaign—in which the socialist candidate received a respectable 155,000 votes, 22 percent of the overall vote—Helen once again took advantage of the access that no other radical figure in America enjoyed. In December, she wrote a letter to the president pleading on behalf of her recently incarcerated IWW friends Elizabeth Gurley Flynn and Arturo Giovannitti, who had been rounded up with hundreds of other radicals under the Espionage Act in September 1917, despite the fact that, unlike herself, they had taken no part in anti-war propaganda after America entered the war. "They seem to have been arrested because they are associated with the Industrial Workers of the World," she wrote Wilson. "True, they are honest exponents of a social revolution which they believe will overthrow the present economic system. Their crime is that they see the evils of their time and speak out against them, not always wisely or well."[34]

Meanwhile, such was her faith that a better world was right around the corner that she chose an unlikely figure with whom to share her excitement about a recent historic event that had captured her imagination. "For to me the Russian Revolution seems the most wonderful thing that has happened in two thousand years," Helen wrote President Wilson in December 1917, only a month after the Bolsheviks seized power. "It is like a conscious sun bursting upon a gloomy, disastrous world—a sun which shall heal the nations."[35]

It was the first sign of a dramatic shift in Helen's political philosophy. It would be decades before there was any hint that she had changed her mind.

Chapter Fourteen

. . . .

"The Human Wonder"

At the beginning of February 1920, the marquee of New York's famed Palace Theatre heralded a prominent new entertainer on the vaudeville circuit:

FEATURE EXTRAORDINAIRE:

HELEN KELLER

The Most Talked of Woman in the World!

Blind, deaf, and formerly DUMB, in

"The Sweetest Love Story Ever Told."[1]

It was not Helen's first foray into show business. Two years earlier, she had been approached by a Hollywood producer named Francis Miller proposing a movie about her life. "I believe we have a combination of genius—materials with which we can appeal to the public with the most powerful human drama that the world has yet seen. Its possibilities far exceed the *Birth of a Nation*," Miller gushed, a reference to the D. W. Griffith Reconstruction-era silent epic that had grossed millions of dollars at the box office.[2] Given the immense interest in her life story, he predicted that Helen would make as much as $100,000 from the project.

Besides the appeal of a large payday, Helen was excited about the prospect of using the medium of film to gain a wider audience for her political beliefs. She was quickly disabused of this idea when the director made it clear that he wanted a "commercial thriller" and that the public was more interested in a heartfelt inspirational story than seeing a headstrong woman with fierce political convictions. Despite engaging in what she described as a "battle of words" with the filmmaker, she sensed early on that it was futile and that none of her cherished ideas would make it into the movie, though she had agreed to appear as herself in the section portraying her life as an adult. "I doubt if the picture will carry any radical message to the people," she wrote her socialist friend Horace Traubel. "The great forward moving spirit of the world—Marx, Proudhon, Tolstoy, Lenin, Roland Liebknecht—in it among the vital influences shaping and moulding my thought and sympathies."[3] As she expected, the 1919 film—titled *Deliverance*—failed to capture any of her true spirit. Instead, the finished product was a tawdry melodrama filled with what she would describe as "flights of fancy" and "absurdity." Although the silent film ignored her socialist politics, it did show her pleading with President Wilson to keep America out of the European war and even included a scene with Helen mounted on a horse as a modern-day Joan of Arc bearing "the standard of justice and humanity."[4]

For Helen, the lone bright spot from the experience came when she and Teacher met Charlie Chaplin while filming in Hollywood. Though she had been feted during the trip by a number of the greatest movie stars of the era, including Douglas Fairbanks and Mary Pickford, she was left with a "defrauded feeling" because each of the celebrities had ignored Annie—with the lone exception of Chaplin, who had appeared to bond with Teacher. "They had both endured poverties, and the deformations it creates in body and soul," she later wrote. "They had both struggled for education and social equality... So, it was natural that they should understand each other and form one of the friendships that afford solace to great artists in a world too often unfaithful to the children of genius."[5] He even invited Helen and Annie for a screening of his film *A Dog's Life*, and then let her touch his trademark bowler hat and mustache so that she could have a clearer idea of how he appeared on-screen. "He sat beside me and asked again and again if I was really interested and if I liked him and the dog in the picture," Helen recalled.[6] We can only speculate at what Chaplin and the other attendees must have thought at the sound of peals of laughter coming from the famously deafblind woman throughout the screening. Whether or not her encounter with Chaplin was the impetus, Helen would remain a lifelong devotee of movies, especially comedies, attending the cinema on a regular basis while Annie and later companions relayed into her palm the story and action taking place on the screen.

While the film was in postproduction, Helen flew back to New York where the union representing actors and stagehands was locked in a bitter labor dispute. As a newly minted actor herself, she found herself in common cause with the strikers and could be found daily marching down Broadway carrying a picket sign. On more than one occasion, she even led a "strike parade" to New York's Rialto Theatre.[7] Helen had been expected to deliver a speech to the gathering of prominent figures and critics who had been invited to the film's gala premiere. Instead, she sent a note to the producers declining her box seats and informing them of her decision not to attend. "I am afraid that the actors and some of my friends may construe my presence as a lack of sympathy with the strikers," she informed the producers.[8] "I would rather have my picture fail," she told reporters, "than not be with the actors and the Actors' Equity Association in this glorious fight."[9]

Deliverance was a commercial flop and failed to deliver the vast sums that she had been promised when she signed on. "We are the kind of people who come out of an enterprise poorer than we went into it," she wrote about the experience.[10] They returned home and Helen soon resumed her political efforts where she had left off—continuing to battle for her radical comrades, including Eugene Debs. Although she had long been disillusioned by the influence of reformers within the Socialist Party, she had not lost faith with Debs, who repeatedly resisted efforts to push his party to the right. Announcing his admiration for Lenin and Trotsky in February 1919, the party leader delivered a fiery speech calling on socialists to "scorn and repudiate the cowardly compromisers within our own ranks, challenge and defy the robber-class power, and fight it out on that line to victory or death."[11] After the Supreme Court upheld his conviction under the Espionage Act in the spring of 1919—concluding that he had intentionally obstructed the draft and America's military recruitment efforts[12]—Helen was compelled to write expressing her solidarity:

> Once more you are going to prison for upholding the liberties of the people...When I think of the millions who have suffered in all the wicked wars of the past, I am shaken with the anguish of a great impatience...With heartfelt greetings, and with a firm faith that the cause for which you are now martyred shall be all the stronger because of your sacrifice and devotion, I am Yours for the revolution—may it come swiftly, like a shaft sundering the dark![13]

She was still so shaken by the assault on her comrades' political rights that she agreed to sign on as a founding board member of a new organization, the American Civil Liberties Union (ACLU), which sought to secure an amnesty for political, industrial, and military prisoners. Although it would later come to be identified as a bastion of liberal rather than leftist values, the ACLU was widely embraced by the far left during these early years as it fought to free an assortment of radical figures imprisoned for their political beliefs.[14] By the beginning of 1920, she was so preoccupied with her political battles that income-generating opportunities were in short supply, and Helen and Annie once again found themselves in financial straits—most of the $10,000 advance they had received from *Deliverance* already spent. When the vaudeville offer came in, it seemed like an answer to their prayers.

Money concerns had, in fact, long weighed on the duo, despite the fact that Helen had earned vast sums since she graduated from Radcliffe—more than enough for the average American to live comfortably many times over. Although Andrew Carnegie had died a year earlier, she was still receiving the $5,000 annuity he had bestowed as a life trust. She also received income of more than $800 a year from a trust established before she entered Radcliffe, plus significant royalties from *The Story of My Life* along with a smaller trickle from the sale of her other books.[15] In addition, she and Annie were receiving dividends from various investments totaling thousands of dollars per year. Their earnings in 1920, in fact, were more than six times the average household income in the United States.[16] And yet it was never enough.

A complete picture of their finances is still murky, but there is evidence that the financial problems led directly to John Macy. It had been more than five years since John left Annie for good in early 1915. Annie had steadfastly refused to grant him a divorce, although there were reports that in the years since their separation John had taken up with a "deaf-mute sculptress" named Myla and was supporting a child he had with her out of wedlock.[17] Annie had taken the separation hard and was still grief-stricken by the breakdown of the marriage. Taking full advantage of the situation, Macy had been bleeding Annie dry for years—well aware that Helen had always shared her vast financial resources with Teacher and that Annie considered herself a partner in Helen's enterprises. "The genius is hers, but much of the drudgery is mine," Annie wrote a friend in 1905 explaining their financial partnership.[18] She was from all indications a soft touch, unable to say no to the husband who had abandoned her.

Helen expressed her frustration in a letter to her mother in 1920 updating Kate about their financial troubles. "We don't see John now," she wrote. "I was really disgusted with him, mother. He kept asking, dunning Teacher for money. Now, you know it is money I am trying to earn to provide for Teacher, not to waste on John."[19] In a letter she sent to her sister, Mildred, she explained that the income the two had earned on the lecture circuit before the war had been "largely spent improving our house in Wrentham and paying debts incurred by John...I am telling you all this, Mildred, to show you that we had a hard row to hoe most of the time. No doubt, we might have managed better if we had

had 'business sense.' I do not have to tell you that Teacher and I do not know anything about money, except to spend it."[20]

To protect their dwindling finances, as well as Annie's fragile emotional state, Helen appears to have finally made the decision to cut John off from their lives for good, despite the fact that there were continued business-related matters relating to *The Story of My Life*, which he had coauthored, and two other books for which he had acted as literary agent. Helen and Annie had long since sold the Wrentham house and moved to Maine for a period before buying a house in Forest Hills, New York, in 1917—seemingly without leaving him a forwarding address.[21] His frustration is reflected in a series of revealing letters he wrote during this period, which provide important clues about both John's character and the nature of his complicated relationship with Helen.

Despite his estrangement from Annie, John persisted in writing to Helen on a wide range of topics ranging from the political to the mundane. Most of these letters went unanswered, but it did not stop him from begging her to meet. Two years after he left, Macy had written an acclaimed history of the US radical movement titled *Socialism in America*—siding with the militant wing of the party. It should have cemented his place as a leading light of the movement. Years earlier, the trio of John, Annie, and Helen had entertained many of the best-known figures of the American Left at their lively Wrentham home. The conventional narrative suggests that these figures were part of John's circle—friends he had cultivated since he first joined the Socialist Party. In the years that followed, however, many of these high-profile radicals had maintained strong friendships with Helen rather than John, as evidenced by her voluminous correspondence with figures such as Emma Goldman, Max Eastman, Horace Traubel, Arturo Giovannitti, and Joseph Ettor. The letters from John during this period provide a strong clue as to his attitudes around her political activities. They are in turn condescending, insulting, and petty, while revealing him to be vain and tremendously insecure.

"I wanted to see you... but you were not in the phone book," he wrote Helen in January 1918. "I don't know what Annie's ideas are now or how clearly she sees things. Perhaps she will not trust my judgment. But it is very good, because I am in constant communication with two or three wise men."[22] Helen had continued to write political essays in the radical press and John was evidently following them closely. "As for your writings, 'The Invincible Revolution' is right in spirit, and will do good," he wrote her. "But you go up in the air and say things you can't back up, can't make good. For example, my dear, you say, 'Read the literature of France, Germany, and Russia the last sixty years and you will be convinced.' Then you mention a string of people, three of whose names you misspell. And then, how much of the European literature of the last sixty years have you read?"[23]

After Helen wrote President Wilson pleading for the release of her IWW colleagues rounded up under the Espionage Act—a letter widely reprinted in the socialist press—he wrote again, admonishing her:

> Your letter to the President might be useful as an open letter to be published in the *Call* for the sake of propaganda. But don't send it to the President. It is too much like his own way of thinking! Forgive me for saying that, but it is true. And you put impertinent things. For example, "a Bolsheviki mind." Bolsheviki is plural, and you would not say an Englishmen mind. And besides, what the dickens do you know about the Bolsheviki? I cannot tell you what to do with your letter. It is admirable and adorable in spirit as you are, but regarded as a useful intellectual production, as something I should like to see under your signature, no, it won't do. Irony is not your strong suit. You don't know that game at all.[24]

One of their longtime mutual friends was John Reed, a socialist comrade who had traveled to Russia to cover the revolution and had spent time with many of the Bolshevik leaders, including Lenin and Trotsky. Shortly after the Bolsheviks seized power, Helen sent Reed money to book a return passage to America, where he would soon publish his landmark work, *Ten Days That Shook the World*, about the October Revolution. Learning about her patronage of their old friend, Macy sent Helen another letter chiding her for her support. "I don't like your having sent money to Jack Reed," he wrote in February 1918. "He is able to take care of himself. Besides, it makes no difference whether he stays in Russia or comes home or is stranded on the remotest South Sea island. No difference, I mean, to you or any idea or cause or principle that you are interested in. NO American correspondent who doesn't know Russian can tell us anything of value...You will also get much out of Trotsky's book...but Jack Reed is not worth ten cents, except to himself, in Russia." And in an inappropriately controlling turn, he requested that "if anyone asks you for money, you might let me know. I have many excellent sources of information and the steadiest of advisers."[25]

In another missive complaining about her public support for her IWW comrades, he implies that she has a messiah complex:

If you could do any practical good now by coming out in support of the IWW, I should cheer you on, no matter what the cause or sacrifice. But you can do nothing, precisely because you are you. You will alienate sympathy and rouse increased resentment against the IWW, which will be accused of having misled your dear innocent soul...The worst possible person to plead for the IWW now would be Jesus. Besides, don't you see that it will be a good thing to send a few men and women to jail now? It will strengthen the organisation. The victims can stand it, but YOU KEEP OUT.[26]

Aside from providing a rare window into his own personality, these letters offer some revealing clues to John's feelings about Helen's status as a celebrity of the American Left. Even as he desperately craved acceptance in radical circles, he had repeatedly found himself overshadowed by Helen and her fame. With this in mind, we might also reevaluate the circumstances surrounding his resignation as secretary to Mayor Lunn shortly before Helen's scheduled arrival in Schenectady in the fall of 1912. Could Mayor Lunn's unexplained failure to offer Helen a post on the Board of Welfare—after previously announcing his intention in the press—have a different explanation than Helen had been led to believe? Could John have, in fact, derailed the job offer in a fit of jealousy after her imminent arrival became national news?

Whatever his private motivations, there is no question that his profligate spending and debts were the primary reason Helen agreed to exhibit herself on the vaudeville stage, which she would later explain as her desire to protect Annie. She feared Teacher would be left "destitute" if Helen predeceased her.[27] "Years later when Teacher and I did 'exhibit' ourselves in Vaudeville, we had no other means of support. My writings had not brought in enough," she wrote. "At first everything seemed to be against us. We had gambled for big stakes at Hollywood and lost... I almost lost heart when I reflected that if I failed, I knew that Teacher would suffer even more from the snarl of the tiger and the tooth of the wolf that constitute part of man's nature."[28]

In the 1890s, Arthur Keller, mired in debt, had been approached by a vaudeville promoter to feature the teenage Helen on the circuit at a staggering salary of $500 per week, but Annie had refused to entertain the prospect at the time. Now, Helen was once again being offered vast sums of money to display herself in a "dignified" fashion, and this time the offer was too good to pass up.

The act was built around a drawing room set. Annie launched the show with a twenty-minute description of Helen's life beginning with the miracle at the water pump followed by her acquisition of speech, her graduation from Radcliffe, and her friendship with Mark Twain. At this point, Helen herself would enter the room, walk toward a piano onstage, and declare, "It is very beautiful," followed by a demonstration of lipreading, finger spelling, and a mawkish speech. "Alone we can do so little," she addressed the audience. "Together we can do so much. Only love can break down the walls that stand between us and our happiness. The greatest commandment is: 'Love ye one another.' I lift up my voice and thank the Lord for love and joy and the promise of life to come."[29]

The press and the public ate it up. "Before she had been on the stage two minutes," wrote one New York paper, "Helen Keller had conquered again, and the Monday afternoon audience at the Palace, one of the most critical and cynical in the world, was hers."[30]

Many reviewers were especially struck by Helen's "bright blue eyes," which one paper wrote had "the deceptive appearance of being unusually strong and clear."[31] This was the first time most of the audience had ever seen her in person. Few realized that one of those eyes had been implanted years before to replace a protruding eye, presumably resulting from the original childhood ailment that left her deafblind. As a result, for most of her early life, Helen was almost always photographed from a strategic angle to avoid portraying what must have been considered a "deformity." In 1911, she had paid $10 to a Boston optician for an artificial left eye to prepare her for public display on the lecture circuit.[32]

Although the first half of the show followed a carefully conceived script, the highlight for many audience-goers was Helen's impromptu responses to audience questions following the main performance. "Miss Keller displayed a pretty wit in reply to some questions asked by the audience," wrote one reviewer, "and she 'came back' several times with a quickness and good humor that the keenest of experienced monologists might well have envied."[33]

A year before Helen made her vaudeville debut at the Palace, a group of writers and show business figures had begun meeting at the nearby Algonquin Hotel, where their wit would earn them a glittering reputation as they traded fast-paced repartee and gossip—exchanges that would often find their way into the columns of New York newspapers. Helen, in fact, would later befriend three of the most prominent denizens of the famed Algonquin Round Table—writer Dorothy Parker, drama critic Alexander Woollcott, and film star Harpo Marx.[34] Harpo would later tell a reporter that he often found it difficult to keep up with Helen's droll sense of humor, despite his own reputation as a comedian and member of the celebrated Marx Brothers. "I'll best her yet!" he vowed to one reporter. "I'll learn a new joke."[35]

Judging by Helen's responses to some of the questions posed to her onstage during her vaudeville career, she would not have been out of place herself at the Round Table. A sample of the questions and answers during these sessions provides a good example of the lightning wit that often left the audiences roaring with laughter.[36]

Q: (During Prohibition). What do you think is the most important question for the country today?
A: *How to get a drink.*

Q: Do you approve of giving every man a job to fit his brain?
A: *I'm afraid if we tried to do that, it would throw too many people out of work permanently.*

Q: Do you think women are men's intellectual equals?
A: *I think God made woman foolish so that she might be a suitable companion to man.*

Q: Do you think all men are born equal?
A: *I think all men are born equally stupid.*

Q: What is the slowest thing in the world?
A: *Congress.*

Q: Does Miss Keller think of marriage?
A: *Yes, are you proposing to me?*[37]

While her radical political opinions had been excised from *Deliverance*, over which she had little creative control, vaudeville offered a chance to share her beliefs about politics and disability issues. The audience was often taken aback by her fiercely held convictions, many of which hold up remarkably well today:

Q: What do you think of capitalism?

A: *I think it has outlived its usefulness.*

Q: Do you think that all political prisoners should be released?

A: *Certainly. They opposed the World War on the ground that it was a commercial war. Now everyone with a grain of sense says it was. Their crime is they said it first.*

Q: What did America gain by the First World War?

A: *The American Legion and a bunch of other troubles.*

Q: Do you think the voice of the people is heard at the polls?

A: *No. I think money talks so loudly that the voice of the people is drowned.*

Q: Who are the three greatest men of our time?

A: *Lenin, Edison, and Charlie Chaplin.*

Q: What is the greatest obstacle to universal peace?

A: *The human race.*

Q: What do you think of Soviet Russia?

A: *Soviet Russia is the first organized attempt of the workers to establish an order of society in which human life and happiness shall be of first importance, and not the conservation of property for a privileged class.*

Q: What do you think of Harvard College's discrimination against the Jews?

A: *I think when any institution of learning applies any test other than scholarship, it has ceased to be a public service institution. Harvard, in discriminating against the Jew and the Negro on grounds other than intellectual qualifications, has proved itself unworthy of its traditions and covered itself with shame.*

Q: Which is the greatest affliction, deafness, dumbness, blindness?
A: None.

Q: What then is the greatest human affliction?
A: Boneheadedness.[38]

The tour was lucrative, sometimes paying as much as $1,000 for a single night's appearance. For a time, vaudeville provided the much-needed financial security that the two women had been seeking. More importantly, Helen appeared to be enjoying herself immensely, even if Annie found the experience decidedly unpleasant. "My teacher was not happy in Vaudeville," she later recalled. "She could never get used to the rush, glare and noise of the theatre, but I enjoyed it keenly...I found the world of Vaudeville much more amusing than the world I had always lived in, and I liked it. I liked to feel the warm tide of human life pulsing around me." Employing the figurative language she often used to describe experiences vividly communicated to her by her companions, she added, "I enjoyed watching the actors in the workshop of faces and costumes."[39]

As lucrative as the vaudeville circuit was, there were those who did not approve of Helen displaying herself for entertainment purposes. "At first it seemed odd to find ourselves on the same bill as acrobats, monkeys, horses, dogs, and parrots," Helen recalled, "but our little act was dignified and people seemed to like it."[40] Dignified or not, Helen's four-year vaudeville career is another aspect of her life that hasn't held up well under the harsh light of history. Disability historian Susan Crutchfield has noted that vaudeville was often noted for featuring "freak acts," and that the marketing of Helen's performances was often indistinguishable from other such attractions. "Reviews continued to place her routine in the freak act category by means of language one might expect to hear from a sideshow barker luring his audience into the tent," Crutchfield writes. "Thus, these reviews illuminate the freak show appeal of her act, the degree to which its interest turned on Keller's unique persona rather than her unique talents."[41] She cites one ad that illustrates this phenomenon:

SHE'S A HUMAN WONDER: DEAF, DUMB AND BLIND, HELEN KELLER HEARS AND SPEAKS. Appearing at Orpheum This Week, Woman Answers Questions Through Her Teacher by Tapping of Her Fingers[42]

In fact, the unseemly nature of the vaudeville appearances attracted criticism even from contemporary critics. During Helen's tour, the renowned deafblind French writer and disability rights advocate Yvonne Pitrois—who was often billed as the "French Helen Keller"—published a brochure in which she disparaged Helen's vaudeville act. She derided the "deplorable theatrical exhibitions" and accused Helen of "allowing herself to be dragged" and displayed "like a wild animal."[43] These appearances, she decried, were "painful, offensive and exhibitionistic." She hoped that the memory of these performances and the criticism that they inspired would eventually be lost and that Helen would instead be remembered for her many fine traits.[44] Helen, however, had no apologies for her vaudeville career, as she told Pitrois when she received word about the critique. "As a matter of fact, in the United States I was not criticized for going into Vaudeville," she wrote the French activist. "But I have been severely handled by some on account of my radical opinions. I do not possess the happy faculty of telling unpleasant truths without giving offence."[45]

Despite the criticism, she appeared to have had no regrets. "I had many delightful experiences and everyone, on the stage and off, was kind to me," she wrote a friend. "I learned that Vaudeville is life in a nutshell; it has its wars, its adventures and romance, its laughter and tears, its good side and its ignoble, vulgar side."[46]

Chapter Fifteen

The Foundation

Although the vaudeville circuit had appeared for a time to offer the financial security to allow Helen and Annie to settle down comfortably, they were still vulnerable to the unpredictable nature of show business. While some bookings could bring as much as $2,000 a week, there were often weeks and even months at a time when they didn't hear from their booking agent at all. "No Vaudeville work in sight, not a peep from Harry Weber's office," Helen wrote her sister, Mildred, at the end of 1922. "Our funds are disappearing rapidly." She even claimed that she had to "go to court" to access money from her trust to use to meet expenses.[1] A year later, things had evidently not improved: "We have no work in prospect, and I don't know what is to become of us. Expenses go on, whether money comes in or not...The legitimate theatre business is so dull that some of the best actors and actresses have gone into Vaudeville, and we are crowded out. We were never a real Vaudeville attraction, I guess."[2]

In her annual Christmas letter to Mildred in December 1923, she hinted at the tantalizing prospect of an opportunity to finally achieve a semblance of financial stability that would allow them to retire from show business. "It is possible that we may get work to do in the coming year," she wrote. "A gentleman who is deeply interested in the movement is coming to see us Thursday afternoon, and we hope he will make us some sort of proposition."[3] The gentleman happened to represent an organization known as the American Foundation for the Blind (AFB), which had been founded in 1921 to act as a national advocacy group to build on the work of a scattershot series of agencies throughout the country. It aimed to merge the efforts of existing national organizations that had been working to create both vocational and educational opportunities for the millions of Americans with vision loss.[4]

By the end of 1923, the AFB was still suffering from a series of organizational growing pains that threatened to derail the new foundation almost before it could get off the ground. These had been smoothed out considerably with the addition of a bold staff—including two men who would have a profound effect on Helen for decades to come. One was Moses Charles Migel, a retired silk manufacturer who had developed an interest in the blind community when the American Red Cross asked him to arrange for the return and adjustment to civilian life of American servicemen blinded in battle during the First World War. His service earned him the honorary rank of major—a designation he would use throughout the rest of his life. After the war, Migel served on the board of the recently created Red Cross Institute for the Blind in Baltimore, where he developed a passion for issues involving visual impairment. His reputation at the institute had caught the attention of an AFB official named Robert Irwin, who had been left completely blind at the age of five by an eye infection. Despite his condition and a childhood marked by poverty, Irwin managed to claw his way to an education and eventually earned a graduate degree from Harvard. From there, he was hired by the Cleveland Board of Education to organize the city's first day-school classes for blind children. By 1922, he came to work for the recently created AFB as the director of research, and by the following year, he had emerged as a powerhouse within the organization.

It was Irwin who first convinced Migel to come aboard as president of the Foundation, and by 1923, the two men had entered into an effective partnership and begun to consolidate the mission of the organization, sorting out the hiccups that had briefly threatened its existence.

Still, it was clear that if the AFB hoped to become a truly effective force for the interests of the blind community, it would need to raise significant amounts of money.

Enter the most famous blind person in America.

The idea to enlist Helen as a fundraiser appears to have come from her old friend Charlie Campbell, who Helen and Annie had come to know well when he headed the Detroit League for the Handicapped years earlier. Migel had enlisted Campbell's input about a plan recently formulated by the trustees to expand the membership nationwide. "As you probably know, no work in a large way can proceed without the necessary financial resources," he wrote. Migel hoped to enlist a group of prominent people to underwrite the Foundation's efforts to the tune of $50,000. "With this accomplished, the Foundation would be safe for a period of three years," he explained.[5]

Campbell knew exactly how to achieve this goal. "For years, I have felt very keenly that the most practical method of raising money is to avail oneself of the services of Miss Helen Keller and her teacher," he wrote. "I am convinced that nothing would please them more than to do their part in a campaign to raise funds for the Foundation." He noted that when Helen was young and studying at Perkins, Michael Anagnos raised vast amounts of money for a new kindergarten for the blind by using Helen to make the appeal. "Those of us intimately acquainted with Miss Keller scarcely realize the psychological effect of having such a person speak on behalf of her own people."[6]

Migel was very much on board with the idea of enlisting Helen in the fundraising effort but wondered how she would be compensated. "It goes without saying that Mrs. Macy and Miss Keller should receive a very handsome honorarium for this service," Campbell responded.[7] Evidently, the Foundation trustees didn't agree. When Helen was originally approached, it was suggested that she hold a series of donor meetings with compensation set at a paltry $50 honorarium per session. These gatherings—featuring a performance by blind musicians and a talk by

Helen and Annie—proved tremendously successful. In the first seven meetings, attended by more than ten thousand people in the New York area, $8,000 was subscribed to the Foundation, which Migel described as a "most wonderful record." He reported to Campbell in April 1924 that both Annie and Helen had been "indefatigable, most willing and disinterested," asserting that they were motivated first and foremost because "they really feel that they wish to help the cause."[8]

Witnessing this initial success, Annie sensed that Helen would be very valuable to the fledgling AFB, which had initially resolved to wait three years before embarking on a $2 million endowment campaign to permanently establish the Foundation as a going concern. Knowing that such a campaign could only be successful with Helen as its public face, she proposed that the Foundation move up its campaign. Migel and the trustees were thrilled with the idea, but initially balked at Annie's insistence that they should be generously compensated for their services. While Migel agreed that Helen would need to be paid far more than the $50 stipend she had received for the initial tour, he hadn't counted on the hard line that he encountered from Annie during the negotiations. When the major suggested that the "Helen Keller Party" receive $750 per month plus expenses, Annie insisted on at least $2,000 per month for a six-month campaign, which would cover four public appearances per week.

"The situation is very distressing to me," Annie wrote Migel at one point, informing him that the women were at "the end of our resources." Their house, she explained, was heavily mortgaged, and the work they were doing for the Foundation meant a vaudeville engagement would be out of the question. "In addition to our usual household budget, our bills this month are unusually large, as they include doctors' and dentists' bills and expenses incidental to preparations for the tour. To cut down expenses, I am selling our car, which is the only luxury we possess, and which in a real sense is not a luxury, as Helen and I find it very difficult to get about in the city on account of our combined limitations."[9]

When Migel still bristled at her demands—especially after she brought in a lawyer to conduct the negotiations—he implied that the Foundation could carry on the campaign without Helen, noting that a series of private fundraising firms had offered their services. To his probable surprise, Annie called his bluff, responding that "if you think other agencies can raise the two million dollars without Helen Keller, we shall be most willing to withdraw, and further negotiations will not be necessary."[10]

Eventually, Migel acquiesced, but he appeared reluctant to contract Helen as a staff member of the Foundation. Instead, he offered to underwrite her $2,000 salary out of his own pocket—allegedly to protect the Foundation from accusations of "extravagance."[11] Helen and Annie likely had no idea that there may have been other factors behind Migel's apparent reluctance to add Helen to the AFB payroll. On the surface, hiring Helen on as the public face of the Foundation was in fact a logical step to solving the AFB's organizational woes and providing the stability that it desperately needed to entrench itself as the country's premier organization working for the welfare of the blind community. It seemed a perfect conjunction of mutual need and opportunity, observed historian Frances Koestler in her 1976 social history of blindness in America, *The Unseen Minority*. Of the natural alignment of interests, Koestler writes, "No inspired stroke of genius was needed to conceive the plan that Helen Keller should join forces with the Foundation. Helen Keller was not only the perfect symbol, her name was a household word. She could be counted upon to attract large audiences to any public meeting at which an appeal would be made for support of a new movement to assist America's blind people."[12]

And yet there appeared to be one major hurdle. Her radical politics were still notorious, and the trustees were nervous that the wealthy benefactors they were hoping to attract would be scared off by somebody who had spent years painting them as the epitome of society's evils. Compounding the problem, it appeared, was Helen's recent habit of glorifying the Bolshevik regime. In February 1924—weeks after Helen had embarked on her first AFB fundraising tour—Major Migel received a note from Stanwood Menken, president of the fiercely right-wing National Security League, lamenting Helen's recent political declarations. "Is it not rather a pity," he wrote, "that one for whom our system of education has done so much as it has for Miss Keller—notwithstanding her remarkable achievements under great affliction—should be induced to write as she does? The pity of it is that it does not reflect upon Miss Keller, but upon those responsible for her education, and for the contact she has had with persons who bear the taint of Communism... We have known of Communists occasionally in the schools and colleges but did not know that they sought out those without complete physical equipment for the purposes of deception."[13] Like many before, he presumed that Helen's political predilections were the result of manipulation, inflecting his criticism with an ableist perception of her ability to come to her own intellectual conclusions.

Helen had made no secret of her continuing support for the Soviet Union. In a letter she had recently written accompanying a donation to the "Friends of Soviet Russia" to benefit Russian children, she alluded to a number of recent anti-Bolshevist attacks by American labor unions, especially the American Federation of Labor led by Samuel Gompers.[14] "The hostility of labor organizations to the Russian Revolution has been one of the darkest tragedies of the class struggle. Oh, the ignorance of the workers. They fall with both feet and open eyes into the traps set for them by those who profit by their folly."[15]

Still, in some ways, Helen's iconic status continued to help immunize her from the fallout over her political beliefs. As infuriating as it was for her to know that those beliefs were often dismissed because of the assumption that she had been manipulated by those around her, it also provided a shield that helped her avoid the fate of her comrades, many of whom had been arrested or even framed for horrific crimes thanks to their political activities. Just weeks before Menken's letter to Migel, Helen had written a letter to the wife of one of those comrades, IWW organizer Joe Ettor. "Russia seems to be the only light in the universal gloom," she wrote Iva Ettor. "Already her voice is heard like the sea all round the world. I can't tell you, dear comrade, what a warm glow it spreads over my heart. I for one believe that the Russian way is the right way—the only possible route to the Promised Land."[16]

By the summer of 1924, Helen had shown no signs of dialing down her outspoken political convictions. In July, she closely followed Robert La Follette's third-party presidential candidacy under the banner of the Progressive Party—battling the Republican incumbent, Calvin Coolidge. Helen had become enamored of the Wisconsin senator when he voted against America's entry into the First World War and opposed the Espionage Act that had rounded up many of Helen's fellow socialists. Now, he was running on the platform of nationalizing the railroads and utilities while taxing the rich and outlawing child labor—positions endorsed by the Socialist Party and a coalition of unions.

In a private letter to La Follette that summer, Helen wrote, "I have hesitated to write to you because I know that the newspapers opposed to the Progressive movement will cry out at the 'pathetic exploitation of deaf and blind Helen Keller' by the 'motley elements' who support LaFollette. It would be difficult to imagine anything more fatuous and stupid than the attitude of the press toward anything I say on public affairs."[17] It is especially interesting to take note of the concluding passage:

> So long as I confine my activities to social service and the blind, they compliment me extravagantly, calling me "archpriestess of the sightless," "wonder woman," and "a modern miracle." But when it comes to a discussion of poverty, that is a different matter! It is laudable to give aid to the handicapped. Superficial charities make smooth the way of the prosperous; but to advocate that all human beings should have leisure and comfort, the decencies and refinements of life, is a Utopian dream, and one who seriously contemplates its realization must indeed be deaf, dumb and blind.[18]

DR. HOWE TEACHING LAURA BRIDGMAN.

An illustration from the 1887 Perkins School Annual Report shows the deafblind girl Laura Bridgman sitting on the lap of Perkins founder Samuel Gridley Howe, who made it his mission to prove that deafblind children could be educated. After Laura learned the manual alphabet and learned to formally communicate, her story captured the imagination of Americans and helped humanize people with disabilities. Years later, Helen Keller would become known as the "Second Laura Bridgman." *(Courtesy of Perkins School Archives)*

Sitting on a window ledge, John Macy uses the manual alphabet to spell into Helen Keller's hand in 1909 while holding a document at their home in Wrentham, Massachusetts. His wife, Annie Sullivan, stands behind Helen. As editor of Helen's 1903 memoir, *The Story of My Life*, Macy was instrumental in helping shape the narrative of Sullivan as a "Miracle Worker" who had almost single-handedly been responsible for Helen's extraordinary achievements. Later, Macy would be credited with influencing Helen's conversion to socialism despite the fact that Helen herself may have been a socialist before him. *(Courtesy of American Foundation for the Blind, Helen Keller Archives)*

Mark Twain stands behind fifteen-year-old Helen Keller, who is seated in a chair. Twain was instrumental in publicizing Helen's achievements, describing her as the "Eighth Wonder of the World." Many chroniclers have highlighted their long friendship by writing about their gentle banter, humor, and mutual admiration. Often ignored are their frequent discussions on world affairs and the fact that they shared a dark bond. They were both transplanted Southerners who believed they were tainted by their families' connections to the evils of slavery. Like Twain, Helen would use her fame to become a radical firebrand intent on transforming American society. *(Courtesy of 4.0 International)*

Fourteen-year-old Helen Keller sits outside with Alexander Graham Bell at his summer home in Cape Breton, Canada, while Annie Sullivan stands behind them. Bell, who devoted his career to the education of deaf people, was so influential in Helen's life that she dedicated her first memoir to him. Although best known for his invention of the telephone, Bell was a believer in the pseudoscience of eugenics and used Helen to wage a successful war against the use of American Sign Language, which he believed would encourage deaf people to marry and create a "defective variety of the race." It is uncertain whether Bell influenced Helen's own brief embrace of eugenics, which would forever taint her legacy. *(Courtesy of Library of Congress)*

TRANSFER RECORD	
Date Admitted	
Date Withdrawn	
Local	
Branch	
Secretary	
Date Admitted	
Date Withdrawn	
Local	
Branch	
Secretary	
Date Admitted	
Date Withdrawn	
Local	
Branch	
Secretary	
Date Admitted	
Date Withdrawn	
Local	
Branch	
Secretary	

Socialist Party of America

State _of Massachusetts_
Local _Member at large_
Branch _____

MEMBERSHIP CARD

Name _Hellen Keller_
Address _Wrentham_
Admitted _Sept. 24th_ 1912
No._____ Page._____

Squire E. Putney
State Secretary
Address _14 Park Sq. Boston_

ISSUED BY AUTHORITY OF THE
National Committee, Socialist Party
20

Helen's 1912 membership card in the Socialist Party of America. Between 1912 and 1924, she would be among the most prominent socialists in America—extolling the merits of "revolution" while waging crusades against racial discrimination, child labor, and American involvement in the First World War as a member of the IWW. She also frequently linked blindness and disability to capitalism. Although she would tone down her public rhetoric after she went to work for the American Foundation for the Blind in 1924, she retained her lifelong belief in socialism and would move sharply to the left following the Russian Revolution in 1917. For decades, she was a champion of the Soviet regime, and the FBI kept track of her involvement in many Communist front groups during the 1930s and '40s. *(Copyright © American Foundation for the Blind, Helen Keller Archives)*

A newspaper clipping from 1918 shows Helen with Annie Sullivan and two picketers under the headline "Helen Keller Cheers Actors' Strike Pickets." After Helen appeared as herself in a silent film about her life called *Deliverance*, she refused to attend the gala premiere because the union representing actors and stagehands was involved in a bitter labor dispute. Helen could often be found leading "strike parades" down Broadway. "I would rather have my picture fail," she said, "than not be with the actors and the Actors' Equity Association in this glorious fight." *(Courtesy of Greenwich Village Society for Historic Preservation)*

Helen Keller runs her fingers over Charlie Chaplin's face to read his lips on the Los Angeles set of his silent film *Sunnyside* in 1918. Although she and Annie had been feted by many of the leading movie stars of the era while she was filming her biopic *Deliverance* in Hollywood, she was left with a "defrauded feeling" because each of the stars, with the exception of Chaplin, had ignored Teacher. During the McCarthy era, both Helen and Chaplin would be targeted for their left-wing political beliefs. *(Copyright © Roy Export Company Limited)*

German students give the Nazi salute in Berlin in May 1933 while thousands of books smolder in a huge bonfire—the first wave of book burnings ordered by the new regime to cleanse Germany of "degenerate" works. The burning of Helen Keller's book *How I Became*  *a Socialist* made her one of a handful of Americans targeted as an enemy of the New Order. "Don't think your barbarities to the Jews are unknown here," Helen wrote to Hitler that same week. The Nazis would later censor her 1929 memoir, *Midstream*, because of its paean to Soviet founder Vladimir Lenin, and banned her 1938 *Journal* because of her frequent criticism of Hitler's "demoniac" forces and "insane pursuit of power." *(Courtesy of U.S. National Archives)*

First Lady Eleanor Roosevelt (left) greets Helen Keller (center) and Helen's longtime companion Polly Thomson in 1936. Helen regarded Mrs. Roosevelt as a kindred spirit and in 1940 would enlist her in a mission to transport Spanish Loyalist refugees out of France following the fascist takeover of Spain by Francisco Franco a year earlier. The First Lady would abruptly resign from the mission after it was revealed to be a Communist front. Despite standing her ground at first, Helen also resigned under intense pressure from those around her, worried that her association would harm her reputation amid growing anti-Communist stigma in America. *(Courtesy of Library of Congress)*

Helen stands on stage with Polly Thomson addressing an outdoor gathering of Black South Africans on a 1951 tour. As a lifelong opponent of racial discrimination, Helen was deeply troubled as she toured the country, which had adapted the racist apartheid system three years earlier, allowing a tiny white minority to oppress a large Black majority. She would spark controversy on the tour when she told a reporter that she was "appalled" by the plight of Black South Africans. A few years later, she would help raise money for the defense of the still-unknown Nelson Mandela and other dissidents who were charged with high treason and facing the death penalty. *(Courtesy of American Foundation for the Blind, Helen Keller Archives)*

It is impossible to know whether the Foundation made Helen's political silence a condition of employment when they finally acquiesced to
Annie's demands and placed Helen on staff at a salary of $5,000 per
year, or whether she simply instinctively understood that the first rule of
fundraising is not to bite the hand that feeds you. Whatever the reason,
her new affiliation with the AFB marked the end of her public rhetoric
about the merits of revolution. Now, instead of fiery speeches laying the
blame for disability at the hands of the capitalist system, her appeals
were designed to play on the image that had captured the public imagination all those years ago.

"I like to think that you have come here because you want to make
blind people happier," she told a Washington, DC, audience in 1925
while fundraising for the AFB. "That is what this work means. It also
means helping the deaf blind children who are scattered in the different
states. They are in the same sad plight I was in before I was taught. Will
you not help me to lead these little captives out of the shadow into the
light and freedom of the spirit?"[19] The audience ate it up and vast sums
poured into the endowment campaign.

If Migel and the trustees had thought that Annie was a formidable
opponent, they would soon discover that Helen was a challenge unto
herself. Her years of advocacy on behalf of workers meant that she
immediately recognized exploitation when she encountered it. This was
underscored when the Foundation treasurer, Herbert White, sent Helen
a "bonus" check of $1,000—presumably as a reward for her success in
the fundraising campaign. And while this was no small amount in 1926,
when the median salary in New York City—where AFB headquarters
was located—was $1,250 per year,[20] Helen was acutely aware of the hun-
dreds of thousands that the Foundation had raised to date because of
her efforts. She clearly believed that she deserved more, as evidenced by
the angry letter she sent White from Montgomery where she was staying
with her sister in July 1926. "I have not written to you before because
I needed to consider very carefully the advisability of accepting the

check," she wrote. "My first impulse was to accept it; for I felt that Mrs. Macy and I had earned it... Besides, we needed the money badly. As we told the Executive Board, every cent of our salary went for expenses."[21]

In addition to Annie and Helen, Polly Thomson had by now become an indispensable member of the household, which only added to the financial burden. It is utterly impossible for three women to live on such a "meagre salary," she complained. "Frankly, the attitude of the Foundation towards Mrs. Macy and me has always been that of an employer, governed solely by practical considerations. It has assumed that we were for sale and has negotiated to buy us as cheaply as possible... But we are not for sale at a bargain anymore. We are capable of earning our living with much less effort and strain... Under the circumstances, we feel quite disinclined to work for the Foundation next year. I doubt even if a more equitable arrangement would induce us to continue."[22]

Although the women needed the financial stability that the job provided, it was evident that Helen had little passion for her new job, notwithstanding the important work the Foundation was doing on behalf of the blind community. A number of factors could explain her lack of enthusiasm—not least her long-held opinions on the nature of such work. "It is perfectly true that my work for the blind is a trust, and in order to fulfil its duties justly I must keep it as the centre of my external activities," she would later confide to Nella Henney. "But it has never occupied a center in my personality or inner relations with mankind. That is because I regard philanthropy as a tragic apology for wrong conditions under which human beings live, losing their sight or hearing or becoming impoverished, and I do not conceal this awkward position from anybody."[23]

She could also barely disguise the emotional toll of the hundreds of public appearances and functions necessitated by her new role, which usually involved a reception where each guest was eager to meet her. "I do not know of a more disturbing sensation than that of being ceremoniously ushered into the presence of a company of strangers... especially if you have physical limitations, which make you different," she later wrote. "As a rule, when I am introduced to such people, they are excessively conscious of my limitations. When they try to talk to me and find that their words have to be spelled into my hand, their tongues cleave to the roofs of their mouths and they become speechless. And I am quite as uncomfortable as they are." She felt also a need to perform, to smooth over the discomfort, remarking, "I know that I should have clever things to say which would tide over the embarrassing moment, but I cannot remember the bright casual remarks which I intended to grace the occasion."[24]

Although she had arguably done more than almost anybody in history to humanize people with disabilities, she still encountered ableist attitudes at every turn, and these indignities couldn't have failed to take an additional toll. In a 1914 lecture she delivered about Helen's education, Annie provided a telling example. "A few months ago, Miss Keller and I were at supper with a learned foreign physician," she recalled. "Miss Keller had been arguing with him about some problems of economics. They were speaking in German, she reading his lips. Apparently, he was interested in the discussion, taking up her points and replying to them. Presently, he turned to me and asked, 'Has she any conception of an abstract idea?' I did not know what to say. They had been arguing about abstract ideas for half an hour!"[25]

If such experiences were exceedingly frustrating, another frequent obstacle in her role with the AFB was the difficulty of holding her tongue while begging money from people whom she had long held in contempt. Since her Radcliffe days, Helen had often relied on philanthropists for her livelihood, but she had never personally asked for their assistance. It was usually others who solicited the funds on her behalf. Now, her central job function involved approaching prominent industrialists, hat in hand, begging for money—including more than a few figures who offended her deeply held convictions.

A decade earlier, she had publicly called out John D. Rockefeller after thugs working for his Colorado Fuel and Iron Company gunned down twenty-five people, including eleven children, in an incident that would become known as the Ludlow Massacre. "Mr. Rockefeller is a monster of capitalism," she told a reporter after the incident, suggesting that a monument should be built to the businessman called "the Shame of America." At the same time, she also called into question his well-publicized reputation as a philanthropist. "He gives to charity and in the same breath, he permits the helpless workmen, their wives and children to be shot down," she charged.[26] Years later, it was the Rockefeller family to whom she was asked by the Foundation to appeal, notably John D. Rockefeller Jr., who had prominently defended his father's role in the massacre years earlier. "It is unjust in the extreme to lay it at the door of the defenders of law and property, who were in no slightest way responsible for it," the younger Rockefeller lamented at the time.[27] Now, thanks in part to Helen's efforts, Rockefeller Jr. had been persuaded to pledge a total of $100,000 toward the Foundation's $2 million goal, making him the largest single donor to the AFB endowment campaign.[28]

As it turned out, Helen's indignant letter to Herbert White complaining about the bonus wasn't an empty threat. Nor was she appeased when the trustees voted to offer an extra $5,000 in salary, though her letter turning down this offer was considerably more conciliatory than the one she had written earlier. "After thinking the matter over all summer, I decided that I owed it to myself and to others beside the blind to lay off for a year and bring my autobiography up to date," she wrote the trustees in October 1926.[29] Her financial troubles had not improved, she added, but she could always supplement her income through lecturing. Not long after she completed her new memoir, *Midstream*, the Wall Street crash and the ensuing Depression would change the fundraising landscape considerably. Although she occasionally returned to lend support to various campaigns, it was 1932 before she returned full-time to the Foundation. Within a year, world events would effect a profound change on her life and legacy.

Chapter Sixteen

. . . .

Helen vs. the Führer

On the night of May 10, 1933—only a few months after Hitler took power—thousands of torch-bearing students converged in university towns all over Germany chanting Nazi slogans. Each chilling procession had a similar destination: the town square. In Berlin, forty thousand people gathered to hear Joseph Goebbels—Germany's new minister of public enlightenment and propaganda—declare that "the era of extreme Jewish intellectualism is now at an end... The future German man will not just be a man of books, but a man of character. It is to this end that we want to educate you... And thus, you do well in this midnight hour to commit to the flames the evil spirit of the past." When Goebbels finished speaking, torches were applied to a massive pile of logs and the flames illuminated the square, setting the stage for the arrival of a convoy of trucks and cars each bearing the same cargo: books and pamphlets.[1] An observer described the scene: "The cars carrying them stopped at a distance and each group of students brought an armful and tossed it into the fire." The crowds cheered as the student union president, wearing a Nazi uniform, declared that he and his fellow students had gathered to consign to the flames "un-German" books that threatened to disintegrate the national movement. "There must be purity in German literature," he announced.[2]

Occasionally, a student would bark out the author's name as a book was tossed onto the raging inferno. "Sigmund Freud for falsifying our history and degrading its great figures. Emil Ludwig for literary rascality and High Treason against Germany!" Their works were soon joined by the "degenerate" volumes of other Jewish authors along with a predictable list of left-wing figures, including Marx and Lenin. In an apparent recognition that books are valuable learning tools, the students had spent days sorting through the piles to ensure that no books on the German "Expurgatorius" index were spared. Many volumes that were mistakenly designated for the bonfires were returned to libraries.[3]

So, when Helen Keller's book *How I Became a Socialist*—a German-language compilation of her radical writings—joined thousands of others in the flames that night, she became one of a select group of American authors, including Upton Sinclair and Jack London, who had been singled out by the Nazis as an enemy of the new order.[4]

Noting that the great nineteenth-century German poet Heinrich Heine had been one of the authors whose works were consigned to the flames, more than one observer would later point out a passage that Heine had prophetically written decades earlier: "Where they burn books, they will, in the end, burn human beings too."[5]

Media reports had circulated days earlier that the Nazis had chosen Helen's work to be purged,[6] but even if her name hadn't been among those targeted for the flames, she would have almost certainly been irate at the Jew hatred that was central to the crusade. She had long abhorred anti-Semitism with the same sense of moral outrage as she had decried discrimination against Black Americans. In 1920, thirteen years before Hitler took power, she was roused to fury when the auto magnate Henry Ford launched the most sustained hate campaign in American history in his weekly newspaper the *Dearborn Independent*. Week after week, the paper blamed Jews for all the evils in American society, along with an assortment of mundane complaints. "If fans wish to know the trouble with American baseball, they have it in three words: too much Jew," the paper once declared during its seven-year campaign.[7] Ford's paper also introduced Americans for the first time to a notorious conspiracy theory that had originated in Russia at the beginning of the twentieth century, known as the Protocols of the Elders of Zion, warning of a fictional Jewish cabal intent on ruling the world by manipulating the economy, controlling the media, and stirring religious conflict.[8]

Not long after Ford's hate campaign first came to her attention in December 1920, Helen fired off a letter to the *Jewish Advocate* newspaper, becoming one of the first prominent Americans to publicly call out Ford for his poisonous diatribe. "The attacks upon the Jews in the *Dearborn Independent* fill me with shame and indignation," she wrote. "Such utterances are stupid, cowardly and false. Obviously, they have not taken the trouble to investigate the sources of the 'protocols' upon which they base their allegations. One has only to glance at these slanders to see that they are the work of ignorant persons who set themselves the ignoble task of keeping alive in men's minds hostilities and prejudices which originated in times far removed from the present."[9]

In the years since she had first spoken out against the *Independent*, a selection of its columns had been compiled into a book, *The International Jew*. The book would have a particularly poisonous influence in Germany, where it would stoke the anti-Semitism of many future Nazis. Hitler himself hung a portrait of Ford over the desk at his Bavarian party headquarters and later told a Detroit columnist that he regarded Ford as "my inspiration."[10] Now, watching the hate-mongering she long abhorred manifest itself in the new Nazi regime, she sat down at her typewriter to compose a letter to Adolf Hitler:

History has taught you nothing if you think you can kill ideas. Tyrants have tried to do that often before, and the ideas have risen up in their might and destroyed them. You can burn my books and the books of the best minds in Europe, but the ideas in them have seeped through a million channels and will continue to quicken other minds. I gave all the royalties of my books for all time to the soldiers blinded in the World War with no thought in my heart but love and compassion for the German people. Do not imagine your barbarities to the Jews are unknown here.[11]

For reasons unknown, at the conclusion of her letter, she crossed out Hitler's name on the address line and directed it instead to "the student body of Germany."[12]

Having apparently set aside their differences, Helen had returned to work full-time at the AFB in 1932 when Major Migel concluded that her talents could be useful for more than just fundraising purposes—especially after the election to the White House of a candidate who the Foundation believed would be more sympathetic to its cause, given his own disability.

In 1929, during a period when she occasionally undertook work for the AFB, Helen had sent a letter to the then governor of New York, Franklin D. Roosevelt, asking him to join the board of the Foundation. FDR politely declined. Discovering that he had failed to sign the note refusing her invitation, Helen sent it back accompanied by a handwritten letter in her distinctive block handwriting. "Please Dear Mr. Roosevelt sign your name," she wrote. "Something tells me you're going to be President of the Land of the Free and the Home of the Brave and this seems a good time to get your autograph."[13] Her prediction would prove prophetic when FDR was elected to the Oval Office in 1932, though she didn't personally vote for him, telling the *New York Times* two weeks before the election that she was "still a socialist" but that she was too busy with her work to "bother with politics."[14]

Stricken with polio when he was thirty-nine—leaving him permanently paralyzed from the waist down—Roosevelt became the first person with known disabilities to occupy the Oval Office. Whether or not she felt a kinship with the new president because of his disability, Helen developed a warm relationship with Roosevelt and a special friendship with his wife, Eleanor, whom she regarded as something of a kindred spirit. "We have met only twice for a moment, but I have been drawn to you by your earnest, constructive efforts on behalf of the unprivileged, and since Election Day I have felt the bond of sympathy grow stronger and stronger between us," she wrote the First Lady in February 1933. "I cannot tell you with what pride and satisfaction I have followed your courageous activities. Your talks over the radio have in them the ring of conscience and vision."[15]

She wasted no time in calling on the new president to aid her cause. Within weeks of his inauguration, she had won FDR's approval for an initiative to allow blind people to set up stands in federal post office buildings to sell a variety of wares, and thus be enabled "to earn a good living."[16] Seeking vocational opportunities for people with disabilities, in fact, would be a central focus of her activism for the remainder of her life and she was especially passionate about her belief that, given the right opportunities, deafblind people could be "fully self-supporting."[17] Two years later, she helped win a more substantive concession when Roosevelt signed the Social Security Act—a far-reaching piece of social legislation that provided federal old-age benefits and unemployment insurance for the first time, along with a monthly allowance for Americans with disabilities. Thanks in large part to fierce lobbying by Helen and the AFB, an amendment was added to the act that explicitly included blind Americans in the category of those eligible for financial assistance after the original draft contained not a word about blindness, which had always been considered under state jurisdiction. The Social Security Act almost certainly did more to improve the lives of blind Americans than anything that came before it.[18]

But if Helen could look on such victories with satisfaction, she also frequently pushed back when she believed the Foundation's priorities didn't align with her own. This was driven home in 1933 when Major Migel suggested that she take part in the Foundation's new Talking Books campaign—the effort to record books on phonograph records so that the blind could listen to them. It was an idea that had first been proposed by Thomas Edison decades earlier when he applied for the patent on his tinfoil phonograph in 1877.[19]

Helen was vacationing in Scotland with Annie and Polly when she received Migel's request. Her telegram in response was succinct: "TALKING BOOKS A LUXURY THE BLIND CAN GO WITH-OUT FOR THE PRESENT. WITH TEN MILLION PEOPLE OUT OF WORK AM UNWILLING TO SOLICIT MONEY FOR PHONOGRAPHS."[20]

Four years into a Depression that had plunged the nation into a morass of economic despair from which it had still not begun to recover, her refusal lays bare her philosophy around privilege and disability that she had begun to articulate years earlier. Decades before social movements began to include a critique of privilege, Helen was already acutely conscious of her own privileged position and had long resolved to incorporate that understanding into her disability activism. As she had written in 1916, she understood that, although she came from a background of oppressors, her values compelled her to stand with the subjugated:

> My family all belonged to the master class, and were proud of their birth and social prestige, and they held slaves. Now, ever since childhood, my feelings have been with their slaves. I am dispossessed with them. I am disenfranchised with them. I feel all the bitterness of their humiliation when a white man may take a job or a home he wants, while they are driven out of their houses and churches—nay and are even terrorized and lynched if they compete in doing profitable work for the master class. And my sympathies are with all the workers who struggle for justice, decency, higher education, equality of opportunity and fair play for everybody. Their fight is my fight, I want what they want, and I am against what they are against.[21]

Although it had been years since she publicly waded into radical politics, it was clear during these years that her political convictions still ran deep. Three years earlier, she had successfully lobbied Congress for an appropriation to fund the distribution of braille books to American libraries. "Books are the eyes of the blind," she told the congressmen at the time.[22] So her abrupt refusal to support the new endeavor came as something of a shock to Migel and the others following her enthusiasm for the braille campaign. "Helen's resistance to participation in the Talking Book campaign surprised and dismayed the Foundation trustees," notes AFB historian Frances Koestler. "Some attributed her attitude to her own deafness, which might cause her to underestimate the importance of the spoken word. Others thought it to be a reflection of her lifelong Socialist convictions, which understandably put bread ahead of 'luxuries.'"[23]

It wouldn't be the last time that she would place her principles over her duties as a Foundation staff member. In December 1943, AFB executive director Bob Irwin wrote Helen asking her to lobby for an amendment to the income tax act that would allow blind people to take a $500 tax deduction for miscellaneous expenses related to their condition. Once again, Helen wasn't the least bit interested in a provision that would benefit a small minority of affluent individuals. "Of course, my interest in the blind embraces all large movements for their benefit," she wrote Irwin, "but it seems to me that H. R. 3687 is not vitally important like the proposed legislation for insurance against blindness. The particular income tax hardships of a fairly comfortable group like yours and mine are in my view overshadowed by the fact that the great majority of the blind have no income tax." Instead, her focus remained on how disability and poverty often overlapped, asserting that "my main objective has always been to promote the well-being of those who are caught in the tragedy of being both poor and blind, and I shall continue to stick to this central endeavor."[24]

The trustees may have been correct in attributing her refusal to her once notorious political ideology, and yet she couldn't be accused of simply following a party line. For Helen, socialism had merely crystallized her own deeply held beliefs—many of which had formed long before she read Marx, encountered John Macy, or joined the Socialist Party.

"Blindness with a big 'B' has never interested me," she told the *New York Times*. "I have always looked upon the blind as a part of the whole society, and my desire has been to help them regain their human rights so as to enable them to keep a place of usefulness and dignity in the world economy. What I say of the blind applies equally to all hindered groups—the deaf, the lame, the impoverished, the mentally disturbed."[25]

An examination of what projects she gladly undertook on behalf of the Foundation and which ones she flatly refused provides a stark indication of her priorities. Time and time again, she chose to advocate for those she considered the most vulnerable members of society. In fact, she would eventually take an active role in the Talking Books campaign, but not until after FDR's New Deal programs began to alleviate the worst effects of the Depression.

⠗⠋⠎⠃ ⠙⠓⠐
⠎⠄⠃⠄ ⠍⠃⠐

By the mid-1930s, Helen's duties at the Foundation had increasingly taken a back seat to caring for Teacher, whose health had been steadily deteriorating for years. At the end of 1935, she traveled with Annie to Jamaica, hoping the warmer climate would improve her condition and her mood, as it had done when she spent months in Puerto Rico recovering from tuberculosis two decades earlier. Even here, among the beauty of the tropics, Helen couldn't help dwelling on the plight of the locals. "Poverty and ignorance seem more terrible in a setting of such natural splendor," she wrote a friend. "It may sound a little shabby to dwell on the dark aspects of the island when it offers such an abundance of charm and delight, but for one with imagination the charm is overshadowed by the degradation of most of the natives."[26]

By the following summer, Helen sensed that her beloved teacher didn't have long—especially after she lost her remaining sight. After they rented a seaside college in Long Island, Annie reassured Helen that she was anxious to return home so as to put herself into a different frame of mind. "Her words did not deceive me, I knew that she had begun to die," Helen recalled.[27] During these final months, friends who visited reported a poignant reversal. After Annie lost her remaining vision, and she discovered that she had forgotten how to read braille, Helen spent hours by her side guiding Teacher's hands over the raised characters as she retaught her to read. A half century after Annie had introduced her to braille, the pupil had become the teacher.

On October 15, 1936, Polly Thomson—who had increasingly assumed many of Annie's former duties—sent a telegraph to Lenore Smith in Washington after Annie suffered a coronary thrombosis: "TEACHER SINKING RAPIDLY."[28]

"In the days that followed it seemed my heart would stop beating," Helen later recalled. "Teacher would shift from mood to mood. She would yield to despair and much of the time did not seem to care that Polly and I were full of anguish. When someone tidied her room, she kept talking to me about the Angel of Death coming for her soon and we should have everything in order at his arrival."[29]

Helen's last memory of Annie was an October evening while she and Polly gathered at her bedside along with their friend and neighbor Herbert Haas.[30] "She was laughing while Herbert told her about a rodeo he had just seen. She spelled to me all he said, and how tenderly she fondled my hand. Afterwards, she drifted into a coma from which she never awoke."[31]

While tributes poured in from around the world, a funeral service was held in New York before her ashes were interred at Washington's National Cathedral—an honor ordinarily reserved for a select group of national figures, including presidents. But Annie's story had so captured the imagination of the nation that it was as if her spirit belonged to the people. "Here ends the mortal chapter of one of the most extraordinary stories on the human record," the Reverend Harry Fosdick declared in his eulogy. "She who lighted the life of her friend like sunshine through an eastern window."[32]

None of the maudlin sentiments, however, captured the magnitude of what the two women had meant to each other as poignantly as did Dorothy Herrmann in her 1998 biography:

> For nearly fifty years the two women had enjoyed a friendship that was as all-encompassing as the most passionate love affair between a man and a woman...Like the relationship between most couples, their alliance had been a complicated interplay of power and dependence. Although Annie came to rely on Helen's fame to provide their livelihood and on her seemingly tranquil disposition to lift her out of her dark moods, it was Helen, with her afflictions, who appeared to the world as the helpless one.[33]

According to Nella, a number of Helen's friends believed that Annie's death meant that her public life must come to an end. Without Teacher to guide her, they felt there was nothing for Helen to do but go home to Alabama and live out her days with her sister, Mildred. The general sense was that Polly Thomson was not up to the task of stepping into Annie's shoes.[34] Teacher had reportedly expressed a similar worry to her nurse during her final days, even as she was assured that Helen would be taken care of. "I know how many people will fight not to stand back of Helen, but beside her," Annie responded. "I don't know if Polly will be strong enough."[35] But the dour Scotswoman had, in fact, shown herself quite capable for many years. Even as she was content to take a back seat to Teacher, Polly had gradually taken on more of Annie's duties as her health failed and, while the bond would never be the same, Helen had come to trust her, and even felt a political kinship that she had never enjoyed with Annie. Polly was "conservative in every field except politics," noted Nella Henney, suggesting that the Scotswoman frequently sympathized with Helen's left-wing beliefs, but that she held a number of biases that frequently rubbed people the wrong way. This included an apparent disdain for Catholics—ironic considering Annie's

Irish Catholic heritage. "She was as intolerant as John Knox," Nella observed.[36]

While Helen had no intention of retiring from public life, she had begun to reconsider her future and the shackles that had been placed on her by her continuing relationship with the AFB. For some time, she had contemplated resigning from the Foundation, and had already threatened to do so a few years earlier in a letter to Major Migel following a dispute over the administration of the endowment fund not long after she returned full-time in 1932.[37]

Now, still grief-stricken, she had not yet made up her mind what the future held in store. "Teacher's departure so disorganized my life that many months passed before I could disorientate myself," she recalled.[38] Polly had suggested they sail for Scotland where Helen could lift "the mists of grief" from her mind while spending Christmas with the Thomson family. After they set sail on the SS *Deutschland* in November, Helen began compiling a shipboard diary to record her thoughts and emotions—her first attempt at a journal since she was a teenager. Her daily musings during this period strongly suggest that something had changed in her outlook. No longer distracted by Annie's failing health, the journal appears to signal her new determination to emerge from the political cocoon into which she had placed herself since going to work for the AFB more than a decade earlier. It provides a unique perspective into the depth of her knowledge about current affairs and her diverse and extensive reading habits. It also reveals a sophisticated political analysis demonstrating a profound understanding of global currents—especially her growing alarm at the menace of fascism sweeping through Europe.

Among her most prophetic musings during this period was an entry from April 1937: "Apprehension has filled my thoughts since I read two weeks ago that Hitler had ordered the army to be ready in case of a sudden coup d'état. He would not attempt it alone, surely, but there is no conjecturing as to what direful events may result from his interviews with Mussolini. Those two ruthless leaders may yet lay the train for another war."[39] In another observation, she predicts the combatants in a war still several years in the future. "There is a possibility, nay a probability, that some time Germany, Italy and Japan may combine in a supreme effort to subjugate Russia," she wrote more than four years before Hitler invaded the Soviet Union.[40]

These are just two of numerous entries addressing what she described as Hitler's "demoniac forces" and "insane pursuit of power." When the journal was published in March 1938, in fact, there were so many broadsides against the führer that the regime announced it was banning the book for sale in Germany, citing a number of statements she included about "the injustices and brutalities of Hitler's state."[41] Five years after another of her books had been consigned to the Nazi bonfires, the woman who most people still pictured as a saintly apostle of love and understanding demonstrated that her words had enough sting to make even the world's most ruthless dictator tremble. "Banning of my Journal in Germany challenges me to assert rights of normal people and handicapped alike against brute terrorism, for they are blind who acquiesce in slavery and fail to distinguish principle from lust for power," she told the New York–based anti-Nazi newsletter, *The Hour*.[42]

Her outspoken comments about the Nazis and her decision to publish her journal appeared to herald a new determination to once again speak out on subjects other than blindness.

Meanwhile, as she watched the Germans wreak havoc in Europe virtually unchecked, she had become increasingly frustrated by the failure of the American media to pay sufficient attention to Hitler's crimes. She was alarmed enough by the "dread menace" that she accepted an invitation to join the American Council against Nazi Propaganda, where she raised the alarm about reports circulating out of Germany of a monstrous euthanasia program targeting the disability community. As she redoubled her efforts to publicize their plight, she was informed that she had been placed on what she described as a Nazi "blacklist—the list of suspects who are to be sent to concentration camps."[43] She never elaborated on the source of this alarming revelation.

By this time, Helen found her stance toward eugenics had shifted profoundly. Two decades after her troubling intervention in the Bollinger baby case, she found herself wading into another controversy involving an infant requiring lifesaving surgery. Helaine Colan, a Chicago infant, had been born with a cancerous tumor in one of her eyes. After doctors recommended that the baby's eyes be removed to save her life, the parents initially rejected the surgery, implying that they would rather allow their baby to die than live a life of blindness. Although Helen and other advocates had made great strides in humanizing people with disabilities, the reaction of a number of commentators at the time provides a stark reminder about the archaic attitudes that still persisted. "Better no life than a life of darkness," one newspaper weighed in, opposing the surgery.[44] In a stark reversal of the position she had taken supporting Dr. Haiselden's eugenic arguments years earlier, Helen sent a telegram and a public letter to urge the family to consent to the surgery because "blindness is not the greatest evil…Those who say the blind should die are themselves in outer darkness."[45] Thanks in part to her efforts, the parents consented to the surgery and Helaine's life was saved.

Three weeks after the Kristallnacht pogroms targeted the Jews of the Reich during the fall of 1938, she wrote to her friend John Finley, who had just retired from his role as editor in chief of the *New York Times*. She called his attention to a letter she had recently received from a former employee of the Jewish Institute for the Blind in Vienna. It revealed that the Nazis had closed the institute and driven out the students to "beg or starve—reduced to misery even worse than that of Jews who can see, since blindness intensifies every privation." She urged Finley, as "a champion of the oppressed, a counsellor of the bewildered," to use his influence to shine a light on a "nameless shadow worse than blindness, a silence stabbed by inhumanity to the defenceless." Laying bare her growing frustration, she uses the same letter to decry the "perfidy" of France and Britain for allowing Hitler to annex the Sudetenland at the Munich Conference in September—a failure she described as the "folly and cowardice of governments which should have been far-seeing, fearless against dictatorship."[46]

⠲⠴⠆⠃ ⠰⠁⠄⠴
⠰⠴⠒⠃⠄ ⠉⠂⠄⠴

Even as she closely followed world events, Helen continued to read voraciously the novels and poetry that she had loved since she was young. Like millions of Americans, she was captivated by Margaret Mitchell's 1936 bestseller *Gone with the Wind*—the epic story set in Civil War and Reconstruction-era Georgia. It stirred in Helen a "nostalgia for the drowsy sweet, spring and early summer days in Tuscumbia" and its depiction of African Americans reminded her of her Black playmates "who so good-naturedly played with the insatiate tomboy that I was." But as she often did when memories of her childhood turned idyllic, she summoned the harsher reality that she also remembered well: "Sadly I recall the degrading poverty, the ignorance and superstition into which those little ones were born and the bitterness of the Negro problem through which many of them are still living."[47]

In a 1938 interview with the Kansas City African American newspaper *The Call*, she was even more explicit about her feelings. After discussing her personal friendship with the noted Harlem Renaissance poet Countee Cullen, she was asked whether she believed the United States could wield moral influence as long as it tolerated "lynchings and prejudice." As Polly spelled out the word "lynchings" into her palm, the reporter noted a "perceptible sign of horror" come over Helen's face. "I am ashamed in my soul over it all," she declared, invoking the kind of language and tone that had been largely missing from her public utterances about American politics since the days of her public involvement with the Socialist Party and the IWW. She added that the United States would yield far more influence if it "could stand before the world with a clean record of justice and humanity for all its people."[48]

And while the issue of anti-Black racism continued to hit home, she soon demonstrated that she was equally indignant at discrimination against other marginalized groups. In July 1939, shortly after she bought an estate in Westport, Connecticut, that she named Arcan Ridge, she received notice that she had been "adopted" as an honorary member of the Stoney Indian Nation—an honor frequently granted to prominent figures such as movie stars and politicians. Traditionally, celebrities offered only platitudes when this honor was bestowed. But at the ceremony accepting her membership, Helen took the opportunity to speak out about an issue rarely discussed during this era when Native people were still routinely portrayed as "savages" in popular books and movies. "Since my childhood," she told the tribe, "I have read all I could find about the Indians, and my cheeks have burned with shame at the terrible wrongs the white man has done them and his violence against the peaceable disciples of the Great Spirit."[49]

After a long period during which Helen had rarely spoken out around any issue unrelated to her AFB advocacy work, it was clear that something had changed. A few years earlier, Helen had informed Major Migel that her working relationship with the AFB was causing her "friction and unhappiness." If she didn't do something, she told him, she feared that she would live out her life "begging for the Blind the rest of my days—a prospect which does not appeal to me."[50]

As the 1930s drew to a close, it was increasingly evident that she had resolved to unleash the old spirit that she had kept in check for far too long.

Part Three

HELEN AND THE REDS

Chapter Seventeen

"The Spirit of Revolt"

At the beginning of 1939, Helen dispatched a package to Eleanor Roosevelt, along with a brief note. "May I commit the indiscretion of sending you my *Out of the Dark*?" she wrote. It was an unusual gift to send to the First Lady of the United States, considering the book was a compendium of essays that Helen had written during the first phase of her involvement in left-wing politics years earlier, including the most infamous articulation of her political philosophy at that time, "How I Became a Socialist." As she followed Mrs. Roosevelt's tireless efforts to champion progressive causes during her tenure in the White House, Helen appears to have sensed that she had found something of a political soulmate. "Some of the things I said at the time are now out of date, but the spirit of revolt which animated us both remains," she added.[1]

In December 1940, Helen wrote Eleanor again, this time to enlist her in a cause that had captured her attention for some time. As far back as 1938, she had written in her journal about her support of Spain's Loyalist cause. "My heart bleeds for the defenders of Madrid," she wrote. "It is proud tears I shed for the masses who are giving their lives to create a more enlightened and civilized nation."[2] She followed the bloody three-year civil war there closely, and was dismayed when, in 1939, Republican forces loyal to the left-wing Popular Front government in Spain were routed by the Hitler-backed general Francisco Franco.

While the surviving Americans and members of other international brigades were able to return to their home countries after the war, Spanish Loyalists were forced to flee retribution from Franco, who wasted no time rounding up "traitors" after the fall of Barcelona in January 1939. Amid reports of widespread executions, torture, and forced labor, almost half a million refugees made their way over the border to France in an exodus that came to be known as La Retirada (The Retreat).[3] After Nazi Germany invaded France in June 1940 and established a puppet regime in Vichy, most of those refugees ended up in concentration camps or forced labor units.

Since she initially signed on with the AFB in 1924, Helen had largely steered clear of outside affiliations. And with the exception of her increasingly outspoken opposition to Nazi Germany, and occasional candid remarks about racial discrimination, she had mostly kept her political opinions to herself. But 1940 saw her quietly take the helm as the honorary chairperson of a new group calling itself the American Rescue Mission. Under the auspices of the United American Spanish Aid Committee, the group announced that the Vichy government in France had agreed to release Spanish refugees from concentration camps to Mexico—one of the few countries that had supported the Loyalist forces during the war—if transportation could be arranged. To that end, Helen threw herself into a mission to raise $300,000 to charter a rescue ship, which would ferry the refugees out of France.

She wasted no time calling on her extensive network of friends and contacts to join the mission, including her entreaty to the First Lady. "You will remember how the thirteen Colonies stood almost alone in a hostile world fighting for their very life and liberty," she wrote Mrs. Roosevelt at the beginning of December 1940. "It seems to me we cannot commemorate their still unmeasured sacrifices more fittingly than by helping to safety others who have gone through fire and through blood to salvage democracy from a broken Europe."[4]

Years earlier, Franklin D. Roosevelt had told the beloved American entertainer Will Rogers, "Anything Helen Keller is for, I am for."[5] It would appear that Eleanor shared her husband's enthusiasm because she quickly agreed to lend her name to the mission. Days after she signed on to support the cause, the *New York Times* announced that 130 prominent figures—including university presidents, distinguished members of the clergy, H. G. Wells, and Yehudi Menuhin—had joined Helen Keller as sponsors. On December 12, Mrs. Roosevelt even mentioned the Rescue Ship Committee in her widely read syndicated newspaper column, "My Day."[6]

Within days, however, she had done an abrupt about-face. In mid-December, the First Lady wrote a private note to Helen suddenly withdrawing her sponsorship: "I have just discovered that the group sponsoring the American Rescue Ship Mission is the group which left the Spanish Committee, and, much as I regret it, I feel there are other groups serving the same purpose with which I would be happier to be affiliated. Therefore, I am now resigning and hope you will not use my name any further. I feel sure you did not know this, and therefore I am writing to express why I feel I must withdraw my name."[7] It took an additional three weeks for Mrs. Roosevelt's resignation to be made public when the *New York Times* trumpeted the news on its front page in early January 1941. Although the story reiterated the explanation that Eleanor had relayed privately to Helen in December, the *Times* filled in the blanks for its readers by revealing the "inside story" of a split that had taken place months earlier in the Spanish Relief Campaign. The paper claimed that the chief organizers of the United American Spanish Aid Committee had been "ousted" for "preferring to help Communist propaganda rather than relief and for sabotaging the efforts of their associated liberals to get Spanish refugees to safety without regard to politics."[8] Moreover, the group's executive secretary, Fred Biedenkapp, was closely tied to the Communist Party.

For her part, Helen at first seemed unmoved by the revelation that the organization to which she had lent her name was an apparent Communist front. In a statement issued to the media, she appeared to reaffirm her support. "It grieves me that anyone who calls himself a free spirit should be hostile to the Rescue Ship Mission," she declared. "When I gave my name to the enterprise, I did it as an act of pure love for the multitude and because I count it a joy and privilege to help feed the flame of liberty or rekindle it wherever it has been quenched. I look upon any person, conservative or radical, as a renegade to humanity, who holds his own tactic or theory more important than ministering to the agonized needs of a heroic people."[9] Although a wave of resignations followed Mrs. Roosevelt's withdrawal, Helen Keller's name was conspicuously not among the exodus. It appeared at first that she had every intention of standing her ground and continuing her work on behalf of the Spanish refugees.

Behind the scenes, however, a series of events was unfolding among her inner circle, engineered by Nella Henney, who had become one of Helen's closest confidantes since Annie's death. Nella had first entered her life in 1923 when her employer, Doubleday Publishing, assigned her to help Helen work on a sequel to *The Story of My Life*. On the surface, it appeared that the two women had much in common. Born in small-town Georgia, Nella graduated from Wesleyan College before moving to New York to escape the confines of her sheltered Southern upbringing. Before long, she was hired by Doubleday as a junior editor. Commuting from her Manhattan office each day, Nella spent significant time with Helen and Annie at their home in Forest Hills—a leafy residential neighborhood in the New York City borough of Queens—where she quickly learned the manual alphabet while working with Helen on her second memoir, *Midstream*, published in 1929. Along the way, she established a close bond with Annie, who chose Nella to write her 1933 biography, *Anne Sullivan Macy*. After Annie's death, Helen would eventually come to trust Nella enough to grant her power of attorney over her business affairs.

While Nella clearly believed that she had inherited Annie's role as Helen's protector, her chosen methods proved to be very different.

Whenever Teacher disapproved of Helen's increasingly radical political positions, she had always used gentle prodding or humor to express her approbation or to nudge her back to earth if she believed that publicly expressing those opinions would damage her pupil's reputation or interfere with her advocacy work. In marked contrast, Nella frequently performed damage control by maneuvering behind Helen's back. And since Polly Thomson was now the primary gatekeeper between Helen and external forces—the media, the public, and even the AFB—Nella had long since understood that the way to Helen was through Polly. Surviving documentation is spotty about what kind of backlash was brewing behind the scenes at the Foundation as the Spanish aid controversy unfolded, but the correspondence exchanged between Polly and Nella during this period paints a revealing picture.

Polly blamed herself for the controversy and especially for "allowing" Helen to get involved with the Spanish Aid Committee in the first place. Not all the correspondence has survived, but it's clear Nella had implied that Polly had let her guard down. "Alas, Nella, I'll never forgive myself," Polly wrote. "I should have known better. Yes, I did have all the data put into braille for Helen so she would know what she was doing—I am still to blame. The list of sponsors certainly helped to fool us."[10]

Meanwhile, to the dismay of both Polly and Nella, Helen was showing no signs of backing down. The Red smears clearly reminded her of the kind of political attacks that she and her comrades had endured in the heady days of her socialist crusades two decades earlier. One of those comrades, the left-wing cartoonist Art Young, helped steel her against the onslaught by counseling her to hold her ground. "Within my own lifetime, I have watched the capitalist agents of propaganda smear those who belonged or were even tolerant of progressive ideas," Young wrote her days after Eleanor's resignation was made public. "So, harking back to the days when Populism, Pacifism, Anarchism, I.W.W.'s and other movements were anathema to the ruling-class, I try to take it for granted that Communism is next to be feared and condemned."[11]

What she had likely failed to reckon with was the level of growing anti-Communist sentiment in America that had been steadily building from a wide range of powerful forces. If Helen in her idealism underestimated those forces, Nella was savvy enough to understand that the backlash could tarnish her saintly image. Like Eleanor Roosevelt, Helen Keller had regularly appeared on the list of the most admired women in America, and Nella was clearly determined to keep her there. And yet she was also acutely conscious of the fact that Helen wasn't easily moved to change her mind—especially involving a cause she held dear. Days after Mrs. Roosevelt's resignation, Helen issued a public statement declaring that she was making "enquiries" about charges that the organization was Communist controlled, but hinted that she found such charges groundless, adding that she failed "to see any question between that question and this movement."[12]

Dismayed about her apparent reluctance to distance herself from the committee, both Nella and Polly conspired to gather information and provide an exit strategy that they knew would move her. "I am as anxious as anyone else for Helen to get out of the Rescue Ship Mission," Nella wrote Polly in late January, "but I feel that she must have awfully solid ground under her feet when she does it."[13] To that end, she appeared to suggest a road map for persuading Helen to back down:

Helen has already made her statement as to where she stands on that and the issue of communism might be considered as disposed of, except that the organisation as a whole has never defined its position. It would not matter so much if they were communists and said so, but it does matter very much indeed if they are communists and deny it. Nothing that has been published and nothing that has been unearthed is definite enough and factual enough for Helen or anybody else to take hold of—I mean nothing that would stand up in court. You've got to have documents for your distrust, rather than impressions and hearsay.[14]

In what would become a familiar pattern, Nella suggested a path that she was likely certain would lead to the result she desired. She counseled Polly to make enquiries to Helen Bryan—the successor of the Communist-affiliated Biedenkapp, who had withdrawn from the committee following Mrs. Roosevelt's resignation. "If Mrs. Bryan says she cannot answer some of the questions, I think you should then ask who can...Helen might resign on such grounds as having too much else to do or for reasons of health."[15]

Sure enough, according to the script Nella had carefully laid out, Helen suddenly announced on February 7 her withdrawal from the Spanish Aid Committee. As with Mrs. Roosevelt, the news of Helen's resignation was featured prominently on the front page of the *New York Times*. "As a result of this investigation, I conclude that I am not equal to keeping track of the endless happenings, complications and rivalries which surround the mission," she explained. "It was because my heart was pierced by the plight of the Spanish refugees that I tried to help them. But now I find the extra effort for the mission too heavy a burden in addition to my work for the American Foundation for the Blind... My affectionate interest in the refugees remains. It grieves me deeply that the circumstances did not leave me free to do what I should like for them."[16]

Although the implications were clear, nothing in her statement suggested that Helen had resigned because of the accusations of Communist ties. But accompanying the statement, Polly gave an interview to the *Times* reporter elaborating on the context and issuing a disturbing excuse—presumably without Helen's approval—to explain why it had taken so long after Mrs. Roosevelt's withdrawal. Polly attributed Helen's delay to "her handicaps." She also revealed that Helen had made her own investigations—including two separate interviews—and found the answers "vague, contradictory or evasive."[17]

Although Helen had been careful in her statement not to give credence to the accusations tying the Spanish Aid Committee to

Communism, others assumed there was no other logical explanation for her resignation. By 1941, the ACLU had long since moved away from its radical roots and its leaders were eager to position the organization as the liberal defender of free speech it is still known as today. When Executive Director Roger Baldwin heard about Helen's withdrawal, he dispatched a memo to his colleagues about the woman he had recruited as a cofounder of the organization twenty years earlier. He reported that her defection from the rescue mission had occurred because the committee was tied to Communism and was "dishonestly administered." When news reached Helen about the letter, she was furious. "I am indignant that such unauthorized use should be made of my name," she wrote him. Baldwin would later attempt to mollify her by assuring her that the letter was not "official correspondence," but instead a personal letter, and that he had not quoted her directly, but had simply "drawn conclusions."[18]

Decades later, Helen's most celebrated biographer, Joseph Lash, would apparently jump to the same conclusions, writing that she had been "duped by the Communists in the Spanish refugee ship affair."[19] Such an assertion is reminiscent of the countless media accusations during her overtly radical years claiming that Helen had been manipulated by those around her. It was part of a deeply troubling ableist narrative that would eventually attach to Helen's reemergence in left-wing politics and would be taken by many as gospel. The Spanish Rescue Ship controversy, after all, was the first time that Helen had been publicly associated with a radical cause since she had gone to work for the AFB during the mid-1920s.

In his "definitive" 1980 biography, *Helen and Teacher*, Lash also implied that by the time of the Spanish Rescue Ship controversy, her radical politics were mostly behind her, quietly shelved around the time she joined the Foundation:

In reality, Helen's views on society and politics were mellowing. The social revolution no longer was the guiding star of her thought and action. Wartime repressions had destroyed the IWW. Some of its members had joined the Communists, but they were a group of quarrelsome sects, many of them underground. The Socialists were weaker than they had ever been; moreover, Helen had washed her hands of the international socialist movement because of the failure of most of the socialist parties to stand up against the war.[20]

This is a narrative that has been perpetuated by countless others over the years, including members of Helen's own family. "Her early radical political views came about in the earlier 1900s to 1925," Helen's great-nephew William Johnson told a reporter in 2005. "In any event, she apparently didn't pursue it in her more mature years. Everybody gets to be a radical when they're young. It would be fair to view that side of her as almost an historical relic."[21]

Even those who sympathized with those politics appeared to accept this explanation. In 1967, the labor historian Philip S. Foner compiled a selection of Helen's left-wing speeches and writings for a book published by a small Marxist press, titled *Helen Keller: Her Socialist Years*.[22] The selections were mostly confined to the years 1911–1925. A number of recent documentaries have also acknowledged her so-called radical years, focusing on her public involvement with the Socialist Party and IWW. This roughly fifteen-year chapter of her life has often been portrayed as a "phase" that Helen eventually outgrew. Thus, even when Helen's radical politics are acknowledged, conventional wisdom accepts that this chapter of her life was a passing fancy lasting roughly until the period when she went to work for the American Foundation for the Blind. After that, the commonly accepted narrative goes, she became mostly apolitical or shifted to a liberal outlook on society and politics. In this telling, the Spanish Rescue Ship affair was an aberration and Helen was either duped or unwittingly drawn into an enterprise out of line with her maturing political outlook.

As anti-Communist hysteria became an increasing fixture of

American politics during these years, many people became victims of guilt by association. In fact, judging by the exodus of prominent figures from the Spanish Aid Committee following Eleanor Roosevelt, many had jumped aboard without knowing all the facts. It is hardly a surprise that Helen's explanation was readily accepted, as was Joseph Lash's later assertion that she had been "duped." And yet a large body of evidence—including intelligence dossiers, FBI files, private journals, and correspondence—reveals that nothing could be further from the truth. Contrary to Lash's assertion that Helen's politics had "mellowed," the facts demonstrate unequivocally that she had in fact quietly shifted further to the left.

As Lash accurately points out, Helen had become largely disillusioned with the Socialist Party by the time she signed on with the AFB in 1924. In fact, she made no secret of her discontent and had even cited it when she joined the IWW years earlier, claiming the Socialist Party was "too slow." Like many on the left, she also made no attempt to conceal her elation with the Bolshevik revolution in 1917, which she believed marked the culmination of her socialist ideals. Shortly after the Bolsheviks seized power, her friend and comrade Emma Goldman—America's most prominent anarchist—wrote to Helen, "Is not Russia the Great miracle?...I have always lived in the revolutionary tradition, all the 33 years of my life in America, and now all our young dreams for Russia are being realized."[23]

In the immediate aftermath of the revolution, many fellow members of the US Socialist Party, led by Eugene Debs, welcomed the Bolshevik takeover in Russia. Months after the revolution, the Bolshevik Party changed its name to the All-Russian Communist Party. The lines between Socialist Party politics and the goals of the new Communist regime, however, were murky at first. Socialism and Communism, after all, both drew on Marxist principles, and Vladimir Lenin had declared his intention to construct a new "socialist order." This included public ownership of the means of production and the "dictatorship of the proletariat."[24]

Meanwhile, John Reed—whom Helen had supported financially against the advice of John Macy—returned to the United States shortly after the revolution committed to steering the Socialist Party toward support for the new Bolshevik regime. Reed was part of a "left-wing" faction that attempted to seize control of the party from the moderates who still believed in achieving socialism gradually and peacefully through democratic means. In 1918, the left-wingers issued their own manifesto calling for the party to agitate for the "overthrow of capitalism and the establishment of socialism through proletarian dictatorship."[25]

In a dramatic showdown in the spring of 1919, the party's National Committee expelled tens of thousands of pro-Bolshevik members from the party. Months later, Reed and other so-called left-wingers formed the Communist Labor Party—one of three separate Communist parties formed that year by disillusioned socialists.[26] Before long, the three parties would merge under the banner of the Communist Party of the United States of America (CPUSA), which from the beginning declared its strong allegiance to Lenin's regime.

During these early years following the revolution, Helen's comrades chose divergent political paths. In 1919, Emma Goldman was deported to Russia and became thoroughly disillusioned with the regime. Concluding that the revolution was no miracle after all, she accused Lenin of ruthless authoritarianism and severe repression of her fellow anarchists.[27] When John Reed died of typhus in 1920, he was given a hero's funeral in Russia and would become one of only three Americans buried in the Kremlin wall, along with Helen's old IWW comrade Big Bill Haywood. Meanwhile, former militant socialists such as Ella Reeve Bloor and Elizabeth Gurley Flynn would assume leadership roles in the CPUSA, while others such as Eugene Debs remained committed to the Socialist Party cause, despite his frequent battles with the reformers and his initial admiration for the Bolsheviks.

⠗⠹⠏⠀⠙⠓⠄
⠍⠹⠏⠄⠍⠏⠄

As previously noted, there is no evidence that Helen explicitly agreed to downplay her politics after she went to work for the AFB in 1924, though we can presume she knew that her fiery revolutionary rhetoric could only hurt the fundraising efforts for which she had been hired. And even if she was reluctant to tone down her politics at the time, we can be certain that Teacher would have gently reined her in, as she was known to do on more than one occasion. Indeed, not long before she signed on with the Foundation in 1924, Helen was asked by a reporter whether she was a Republican. When she responded that she was in fact a "socialist and a Bolshevik," the reporter noted that Annie responded with a playful slap. "Only red-handed workmen are admitted to the party of the Bolsheviki," Teacher admonished her. "You are poking your nose in where you are not wanted."[28] Helen's dual allegiance suggests that she had not yet fully made up her mind where she stood on the ideological scale.

And while she had largely eschewed political rhetoric in the speeches she delivered on behalf of the Foundation, she occasionally let her guard down in private, revealing her true sentiments. In early 1926, a fiercely anti-Communist campaigner named Fred R. Marvin circulated a nationwide letter to members of his group, the Committee on American Education, calling Helen's loyalty into question. Along with the letter, he enclosed two affidavits from men he described as "officers of the Intelligence Department of the Reserve Corps." One of the men, Henry B. Greisen, attested that while she was promoting the AFB's Helen Keller Fund at a Milwaukee hotel, he heard Helen questioned about her position on Communism. She replied that she "is actively interested in the doctrines and teachings of Communism, Socialism and Soviet Russia, and that the Red flag is the true symbol of the welfare of mankind." The second affidavit, from Robert B. Richards, asserted that when Helen was asked whether she knew that the true purpose of the Communists was to overthrow the government "and to raise the Red flag above the White House," she had answered "that she favored the Red flag because to her it meant 'Brotherhood.'"[29]

Marvin also noted that Helen sat on the National Committee of the American Civil Liberties Union, a "notoriously radical movement." The week before, he claimed, ACLU leader Roger Baldwin had acted as toastmaster at a banquet in New York for Elizabeth Gurley Flynn, "who for many years has been noted for her radical actions, having been connected with both the I.W.W. and the Communist Party." At the same dinner, he added, Ben Citlow—"recently convicted for his urging the overthrow of the Government by force and violence"—was one of the speakers.[30]

"Miss Keller herself is probably not at fault," Marvin stated in his affidavit. "She is far from a normal individual. Wrong impressions have been given her by those who surround her and these impressions she but repeats. Her popularity and her prominence are being cleverly used by those who would destroy this Government. However innocent Miss Keller may be, the facts as herein stated should be known to you and others in your community."[31]

Helen's candid comments were captured during the period when her excitement over the Bolshevik revolution was still fresh and while Russia had not yet fully emerged as the bogeyman it would later become. So, perhaps they can be dismissed as a brief holdover from her so-called radical phase. A few years later, however, she sat down to update her memoirs—expanding on what had happened to her in the quarter century since she wrote *The Story of My Life*. Unlike the first memoir, which had been largely devoid of politics, *Midstream* provides a hint that her worldview had expanded considerably by the time it was published in 1929. In one passage evoking her deep-seated religious faith, she explains that she identified with St. Paul and his declaration that he delights in "the Law of God after the inward man." Although she believed that love would eventually make everything right in the end, she notes that she can't help sympathizing with the plight of the oppressed who feel driven to use force to gain the rights that belong to them. "That is one reason why I have turned with such interest towards the great experiment now

being tried in Russia," she writes. "No revolution was ever a sudden out-
break of lawlessness and wreckage incited by an unholy brood of cranks,
anarchists, and pedagogues. People turn to revolution only when every
other dream has faded into the dimness of sorrow." These "mighty dis-
turbances," she adds, are often fed by "streams of discontent and oppression…streams which have their source deep down in the miseries of the
common people."[32]

A decade earlier, while she and Annie toured the vaudeville circuit,
she had frequently described Vladimir Lenin as the world's greatest living figure. There is no surviving documentation about Helen's reaction
to his death in January 1924. But, far from having turned away from
that admiration during her years with the AFB, her memoir five years
after his demise reveals that she was still deeply moved by his spirit:

> The Russian Revolution did not originate with Lenin. It had hovered
> for centuries in the dreams of Russian mystics and patriots, but when
> the body of Lenin was laid in simple state in the Kremlin, all Rus-
> sia trembled and wept. The mouths of hungry enemies fed on new
> hopes, but the spirit of Lenin descended upon the weeping multitude
> as with cloven tongues of fire, and they spoke one to another and
> were not afraid…Men vanish from earth leaving behind them the
> furrows they have ploughed. I see the furrow Lenin left sown with
> the unshatterable seed of a new life for mankind.[33]

Given this paean to the Soviet founder, it is hardly surprising that *The
Story of My Life* is still required reading in thousands of schools while
most people are likely unaware that Helen ever updated her life story
to include her adult accomplishments and beliefs. And in 1934—a full
decade after she signed on with the AFB—her admiration for the "great
experiment" remained intact. That year Helen wrote to her old friend
and mentor Joseph Edgar Chamberlin, who had first introduced her to
socialism when she was a teenager, about the encouraging signs of "a

courage and an idealism" emerging under Soviet-style socialism. "There is strength and hope in Russia," she told the man she still affectionately called Uncle Ed.[34]

And, two years later, when she and Polly embarked on their transatlantic voyage aboard the SS *Deutschland* to visit Polly's relatives following Teacher's death, her journal provides a candid window into the evolution of her beliefs. In one entry, dated December 29, 1936, she notes that she had recently received a letter from her German publisher, Otto Schramm, which has "excited a turmoil of mental insurrection in me." Schramm, she reveals, had written her twice before, "trying to argue away at length my favorable views on Bolshevism." But with the impending German publication of *Midstream* in Germany, his latest letter warned her that he could no longer be responsible for such opinions and that the "laws of Germany forbid the printing of such passages as I wrote expressing a friendly feeling towards the great Russian experiment of economic democracy."[35] In particular, she reveals that Schramm—echoing the fierce anti-Communist doctrine of the Nazi regime—insisted on cutting out the section of the book in which she praises Lenin and talks about the "unshatterable seed" that he has sown for mankind. Justifying this censorship, he claimed that the German nation "feels forced to fight Bolshevism to the death," and that the regime therefore forbids the publication of such sentiments.[36]

"I hope you meantime have become convinced of your error of judgment," Schramm wrote, "and therefore feel obliged to let me know that your attitude now towards Russian Bolshevism has entirely altered since you have learned about the evil and monstrous destruction to which this world-doctrine tends."[37] When Helen recounted this correspondence in her journal, she revealed that her attitude toward the Soviet Union remained largely unchanged from a decade earlier. "If, as Mr. Schramm asserts, millions upon millions of Russia's people had been killed body and soul, that country would not now be emerging, as we know it is, stronger than ever from its age-long fight against hunger and ignorance." She did however, admit that Russia was far from perfect, but suggested some irony in this criticism coming from her German publisher, writing, "No doubt Russia has committed blunders, grave ones; but so has National-Socialist Germany, and now it has reverted to the darkest of the Dark Ages."[38]

The following month, the subject of Russia came up once again while Helen was touring England. During a get-together, she noted that she had engaged in a spirited argument with her friend Charlie Muir about the question of who is "more tyrannical," the Hitler regime or the Russian Soviet? Writing in her journal that evening, she records the discussion:

> He wondered why I am more harsh in my attitude towards Germany than towards Russia. I told him that it seems to me that, considering its abysmal misery during a thousand years, Russia is making wonderful progress under a benevolent if paternalistic government, and that its Asiatic modes of thought and self-expression are fundamentally different from what Germany or any other western country has experienced. I am afraid he thinks I am a heathen. When he deplored the anti-Christian campaign, I said I was glad the Russian Church is overthrown.[39]

On the same trip, she discussed the reaction of her friends, Mac Eagar and Ned Holmes, to Schramm's attempt at censorship. "Mac dispatched a stinging reply to *Der Sturmer* and wrote a noble protest to *The Times* against the spread of anti-Semitic prejudice. Since Germany is anxious to be on friendly terms with England, he said, it is incumbent upon the British Government to warn the Reich that it is an offence against good relations between the two countries to permit the circulation of writings hostile to the Jews outside its borders." Helen went on to recall how "Ned praised warmly the young Soviet engineers whose prodigious feats are astonishing the world. 'Yes,' Charlie and Mac assented, 'the Russian ideals are wonderful, but how can they have lasting results with no religion, no freedom?' "[40]

Considering her devout religious faith, it is somewhat surprising here to watch Helen once again shunt aside arguments about Russia's brutal suppression of religious institutions. Indeed, of all the Marxist principles that she had subscribed to over the years, there is no indication that she had ever agreed with his assertion that religion is the opiate of the masses. "At least they have freedom to develop their special talents," she countered, "which is impossible in present-day Germany, where art, literature, education are being reduced to a dead level, and science turned into a pan-Aryan mania."[41]

A month later, returning to the States after a long period abroad, we get the first hint about what she thought of Lenin's successor, Joseph Stalin, when a reporter asked her who she considered the greatest man in the world. "That depends on the kind of greatness you admire," she responded. "If you refer to science, of course Professor Einstein is the greatest genius in the world. Or are you thinking of statesmanship? If President Roosevelt maintains his high level of achievement and preserves his spiritual balance with the stupendous power he possesses, he will be acclaimed as a truly creative statesman." In her private journal entry that evening, she wrote, "I did not mention Stalin because he himself says he is merely an instrument to execute Lenin's purposes. I do not think he has the imagination or breadth of judgment or generous humanity which were among Lenin's most conspicuous characteristics."[42]

In fact, Helen had already appeared to sour on the Soviet dictator when she read about the Moscow Show Trials that marked the start of the Great Purge in 1936—a period when Stalin used torture, executions, and kangaroo courts to consolidate his power. In her journal, Helen described the purges as "sickening."

"Those trials are utterly incomprehensible to me in a country so progressive as modern Russia," she writes. "They read exactly like a repetition with different names of the hysterical witchcraft trials once held in Puritan New England. Apparently, there is the same frenzied fear among the Soviet leaders and the same determination to force the prisoners to admit to crimes they have never committed."[43]

Despite these misgivings, Helen would continue to maintain her unwavering faith in Bolshevist ideals and ardent defense of the Soviet regime. And yet she steered clear throughout most of the '30s of any public affiliations that would bring her into the sphere of American Communism or give American intelligence agencies reason to target her as a potential subversive. This begins to change in February 1939—only weeks after Barcelona fell to Franco's nationalist forces, signaling the triumph of the fascists in the Spanish Civil War. As surviving members of the international brigades returned home in defeat, a memorial meeting was organized in New York to pay tribute to the Americans who had given their lives fighting for the Abraham Lincoln Battalion—the American brigade organized by the Communist International to combat fascism in Spain. During the emotional ceremony, Helen shared the stage alongside wounded veterans recently returned from Spain. Eulogizing the 355 Americans killed fighting against Franco, she told more than five thousand veterans gathered at the Manhattan Center that the brigade, in its fight for democracy, had furnished a "shining light in a world of darkness."[44]

Although anti-Communist hysteria would not reach its zenith for another decade, it turned out that the FBI and its zealous director, J. Edgar Hoover, were already keeping a watchful eye on various "front" groups— progressive organizations that received the bulk of their funding from the Communist Party or were led by known party figures. In fact, it is Helen's involvement in the Spanish Loyalist cause—known as the Popular Front—during this period that placed her in the crosshairs of the Bureau for the first time. Although the FBI would later claim that it had not conducted a "formal investigation" into Helen's political activities, her heavily redacted FBI file—declassified in 1984, and gathered from what the Bureau describes as "reliable sources"—reveals that those activities had come under intense scrutiny as early as April 1938. That month, the American Communist Party newspaper, the *Daily Worker*, reported that she had signed a petition circulated by the American Friends of Spanish Democracy calling on Franklin Roosevelt to end the arms embargo against Spain so as "to give the Spanish people a fighting chance."[45]

Reporting on her involvement, the FBI file notes that "the Communist Party threw itself wholeheartedly into the campaign for the support of the Spanish Loyalist cause, recruiting men and organizing multifarious so-called relief organizations...such as...the American Friends of Spanish Democracy." Months later, in October 1938, the *Daily Worker* again took note of Helen's support for the Loyalists when it reported on two letters that she sent to Robert Raven, a veteran of the Abraham Lincoln Batallion who had been blinded fighting in Spain and was touring the country on behalf of the brigade.[46]

Her association with the Loyalist cause as early as 1938 provides the missing link to connect the dots around how she eventually assumed a leadership role in the Spanish Rescue Ship mission two years later. Still, many non-Communists had supported the Loyalists and the FBI's record of identifying Communist sympathizers was spotty at best and often involved guilt by association. In later years, the role of American Loyalist supporters during the Popular Front would be reevaluated and come to be regarded as prescient since they were among the first to warn of the dangers of fascism. Many supporters accurately cited Hitler's strong support of Franco to argue that Spain was simply a dress rehearsal for his master plan. As far back as 1937, in fact, Helen had read about "secret interviews between Hitler and Mussolini," which to her seemed to point to some "conspiracy alarmingly imminent" involving their support for Franco's nationalists. "I hope they may be foiled in their efforts to isolate France from its allies and reinforce the nationalists in Spain," Helen opined in her journal. As if she already anticipated the imminent seismic shift in world affairs, she noted that "such personalities are as terrible as natural forces that may cause a devastating earthquake or volcano any moment."[47]

Helen's strong support of the Loyalist cause could perhaps be dismissed as an extension of her anti-fascist beliefs rather than an alignment with American Communism, but that argument begins to fall apart with an analysis of her actions around World War II.

Chapter Eighteen

Fellow Traveler

When Germany invaded Poland on September 1, 1939—marking the beginning of the Second World War—Helen was uncharacteristically quiet about the prospect of finally crushing the Nazi regime that she had been publicly calling to account almost since the beginning of Hitler's ascension to power in 1933. Nine days before the Nazis stormed Poland with the greatest assembly of military might ever deployed, Germany and the Soviet Union had signed a nonaggression pact ensuring that the two bitter enemies would refrain from attacking each other for ten years while each carved up its own sphere of influence in Eastern Europe. It also marked a decided shift of tone for Communists and their allies.

"The Nazi-Soviet pact came as a surprise to American Communists," writes historian John Earl Haynes, "but they dutifully and swiftly shifted their political stance in response to a series of messages from Moscow instructing them on their new policy."[1] Not long after Hitler invaded Poland, the American Communist Party adopted a new slogan, "Keep America Out of the Imperialist War."[2] Despite the apparent hypocrisy of this anti-intervention stand, and its rapid embrace by a large segment of the American Left, many members of the movement believed that neutrality was necessary to give the Soviet Union time to arm itself for an inevitable war with Germany.[3] Historians Bernard and Jewell Bellush documented the dramatic overnight shift:

For some three years, Browder and the Communist Party had been urging upon Roosevelt a vigorous policy of collective action against Hitler and Mussolini in order to "cleanse the earth of the typhus of fascism" while insisting that "humanity can no longer live in the stifling atmosphere of Hitler." In November, the international Communist leader Georgi Dimitroff dictated the new Party line from Moscow when he described the "present war, on the part of both warring sides, is an imperialist unjust war."[4]

Meanwhile, as England and France braced for a German onslaught, President Roosevelt looked for ways to support the beleaguered European nations short of direct military intervention. After Roosevelt backed a bill to allow the sale of arms to England and France, the *Daily Worker* asserted that the majority of Americans firmly resisted "involvement in a dirty imperialist war." The Communist paper denounced the president for pushing the legislation in an atmosphere "strongly tainted with war hysteria."[5]

Following these developments from her Connecticut home in early 1940, Helen wrote a letter to her brother Phillips Keller that reveals her astonishing political shift and a surprising new attitude toward FDR: "I am keenly disappointed in President Roosevelt because, it seems to me, his chief concern is to win a glorious name dragging America into the war, instead of confining himself to the task of strengthening democracy within our borders and reconstructing the people's life on humane principles as he declared we should do years ago." She was never sure, she confided, that Roosevelt possessed "real greatness," and she looked forward to future presidential administrations that might demonstrate genuine statesmanship. "In the meantime, I pray that the United States may stay out of the conflict, since it is a struggle between rival empires. All statements to the contrary, no empire has ever sincerely championed democracy, and I cannot believe that either Britain or France is an exception."[6]

Four months later, as France was falling to the Nazis, she took a similar anti-intervention line in a *New York Times Magazine* profile, suggesting that the effort to defeat Hitler was unnecessary because he would destroy himself eventually. "War is a form of blindness much more difficult to cure than mere lack of eyesight," she declared.[7] Undoubtedly remembering Helen's high-profile campaign to keep America out of the First World War, the reporter noted that her "abomination" of the war was likely motivated by her status as a "convinced pacifist." He was perhaps unaware that her long campaign against "preparedness" from 1914 to 1917 came during the height of her public affiliation with the Socialist Party when anti-intervention was a central platform of the party line. In fact, she had repeatedly emphasized that she decried pacifism for its own sake and had cited the French Revolution to illustrate her belief that "bloodshed" was sometimes necessary in pursuit of democracy.

As late as April 1941, she was still conspicuously preaching a similar stance when she told a gathering in Tallahassee, Florida, that she has a "great fear that the United States will enter the war," but "hopes against hope that this country will not become involved."[8]

Two months later, on June 22, 1941, Hitler betrayed his tenuous pact with Stalin when he launched Operation Barbarossa, the German invasion of the Soviet Union. Again, almost overnight, the American Communist Party reversed its stance against American involvement in the European war. "After the Nazi invasion of the Soviet Union in June 1941, the Communist party hastily shifted from uncompromising opposition to US involvement to fire-eating support for American intervention in the war," writes historian Harvey Klehr.[9]

Not coincidentally, the German invasion also marked a noticeable shift in Helen's own position. She quickly became an avowed supporter of American intervention. "I'm afraid America must enter the war," she told an audience in Dallas during the period when the Nazis were closing in on Moscow. "The world crisis grows terrible each day. It would be better to give millions of lives defending our divine right to liberty than to live in thralldom as

Europe is living now."[10] The same month, she addressed a Denver audience where she once again took a pro-war line. "The present war grieves me more than I can express," she declared. "Yet, strangely enough, it also rouses an exaltation in me because of the splendid courage the people are showing in their struggle for liberty." Noting her justification for American intervention, the reporter covering the event for the *Rocky Mountain News* made a keen observation linking her stance to her once notorious left-wing politics. "That her early sympathy with Socialism has not waned was indicated by her interest in Russia's fight against Germany," the paper noted, quoting Helen's unusual exaltation. "I have always had faith in the Russian people," she told the audience. "I know that no matter what windings of diplomacy occur, they will rise to their ideals of freedom and honor."[11]

Her changing position around American intervention leaves absolutely no doubt that Helen had become a Fellow Traveler—the term for a figure who embraced the Communist Party line without formally taking out a membership in the party.[12] During the later McCarthy era, the term would be frequently used as a pejorative by the Right to tar liberal and progressive figures, but Helen was anything but a liberal. Historian John Haynes, who specializes in the history of American Communist movements, notes that Helen's abrupt shift closely echoed the position of the Communist Party and its Fellow Travelers during this period. "In the mid- and late-'30s, a number of liberals and leftists adhered to a Popular Front position. Many dropped that stance after the Nazi-Soviet Pact," he explains. "If one continued in a Popular Front mode after the pact and supported the CPUSA's anti-interventionist stance from the pact to the Nazi invasion and then switched to a pro-intervention position, that suggests a strong alignment with the Communist Party."[13]

Within a week after the invasion of Russia, observed historians Bernard and Jewell Bellush, "Communists had called for the full collaboration between the United States, Great Britain and the Soviet Union to ensure the military defeat of Hitler... The 'imperialist' war had become a 'people's' war."[14]

Helen's rhetoric provides further evidence that her change of heart was not a coincidence. Writing to Nella Henney, she later explained her abrupt change of position using language virtually identical to that of the Party. "I know that the conflict began as a rankly imperialistic one, but what could I do when it appeared to develop into a people's war of liberation?" she wrote Nella.[15] Emory University professor Harvey Klehr, a historian who has written extensively about the role of Fellow Travelers during the heyday of the CPUSA, agrees that Helen's changing rhetoric around the war suggests that she was following "the standard Communist Party line."[16] At its height in 1939, Klehr observed, the party had sixty-six thousand registered members and almost ten times as many sympathizers.[17]

America was finally thrust into the war when the Japanese attacked Pearl Harbor in December 1941. Upon hearing the news, Helen's first reaction was to think back to the trip she had taken with Polly to Japan in 1937. "Hardly had we returned home when the thunderbolt news burst upon us that the United States is at war," she wrote her friend Walter Holmes two weeks after Pearl Harbor. "My body shook like a taut rope not from fear. I had expected it a long time but it was an abrupt shock for me to discover that all the Japanese friends whose kindness I so gratefully remembered had been thrown into the ranks of our enemy aliens."[18]

⠗⠦⠃⠏⠀⠘⠃⠅⠈
⠗⠄⠏⠈⠀⠂⠉⠄⠈

With the entry of the United States into the war, the Soviet Union was now America's erstwhile ally in the fight against Hitler. For the next four years, this would leave Helen free to publicly align herself with Communist institutions without attracting controversy. Only a month after Pearl Harbor, in fact, she wrote a letter of solidarity to the Women's Anti-Nazi Conference in Moscow welcoming America's new alliance with the Soviets. "The renewal of official amity between the United States and

Soviet Russia is a cause for thankfulness," she wrote the delegates. "Of course, it is only a seal to us who have read the throbbing sympathy between groups in the two countries that understood each other's ideals and experiments to create a genuine democracy, but it is undeniable proof that ignorance and prejudice cannot separate forever people into whom freedom has breathed a soul. I am on the way with you, and therefore I love you."[19]

Months later, she chose the American Communist Party magazine, *New Masses*, to publish an impassioned attack on segregation under the headline, "WHAT THE NEGRO MEANS TO THE WAR":

> It is almost universally declared that the global conflict is being waged to secure equal right and opportunities for everybody in other lands...The obstinate prejudice that perpetuates hostility between two equally God-created American populations is inexcusable at this crucial time...It is a ghastly *reductio ad absurdum* for America to defeat Nazism and brute force while in its borders discrimination and inertia are allowed to rob the colored folk of their hard-won advances towards justice and intelligent citizenship...Therefore it is incumbent upon us to help the Negroes safeguard their bulwarks against injustice, remembering from bitter experience that if those rights are cancelled, the war cannot end in a genuine victory for democracy.[20]

Although American Communists had long been in the vanguard opposing lynching and anti-Black racism, their record around another issue involving racial discrimination paints them in a less favorable light. After Pearl Harbor, apparently anxious to demonstrate its patriotism, the CPUSA responded by expelling Japanese Americans en masse from its ranks.[21] What's more, the party failed to speak out two months later when federal authorities began to round up more than one hundred thousand Americans of Japanese ancestry and place them in internment camps, claiming they were a "threat to national security." It would later emerge that the government had no evidence that these Japanese Americans posed a threat and that the internment was instead fueled by what a 1980 US congressional commission described as "race prejudice and war hysteria."[22]

In the summer of 1943, Helen received a letter informing her that the US War Relocation Authority had established the Helen Keller School for children with disabilities at Camp Tule Lake—one of the "relocation facilities" set up to intern Japanese Americans. The letter came from a fifteen-year-old deaf girl named Hannah Takagi. "We are but a few of the thousands of Japanese Americans who were evacuated from our homes on the West Coast, over a year ago," she wrote. "Our school is called 'Helen Keller' in honor of you, Miss Keller, because you tried so hard to succeed and became famous."[23]

As near as can be determined, Helen never spoke out publicly or privately during the war about the forced confinement of American citizens in domestic concentration camps, despite her often-outspoken criticism about the "shameful" racial segregation experienced by African Americans. She did, however, respond to Takagi's letter, hinting that she was not unaware of the horrors the girl and her people were experiencing. "Truly it is wonderful that you and the children at the Tule Lake School should think so kindly of me, a stranger. You must miss your homes and many other things dear to you…I am glad of the chance that the children there have to learn to read books, speak more clearly and find sunshine among shadows. Let them only remember this. Their courage in conquering obstacles will be a lamp throwing its bright rays far into other lives beside their own."[24]

At the height of the war, she would contribute once again to a Communist publication, *Soviet Russia Today*. Following the siege of Stalingrad, she composed a glowing missive to the Red Army, which, she wrote, was born under the "creative inspiration and drive of Lenin's great dream," destined to preserve world peace. In its ranks are "all colors, races and religions, welded into one glorious fighting force by the genius of Stalin."[25] A month later, she lunched with Countess Alexandra Tolstoy, daughter of the famed Russian author of *War and Peace*. Writing to a friend after the lunch, she made it clear that she still had little patience for anti-Soviet sentiments. "I had all I could do to curb my argumentative tongue when the Countess spoke of Russia as if it was hopelessly lost to Christianity and civilization," she wrote.[26]

Meanwhile, she enthusiastically supported the war effort—embarking on a patriotic coast-to-coast tour of military hospitals. "Next to the doctors, her visits are probably the most healing that can come to them," wrote Eleanor Roosevelt in her column, "My Day."[27] Although she continued to carry on her fundraising and advocacy work for the AFB during the war, her enthusiasm for this work often only truly surfaced when she was advocating for further marginalized groups within the blind community. In October 1944, she testified before a congressional committee, where she delivered an impassioned plea asking legislators to provide more funds for Americans with disabilities. Helen and the AFB had been instrumental in lobbying for the inclusion of financial aid for blind Americans when FDR first introduced the act in 1935 as a cornerstone of his New Deal.[28] But it had failed to account for the increased cost of living many blind people incur as the result of their disability. "The Social Security Act has not provided sufficiently for the particular needs of the poorer blind or taken into account their severe curtailments in bread-winning opportunities," Helen told the committee. "Most of them cannot afford braille writers or typewriters. Can you imagine yourself in the dark, unable to send a written message to a son or brother overseas?"[29]

There were two groups, she told the congressmen, for whom she had especially come to plead—"the hardest pressed and the least cared for among my blind fellows." The first was blind African Americans. "In my travels up and down the continent I have visited their shabby school buildings and witnessed their pathetic struggle against want,"

Helen shared. "I have been shocked by the meagreness of their education, lack of proper medical care and the discrimination which limits their employment chances. I feel it a disgrace that in this great wealthy land such injustice should exist to men and women of a different race—and blind at that! It is imperative that colored people without sight be granted financial aid worthy of their human dignity and courage in the face of fearful obstacles."[30]

She concluded her testimony pleading for the deafblind community: "In every state there is an agency trained and willing to help the blind in their economic problems and diversions, but not one has been organized to rehabilitate the loneliest people on earth, those without sight or hearing. They have no funds to buy little advantages or enjoyments that would bring sunshine into their double dungeon—darkness and silence."[31]

Shortly before the 1944 presidential election—with FDR running for an unprecedented fourth term—Helen told the *New York Times* that she was planning to vote for Roosevelt for the first time, which may have come as a surprise to most Americans and even the president himself, who had often sung her praises during his nearly twelve years in office. "If re-elected, he will conduct the war to victory and do his best to help secure a peace that will justify the hard sacrifices made by the peoples of the earth for decency and justice," she told the paper about her decision to support the president.[32] Her announcement that she was planning to vote for one of the mainstream party tickets for the first time in her life may appear as conclusive evidence that she had abandoned her radical politics and was now a liberal Democrat. But given the political landscape of wartime America and Helen's recent ideological shift, there is a more logical explanation. Four years earlier, Helen had echoed the CPUSA party line when she accused the president of "dragging" the United States into the war after he offered military aid to England and France in 1940. Since then, however, the Soviet Union had become a wartime ally and Helen's attitude toward FDR appeared to shift dramatically.

During the waning days of the Second World War, the Communist Party had also offered their endorsement to the incumbent president. The party "threw themselves into the campaign for FDR's re-election," noted historians Bernard and Jewell Bellush in a 1980 study examining the response of the American Left to the Roosevelt presidency.[33] Thus, it would appear that Helen was not turning from her leftist politics, but once again echoing the Communist Party line when she announced her support for the president. Privately, however, she appeared to have misgivings about her choice. For three decades, after all, she had been resolute in her antipathy to the traditional political parties, which she had once characterized as a choice between "Tweedledum and Tweedledee." In a letter to Nella two months before the election, she revealed her conflicted emotions: "I have again examined the possible consequences of casting my vote for F. D. Roosevelt, and I shall march up to the cannon's mouth just the same. Seriously, Nella, my voting for Roosevelt seems to me no worse than taking part in this war after I had been a pacifist from my youth up. I still feel like a deserter." She felt some guilt at voting for a Democrat, that doing so may seem like an unequivocal endorsement of his leadership. On the contrary, she asserted, "Oh no! I do not mean to imply that I look upon Roosevelt as a leader of the masses. I do not think America has had a genuine people's president since Lincoln's day, and the people's party does not yet exist which would command my allegiance."[34]

Within a year, the war would be over, FDR would be dead, and Helen would find herself in a pitched battle to restore his legacy.

. . . .

Chapter Nineteen

Gathering Storm

As the Greyhound bus made its way north, Isaac Woodard was looking forward to seeing his wife for the first time since being shipped out four years earlier. It had been a long journey home—a route that started in Manila following demobilization and then a troop train to Camp Gordon in Georgia, and finally on to his ultimate destination, Winnsboro, South Carolina. The twenty-six-year-old soldier had recently been discharged after serving more than three years in a segregated US Army "Negro unit" where he had earned a battle star for his courage under fire in the Pacific theater—distinguishing himself during the multiyear battle to take New Guinea.

Despite the arduous conditions, the Army had served as something of a welcome refuge for Woodard, who left home at the age of fifteen seeking relief from the crushing poverty of his childhood in a majority-Black county fifty miles southeast of Raleigh. His mother would later observe that the local white community did not "think of a Negro as they do a dog...All they want is our work."[1]

Now, on a chilly evening in February 1946, he was nearly home. According to Woodard, his ordeal started after a tense confrontation with the bus driver, Alton Blackwell, when he requested a bathroom break. After the driver cursed him and refused to stop, Woodard defiantly demanded Blackwell treat him like a man and was finally allowed off the bus to relieve himself.

Later, as the bus passed through Aiken, Blackwell summoned two police officers sitting in a patrol car, including local police chief Lynwood Shull, and informed them that the soldier had been causing a "disturbance."[2] As Woodard later recounted, he attempted to tell the officers about his testy exchange with the bus driver but before he could complete his explanation, Shull removed a baton from a side pocket, struck him across his head, and told him to "shut up." A white soldier, Jennings Stroud, later told the FBI he saw a policeman "hit the colored fellow a fairly good lick which did not knock him down but seemed to show the colored fellow [his] authority."[3] As he was being dragged to the police station, Woodard claimed that Shull repeatedly struck him in the face and knocked him unconscious.[4] When he woke in a cell the next morning, he could not see. By the time he was finally admitted to a veterans' hospital for treatment, doctors concluded that his eyes were damaged beyond repair. It would take an additional two months for Woodard to be reunited with his family.

After President Truman ordered a federal investigation, Shull was charged with excessive force, but he claimed that he had struck Woodard in self-defense. An all-white jury acquitted him after deliberating for only thirty minutes.[5]

Although the case received little attention at first, Orson Welles singled out Woodard's plight and demanded justice in a series of broadcasts on his weekly ABC radio show that summer, where he highlighted the blinding of the soldier as an example of the indignities being suffered by returning Black veterans.[6] The case would soon become a rallying cry for the African American community, and in August 1946, twenty thousand people attended a rally in Harlem to raise money for Woodard's living expenses.

Not long before the case of Isaac Woodard first came to her attention, Helen had visited the home of her younger sister, Mildred Keller Tyson, who lived with her husband and three children in Montgomery, Alabama—the town where Helen had moved with her mother for a period after Arthur Keller's death and again after her thwarted engagement with Peter Fagan. While Montgomery had once celebrated her as a favorite daughter, her celebrity had dimmed considerably after her letter to the NAACP in 1916 chided the South for its treatment of African Americans and revealed that she was "ashamed in my soul" of her Southern heritage. In the years since, she had made it a point to slip in and out of town with little fanfare, and Mildred was forced to downplay their family ties among her friends and neighbors. For her part, Helen was also deeply uncomfortable during these visits. An entry in Nella's journal recorded Helen's feelings after returning from one trip to Montgomery, writing, "The visit to Mildred was not happy. M and her family are rock-bound, old-fashioned Southerners, not interested in the things Helen cares for, not interested in trying to catch a glimpse of the horizons that Helen has seen."[7]

There is no record of whether Helen ever paid a visit to the local NAACP office during these periodic family visits. If she had, she may have come across a young woman named Rosa Parks who had been named secretary of the Montgomery branch in December 1943. It would be another decade before Parks refused to give up her seat at the front of the bus. Her arrest launched a yearlong boycott of the Montgomery bus line that would vault a local minister onto the national stage. Before Dr. Martin Luther King Jr. and Rosa Parks sparked a national dialogue on civil rights in 1955, it was rare for any prominent white figure to speak out publicly against racism in America. But when Helen came across the case of Isaac Woodard in the summer of 1946, she could not conceal her indignation.

In September, she accepted an invitation to give a talk at a meeting in Danbury called to urge "justice to Negros in Connecticut." There is no record of the speech she gave that afternoon to a large audience that included the celebrated Black contralto, Marian Anderson, with whom she dined afterward. But a letter to Nella reveals that she used the occasion to express her deep-seated feelings around anti-Black racism and reflect on the discrimination she had witnessed over the years:

As you can easily surmise, what I said at the Danbury meeting was only a sign of the unquenchable shame I feel over the situation of our colored people today. This revolt has never slumbered within me since I began to notice for myself how they are degraded...I cannot forget my humiliation when a colored teacher of high culture and noble dignity who called on me at a hotel in a Southern city was ordered into the freight elevator. It stabs me to the soul to recall my visits to schools for the colored blind which were shockingly backward, and what a hard struggle it was for them to obtain worthwhile instruction and profitable work because of race prejudice. The continued lynchings and other crimes against negroes, whether in New England or the South, and the unspeakable political exponents of white supremacy, according to all recorded history, augur ill for America's future.[8]

In the same letter, she singled out the case of Isaac Woodard, writing that she had "a glimpse into another abyss of evil, learning how a police officer blinded a colored veteran, reportedly in 'self-defence.' I cannot help adding that the rights of the blind, the deaf and other handicapped groups are invaded wherever brute force defies the law to maim a limb or put out an eye, then calls its conduct 'self-defence.'" In the thirty years since Helen had expressed her "outrage" at racial discrimination in her letter to the NAACP, the Woodard case was a painful reminder that not a lot had changed in America even after he and countless other Black veterans fought a world war in the name of freedom. Helen appeared to recognize the implications, as if she sensed that, seven decades later, similar cases would continue to dominate the headlines of American newspapers. "An atrocity of such an ultimate nature is not only an impeachment of the inertia through which it occurs," she told Nella. "It also indicates an undercover of moral infection by traitors to Christianity and to the whole democratic spirit in the best traditions of America—a sinister danger of our being dragged down to the standards of the Middle Ages."[9]

Helen's repeated outspoken condemnation of anti-Black racism underscores a conspicuous feature of her activism—the fact that she often appeared to get more worked up about racial prejudice than discrimination against people with disabilities. "She neither experienced, nor saw herself as part of an oppressed group, only as an individual who had difficulties," observed Kim Nielsen.[10] And yet she consistently highlighted the plight of marginalized people within the disability community as illustrated by her defense of Isaac Woodard and her lifelong advocacy for people with disabilities living in poverty, including blind and deaf racial minorities. Nonetheless, the fight for disability civil rights would have to wait for a future generation of activists.

⠗⠁⠝⠃ ⠄⠁⠈⠄
⠐⠁⠃⠐ ⠐⠊ ⠄

Meanwhile, Helen showed no sign of losing her admiration for Soviet Russia, feelings that had come to the forefront during the recent world war. She would soon find her left-wing ties under renewed scrutiny thanks in part to her burgeoning relationship with the sculptor Jo Davidson, whom she had counted among her closest friends since they first met in 1942. Having learned the manual alphabet from a deaf sculptor years earlier, Davidson wrote that he had developed "a spontaneous sympathy" with Helen, who often stayed at his farm in Pennsylvania.[11]

Davidson had emerged as one of America's most celebrated sculptors since befriending the powerful art patron and collector Gertrude Vanderbilt Whitney in Paris in 1908—two decades before she founded New York's Whitney Museum. In 1923, he accompanied Robert La Follette to Russia, where he hoped to do a bust of "one of the most talked-about" men in the world, Vladimir Lenin.[12] By the time Davidson arrived, the Soviet leader was too ill to sit for him, but he ended up sculpting a number of other prominent Bolsheviks, including the acting prime minister, Alexei Rykov. During his time in Russia, he also befriended Helen's old political mentor, the IWW leader Big Bill Haywood, and the left-wing

American journalist Lincoln Steffens. Whether or not this trip marked his entrée into radical politics, the rest of his life would see him move steadily to the left. Like Helen, Davidson threw himself into the Loyalist cause during the Popular Front and he even traveled to Spain during the civil war to create portraits of prominent anti-fascist leaders.

Although there's no evidence that Davidson ever joined the Communist Party, it is clear that he hewed closely to the party line and was, like Helen, almost certainly a Fellow Traveler at the very least. There is a possibility that he may have even been a "concealed Communist." In 1948, a former Soviet spy named Louis Budenz, who had renounced Communism and defected to the FBI three years earlier, claimed that Davidson had been selected by the "Politburo" for a leadership role because of his "long relationship with the Party" dating back to the days when he befriended the left-wing journalist Lincoln Steffens during his visit to Russia in 1923.[13] A confidential informant would later tell the FBI that the US Communist Party leader, Earl Browder, claimed Davidson was a suitable candidate to lead a party front group because he would "accept Communist discipline"—a principle that required followers to subordinate their own beliefs to the will of the party.[14]

Coincidentally or not, Davidson threw himself into the Roosevelt campaign right around the time that the Communist Party endorsed FDR's reelection in 1944. He even organized a group of prominent friends under the banner of the "Independent Voters Committee of the Arts and Sciences for Roosevelt" and convinced Helen to sign on along with numerous other celebrities, including actresses Ethel Barrymore and Tallulah Bankhead.[15]

Despite his committee's affiliation with the FDR campaign, Jo was especially close to Vice President Henry Wallace, who had recently been ousted from the 1944 presidential ticket in favor of Harry Truman at the last minute. Conflicting theories speculate that he may have been dropped because he was perceived as being too friendly toward the Soviet Union, or because of his outspoken opposition to racial discrimination, which would have threatened the fragile coalition of segregationist Dixiecrats and more progressive northern Democrats. This tenuous alliance kept much of the South in the Democratic Party camp for decades, but had always prevented Roosevelt from speaking out against Jim Crow for the sake of political expediency during his long tenure in the White House.

Although Wallace was dumped from the ticket, he had gained a rather sizable following—so large that Davidson was able to fill Madison Square Garden for a political rally featuring him as the keynote speaker a week before the 1944 election. The enthusiasm for Wallace among the mostly left-leaning crowd was not lost on Davidson's circle, who sensed the birth of a powerful new movement centered around the outgoing vice president. After the rally, where Helen met Wallace for the first time following a speech she delivered on Roosevelt's behalf, she wrote him a gushing letter describing him as a "new type of statesman for whom the times cry aloud" and reflecting her continuing preoccupation with a country that would soon transform from a wartime ally into America's bitterest enemy: "Your understanding appreciation of the Soviet Union is refreshing to me, especially because of the obstacles I encounter in persuading people to judge generously a country that has had only twenty-six years in which to achieve a stupendous social and economic renaissance."[16]

Wallace's response revealed that he was equally enamored of Helen, describing her message as "one of the most inspiring letters which I have ever received."[17] For both Helen and Davidson, Henry Wallace represented the progressive ideals they claimed were embodied by President Roosevelt when they decided to support his reelection. In contrast, Wallace's successor as vice president, Harry Truman, represented the reactionary forces intent on undoing the New Deal reforms that FDR had championed.

Following Roosevelt's death in April 1945 and Truman's ascension to the Oval Office, all their worst fears appeared to have been confirmed.

They had been temporarily mollified when the new president kept Wallace on as his secretary of commerce, anxious to keep New Deal Democrats in the fold. Many looked on in dismay while Truman used Wallace time and time again to run interference for him while he moved the party to the right—especially when it came to relations with the Soviets.

Watching this shift, many of the liberals and leftists who had once supported the Roosevelt-Truman ticket looked on with alarm—not least Jo Davidson, who had reconstituted his FDR reelection committee into a new political action group called the Independent Citizens Committee of the Arts, Sciences and Professions (ICCASP). By the end of 1945—only months after two atomic bombs were dropped on Japan—the committee seized on the issue of nuclear arms control as one of its guiding doctrines. Its mission paralleled the position of Wallace, who had remained close to Davidson and signaled his close adherence to the committee's principles even as he continued to serve in the Truman administration.

It would be another two years before financier Bernard Baruch coined a term to describe the increasingly hostile relations between the United States and the Soviet Union, but the Cold War was already very much underway, and Harry Truman readily embraced the growing anti-Communist hysteria that had begun to grip the nation. Wallace appeared to be one of the few willing to dial down the tension. In July 1946, he wrote a private letter to Truman arguing that the Soviets had reasonable grounds for "fear, suspicion and mistrust" of the American military program and urged the president to concede "reasonable guarantees of security."[18] He also called for a continuation of American-Soviet friendship, claiming that close economic ties would be mutually beneficial for both nations. The president, however, appeared indifferent to his pleas.

Frustrated by Truman's intransigence, Wallace had already made up his mind to resign following the November midterm elections. Meanwhile, he resolved to make his case to the American people. On September 12, 1946, Wallace delivered an address at Madison Square Garden urging an independent foreign policy. "We should recognize that we have no more business in the political affairs of Eastern Europe than Russia has in the political affairs of Latin America, Western Europe and the United States," he declared. Though the speech was booed by the left-leaning audience for its apparent rebuke of Soviet interference, it was immediately seized on by Republicans who accused Wallace of attempting to align the United States with the Communist bloc. Although the White House had cleared his speech in advance, Truman bowed to the pressure and demanded the secretary's resignation from his cabinet.

For her part, Helen had become long convinced that the Truman administration was "working towards imperialism" and the firing of Wallace was the last straw for her.[19] If there was any doubt about whether Helen's politics had mellowed in the twenty years since she had gone to work for the AFB, or whether she had abandoned her leftist political beliefs, it is convincingly allayed by the angry letter she fired off to Nella after she learned the fate of her new friend:

> Friday night I was stunned by the radio announcement of Henry Wallace's forced resignation...The indignant remarks of various commentators bore out my feelings with regard to the Administration, which has never given me the slightest cause to renounce my extreme left-wing views...The American people including myself have, I think, been ignominiously slow about supporting Wallace in his struggle to check the disgraceful squabbles between the supposed Allies and restore F. D. Roosevelt's magnanimous foreign policy as a counsellor and friend of mankind.[20]

Less than a month after Wallace's firing, a number of left-leaning groups met to form a coalition that would lead to the creation of the Progressive Party of America with Henry Wallace as its standard-bearer. Weeks later, the Senate elections of 1946 saw the ascension of an obscure Republican politician from Wisconsin who would soon have a profound effect on Helen's life and legacy. Although the worst excesses of Joe McCarthy were still a few years in the future, the dark clouds of the movement he would come to symbolize were already beginning to gather. When the storm came, Helen would find her resurgent political beliefs directly in its path.

Chapter Twenty

. . . .

Red Scare

The phenomenon that would become known as McCarthyism first reared its ugly head in the fall of 1946 when President Truman appointed David Lilienthal to head the newly created Atomic Energy Commission.

Months after the atomic bombs dropped on Hiroshima and Nagasaki, Congress had established the commission to foster and control the peacetime development of nuclear technology. Lilienthal had distinguished himself as the head of the Tennessee Valley Authority, the enormously successful federal public works project that distributed inexpensive hydroelectric power to rural areas throughout the South. He seemed a shoo-in for confirmation to the position—until a Democratic senator from Tennessee named Kenneth McKellar attempted to block the appointment. Months earlier, McKellar had told a reporter that he believed Lilienthal to be "the head Communist of my state" and that he would probably give the "atomic secret" to Russia should he ever gain control of the commission.[1]

Eventually, what was expected to be a nearly unanimous confirmation became a full-fledged battle as more senators—both Republican and Democrat—joined the effort to derail the nomination. At the height of the controversy, Helen publicly waded into the battle when she wrote a letter to the *New York Times* demanding Lilienthal's confirmation. "As a free citizen and a thinking daughter of democracy," she wrote, "I am moved to speak my mind in the present conflict between light and darkness symbolized by the conscienceless campaign of political goring and tossing against David E. Lilienthal...It is an issue vital to the nation and the world whether Mr. Lilienthal shall act as Chairman of the Commission of Atomic Energy or be repudiated, and its decision is the duty of the American people, not of a static group tied to vested interests and provincial bigotry."[2]

Although Lilienthal would eventually be confirmed, it foreshadowed the ugly politics that would dominate the political landscape for decades to come. In July that year, a man named Walter Steele appeared before the House Un-American Activities Committee (HUAC) and set off a political firestorm. Steele, publisher of the fiercely anti-Communist publication *National Republic*, claimed to represent "twenty million patriots" in support of legislation outlawing the Communist Party. During his testimony, he leveled a number of sensational charges and claimed that the Communists were contemplating the creation of a dictatorship by violence if necessary.[3] Among its leading forces, he singled out Jo Davidson and his Independent Citizens Committee of the Arts, Sciences and Professions (ICCASP)—an organization in which Helen had become increasingly active. Steele described the group as a "Red front" linked to the recently created political party headed by Henry Wallace.[4] In states that had outlawed the Communist Party, he claimed, "the Reds lend their support to so-called 'progressive' candidates sponsored by Progressive Citizens of America. It is to be expected that this movement will assume the role of an iron curtain, behind which the Communists will parade in the political field in the states barring them from the ballot."[5]

Many of the names cited by Steele at the hearing—including Hollywood figures such as Charlie Chaplin and Gene Kelly—had only peripheral links to the myriad front groups he cited. Even Ronald Reagan, who was once a New Deal Democrat, had served on the board of Davidson's ICCASP for a time before he stepped down when accusations of Communist influence first began to circulate.[6] Many liberals, in fact, would find their names tarnished for joining left-leaning groups, attending a meeting, or even signing a petition that was later revealed to be tied to a Communist organization or alleged front group. For those inadvertently caught up in the murky atmosphere of progressive politics, it was often difficult for observers to know where to draw the line when the witch hunts began.

As the FBI kept track of Helen's political activities, however, there was little question which side of the line she stood on. If her open association with Communist institutions during WWII had been largely overlooked because the Soviet Union was an ally at the time, her continued sympathies a few months after the war ended once again caught the attention of the Bureau. They took note of a piece published in the Yiddish-language Communist newspaper, *Morgen Freiheit*, which reported that Helen had been one of the guests at the Soviet consulate in Manhattan on November 8, 1945, at a reception marking the twenty-eighth anniversary of the Soviet revolution. When she entered the consulate, she was heard to declare to her hosts, "Finally I am on Soviet Soil."[7]

Three months later, the Bureau once again took note when Helen's name appeared on a list of groups and individuals who sent messages of greeting to a conference of the Veterans of the Abraham Lincoln Brigade—Americans who had fought against fascism during the Spanish Civil War. In the seven years since Helen had first appeared with the brigade in the earliest days of her involvement with the Popular Front, the group had been officially listed by the United States attorney general as a "Communist organization."[8] At the end of 1946, she publicly extolled the USSR once again in the magazine *Soviet Russia Today* when she contributed an article headlined "We Are Judged by What We Do to Them," calling for friendship between the United States and the Soviets. "There are solid grounds for faith to celebrate the 29th anniversary of the USSR," she wrote. "May its founding ever be hailed as a new daystar of healing influences dawning upon man's strife-blurred vision!"[9]

Initially, her explicit associations with Communist institutions and media outlets mostly escaped public scrutiny in the postwar period. But with the rapidly shifting American political climate, that was about to change. It was increasingly clear that she had become disillusioned with the direction the country was taking under Truman. "Here in America, we are living through a bitter period of retrograde," she wrote her friend Eric Boulter in February 1947. "Since Franklin Delano Roosevelt's death, an uninspired, short-sighted administration has made havoc of the far-seeing, beneficent global policies for which he gave his life." Racial discrimination, she complained, is "rampant" and every effort is being put forth to "stifle radicalism. Liberals are not allowed the use of any broadcasting stations, the manufacture of bombs continues, and it dismays me to see how little the people are doing individually to prevent atomic warfare."[10]

Although Jo Davidson's ties to the Communist Party—if any—are still uncertain, other figures around Helen during this period were undeniably party members, as Nella Henney observed with dismay in her journal in March 1947. Nella was especially concerned about Helen and Polly's association with the future author of *Spartacus*. "Howard Fast, a close friend of theirs, a Jewish young man with a distressing background is an avowed Communist," she wrote. "He has a dramatic sense and no small amount of literary ability, but he lacks integrity (see the way in which he manipulates American history to serve his thesis) and I am sorry to see Helen and Polly tangled up with him."[11] Her relationship with another prominent left-wing writer, Dorothy Parker, dated back to at least 1940 when Parker served on Helen's ill-fated Spanish Rescue Ship mission to ferry anti-fascist refugees out of Vichy France.[12] Parker had been named as a "Concealed Communist" by the former Soviet spy Louis Budenz, who served as a member of the CPUSA Central Committee before defecting in 1945. He provided no concrete evidence against Parker and, like McCarthy, Budenz was known for reckless accusations, although a confidential informant also told the FBI that Parker was a "concealed" member of the Party. Her file also revealed that she was a member of dozens of front groups and Communist "enterprises."[13] Helen's involvement with other alleged party figures during this period underscores the fact that we can't definitively pinpoint her close friendship with Jo Davidson as the linchpin of her continuing associations in the orbit of the Communist Party—especially since she was already a Fellow Traveler at least three years before she first met Jo in 1942. If a paper trail once existed pointing to her earlier party contacts, it almost certainly disappeared in the 1946 fire that destroyed Arcan Ridge and most of Helen's cherished possessions while she and Polly toured Europe.

Meanwhile, the prospect of Wallace taking on Truman in the 1948 election was already causing trepidation among both the anti-Communist right and the leadership of the Democratic Party as they watched the Left champion a presidential run. Helen's circle was undeniably excited at the prospect of a Wallace candidacy, as Nella observed after attending a party at Arcan Ridge in November 1947. She made particular note of the discussion after Jo Davidson arrived with his wife, Florence:

> They both were on fire, for they had just had lunch with Henry Wallace and Wallace had agreed quietly to run for the presidency, if asked, knowing that he would fail...The Davidsons believe that Wallace is Christlike and that he is ready to be crucified for the people...They want it to be an upsurge of liberal-progressive thought and though they are all ready for failure, Jo says, 'And by God we may win.'... Helen says that Wallace is her man.[14]

That same month, American Foundation for the Blind director Bob Irwin sent Helen an ominous note: "Enclosed is a clipping from the *Daily Worker*. There is a rumor going about that [the House Un-American Activities Committee] is going to investigate the Foundation very soon."[15] The clipping he attached is missing from the files, but the Communist Party paper had recently reported that Helen sent a statement of greeting to be included in a booklet commemorating the presence of Ella Reeve

"Mother" Bloor at a gathering of the Philadelphia Communist Party. Bloor was a former Socialist Party comrade, who had moved sharply to the left after the birth of the Soviet Union to become one of the cofounders of the Communist Party USA. A beloved figure in left-wing circles, she was widely known as the "Mother of the Communist Movement." It would also soon emerge that Bloor's son, Hal Ware, had headed one of the largest Soviet spy rings in American history, known as the Ware Group. Before his death in a car accident in 1935, he recruited dozens of spies to infiltrate the New Deal administration in underground cells scattered throughout the federal government.[16]

When Helen sent a greeting to Ella Bloor in the summer of 1947 that read simply, "Fraternally Yours, Helen Keller"—printed in the program of the Communist Party gathering—Ware had not yet been named publicly as a spy.[17] Still, the attention of the witch hunters and the threat of an investigation made the AFB undeniably nervous and marked a dramatic turning point in Helen's relationship with the Foundation to whom she had devoted so much of her life.

Only weeks after Irwin warned her that HUAC was threatening to turn its attention on the AFB, the most ominous threat to date presented itself in December 1947 when Westbrook Pegler devoted most of his popular syndicated column disparaging a piece that had recently appeared in rival Ed Sullivan's "Talk of the Town" column.

Sullivan, the future TV variety show personality, reported that Helen Keller had recently visited the New York nightclub Café Society with Jo Davidson and that she had "followed the harmonic rhythms" of the headliner, Larry Adler, while he played harmonica. Pegler, a notoriously right-wing columnist, took note that the club was owned by brothers Leon and Bernard Josephson, both of whom had been associated with American Communism. Leon Josephson, he informed his readers, had told the State Department that he was a member of the "inner circle" of the US Communist Party and that he would "commit any act short of murder" to carry out the orders of the Communist Central Committee.[18]

Having convincingly established that the nightclub was a Communist front, Pegler blasted Ed Sullivan for providing "political publicity and propaganda" by reporting on Helen Keller's outing under the guise of "innocent babble."

He notes that by 1943, the headliner, harmonica virtuoso Larry Adler, had appeared "three times in the reports of the Dies Committee"—a congressional committee chaired by Martin Dies that was formed before the war to investigate "disloyalty and subversive activities." It was now better known as the House Un-American Activities Committee (HUAC). Helen's companion Jo Davidson, he adds, was also "cited" by the committee a number of times. Despite these references, it is clear from the tone of Pegler's column that it was designed to out Helen as a Communist sympathizer—the first time the mainstream press had ever linked Helen directly to Communism.

"Helen Keller is cited 11 times down to 1943," Pegler wrote, apparently referring to the number of times her name appeared in the committee's internal investigations. "She knowingly chose her political company a long time ago. No news here."[19]

Both the timing of Pegler's column and the rumor that the Foundation would soon be investigated were precipitous. On November 24, 1947—only two weeks before Pegler singled out Helen and implicitly tied her to American Communism—the US Congress had cited ten Hollywood figures with contempt for refusing to cooperate at hearings called by HUAC to investigate alleged subversive activities within the film industry. The men, soon to become known as the Hollywood Ten, would be handed sentences of up to a year in jail—among the first victims of the blacklist that would destroy many lives over the next decade. Many, in fact, were members of Jo Davidson's ICCASP. Their indictment would send a chill through the American Left that would last for years as countless progressive figures were hauled before the committee and given the chance to "name names" to save their careers. Others were forced to sign loyalty oaths. "Those who aren't loyal should be put in concentration camps before it's too late," wrote the influential gossip columnist Hedda Hopper.[20]

Among the most worrying words in Pegler's column was his assertion that Helen had been cited multiple times by the Dies Committee. It suggested that he had been leaked information by the FBI or the committee and appeared to confirm the rumor that Bob Irwin had recently heard about a potential investigation. The fact that the committee had never *publicly* named Helen or summoned her to testify suggests that the Pegler leak may have been designed as a shot across the bow—a warning for her to dial down her radical associations.

The pattern of the Red-baiters over the following decade indicates that her status as a beloved icon almost certainly shielded Helen herself from persecution. It is likely no coincidence that HUAC had chosen to turn its attentions first on a group of screenwriters and directors, rather than any number of stars who had been party members or Fellow Travelers during the 1930s and '40s. Indeed, even when the committee eventually singled out actors, many of the names it targeted were relatively obscure, while both J. Edgar Hoover and the blacklisters often gave bigger names a pass during the witch hunts that followed. A few years later, the experience of one of those names would provide a telling example that suggests a figure of Helen's stature was probably in no danger of public exposure.

When *I Love Lucy* debuted on CBS in 1951, it would transform a bubbly redhead named Lucille Ball into one of America's first television superstars virtually overnight. Although she had already been a B-list movie actor for many years, her newfound fame brought unwanted attention to her political past. It didn't take long for intelligence agencies to uncover the fact that Lucy had registered to vote for the Communist Party in 1936. That same year, according to her FBI dossier, there was a report that she had also been appointed to the State Central Committee of the California Communist Party. In addition, California Secretary of State records revealed that she sponsored a Communist Party candidate for the state assembly named Emil Freed.[21] In 1938, Lucy registered to vote Communist once again, and on at least one occasion allowed her Beverly Hills home to be used to host a Communist Party gathering.[22]

Here was explosive evidence of a direct link between television's biggest star and American Communism, far more concrete than the innuendo or secondhand rumors that had already destroyed more than one career. But America loved Lucy, and J. Edgar Hoover would later describe her and her husband, Desi, as among his "favorite stars."[23] Rather than expose her to a damaging public hearing, she was given the opportunity to meet privately with a member of the committee, William Wheeler. Here, Lucy offered a dubious excuse for her Communist past—telling Wheeler that she had never been a member of the party but had registered to vote as a "favor" to her ailing grandfather Fred Hunt, who had been a "Socialist all his life."[24] Despite this fairly flimsy and disingenuous explanation, the committee allowed the matter to rest there. She later signed an affidavit claiming that she had "no knowledge or recollection" of ever being appointed to the state committee.[25] When Lucy's Communist ties later became the subject of a "blind item" on Walter Winchell's popular radio show in 1953, her husband, Desi Arnaz, deftly dismissed the rumor that the item pertained to his wife. "The only thing red about this girl is her hair and even that we're not so sure about," he quipped.[26]

As with Lucy, it's very unlikely that Hoover or HUAC would have dared risk the approbation of the public and its mostly unwavering acceptance of the witch hunts by targeting a figure as beloved as Helen Keller. "I wouldn't disagree with that assessment," John Fox, the FBI's in-house historian, confirmed.[27]

But even if she was safe from persecution, the same wasn't necessarily true for the Foundation, which clearly feared the lasting repercussions from the Pegler column. We have no record about how the backlash was communicated to Helen, but an entry in Nella's journal in December 1947 provides a revealing picture about what was going on behind the scenes, along with Helen's colorful reaction to the accusations against her and Jo:

> [Pegler] intimated that they were both communists without ever saying so (believe it is now libellous to call anyone a communist). The American Foundation for the Blind was somewhat disturbed. There are several reasons. One is that Helen is a national—rather an international—saint, and we demand austerity of our saints. The other (the main one so far as the Foundation is concerned) is that she is begging for money and the group that Pegler represents has more of it than any other. Helen called Pegler a dung-beetle and the rest of us called him worse names than that.[28]

The growing alarm within the Foundation only intensified after a financial contributor, Mrs. Walter Fosnot, enclosed a copy of Pegler's column along with a note declaring that she would not see her money going to fund Helen's "Communist activities." Irwin immediately sent a memo to AFB president William Ziegler expressing alarm.

"I have heard a good deal of repercussion from this article of Westbrook Pegler but this is the first time I have had any direct evidence it is affecting our contributions," he wrote. "I don't know whether we should ignore this woman's letter or write to her. Would you think something like the attached might be sent over your name? Helen Keller's habit of playing around with Communists or near Communists has long been a source of embarrassment to her conservative friends. Please advise me."[29]

Attempting damage control, Ziegler immediately fired off a letter to Mrs. Fosnot downplaying Helen's activities with an all-too-familiar excuse—the implication that she was being unwittingly duped by those around her:

> Helen Keller has long been interested in downtrodden human beings and years ago the philosophy behind some of the Socialistic writers

appealed to her feeling of universal brotherhood...Naturally some of the Socialistic and Communistic leaders have taken advantage of her Interest in the humanitarian side of their professings...No money however raised by Helen Keller goes to her, but to either the American Foundation for the Blind or the American Foundation for Overseas Blind...You will see therefore that there is little chance of your contributions being used to further the cause of Communism.[30]

Meanwhile, Jo Davidson had assumed a higher-profile role in the Wallace presidential campaign, which was gathering momentum as the 1948 elections drew near. Having already convinced an array of distinguished figures to jump aboard the campaign, Jo was now very eager to add Helen to the roster in a leadership role. Not long before, she had agreed to lend her name to the newly created "Committee of 1000"—a group of prominent progressive figures working to abolish the House Un-American Activities Committee.[31] The Committee of 1000 would be cited in 1948 as a "Communist-created and controlled front organization."[32] Her involvement in one more alleged front group almost certainly caused additional consternation at the AFB, although Helen had not yet agreed to join the Progressive Party campaign in a formal capacity.

While Helen considered whether to publicly endorse a Wallace presidency and take an active leadership role, his campaign had begun to attract increasing scrutiny. There was rarely a suggestion, even from his critics, that Wallace himself was a Communist. It was clear from his economic theories and background that he was what he described as a "progressive capitalist,"[33] but the media had begun to focus on the array of radical figures who surrounded him, many of whom were known members of the Communist Party. A 1948 profile in the *Atlantic* provides a clue to the political climate as Helen grappled with her decision. "It is not a Communist Party campaign despite the closeness with which he has hewn to the Kremlin's Party line and despite the number of Party members and Party-liners manning the machinery of the campaign," the magazine wrote in 1948. It revealed that many of his friends and associates had urged him not to run, "but their earnest arguments were deflected by the Communists and other voices, both from outside and from within himself, which impel Wallace on."[34] Other Wallace supporters, however, were socialists who had always steered clear of any Communist affiliations. The most notable of these was Albert Einstein, who had recently agreed to join Jo Davidson as cochair of a committee of artists and scientists for Wallace. Helen first met Einstein two decades earlier when she gave a speech at a dinner in his honor in 1930. After she met with him again privately a year later in New York, she wrote about the encounter for a national magazine: "Some wag has said that America loves Einstein because it understands his mathematical formulas not at all. This is a jocose untruth. Einstein is a genius all to himself. We like his democratic feeling, his inclusiveness, his freedom from petty prejudices and intolerances."[35] More recently, she had agreed to join the Emergency Committee of Atomic Scientists—the organization he had founded in 1946 to warn the world of the dangers of nuclear weapons.

As she was still weighing her decision, Polly intercepted a telegram from Dorothy Parker asking Helen to join the national reception committee for the impending visit to America of Madame Irène Joliot-Curie, a prominent Communist figure. Curie—a Nobel Prize–winning chemist and the daughter of the famed scientists Marie and Pierre Curie—was coming under the auspices of the Joint Anti-Fascist Refugee Committee. On March 3, apparently worried that Helen would get mixed up in yet another Communist front, Nella wrote Polly counseling her to "ignore" Parker's telegram.[36] "It is hard for Helen to refuse such requests," Nella wrote in her journal, rationalizing her clandestine intervention.[37]

Meanwhile, caught between her allegiance to a candidate who shared her progressive ideals and the growing backlash within the AFB since the Pegler column had appeared, Helen found herself in an untenable situation. "The pressure against Helen to take active part in the presidential election on behalf of Wallace is tremendous," Nella noted. "Florence Davidson wants Helen to give her name to the Women for Wallace group and she and Jo are both so insistent that I am afraid a chilliness is about to develop in this friendship."[38]

In March, Helen finally caved to that pressure when she wrote Jo politely declining involvement in the presidential campaign on the grounds that her "pressing work" on behalf of the blind community meant that she had "no time at all to read the ever-changing statements, editorials and comments upon Wallace."[39]

Her decision would mark the beginning of the end of her decade-long public reemergence into left-wing politics. For the next two years, instead of speaking out on pressing social issues, Helen steadfastly avoided controversy—lending her name to a national braille reading contest and helping to enlist the recently created United Nations to work for the welfare of the blind community.

By 1950, however, the fallout was still very much in evidence when Robert Barnett—a blind Floridian who took over as executive director of the AFB in 1949—dispatched his assistant to the office of the New York *Journal American*. Mary Blankenhorn was assigned to dig up the Westbrook Pegler column, along with any other controversial press coverage about Helen that preceded his tenure at the Foundation. Days later, she reported back on her findings. The only incident she could find "which bore on the Pegler attack," she informed Barnett, was Helen's resignation from the Spanish Rescue Ship Mission in 1941—coinciding with the departure of a number of other figures who resigned because the committee was "Communist controlled."[40]

Why the new director was searching for compromising information about Helen as late as 1950 is uncertain, but an entry in Nella's journal that same week provides a clue. She reveals that the AFB had recently shelved a plan to rename the Foundation the "Helen Keller Foundation for the Blind" because of Helen's "radical views."[41] Nella reported that she shared with Barnett her suspicion that the opposition to the name change was "part of the heritage of malice from the old Foundation." Noting that he agreed with her, she informed him that Bob Irwin had once shown her a "very nasty" letter that the trustees had sent to Helen and Polly saying "they might be better if Helen would stay out of politics."[42] This is the first known evidence that the Foundation had explicitly attempted to put a rein on her political activities, and it likely provides an important clue about why Helen abruptly distanced herself from the Wallace campaign in 1948 despite privately voicing her support.

What Nella didn't know was that Barnett himself had also taken an active role in sidelining Helen. In November 1949, only weeks after assuming his post, the new director sent a memo to Bob Irwin in response to a request from the Service Club for the Blind to use Helen Keller in a joint fundraising appeal. Barnett confided to his predecessor that the Foundation had decided "in the last few days" to "discontinue as soon as we can" using Helen in its fundraising appeals because of the "problems" caused by using her name.[43]

⠶⠢⠰⠾ ⠰⠓⠲⠄
⠐⠶⠄ ⠐⠹⠄

By the time Helen celebrated her seventieth birthday in June 1950, it had been almost three years since Westbrook Pegler implied that she was a Communist. She had remained mostly apolitical since withdrawing from the Wallace campaign. So, when the *New York Times* chose to write a profile on the occasion of her birthday, one might have expected a celebrity puff piece or a retrospective about Helen's "inspirational" life and work. Readers may have assumed it was exactly that when the article appeared in the paper's Sunday magazine under the headline, "AT 70, 'NEW SPIRIT, NEW FREEDOM.'"[44]

The writer, Joseph Barry, begins on a light note, reporting that when he presented her with champagne to commemorate her birthday, Helen referred to it as "bottled sunshine." As always, her sense of humor shines through. When he asks whether she can detect Polly's Scottish accent, she laughs and, to the reporter's delight, mimics her companion's distinctive brogue. "The bur-r-r—rs, the bur-r-r-rns, the br-r-r-rowns." After this light interlude, however, the tone of the interview changes rather abruptly, and it is soon apparent where the piece is headed. "What does Communism mean to Helen Keller?" Barry asks. Her response is unequivocal. "To me, Communism is another kind of tyranny over human minds and bodies," she declares, in what may have been a deliberate attempt to restore her tarnished image.

If she thought that would be enough to change the subject, she hadn't counted on the persistence of his questioning. Having previously toured her library, Barry had noticed a braille copy of the *Communist Manifesto* on the shelf. "If it's not imposed as tyranny, it's one of the finest pieces of literature ever written," she explained. He notes that Helen had seemed to be a great admirer of Lenin, who, she once wrote, had left a furrow "sown with the unshatterable seed of a new life for mankind." To this, she offered the kind of noncommittal explanation one might expect from a politician: "Lenin had a great influence over a great part of the world, not only as a thinker but also as the molder of the future for perhaps half the earth."

Did Stalin, in her opinion, inherit this particular genius? Barry enquired.

"I think not. He has not the same creative thought as Lenin and is on the defensive," she responded.

Probing her opinion on what had happened to the Russian Revolution, he notes that Helen took the "long-range point of view."

"It took one hundred years," she said, "for the American Revolution to be successful. Now the pendulum in Russia is swinging from the spirit of Lenin to the old state of power exercised by the Czars, so that people dare not express opinions of their own. It's sad."[45]

The surprising tone of the piece suggests that somebody in Helen's circle had likely arranged the profile as a way for her to distance herself from the lingering fallout over the Pegler column. Nella and the AFB may have believed that Helen's repudiation of Communism in the pages of America's most prominent newspaper would be enough to permanently silence the doubters and convince her critics within and outside the Foundation that she had finally put her left-wing sympathies behind her. But, as she would soon demonstrate during her last decade of public life, her passionate beliefs had not diminished with age.

Chapter Twenty-One

Helen vs. Apartheid

A t the dawn of the 1950s—with the United States embroiled in a Cold War that threatened to destroy her reputation—Helen quietly shifted her focus from domestic affairs to the international stage. Although she had traveled widely during the 1930s, including a successful visit to Japan in 1937, the war had interrupted plans to expand her work internationally. As late as November 1941, Major Migel had been involved in negotiations with the State Department for Helen to embark on a "goodwill tour" of South America, but that plan was derailed by the bombing of Pearl Harbor.[1]

The end of the war saw her resume her periodic international travels. In 1946, she embarked on visits to war-ravaged Western Europe to raise funds to aid the "destitute sightless" on behalf of the American Foundation for the Overseas Blind—an AFB sister organization where she served as a "Counsellor on International Relations." Two years later, she traveled to Hiroshima and Nagasaki to meet residents whose lives had been devastated by the atomic bombs dropped on their cities. She later wrote of touching the burnt face of a survivor, reflecting on the "desolation, irreplaceable loss and mourning."[2]

During these trips abroad, the media were always eager to report on the activities of the famous visitor, whose celebrity appeared to burn as bright overseas as it did at home, thanks in part to the international popularity of *The Story of My Life*, which had been translated into more than fifty languages, including Arabic, Japanese, Mandarin, Korean, Urdu, Persian, and Vietnamese.[3] In 1946, European papers breathlessly reported that Helen had taken over the controls of a Douglas Skymaster airplane and flew by herself for twenty minutes over the Mediterranean on a flight from Paris to Rome. "She sat in the co-pilot's seat with the pilot behind her and I relayed to her his instructions," Polly told reporters later, adding yet another impressive accomplishment to a long list.[4]

These sporadic international trips, however, had always taken a back seat to her packed schedule of fundraising and advocacy work on behalf of the AFB in the United States. But now, with the Foundation apparently still uneasy about her value on the home front since the Pegler attack, it once again renewed its efforts to employ Helen as an international ambassador. It was never clear what the Foundation intended these tours to achieve, other than to present Helen as a shining symbol of resilience and "overcoming adversity"—a message that had remained largely unchanged since she was a child. For her part, Helen took every opportunity during her travels to drive home the message that blindness was often caused by "poverty, ignorance and greed."[5] She was especially adamant about her belief that people with disabilities could earn a good living if given the opportunity and that governments had a moral obligation to fund schools and programs for citizens with disabilities.[6]

Despite some lingering fallout remaining from her decade-long flirtation with various Communist front groups, Helen remained essentially universally beloved. "Criticism, hysteria and sanctions that destroyed the careers of many of Helen's comrades usually exempted her," noted Joseph Lash, "and those who did attack her were largely ignored...Nothing ever shook the public's conviction that here was someone who wished only to do good, and even more important, someone who had prevailed against the most extraordinary odds, whose joyousness and tenderness had survived some of the greatest trials in American history—an authentic American heroine."[7]

Historian Kim Nielsen discovered that the US government was eager to capitalize on that popularity overseas to boost American prestige abroad. "State department records leave little doubt that the government considered Keller an effective propagandizing tool on behalf of the United States," Nielsen writes. "In the postwar and early cold war period, she fostered an image that resonated profoundly on the international stage."[8] A few years earlier, while her left-wing sympathies repeatedly surfaced, the government may have been wary of using Helen for these purposes. But with her denunciation of Communist "tyranny" in the *New York Times*, she now appeared to have put her radical politics behind her for good and transformed into what Nielsen describes as a "Cold War liberal in support of the spread of Americanism."[9] That assessment would prove to be premature, but by the early 1950s, both the AFB and the government appeared to believe that she would be an asset on the world stage, despite the fact that Helen herself still privately had severe misgivings about her country's international agenda. In a 1952 letter to Nella, in fact, she would complain about the "tragic blunderings" of America's foreign policy, still unhappy about how the Truman administration continued to fan the flames of the Cold War.[10]

While plans were still being finalized with the State Department to determine a suitable itinerary for her foreign travels, Helen decided on her own to accept an invitation from an old friend. She had first met the Reverend Arthur Blaxall, director of the South African National Council for the Blind, when he visited New York in 1931. A white, British-born Anglican priest, Blaxall had worked passionately for years on behalf of marginalized groups of all races in South Africa but had taken a special interest in the blind and deaf communities. During his initial visit, Helen had been captivated by his description of the fledgling efforts underway in his country to provide services for people with disabilities. At the end of 1949, Blaxall wrote her, urging her to visit his country to campaign for blind South Africans, who had encountered many obstacles in recent years. It would take an additional year to arrange the funding, but once the logistics were in place, the tour was scheduled for the spring of 1951.

The political landscape of South Africa had changed dramatically since Helen first encountered Blaxall two decades earlier. A year before she received Blaxall's invitation, the white supremacist National Party had come to power in South Africa and enacted the first apartheid laws dictating the formal separation of the races and the subjugation of the Black majority by the white Afrikaner-dominated minority. At the time, white South Africans constituted less than 20 percent of the country's population.[11] While she had always expressed eloquent indignation whenever she discussed racial discrimination in the past, her explanation for accepting Blaxall's invitation employs uncharacteristically paternalistic language, while implying that the situation of Black South Africans reminded her of the Black Southerners from her youth. "I remembered the earliest years when little Afro-Americans were my playmates," she later wrote. "I have never ceased to follow with affectionate interest the development of the colored people in America."[12] It's entirely possible that the Cold War climate was responsible for chilling her once fiery rhetoric around racial discrimination, in which she had often talked about her "outrage" or "shame" at the treatment of African Americans.

Helen had first taken an interest in South Africa when she was a student at Radcliffe during the Boer War at a time when the Afrikaners were being brutally suppressed by the British, who had acted swiftly to quell an uprising against the colonial empire in 1899. In a letter she wrote to Alexander Graham Bell in 1900, she told him about a paper she had recently written about the conflict: "I began by being strongly in favor of Great Britain; but after I had done all the reading required, I found myself in sympathy with the heroic Boers."[13] Five decades later, the oppressed had become the oppressors, and Helen's sympathies had shifted considerably. The more she learned about apartheid, the more it aroused her ire.

In contrast to her previous international tours, it was clear from the start that her mission this time was more explicitly political. She was determined to do something to help South Africa's "native" population—the term she used to describe Black South Africans. As always when a subject captured her imagination, she threw herself into learning more. She read Alan Paton's *Cry, the Beloved Country*—a poignant novel about the country's racial tensions set in the days leading up to apartheid. After that, she read two books about Gandhi—a braille edition of his autobiography and a book about his sojourn in South Africa as a young lawyer, when he was thrown off a train for refusing to give up his seat in the first-class compartment reserved for whites. "Gandhi knew well the racial problems of South Africa, and the sturdy philosophy and fraternal love that infuses these extraordinarily inspiring books braced me for the peculiar difficulties I was to encounter," she later recalled.[14]

She was experienced enough in international affairs to know that her efforts could be jeopardized if she wasn't cautious. She probed a variety of sources about how best to approach her advocacy work. "I realize the tensions which prejudice and exasperation have created between the various races," she wrote Blaxall, "and one requires skill and tact as well as enthusiasm to obtain the right help for the colored blind who, owing to their handicap, are more subject to the arbitrary will of white society than their seeing fellows."[15]

Shortly before her departure to South Africa, Helen arranged to attend the Colored Debutantes' Cotillion in Harlem at the invitation of her old friend, Dr. Clilan Powell, editor of the influential African American newspaper, the *Amsterdam News*. Although it may have seemed an unlikely gathering to find an elderly white woman, Helen was anxious to attend the ball so that she could consult with the guest of honor, one of America's most famous diplomats, about her upcoming tour. Ralph Bunche had been awarded the Nobel Peace Prize a year earlier for his part in mediating an armistice between Israel and Egypt—making him the first-ever Black Nobel laureate. Helen had first met with him at the United Nations in 1949 and described him as one of her "heroes" while Bunche told her that she had been one of his "inspirations" since he was a little boy.[16] Having spent significant time traveling through the

African continent, Bunche took time off from the festivities of the ball to apprise Helen in detail about what he knew of current conditions in South Africa. In addition to briefing her about the new racial laws, he talked passionately about the deplorable conditions facing the country's Black workers.

"He told me that he had found the native workers in mines, factories and on the land more than a century behind the progress of the workers in Britain after the industrial reform legislation of 1832," she wrote Jo Davidson after the meeting. "From what Dr. Bunche said, I fear that it will be a long while yet before an enlightened attitude is adopted towards the native workers in Africa."[17]

En route to South Africa with Polly, Helen stopped in London where she met with John Wilson, secretary of Britain's Empire Society for the Blind, who had recently written offering a cautionary tale about a trip he had taken to East Africa where he openly expressed his disapproval of racial discrimination with "disastrous" results: "The Africans were embarrassed, the Europeans were appalled, the Indians and 'Coloured' (a mixture of white and black) were distressed. The problem is much more subtle than you at first realize, and you can do far more harm than good by inflaming racial controversy. The rule I follow nowadays is quite simple. Never start a racial controversy but be quite honest about it if someone else does."[18]

If she had intended to heed Wilson's advice, the reality of what she encountered when she arrived in the country was shocking enough that she would soon disregard his caution. The schedule was ambitious, with visits to more than twenty-five schools planned during the two-and-a-half-month duration of her tour along with countless ceremonial and civic engagements. The sheer scale of the itinerary, she later complained, was driven primarily by the segregation that forced separate meetings with different races. The initial media coverage was mostly laudatory, as Helen shared platitudes with reporters about how much she was enjoying her visit, but in private correspondence with friends, she confided her mounting frustration. In the midst of her travels, she wrote back to John Wilson about the challenge of following his advice to hold her tongue. "I too find it difficult not to blurt out my indignation at the blindness and cruelty of racial prejudice," she confessed.[19]

Finally, she appears to have reached her breaking point. At the end of March, the *Cape Argus* reported remarks that she shared with a reporter as she left Capetown under a headline announcing, "Miss Helen Keller is Saddened." "I have been very impressed with the work being done for the blind and the deaf, but how much more needs doing!" she exclaimed. One thing that had "saddened" her a great deal, the reporter noted, was the fact that "non-Europeans" were always segregated from Europeans. "It hurts me indeed to see one group served first and the other waiting in darkness and silence," she lamented, once again making use of the common figurative refrain around the isolation of blindness and deafness. "God was never for any special group among the unfortunate." The reporter added that Helen had been "appalled" to learn that in some Black townships—where the incidence of blindness was as high as one in seven or eight people—there were virtually no facilities to serve them.[20]

There is no record whether her explicit criticism caused the kind of racial controversy that Wilson had told her he once encountered. It could not have escaped notice to have such a beloved figure publicly disparage the system. The AFB had sent its assistant director, Alfred Allen—a white South African expatriate—to chaperone Helen and Polly on the tour, and it is very possible that it was Allen who counseled Helen to tone down her criticism. Nella hinted as much when she later recorded Helen's thoughts about the trip in her journal, writing that "Alfred Allen was a thorn in their side almost from the moment they got on the boat. This was not the fault of P & H. He is indeed an obnoxious little man... A most odd-looking creature who rather fancies himself as an authority on South Africa where he lived for some time but which he has not seen for 30 years."[21]

It seems likely that she had, in fact, been advised to temper her public criticism following her remarks in the *Cape Argus*, because it was the last time she explicitly criticized racial segregation during the course of her visit. In her private correspondence, however, she did not hold back. "Johannesburg is a truly astonishing city, considering the fact that it has been in existence only 67 years," she wrote Jo. "We did not like it at all on account of its bitter racialism, its ugliness in many sections and its 'gold fever,' but I believe there is a nobler spirit growing up that will direct its wealth ultimately towards the well-being, education and brotherhood of all races within the city."[22]

Racial segregation wasn't the only aspect of South African society that troubled her. Since the 1912 Lawrence Textile Strike decades earlier, Helen had been immensely concerned with the plight of oppressed workers of all races. A visit to the Kimberley diamond mine—nicknamed the Big Hole because of its claim to being the deepest hole ever excavated by hand—left a lasting impression and confirmed what Ralph Bunche had told her about the deplorable conditions faced by Black South African miners. "I was fascinated as I felt diamonds in the natural state and learned of their amazingly varied colors," she wrote Jo, "but oh the desolation that swept over me as I considered the Big Hole (mine)—an immeasurable symbol of misery, ill-paid labor, and wasted lives."[23]

Decades earlier, she had no compunction about calling out the industrialists she held responsible for such conditions, but now she decided discretion was in order when she was invited for tea at the home of the country's most prominent mining magnate, Ernest Oppenheimer, whose company De Beers owned the Big Hole mine. "He entertained us pleasantly, and Lady Oppenheimer was very sweet indeed," she wrote Jo after the trip. "That was one of many occasions for us to keep watch over our mutinous lips."[24]

As she spoke at more than forty-eight meetings—addressing an estimated fifty thousand people in total[25]—she kept those mutinous lips in check time and time again while sharing her true thoughts in private correspondence to friends. In her journal, Nella noted Helen's candid assessment of the trip: "They did not like SA; as a group they cared less for the Afrikaners than any other, but the racial tensions made them unhappy in every way."[26]

On occasion during the rest of her two-and-a-half-month tour, she would gently allude to her disapproval of the system, as when she told a local newspaper in Bloemfontein that it was important to make blind people self-reliant instead of a burden to their families. "And that applies to natives as well as Europeans," she added.[27] She told the same newspaper that her tour was "very strenuous" because of the separate meetings required for the multiracial population.[28] Finally, on the eve of her departure back to America in May, she was asked by a reporter from the *Cape Argus* whether there were aspects of South Africa that had disturbed her. "South Africa has terrible racial problems, and it is always depressing when such disturbing elements keep the country tense," she responded, without explicitly criticizing segregation as she had done to the same newspaper two months earlier.[29]

The trip was grueling for the seventy-year-old visitor, who at each stop was feted by a wide assortment of local dignitaries eager to meet the famous American. She complained to a friend that the sheer number of events forced her to work on new speeches until her head was "in a whirl." She welcomed the opportunity for a brief respite at South Africa's famed Kruger Park, where she spent two days on safari encountering wildlife, including herds of lions, giraffes, zebras, and even a hippopotamus—an excursion that she described as "one of the most thrilling experiences imaginable."[30] Although she was forced to rely on Polly for descriptions of the wildlife, she felt the tall grasses rustle around her and "drank with delight the clean air of the jungle and the sense of freedom in which the animals could roam."[31]

One of the stops on her itinerary that she had been looking forward to most was a visit to the city of Durban, where Mohandas Gandhi had lived for more than a decade at the beginning of the twentieth century before eventually returning to India to lead the fight for independence from British rule. It was in South Africa, in fact, that Gandhi first acquired the honorific *Mahatma*, Sanskrit for "great soul," in recognition of his work on behalf of the poor.[32] Helen had closely followed his later struggle for independence with great interest. In 1936, she recorded in her journal her admiration for his recent declaration that he was "prepared to be hanged" in his campaign against British colonialism. But characteristically, she took notice at the same time of another issue that she considered "equally fraught with tragic significance"—the plight of those victimized by the country's deeply entrenched caste system. "The untouchables of India do not appear to desire national independence while their human rights are denied—and why should they?"[33]

In 1951, three years after the mahatma's assassination in India by a Hindu extremist, Helen stood before a large gathering at Durban's Gandhi Hall and invoked his memory. "Somehow, I feel his presence, though unseen, as I speak to you," she told the audience. "My own work for the blind and the deaf has given me experiences that vividly recall Gandhi's passive resistance principles. I have observed that if we struggle uselessly against deafness or blindness or succumb, our defeat is inevitable."[34]

Before her talk, she had been informed that the family of the mahatma's son Manilal Gandhi were in attendance, though Manilal himself could not attend because he was staging a well-publicized fast to protest apartheid. Long overshadowed by his father, Gandhi's second son had lived in South Africa as a child and worked for a time at the Phoenix Settlement—a cooperative community founded by Mohandas—before eventually returning to India. In 1918, Manilal traveled again to South Africa where he spent the rest of his life operating the *Indian Opinion* newspaper as a vehicle for carrying on his father's legacy of nonviolence and social justice, which included periodic fasts—a form of hunger strike—to protest discriminatory apartheid laws.

Midway through her speech, Helen acknowledged the presence of the Gandhi family and offered a message meant for Manilal: "I send good wishes to you whose father's teachings I have held affectionately in my heart. I pray that the good cause for which you now suffer may eventually triumph."[35] At this, Manilal's twenty-two-year-old daughter, Sita, spontaneously rushed forward and embraced her, saying that she would bring the message back to her father.

Manilal Gandhi's younger daughter Ela was eleven years old at the time, but remembers Helen's visit as if it were yesterday. "I didn't know very much about her politics, but she was very famous and I remember thinking how amazing it was that somebody who couldn't see or hear could do all that she did, writing books and traveling the world," she recalls. [36] Ela, who remembers spending time at her grandfather Mohandas's ashram on a visit to India as a child, would grow up to become a prominent anti-apartheid campaigner. She served nine years under house arrest for her underground resistance to the South African regime. After the fall of apartheid, she would serve as an African National Congress MP for more than a decade and was a close ally of Nelson Mandela.

"Looking back, it's so important that somebody as famous as Helen Keller spoke out against apartheid and highlighted the terrible racial laws," observes Ela, who today chairs the Durban-based Gandhi Development Trust.[37] Although she was too young to comprehend the American political landscape at the time of Helen's visit, she would later come to understand that what the famous visitor experienced on her South African tour was not altogether different from the situation in her home state of Alabama, where Jim Crow laws also enforced racial segregation and deprived most African Americans of the vote. Why, then, was Helen so shaken by apartheid?

"I suspect that, like many people later on, she was struck by the fact that in South Africa at that time, a vast Black majority was being oppressed by a tiny white minority. That would have been the major difference between our country and the American South in 1951," Ela explains.

Ela's brother, Arun Gandhi, was seventeen at the time of Helen's visit, but he was not present when his siblings attended her speech at Gandhi

Hall. Instead, he was back home at the Phoenix Settlement supporting his father during his fast and running the *Opinion* newspaper in Manilal's absence. He recollects that Helen had already caused something of a ruckus before arriving in Durban. "I remember it was reported in the newspapers that she annoyed the apartheid regime to no end because of her outspoken criticism, but there was nothing the authorities could do about it without creating a scandal," recalls Arun, who today runs the M.K. Gandhi Institute for Nonviolence in Rochester, New York, carrying on the legacy of his grandfather, whom he fondly remembers from visiting India during his youth.[38]

Although Arun wasn't present to hear Helen's message of support for his father's protest, he recalls meeting her when she and Polly came to visit the family for tea at their home later that day. "I had so many questions I wanted to ask her, but I thought it would be intrusive." He remembers Helen passionately criticizing apartheid when she met with Manilal and his mother, Sushila, that afternoon. "I think she did a great service in speaking out and making people aware of the evils of the system. It also helped bring attention to my father's cause. It was very unusual for people, especially Americans, to speak out at that time. She was very famous and admired. Her support was so important."[39]

A few days later, Helen received a message from Manilal thanking her for publicly endorsing his protest. "I wish to express my profound sense of gratitude to you for the most inspiring message I received from you during my fast," he wrote. "I value it more than all the messages I have received. I regard it as your very kind blessings in the great task that lies before me."[40]

She found at least one additional way to signal her disapproval of the system during her tour when she accepted an honorary degree from the University of the Witwatersrand, one of only two integrated institutions remaining in the country despite apartheid prohibitions on race mixing.[41] It was a symbolic gesture, and she refrained from explicitly criticizing apartheid in her acceptance speech, but she left no doubt about her intentions when she wrote about the trip upon her return to America. "I observed that segregation was practiced everywhere in schools and colleges. The one noble exception I came across was the admission of white and colored to the University of Witwatersrand. Every fibre within me revolted against circumstances that threaten the minds of handicapped human beings and narrow their chances of well-being."[42]

Although she had toned down her criticism of apartheid early on, news had spread rapidly by the time she was welcomed at a Zulu gathering weeks after her arrival in the country where the organizers bestowed on her the honorary name of Homvuselelo Matsoseletso—translated as "You have aroused the conscience of many."[43]

Despite this recognition, she often wondered whether her efforts had actually made any difference, or whether her undiplomatic criticism had in fact jeopardized her mission. After she returned home, she wrote a letter to the blind Kobe University professor Takeo Iwahashi, who had hosted her and Polly on their visit to Japan in 1937 and who was sometimes referred to as the "Japanese Helen Keller."

"Friends kept assuring us that my appeals stirred the hearts of the people, and I trust that some real good will result from our visit to South Africa," she wrote. "But you know about the racial antagonisms which prevail there, and I cannot escape the fear that they may compromise the welfare of the native blind and the deaf."[44]

Upon her return to the States, Helen published an essay reflecting on the experience titled "An Unforgettable Tour." In this piece—marking one of the first broadsides against apartheid by a prominent white figure outside the country—she was considerably more candid about what she had witnessed than the muted criticism she had been unable to hold back during her recent tour. "Again and again, I have witnessed the failure of society to redeem the blind and the deaf simply because of racial prejudice—an offence against humanitarianism which life never forgives. Uncompromisingly I am at war with any system, societal or educational, that shackles or defiles or distorts them."[45]

In retrospect, one notable feature of the South African tour was the fact that Helen's itinerary included visits to an equal number of schools serving the deaf and blind communities. She had, after all, devoted the majority of her advocacy work on behalf of blind people. In her 1929 memoir, *Mainstream*, she explained her singularity of focus: "Although I was as deeply interested in the cause of the deaf as I was that of the blind and had always thought deafness before the acquisition of language a greater affliction than blindness, I found that it was not humanly possible to work for both the blind and the deaf at the same time."[46]

Her failure to advocate for the deaf community in her domestic advocacy, in fact, is one of a number of factors that have tarnished her legacy within some segments of that community. As it turns out, this wasn't entirely her choice. AFB director Robert Barnett later revealed that she had pleaded with him to expand her work, recalling conversations he had with her after he took over the Foundation. "Robert, I've got to do something about the deaf," she insisted. Barnett, however, was indifferent. "I would have to explain it to her that it was not my job," he admitted.[47] Although she had quietly visited a number of schools for the deaf on her Japanese tours, her foreign travels had always primarily focused on the blind community.[48] Now, as she took an active part in planning the itinerary of the South African tour, she finally had a chance to throw off the shackles that had long prevented her from following her instincts.

No sooner had Helen returned to the States in the summer of 1951 than she began excitedly making plans for her next overseas tour. Jo Davidson and his wife, Florence, had traveled extensively in the Holy Land and returned each time with glowing descriptions of the strides being made by the new State of Israel since its founding in May 1948. Although Israel would later emerge as a bogeyman among the left-wing circles that Jo and Helen frequented, it was still widely embraced at the time as a paragon of progressive values; its creation was endorsed by the Soviet Union, and its Zionist mission was supported by socialists throughout the world. The ruling Mapai Party—a coalition of

democratic socialists—had long dominated the country's political landscape since the days when a Jewish homeland was still an elusive dream.

As far back as the '30s, Helen had strongly endorsed the creation of
a Jewish state, frequently recording her feelings about the burgeoning
Zionist movement. "I have long felt that their problem can be solved only
if they have their homeland where they can develop un-molested their
particular genius in religion, art, and social justice," she wrote in her journal in January 1937.[49] In this and later musings, she would demonstrate
her strong support for the Jewish claim to the Holy Land—occasionally
accompanied by what appeared to be an uncharacteristically chauvinistic
attitude toward the Arabs. "In the disputes between Jews and Arabs over
the occupation of Palestine, the argument is seldom if ever advanced
that the Jews held the land long before an Arab invader appeared," she
wrote in her journal in 1937. "What have the Arabs done to develop Palestine? Have they not remained stationary in their customs…while the
Jews, handicapped by age-long persecution and incredible calumny, have
enriched incalculably the world's heritage of constructive statesmanship,
philosophy and collective neighborliness?"[50]

If these words could be interpreted as simply taking sides in the
increasingly contentious debate over a Jewish state, what followed was
an undeniable streak of bigotry. "I am aware that some Arab thinkers in
past centuries have towered above their countrymen; but as a race they
have not kindled, as the Jews have, a steady light leading on to higher
living."[51]

Jo Davidson—living in Paris to escape the reaches of Joe McCarthy—
was also clearly enamored of the new state, which had gained independence from the British mandate only three years earlier. Responding to
Helen's reminiscence about her recent trip to South Africa, he wrote her
a letter in October 1951 that would almost certainly appear ironic to
modern observers. "Helen dear, your letter telling of your experience in
South Africa, its complexities and the work you did there for the blind,
your having to have three or four meetings in one day because the whites

and the colored people, the natives and the Indians refused to gather in one place. It seems fantastic! How different in Israel where they work together." He went on to brazenly assert that in Israel "there is no discrimination."[52] It would be almost two decades before Israel began to emerge as a pariah among wide segments of the left for its treatment of Palestinians and occupation of the West Bank following the 1967 Six-Day War, so Helen received his words with great excitement.

"Polly and I still dream of visiting that country," she wrote Jo and Florence, but complained that there was "nobody to arrange the visit."[53] Months later, Jo informed her that he had personally urged the prime minister, David Ben-Gurion, to issue an invitation. "Be sure to cable me when Helen Keller is in Paris and I myself will invite them," the prime minister assured him at the time.[54] Helen was excited about the prospect, but before she could follow up on the invitation, Jo died in Paris in early 1952. Nella assumed that the prospective journey would now be shelved. "When I heard the news I thought now, the girls will not go to Israel," she wrote in her journal two days after Jo's funeral, "but last night Polly said they were hoping to—the Foundation and the John Milton Society both desire it—and to Iran and Iraq also. Helen and Polly had hoped to go to Israel with Jo and Florence and I have hoped they would not go at all, but I shouldn't be surprised if by this time the die is cast."[55]

While they planned their trip to the Middle East, the State Department had informed Helen and Polly that if they wanted to visit Israel, they would have to do so as the last stop on their itinerary because they would not be granted entry into the Arab countries with an Israeli stamp on their passport. Finally, the logistics fell into place and the trip was finalized. "It thrilled me to think that I was actually to visit the lands I had read about in the Bible," Helen wrote.[56]

They visited Lebanon, Syria, and Egypt on the first leg of their journey in the spring of 1952. Before the tour, Nella had been worried about what she believed was Helen's "natural antagonism towards the Arabs," but there is no sign of any such hostility during this trip. On the contrary, after attending a meeting of the Arab Women's Federation, she gushed to Nella about her admiration for the women of Damascus, who, she noted, "are moving rapidly towards social maturity and independence, and more of them go to the university than men."[57]

By now, the troubling anti-Arab prejudice she had expressed in her journal almost two decades earlier had been apparently replaced by a disdain for the social conditions that left most people oppressed in Arab countries during this era—perhaps a reflection of her evolving political analysis. Despite her many positive observations, she was frequently left appalled by the striking economic inequality she observed and the indifference from authorities toward people with disabilities everywhere she traveled. As with her South African tour, it appears that she was occasionally less than diplomatic in venting her feelings. Writing to Nella about a public meeting she attended in Damascus, she was forthright. "I gave them the devil because their blind had been utterly neglected," she revealed. "They have little sense of social responsibility and must be pounded and pounded before they adopt an attitude of helpfulness towards the unfortunate. There is an appalling economic and social gap between the poor and the rich in all the Arab countries through which we have travelled, and any attempt to remedy the situation is put down ruthlessly by their rulers."[58]

When they finally reached Israel in May, Helen had mixed feelings at first. Arriving in Jerusalem, she informed Nella that she was "bored stiff" sightseeing after touring the city with the minister of labor, Golda Myerson, who would eventually become better known as Golda Meir when she became prime minister in 1969. "We went to the Church of the Nativity and the alleged tomb of the Virgin Mary, and oh, the sickening commercialism of it all!" she wrote. "We climbed every step of the Via Dolorosa and heard every detail of the vicissitudes which had befallen those sacred places. The smells of the ancient city were horrible, and nearly drove me crazy. It was all I could do to keep from exclaiming out loud. How can any sane person call places containing such filth sacred to any religion?"[59]

Despite these quibbles, she was enamored by what the young country had achieved in the four years since independence. "The atmosphere of Israel, so different from the putrescent decay of civilizations not yet buried," she wrote Nella. "Really, Israel is all that I have read, it is clean, vigorous and rejoicing like a strong man to run a race."[60]

She was less impressed when she was brought to the town of Uriel— a settlement an hour outside Tel Aviv that was known as the Village of the Blind. Here, 420 blind inhabitants were entirely self-sufficient— creating and selling specialized handicrafts, furniture, and woven goods. Although Helen told reporters that the villagers were "the most courageous people" she had ever met, privately she bristled at the idea of segregating blind people from society. Robert Barnett later claimed that Helen "blew her stack" and demanded that authorities break up the village. "I strenuously objected to having the place called a 'village for the blind,'" she later wrote, "because from experience I knew that the public would get a wrong, harmful impression of the workers without sight as abnormal and unable to live naturally among the seeing." Instead, Helen argued, "they should be trained for membership of normal society and not as a society of handicapped persons. Herding them together tends to intensify the regrettable effects of their infirmities."[61] When she received word that authorities had taken note of her criticism and changed the name of the village to "the Light of God," she was briefly mollified, but when she realized that only the name had changed, she made it a point to reemphasize her criticism, telling the *New York Times* that she still believed it was better for blind people to live "among the seeing" than in a separate village.[62]

Although none of these undiplomatic musings during her foreign travels had aroused any controversy at home—nor given the State Department reason to reconsider its support—they were a hint that Helen had once again grown weary of holding her tongue.

Chapter Twenty-Two

Helen vs. Joe McCarthy

Helen returned to America in the summer of 1952 to find the nation still in the grip of the anti-Communist hysteria that had forced so many of her friends to curtail their political activities or, like Jo, maintain a self-imposed exile abroad. Privately, she fumed that nobody was standing up against the witch hunters and the increasingly repugnant tactics of Joe McCarthy.

She was elated in August when the *New York Times* published an editorial criticizing the Republican presidential nominee, Dwight D. Eisenhower, for his failure to publicly oppose McCarthy's bid for reelection in the upcoming senatorial election. "The word 'McCarthyism' is not a 'proper' name," declared the influential newspaper. "It is a symbol of something frightening on our American scene. We suggest to the General that he denounce 'McCarthyism.'"[1] Helen was so thrilled at the paper's stand that she was moved to write a letter to the editor describing McCarthy's tactics as a "tragedy" that runs contrary to the finest traditions of the United States. "I am proud of the *New York Times*, that has so often shown itself superior to the blunderings and irrationalities of erring men," she wrote.[2]

It was the first time that she had publicly waded back into the American political arena since she had ostensibly denounced Communism in the same paper two years earlier (although in the interim she had sent a message of condolence on the occasion of the funeral of her former comrade, American Communist Party leader Ella Reeve "Mother"

Bloor—a message that was duly noted in her FBI file).[3] Predictably, her letter about McCarthy set off an immediate backlash. "Having always held you in the most sincere veneration, was greatly shocked by your letter to the *New York Times*," an irate bookstore owner wrote her. "Am afraid that you have been listening to some confused conversations. Am sending you a copy of Senator McCarthy's new book, with the suggestion that you read what he has to say."[4]

A right-wing think tank also weighed in. "Your letter in today's *New York Times* will be deeply regretted by tens, perhaps hundreds of thousands of readers, who have devotedly admired your many-sided services over the years," wrote a representative of the Institute for Public Service. "They will suffer regrets because they will fear that you have reached conclusions about Senator McCarthy's so-called McCarthyism, with only a small fraction of the official record before you."[5]

No sooner had the McCarthy controversy died down than Helen found herself once again embroiled in Cold War politics, sparking one of the greatest crises of her public life. In November 1952, the organizers of the upcoming Congress of the Peoples for Peace gathering issued a statement announcing that they had just received a message from Helen Keller endorsing the congress, scheduled to begin in Vienna in early December. The congress was an offshoot of the Prague-based World Council of Peace, which had been founded by the Soviet Union in 1950 to oppose "warmongering" by the United States. While many of the Communist-front organizations Helen had joined or lent her name to over the previous fifteen years had a murky leadership structure that allowed for plausible deniability, there was no doubt whatsoever that the congress was directly linked to the Kremlin, which had established the council in 1950 to advocate for nuclear disarmament at a time when only the United States had nuclear weapons.[6]

The first alarm bells within Helen's circle sounded after Helen received a letter from Frédéric Joliot-Curie—the respected French scientist who had shared a 1935 Nobel Prize for Chemistry with his wife, Irène Joliot-Curie (the daughter of famed scientists Pierre and Marie Curie), for their discovery of artificial radioactivity. Joliot-Curie, who also happened to be a devout Communist and president of the council, asked Helen for an endorsement to be sent to the headquarters of the council in Prague, Czechoslovakia. Complying with his request, she cabled, "Am with you in your splendid movement."[7] When Polly discovered too late that Helen had dispatched a telegram behind the Iron Curtain, she immediately contacted Nella, who, as usual, swung into damage control mode, warning the AFB that Helen's name might be imminently linked to Communism once again.

An unsigned internal AFB memorandum from that week illustrates the magnitude of the unfolding crisis:

> The World Council of Peace is the front of the Kremlin and is being used to gather in all the well-meaning and idealistic, as well as non-thinking good citizens who hate war, and are deceived by the use of the name Peace... It is the opinion of various prominent journalists that if it ever became known that Helen Keller received a letter and an invitation to this World Council of Peace that we would not only have the entire press of the United States against us with the exception of the *Daily Worker*—but we would also be investigated immediately by the Senate and especially by Senator McCarthy. It would be one way to get Senator McCarthy to visit the Foundation but I fear nobody would enjoy his stay.

This is a RED FLAG ITEM which should be
HANDLED WITH THE GREATEST DISCRETION...
    for GOD'S SAKE
STOP ANY FURTHER ATTEMPTS ON THE PART OF
HELEN KELLER OR ANYONE ELSE CONNECTED
    WITH THIS

INSTITUTION TO WRITE ANY MESSAGE WHICH
WOULD BE READ AT
THE WORLD COUNCIL TO MEET IN VIENNA
DECEMBER 10.

"Apparently, Miss Keller has sent Joliet-Curie a telegram," wrote the anonymous official. "I hope this letter has not gone out. It will appear in every communist paper in the world...THIS IS DANGER!"[8]

⠿⠿⠿⠿ ⠿⠿⠿
⠿⠿⠿⠿ ⠿⠿⠿

Responding to this intense pressure from the Foundation and likely from Nella as well, Helen sent a second telegram to Joliot-Curie on November 21: "REGRET. HAVE LEARNED OF POLITICAL COMPLI-CATIONS WHICH OBLIGE ME TO CANCEL MY PROMISE OF WRITTEN ENDORSEMENT."[9]

Whether or not he deliberately ignored her cable or it arrived too late, the Communist Party newspaper of Czechoslovakia, *Rudé Právo*, prominently published Helen's original message, which took on a slightly modified translation when it was reported by the American press: "I am with you in your wonderful movement with my whole heart."[10]

Days later, AFB executive director Robert Barnett took to the airwaves of Voice of America to denounce the newspaper: "Even though the editors of *Rudé Právo* knew that Miss Keller had repudiated this statement, Miss Keller would have wished me to make it known that on November 28—nine days before the editors of *Rudé Právo* published her so-called endorsement—Miss Keller had already repudiated the Vienna Congress on the grounds that it was not a true peace movement, but a mask for the Stalinist propaganda."[11]

In America, the newspapers wasted no time publicizing Barnett's remarks. "RED DUPED HELEN KELLER INTO BACKING 'PEACE PARLEY,'" screamed one headline. Conspicuously missing, however, was a statement from Helen herself. Behind the scenes, Nella had continued to urge her to distance herself from the damaging associations. In her journal, she revealed that the Voice of America had been "begging" for Helen to issue "a specific repudiation of Communism in all its forms, but this H refused to give because the blind are free in Yugoslavia to communicate with the rest of the world."[12] It's unclear what she meant by this, but Helen often judged a country by how it treated its citizens with disabilities. Nella noted that Helen subscribed to an Esperanto-language Yugoslavian magazine, where she kept up with developments in the country. "She feels that Yugoslavia is intelligent and advanced in its treatment of the blind," she recorded in her journal.[13]

This time, instead of issuing the explicit repudiation of Communism that those around her demanded, Helen was handed a list of six potential responses and ended up approving a relatively mild rebuke: "I do not believe in despotism in any form. I never have. I resent any attempt by organizations or individuals of dictatorial views to draw me into their schemes. My heart is with the freedom-loving peoples in every part of the world." Meanwhile, among the potential statements that she rejected was one that read, "I do not believe in dictatorial Communism. I never have."[14]

Helen's refusal to issue the requested blanket denunciation of Communism suggests that she may have had second thoughts during the two years since she condemned Communist tyranny in the *Times*. It underscores the evident truth that she had not changed her long-held belief that socialism was the best prescription for ridding the world of poverty, racial discrimination, and other social ills, even if she had reservations about individual state regimes such as the USSR that may have corrupted those ideals by imposing socialism through tyrannical methods.

It is difficult to assess, however, whether she could still accurately be described as a Communist sympathizer or whether her feelings had changed since her days as a Fellow Traveler in the '30s and '40s. With the exception of her public declaration that she was a "socialist and a

Bolshevik" in 1924, Helen never formally declared an allegiance to Communism, despite her evident embrace of the Communist Party line for many years. And yet it was clear from her oft-stated admiration of Vladimir Lenin and the "great Russian experiment" that she had long considered Communism an international manifestation of the socialist ideology she still believed in. Lenin himself, after all, had announced his intention to construct a new "socialist order," so it's certainly possible that she still made little distinction between Communism and socialism even as she drew the line at specific regimes.

Her defense of Yugoslavia as her excuse for refusing to denounce Communism outright is particularly noteworthy. She had visited the country with Annie and Polly in 1931 when it was still known as the Kingdom of Yugoslavia.[15] But in the years since, the monarchy had been deposed—replaced after the Second World War by a Communist government led by Josip Tito. In contrast to Stalinist Russia, Tito's regime was considered more liberal and had made a favorable impression on Jo Davidson when he visited the country in 1949. During that trip, he wrote Helen that Tito was a "remarkable man."[16] For Helen, it was hardly disingenuous to denounce despotism, especially since she had been uneasy about Stalin for years. Although the Tito regime was considerably less harsh than Stalin's ruthless dictatorship, his own repressive tactics and suppression of dissidents nonetheless made him very much a despot, although it's unclear how much Helen knew of conditions inside the country beyond the glowing reports that Jo had dispatched before he died and the laudatory reports she read about the nation's blind community in the Esperanto-language journal.

Although she was better read and usually better informed about world affairs than most of her friends and critics—especially since she regularly digested newspapers and periodicals in multiple languages—news from behind the Iron Curtain was heavily censored. Most Westerners would not fully comprehend the conditions of Eastern Bloc countries or the true extent of Stalin's brutality until years later. If Helen didn't fully understand the political situation of these countries, then, she wasn't alone on the Left, although she often came off as more politically savvy than many of her comrades. In fact, she had deplored the kangaroo court–style Moscow Show Trials as an example of Stalin's brutality in her journal in January 1937—in marked contrast to the majority of American Communists and Fellow Travelers who remained mostly uncritical until Nikita Khrushchev exposed Stalin's crimes at the 20th Party Congress in February 1956.

Helen's Vienna Congress endorsement and her renewed entanglement with left-wing politics once again ruffled feathers at the Foundation. In the short time since Robert Barnett had taken over as director in 1949, she had caused multiple headaches—first denouncing Joe McCarthy and then publicly endorsing a Stalinist gathering. Unlike his predecessor Bob Irwin, who enjoyed a collegial relationship with Helen and regarded her as a legacy of the AFB, Barnett appeared to perceive her repeated political agitation as an existential threat to the Foundation.

"The waters have been troubled," Nella wrote in her journal about the new controversy, noting that Barnett, on a visit to Arcan Ridge, had "intimated to Polly without actually saying so that he wanted Helen to resign." Later, talking to Nella herself, he repeated his request for her resignation more explicitly.[17] Although she had no formal job description with the Foundation, she had long been designated by the AFB as a "counsellor and trustee." Just as Helen appeared on the brink of acceding to his demand—under the pretense that she needed to finish her long-delayed biography of Annie—they discovered that Barnett had gone on an extended "vacation" without telling them. Nella used his absence to suggest that the director may have been having a nervous breakdown, and the matter of Helen's resignation was apparently never raised again.[18]

Her rift with Barnett, however, would eventually find her in the middle of a power struggle between the AFB and the American Foundation for the Overseas Blind (AFOB), which had originally been a separate organization before it merged with the AFB following the Second World War. "I feel strongly that the time has come for it to regain its independence," she wrote the trustees in 1953, arguing that splitting up the two organizations was the only way to "dissipate the doubt and suspicion" that had emerged. In the same letter, she confides her increasing disillusionment with Barnett, who for months had been "indifferent" to her and "ignored" her as a counsellor on international relations. "I wonder what has caused this change," she lamented, though she couldn't have been unaware of the director's misgivings about her political history.[19] Her plea to sever the organizations ultimately proved unsuccessful, although the AFOB would eventually split off and change its name to Helen Keller International in 1977. It would become known as a dynamic progressive force overseas, prominently crediting Helen's influence and her belief that blindness and other health conditions could be eradicated only by overcoming "long-standing cycles of poverty."[20]

Although she continued to travel widely abroad for the AFOB throughout the 1950s—embarking on ambitious tours of India, Pakistan, the Philippines, and Greece, among other countries—her domestic involvement with the AFB had slowed significantly and her relationship with Barnett remained cool. For a number of years, the two had enjoyed playing checkers—Helen's favorite game—but their once spirited matches were now increasingly rare. By mutual understanding, she went from taking an active role in Foundation affairs—which had long included fundraising, public appearances, and speeches—to becoming something of a figurehead. For much of the remainder of the decade, her life would center around her Connecticut home instead of the AFB.

Helen's social circles during the 1950s revolved around an intimate circle of friends who would often congregate at Arcan Ridge—the sprawling colonial home in Easton, Connecticut, not far from where Mark Twain lived out his last years. "We have never loved a place more than Arcan Ridge," she told Lenore Smith, describing the spacious study as her favorite room with its book-filled shelves and windows "hospitable to the sun."[21] She could also often be found at the home of her friends and neighbors, Stuart and Sandra Grummon. Stuart was a retired diplomat who had served as ambassador to Haiti and later as first secretary at the American embassy in Moscow before the war. His wife, Sandra, had mastered the manual alphabet so she could communicate with Helen without the need for Polly's constant presence. The couple frequently hosted intimate dinner parties with a wide range of fascinating guests who shared their progressive politics and with whom they knew that Helen would be comfortable. The Grummons could always be counted on to serve Helen her favorite cocktail, an old-fashioned, while she sent Stuart a bottle of scotch every Christmas, which she always referred to as "liquid sunshine" in the accompanying note. Whenever she was invited, Nella's journal entries provide a valuable fly-on-the-wall glimpse at the nature of the conversations during these gatherings.

At a typically lively dinner hosted by the Grummons in November 1951, one of the invited guests was Helen's friend Clilan Powell—editor of Harlem's *Amsterdam News*. Although Nella had long ago established herself as a reputedly worldly New York literary figure, hints of her Southern upbringing often surfaced when it came to racial matters. On this occasion, she notes in her journal that the dinner with Powell was the first time that she had ever dined in an "intimate" setting with a Black person. "I had no feeling about it one way or the other," she wrote, "except when Powell began his third martini before dinner and I was afraid we were in for a bit of noise and rowdiness, but this soon passed."[22] Nella reveals that the group engaged in a spirited discussion over dinner about whether Dwight Eisenhower would throw his hat in the ring and run for president in 1952. Somebody mentioned that the "scandal" would be his greatest obstacle—the open secret that Eisenhower had engaged in an affair with his chauffeur and personal secretary, Kay Summersby, during the war. To this, another guest noted that the same thing had been rumored of nearly every president and that it was well known that Grover Cleveland had an illegitimate daughter before his election to office in the 1880s. At this point in the conversation, Polly remarked that she had read Summersby's memoir and there was nothing damaging in it. "Ah, but we know what was left out," Powell piped in, alluding to Ike's affair.[23]

Among Helen's other close friends, a regular guest at Arcan Ridge during these years was the well-known actress, lyricist, and producer Nancy Hamilton, composer of the Broadway standard "How High the Moon." Hamilton's longtime lover, Katharine "Kit" Cornell—one of the greatest Broadway actresses of the era, known as the "First Lady of the American Stage"—was married to the prominent theater director Guthrie McClintic. However, theirs was a "lavender marriage"—a marriage of convenience designed to keep up appearances for the general public—and her relationship with Hamilton was an open secret, as was McClintic's own homosexuality.[24]

Cornell had long expressed interest in appearing in a movie about Annie based on *Anne Sullivan Macy*, Nella's 1933 biography, but nothing had ever come of it.[25] Instead, the two women arranged, with Helen's blessing, to produce a documentary directed by Hamilton and narrated by Kit. The resulting film, *The Unconquered*, was released to great acclaim in 1954. It showed Helen and Polly at work and at home, along with archival footage of Annie, capped by a visit to the White House where Helen is shown feeling the face of President Eisenhower after she asks whether she might "have the privilege of seeing" him. When the film won the Oscar for Best Documentary in 1955, Hamilton became the first female director to ever win the award.[26]

Helen was also a frequent visitor to Kit Cornell's vacation compound in Martha's Vineyard—nicknamed Chip Chop—where Kit and Nancy spent their summers. Hamilton later recalled that on one of those visits, she informed Helen that she always swam in the nude and invited her to do the same. Since she could not have the pleasure of seeing, Helen retorted, she would wear a bathing suit.[27] Helen delighted in escaping the "villainous heat and humidity" of Arcan Ridge and reveling in the sea breezes of Cape Cod, which she claimed helped renew her "vitality." On more than one occasion, Helen's friend Eleanor Roosevelt—who contributed a glowing foreword to a newly released edition of *The Story of My Life* in the 1950s—joined the three women at Chip Chop. It was here, in fact, that Helen would first encounter her future biographer Joseph Lash, who also had a home on Martha's Vineyard, at an afternoon gathering he attended with Eleanor in 1954.[28]

Despite her fondness for Helen, Kit was known to have severe misgivings about her friend's political beliefs. "Helen's Redness troubles her," Nella recorded in her journal at the height of Helen's friendship with Jo. "She fears the Jo Davidson influence, but I told her not to worry—that [Helen's] radicalism was much older than [her] acquaintance with him, that it was deep and fundamental."[29] Nella's cavalier attitude here about Helen's politics is a little surprising, given how frequently she attempted to suppress those beliefs from becoming public.

Other than Kit and Nancy, Helen's circle of friends at Arcan Ridge included an increasingly diverse group reminiscent of her bohemian circle during the Wrentham days when Helen, Annie, and John Macy frequently hosted an array of radicals and nonconformists. Robert Barnett implied that Kit and Nancy were not Helen's only LGBTQ friends when he later described the "obviously gay guys running in and out" of Helen's house during this period. This almost certainly referred to a local couple who lived together nearby, John Skilton and Ernest Hillman Jr.—frequent visitors to Arcan Ridge whom Helen always referred to as "the boys."[30] In an unpublished interview with Joseph Lash, Barnett referred to her circle as "long hairs and gay friends—people high in state affairs and the art world."[31]

Among those art world figures, in fact, she had struck up an enduring friendship with the celebrated actor/playwright Ruth Gordon through their mutual friend Alexander Woollcott, the prominent drama critic and radio personality. Helen and Polly could frequently be spotted out and about in Manhattan dining with Gordon or accompanying her to the theater. After Helen's death, Gordon—who would later go on to win an Oscar in 1969 for her role in *Rosemary's Baby*—wrote a piece for the *New York Times* about Helen's sense of humor that had endeared her to many of her friends, including Woollcott, an original denizen of the Algonquin Round Table.

"Helen always laughed loudest when the joke was on her," Gordon wrote, recalling one memorable get-together over drinks with Helen and Woollcott at New York's Gotham Hotel. "To remember Alec's face, she patted it over and over. Then she patted his moustache. 'Helen says she thinks your moustache has gotten smaller,'" Gordon remarked. At that, Woollcott leaned over and patted Helen's face. "Tell her that hers hasn't," he responded, at which Helen laughed "louder than anybody."[32]

Despite Helen's unusually diverse circle, there was one thing conspicuously missing from her eclectic group of close friends—other people with disabilities. Kim Nielsen has gone as far as to claim that "none of her close friends were disabled" with the possible exception of the blind Japanese professor Takeo Iwahashi.[33] This is complex territory and ignores the fact that her constant companion for almost half a century, Annie Sullivan, was legally blind for a period of the time that Helen knew her and suffered from a variety of debilitating physical and mental health issues during the last decades of her life. Beyond her relationship with Annie, however, it is not quite accurate to claim that Helen had no close friends with disabilities, though it's certainly true that people with disabilities were never among her intimate circle. By the 1950s, she had, in fact, established key friendships with at least two figures with disabilities who would come to play an important role in her life.

Like Annie Sullivan, Peter Salmon had been admitted to the Perkins School for the Blind as a "partially sighted" student, graduating in 1914. Three years later, he was hired by the Industrial Home for the Blind in

Brooklyn, which had been established during the late nineteenth century to "teach a trade to the blind so that they may earn their own
living and become self-supporting."[34] Salmon subsequently served in a
number of posts before assuming the position of executive director in
1945, where he worked closely with Helen establishing vocational place-
ment services for deafblind Americans. According to Robert Barnett,
Salmon—who was legally blind by the time Helen met him—was one
of her few friends who could get by her ever-vigilant companion. "Polly
Thomson would get furious if anybody talked directly to Helen," he
recalled. "Peter had learned manual language. He would wait for a party
and get on a couch with Helen to circumvent Polly. He would tell her
dirty jokes and Helen would laugh."[35]

Salmon was also responsible for initiating what may have been Hel-
en's only known personal friendship with another deafblind person. In
1953, Robert Smithdas had become the first deafblind student to earn
a graduate degree when he received his master's from New York University. "Proud of your courage and perseverance," Helen cabled upon
his graduation from NYU. "The obstacles you have overcome are pre-
cious laurels."[36] In the following years, however, there was little contact
between them, and friends of Smithdas—who was often described as
"the male Helen Keller"—would later suggest that he resented her to
some degree, perhaps for hogging the limelight as the only deafblind
figure that most people had ever heard of.[37] Thanks to Salmon, whom he
considered his mentor, Smithdas would finally get a chance to establish
a real relationship with Helen during the last years of her life, but only
after a considerable obstacle was removed. Polly Thomson had always
been notorious for strictly controlling access. Smithdas would even later
claim that Polly, for unknown reasons, had a habit of keeping people
with disabilities away from Helen, which is why he only joined her circle
of friends after Polly suffered a stroke in 1957 and could no longer exert
the tight control she once did over every aspect of Helen's day-to-day
life.[38] Although Robert Barnett never addressed this question, he did

observe that she "hated Catholics and wouldn't have a Catholic in the house." He also claimed that Polly was determined to be the "only channel of communication between Helen and the outside world."[39]

Once Polly became less of a constant presence given her declining health in the late 1950s, Smithdas and Helen began to form a newfound bond, thanks in part to Salmon's concerted efforts to bring them together. Most notably, Smithdas claimed that he was instrumental in enlightening Helen about what he believed were Alexander Graham Bell's misguided eugenic views about deaf people. Smithdas revealed that during the course of their friendship, after he filled her in about the inventor's history, Helen told him that Bell had "lied" to her.[40] He was a close enough friend by 1960 that he was among a small group invited to attend her eightieth birthday party that year.[41] Thirteen months later, Helen included both Smithdas and Peter Salmon on a list of honorary pallbearers she wished to have at her funeral,[42] and Helen would end up leaving a substantial portion of her estate to Salmon to fund his work for the deafblind community.[43]

Whatever role Polly may have had in shielding Helen from people with disabilities, there is no question that Helen herself had conspicuously pulled back from involvement with domestic causes and appearances tied to disability during her final years, and not necessarily because she was slowing down due to age. It appears, rather, that she had become deeply uncomfortable with the public adulation and her status as a symbol, which pulled her in many directions as people tried to claim her as their own. "Everybody wanted to adopt Helen Keller...to their own aggrandizement," noted Robert Barnett, who revealed that during the 1950s, Helen refused to lend her name to any cause unless she could study it firsthand—demanding to see the budget and plans before she would grant approval, even when it involved naming a high school after her.[44] This observation would suggest that she likely applied the same due diligence before attaching herself to the various political causes that those around her always claimed she had embraced without knowing all the facts.

Although she met with tens of thousands of people with disabilities during her foreign travels, she refused almost all invitations from American organizations dedicated to disability issues during the last decade of her life. While she happily accepted an honorary degree bestowed by Harvard in 1955, for example, she rebuffed numerous requests to attend the dedication of schools and organizations for blind Americans that proliferated during the 1950s.[45]

Although Helen was spending less time at the AFB, she still kept an office at the Foundation's Manhattan headquarters and would commute in from Connecticut at least once a week to attend to correspondence or business matters. In the evenings, Helen and Polly would usually meet Nella for drinks and dinner at the Harvard Club and take in a Broadway play with Ruth Gordon or Kit Cornell and Nancy Hamilton with Polly rapidly communicating the dialogue into her palm. In between, they could often be found shopping at chic Manhattan department stores such as Bergdorf Goodman or Bendel's, where they racked up bills totaling thousands of dollars for expensive hats and dresses. Polly would usually charge these to the AFB expense account, much to Robert Barnett's chagrin. Frances Koestler later explained these extravagances by claiming that Helen was "very vain."[46] But a 1954 entry in Nella's journal suggests that there may have been another explanation. Following a screening of Nancy Hamilton's documentary in January that year, Nella told Helen that her sister, Mildred, had commented about how nice she looked in the film. To this, Helen responded, "I want all the handicapped to look nice, so they won't repel people."[47] While Helen's activism and most of her ideas were quite progressive and forward-thinking, comments like this are a reminder that some of her questionable attitudes and language around disability were shaped by the stigma and entrenched beliefs of her time.

When she wasn't traveling, shopping, or attending eclectic dinner parties with her close social circle, Helen's greatest joy during these years was taking long walks along the sloping hillside to the woods at Arcan

Ridge or tending to her scented garden. She described the "odorous flood of roses and peonies"—her favorite flowers—and could often be found on her knees weeding for hours at a time. Ever since childhood in Alabama and later vacationing at Red Farm, she had regarded the outdoors as a refuge and credited her "friendship with nature" as the most important factor in maintaining her health. On these walks, she was usually accompanied by her Alsatian, Ettu, and her dachshund, Tinker—the latest of the array of dogs that were among her most treasured companions for much of her life, one of which she once described as her "brother that barks."[48] And yet she never employed a guide dog. During this era, it was still widely believed that such dogs were impractical or unsafe for somebody who was both deaf and blind, although deafblind people have used guide dogs since the 1980s when the first organizations started training canines to adapt to their unique needs.[49] She also kept more than fifty bird feeders on the grounds of Arcan Ridge and instructed her household staff to keep them filled with seed at all times. Although she couldn't see or hear the birds, cardinals would often venture onto the balcony and eat from her hands. Her delight in having them near invokes an observation by one of her companions, who once noted that Helen had "ten eyes, one on the tip of each finger."[50]

Meanwhile, in the three years since the tempest over Helen's World Council of Peace endorsement, she had steadfastly avoided public controversy while she finished the long-planned biography of Annie. Her plans to write the book had been dramatically interrupted by the fire that destroyed Arcan Ridge and most of Helen's cherished possessions in 1946. These included Annie's papers and the nearly finished manuscript that she had worked on for years as a tribute to her beloved teacher. Firefighters never ascertained how the blaze started, but the original manuscript was one of many valuable documents lost to history. After the house was rebuilt the following year, friends presented Helen with a new braille typewriter so she could start over. Helen had long complained that Nella's 1933 biography did not "present Teacher as I know her," and she vowed to "write something about her more to my liking."[51] The book was finally published in 1955 titled *Teacher: Anne Sullivan Macy, a Tribute by the Foster Child of her Mind*. Despite its awkward format—in which Helen refers to herself in the third person while she eulogizes Annie—the biography was mostly well received. Reviewing it in the *Kansas City Star*, Ruth Robinson wrote, "One lays the volume down with a sense of having been in contact for a brief while with a truly great soul—the soul of Helen Keller and Anne Sullivan. For the two were virtually one."[52]

During this period, Helen had lost none of her passion for politics. When Eisenhower finally turned against McCarthy after the Wisconsin senator attempted to smear Secretary of Defense George Marshall as a Communist, it marked the end for the demagogue as a political force— if not the end of the Red Scare that he had helped perpetuate. Nella reported that Helen was thrilled while following the televised Army-McCarthy hearings in 1954 that would bring him down. "Much jubilation because of the turn affairs have taken on the McCarthy question," she recorded in her journal.[53]

In the summer of 1955, Helen also closely followed coverage of the murder of Emmett Till—the fourteen-year-old Black Chicagoan who had been brutally killed while visiting family in rural Mississippi, allegedly for flirting with a white woman. When Till's body was recovered from the Tallahatchie River, it was so badly disfigured that he could only be identified by a ring bearing his initials. News of the murder set off a wave of revulsion throughout the country that is often credited with kick-starting the American civil rights movement. Helen had first read about the case in *Life* magazine, which ran photos of Till's funeral accompanied by a heartfelt editorial commenting on the failure of authorities to prosecute those responsible. Although Nella's efforts to rein in Helen's radical tendencies over the years may have been motivated by a desire to shield her reputation from the increasingly anti-Communist hysteria sweeping the nation, *Life* magazine was anything but a radical publication, so her response to the editorial comes off as disingenuous at best. In October 1955, Nella wrote Polly upon learning that the Till case had stirred Helen to action:

> The Emmett Till thing reached me only yesterday. I will talk with you about it by telephone. I see no reason why you and Helen should not contribute to the NAACP if you want to, but I would rather you would not do it merely on the strength of that overwrought editorial in *Life*. I followed the whole hideous and horrible story very closely in the *Times*. It is not as simple as *Life*'s editorial makes it out to be.[54]

When the press reported that Helen had contributed to the civil rights organization, it inspired at least one angry missive from an AFB contributor canceling his financial support for the Foundation and accusing Helen of contributing to a "devil-inspired" group that threatened to divide America "as nothing has ever done since the Civil War."[55]

Leslie Weary wrote, "Until I read some authoritative statement that you have disassociated yourself from the N.A.A.C.P., it would be better that you save postage and stationery wasted on me."[56]

That same year, a week after Helen's seventy-fifth birthday, she suddenly found herself in the middle of yet another tempest when she received a request to send a birthday greeting to an old friend, Elizabeth Gurley Flynn, who had been arrested in 1951 and convicted under the Smith Act with sixteen other Communists. She was accused of conspiring to "teach and advocate violent overthrow" of the government. Flynn, one of the leaders of the American Communist Party, was serving a two-year federal prison sentence in West Virginia when the request arrived from one of her comrades, Muriel Symington. "I felt very close to your life and work last fall when my dear friend Elizabeth Gurley Flynn granted me the privilege of typing her autobiography from the outset of her career to the tragic conclusion of the Sacco and Vanzetti case," Symington wrote Helen in July 1955. "During the chronicle of those crowded years—fruitful fighting on many fronts—your name and the names of many other distinguished Americans crop up many times. But none of them elicited from her pen greater affection and respect than she exhibited for you."[57]

Helen was all too glad to oblige her request and thought nothing of it until the Foundation was informed that Helen's birthday greeting had been reprinted in the *Daily Worker*, the Communist Party newspaper, blown up as a full-page featuring Helen's message:

> Loving birthday greetings, dear Elizabeth Flynn. May the sense of serving mankind bring strength and peace into your brave heart— Affectionately, Helen Keller.[58]

Within days, the most notorious anti-Communist publication in the nation, the *New Counterattack*, reprinted her greeting while encouraging its readers to write Helen and express their indignation. "The name of Helen Keller for millions of Americans has come to mean courage, triumph over adversity, and hope. The name also has a timely and special meaning for the Communist Party: It is being used as part of its propaganda."[59]

By now, the Foundation likely wasn't surprised by yet another crisis involving Helen's purported Communist sympathies and containing these periodic controversies must have seemed like a game of whack-a-mole. The AFB knew what had to be done when dozens of irate letters poured in from indignant funders and "patriots" demanding action be taken. It is unclear whether Robert Barnett enlisted Nella or whether Helen's longtime confidante took it upon herself to undertake damage control, but she soon fired off a letter to the only person she believed could talk sense into Helen. Her letter to Polly strongly suggests that Helen had been resisting the need for an apology, and once again Nella resorts to emotional manipulation to rein in Helen's political fire:

> No one who cares for Helen can fail to be gravely concerned in this crisis and Helen herself is wrong if she looks upon it with indifference.

For many years, she has been the willing and ardent world spokes-man for the blind, the deaf, the deaf-blind and other handicapped groups and whatever she does reflects upon them.[60]

She compared Helen's stature to that of "royalty" and argued that it carried the same type of responsibility. That is why she can't be allowed to make such "impulsive, unthinking statements." Communists "all over the world," Nella believed, would use the statement for propaganda pur-poses. "You both may have passport complications the next time you plan a trip, for whatever purpose," she told Polly. "Helen's film may be affected and her book, but the blind of the world are more important than she is and they are the ones that will suffer most."[61]

Whether or not Nella's letter was the impetus, Helen appeared to grasp the seriousness of the situation to a greater degree than she had after she endorsed the Stalinist World Council of Peace gathering three years earlier. A form letter in her name was promptly dispatched to each of the dozens of people who had responded to the *New Counterattack* plea. "This encounter with the communists has taught me, as I should have known before, how exceedingly alert and careful we must be at all times," she writes, claiming that she had first met Gurley Flynn decades earlier "among the advocates of miners and other unions who were struggling for fair living conditions." Flynn, she explained, was among the many figures with whom she discussed "tormenting questions" while she attempted to "understand labor problems, strikes, and the tangled history that surrounds them." Since that time, however, Helen claimed to have had no contact or correspondence with her except for a message of condolence she sent after the death of Flynn's son. "Since I joined the American Foundation for the Blind in 1924, I have been so absorbed in work for the exiles of the dark that I have had little time to devote to other activities," the letter concluded.[62]

It was a disingenuous response bordering on dishonesty. Gurley Flynn was more than the casual acquaintance that Helen implied here. She had, in fact, once been a close comrade in the IWW for whom Helen had personally pleaded with President Wilson in 1917 after Flynn and a number of other comrades were accused of sedition. In 1920, Helen and Flynn were founding members of the ACLU, served on the board together, and frequently appeared at the same gatherings, though there is little evidence that they had much contact in the years since. Still, as innocuous as the birthday greeting was, Helen was very much aware of Flynn's continuing ties to the Communist Party and the fact that she had recently been incarcerated for allegedly planning to "overthrow the United States government." And yet she could hardly have known that her private greeting to an old friend would become public.

Helen's continuous political vacillation around Communism through-out the 1950s has left a confusing trail for historians and biographers attempting to assess her evolving beliefs. Her repeated acquiescence in downplaying those beliefs—ostensibly to safeguard her efforts on behalf of the blind community—also raises a question that is difficult to answer. Could she have accomplished anything if she had stood firm in her con-victions and used her celebrity and influence to change the hearts and minds of her countless admirers about the social issues and disability politics that she held dear? Except for the period of her public Socialist Party crusades between 1912 and 1924, and her reemergence into radi-cal politics during the 1940s, most of her writing and speeches usually focused on "inspirational" platitudes that fed into an image for which she had long been a willing accomplice. "The infinite wonders of the universe are revealed to us in exact measure as we are capable of receiving them," she wrote in her twelfth and final book, a 1957 volume called *The Open Door*—a selection of writings that professed to set forth her "philosophy and faith."[63] With the exception of *Midstream* and *The Story of My Life*, "she didn't have too much to say in her books," observed her longtime Doubleday editor in chief, Ken McCormick.[64]

Whatever the reason, Helen had apparently long since decided that speaking her mind would do little good and might even jeopardize her disability advocacy efforts. Coincidentally or not, this attitude appears to date back to the period when she was first considering going to work for the American Foundation for the Blind. Just weeks before she signed on with the AFB in 1924, Helen wrote to the left-wing senator Robert La Follette explaining why she hadn't been in contact after he secured the Progressive Party presidential nomination that year even though her "heart rejoiced" at the news. She implied that she had decided against working on his campaign because she assumed the media would inevitably dismiss her beliefs about abolishing poverty and the links between capitalism and blindness—preferring her instead to talk about "superficial" charities that "make smooth the way of the prosperous." Those attitudes, she informed the senator, explain "my silence on subjects which are of vital interest to me."[65] Although she had occasionally broken that silence in the years since, we can assume she concluded that her celebrity could better be served by what she called "channels of satisfying sympathy and work" on behalf of the blind community. To that end, she was all too willing to give the public what she knew they wanted to hear while only occasionally letting her guard down to provide a window into the issues that remained of vital interest to her. It's difficult to assess whether the periodic political controversies involving her leftist affiliations during this decade were inadvertent. Or did they in fact reflect her frustration about the necessity of holding her tongue for the sake of expediency?

The backlash over the Gurley Flynn greeting marked the last time that Helen would be caught up in a public controversy, though privately she continued to hold strong political convictions. Nella's journal entry from December 1956 captures Helen's thoughts on the recent reelection of Eisenhower and Nixon. "She seethes at Nixon just as she did at McCarthy when he was at his height. She has to have some target for her accumulated resentments and I am inclined to think it may be a good idea for her to concentrate them against one person. Not that she can do them all this way, for she has too many. Her dislike of Eisenhower is only somewhat less than her dislike of Nixon, but she is more prudent about expressing it."[66]

If Helen had transformed into a "Cold War liberal" during the '50s, as Kim Nielsen supposed, it was not evident to Marvel Dobbs, who had gone to work in the AFB's Department of Education during this period. Dobbs often worked closely with Helen and later described her as a "sister socialist" during the period that they worked together. "She remained true to her socialist principles to the end. Of that I am sure," Dobbs recalled in 1977.[67] One of Helen's close friends, the literary critic Van Wyck Brooks, also claimed that she remained convinced of the "socialist point of view" throughout her life.[68]

Despite her steadfast efforts to avoid public controversy after the Gurley Flynn backlash, there is a trail of evidence suggesting that her political convictions still burned bright. Eric Boulter, former field director of the American Foundation for the Overseas Blind, recalled a discussion he witnessed around 1957 between Helen and AFB board member George Fitch about Taiwan, where the notorious right-wing dictator Chiang Kai-shek had ruled the breakaway island province since the establishment of Communist China in 1949. "Fitch argued that everybody should support Chiang Kai-shek on grounds that Chiang was a Christian and gave free rein to Christian activity," Boulter recalled. "I've never seen Helen so angry. She was almost rude as she told all she knew about Chiang and the [Taiwanese] Secret Police—you believe all that should be overlooked because he claims to be a Christian?"[69]

Although she was now savvy enough to keep her opinions about the Soviet Union to herself, the death of Stalin in 1953 appears to have rekindled her fascination with the country, though it's uncertain whether it had ever truly dimmed. This included a resolve to learn Russian, one of the foreign languages she had never mastered, and a determination to finally visit the country that she had idealized in her writings for years. She and Polly were scheduled to travel to Russia in the spring of 1957—a trip originally planned during a temporary thawing of the Cold War and "de-Stalinization" following the dictator's death. The US State Department had even granted approval of the itinerary, but the Soviet invasion of Hungary and the brutal suppression of that country's revolution in November 1956 put an end to those plans. "At first the State Department was enthusiastic. Now they say no," Nella recorded in her journal at the end of 1956 about Helen's planned Russia trip.[70]

Ever since her South African tour years earlier, she had never forgotten the experience nor forgiven herself for participating in racially segregated meetings. She was particularly upset by a letter she received during the 1951 trip by a white teacher representing a progressive South African teachers' union. "We have been eagerly looking forward to meeting you in person," wrote P. F. van Mekarh. "We regret to draw your attention to the fact that the arrangements planned by the authorities have proved offensive. They have decided to have, firstly, a white audience and afterwards a non-white audience. We regret that, despite the fact that this was apparently not done in consultation with yourself, we cannot support such a programme when discrimination on the grounds is shown."[71] Helen's response at the time revealed the depth of her feelings. "Your letter about the Teachers' League has filled me with indignant sorrow," she wrote van Mekarh upon her return to the States. "All my instincts cry out against every practice that segregates and in other ways lowers the dignity of human beings. At the same time, I am deeply moved by the faith of the Teachers' League in me which led them to conclude that I was not consulted with regard to my audiences."[72]

Five years after her tour, the situation in South Africa reached a boiling point when the apartheid authorities rounded up 156 activists, including Nelson Mandela along with the entire Executive of the African National Congress. The arrests followed a period of increasingly militant opposition to the apartheid system by a growing number of dissident factions,

Black and white.[73] Years later, the international movement against apartheid would become a liberal cause célèbre, but in 1956 the resistance was still very much considered a radical movement with direct and indirect ties to Communism. Mandela and the others, in fact, had been charged with high treason under the Suppression of Communism Act. Conviction could mean the death penalty.

In 1959, during the height of the trials, Helen received a request from a man named George M. Houser—executive secretary of the New York–based South Africa Defense Fund—who had seen a comment that Helen issued two years earlier printed in a South African newsletter, the *Treason Trial Bulletin*. "Freedom-loving, law-abiding men and women should unite throughout the world to uphold those who are denied their rights to advancement and education, and never cease until all lands are purged from the poison of racism and oppression," she had declared in 1957 when she first learned about the arrest of the dissidents.[74]

Now, Houser was asking Helen's permission to quote those sentiments in a bulletin to be published in the United States to raise money for the defense fund. Her initial support for Mandela and the other defendants, published in South Africa a year earlier, had escaped notice in America at the time. Given the Cold War controversies that had dogged her throughout the decade, one might have expected Helen to hesitate or ignore the appeal for the sake of pragmatism—fearful that any new association with a cause linked to Communism would taint her reputation or her work. Instead, she did not hesitate to lend her name to support the defense. "My sentiments have not changed, and from a full heart I give my consent to have those comments quoted," she wrote to Houser. "I hope earnestly that generous sums may be added to the Treason Trial Defense Fund. There can be no real safety for civilization until governments everywhere uphold the rights of all human beings to a life in accordance with their usefulness and dignity."[75]

If the 1950s had begun with a pragmatic repudiation of her radical political beliefs, the decade ended with a reemergence of the firebrand who placed social justice over political expediency. Although McCarthyism had lost some of its sting during the interval, the Cold War was still very much alive and, before long, would find the world on the brink of nuclear war in a terrifying standoff between two superpowers. If the changing political climate didn't account for Helen's renewed willingness to wade into controversial political terrain, it may have had a simpler explanation. The woman who had been so influential in putting the brakes on those beliefs for decades had ceased to be part of her world.

Part Four

REWRITING HISTORY

The Miracle Worker

The final chapter of Helen's life shines a light on the influence of a circle of personalities and factions that had moved to fill the enormous void created by Teacher's death two decades earlier.

The events that would shake her world can be traced to an innocuous encounter in 1956 when a young, unknown writer named William Gibson approached Nella Henney about a project he had been working on for some time. Little did she know that this fateful communication would soon herald the tragic end of the most significant relationship of her career, nor that the seeds of the events that would permanently redefine Helen's image would be planted with that meeting.

Gibson's wife, Margaret Brenman-Gibson, was a renowned psychoanalyst on staff at the Austen Riggs psychiatric facility in Massachusetts. While Margaret treated patients, he spent his days honing his theatrical skills by staging amateur dramatic productions featuring patients at the facility. His only previous published work had been an obscure novel, *The Cobweb*, set in an institution similar to Austen Riggs. Margaret would later describe him as the "non-earning poet in the family."[1]

William Gibson and his wife had long been fixtures in left-wing literary and political circles—initially inspired by their admiration for the playwright Clifford Odets, who Margaret described as their "cultural hero."[2] Odets's first play, *Waiting for Lefty*, had catapulted him into the literary pantheon in 1936 not long after he joined the American

Communist Party. Eventually, he would go on to a prominent career in Hollywood, where he avoided the blacklist by naming names before the House Un-American Activities Committee as a "friendly witness" in 1952.[3] Gibson had to be aware of Helen's long association with radical politics when he decided to write about her, but it was still the height of the Cold War, and any such controversial subject matter was likely considered beyond the pale for the project he had in mind. He surely knew that it would be safer to confine his literary endeavor to her childhood.

Most of the events that transpired around his relationship with Nella are sketchy and are largely drawn from the accounts in her journal. An entry from December 1956 describes her first meeting with Gibson, who had been directed to Nella by Doubleday editor in chief Ken McCormick:[4]

> From [Gibson's] disembodied voice over the telephone which seemed rather without character and from Ken's description of him as "a dedicated little man," I had formed an entirely wrong impression of him. He is young and vigorous, quite handsome, with heavy eyebrows and fine Intelligent eyes, fond of music, poetry, and people, dedicated only in the way that any sensitive man of high ideals is dedicated. Almost the first thing he said was "You can see that I am enamored of Annie Sullivan."[5]

The aspiring playwright informed her that he had first read *The Story of My Life* when he was in grammar school, but that his involvement in his current project, to be titled *The Miracle Worker*, began when a woman in Stockbridge told him she wanted to stage a "dance" about Helen Keller. Agreeing to write a script for her, he threw himself into reading the letters that Annie had sent to Michael Anagnos after she arrived in Alabama in 1887. The dance never materialized, but Annie had "stayed in his mind." After reading Nella's 1933 biography, *Anne Sullivan Macy*, he committed to the project, though he told her he knew it was "impertinent" to use such material and he was especially worried that Helen might object to the dialogue he attributed to Teacher. It was only after his script for a "TV spectacular" was accepted by CBS in 1956 that he approached Nella about the project.[6]

By the time *The Miracle Worker* came across her radar, Helen had long since stopped believing that show business might be a path out of her never-ending financial insecurity. *Deliverance* had been something of a fiasco and had failed to produce the riches that she had been promised by the producers when the project was conceived following the First World War. Similarly, Nancy Hamilton's Oscar-winning 1954 documentary was well received but had also failed to produce any significant income. So, it is hardly surprising that she paid little attention when Nella first informed her about Gibson's project.

When *The Miracle Worker* appeared on CBS *Playhouse 90* in February 1957, the production was a rousing critical success in no small part due to the stellar cast, which included twice-Oscar-nominated actor Teresa Wright playing Annie, and Burl Ives playing Captain Keller, while a fourteen-year-old newcomer named Patty McCormack took on the role of Helen. A press release issued by CBS before the broadcast announced that *The Miracle Worker* would portray Helen Keller "as the willful girl who, because of her deaf-blind affliction while an infant, cannot be reared except like a small animal."[7]

The original screenplay was somewhat crude but followed the familiar formula that would mark its future incarnations. The productions that followed would probably do more to forge most people's lasting impression about Helen than even *The Story of My Life*. The story focused on the brief period following Annie's arrival in Tuscumbia when Helen was six, culminating in the "miracle" at the water pump. Nella had been immediately taken by the quality of the script. "I became very excited about it," she wrote. "Here at last, I thought, is something of great literary merit and dramatic power."[8]

The television production was well received by almost every reviewer, but it was soon evident that not everybody shared their enthusiasm. In a letter to Ken McCormick, Nella suggested that Helen's companion had doubts about Gibson's script from the start. "Polly did not like *Miracle Worker*," she wrote. "For one thing I think any treatment of the early years of Teacher's life makes her uncomfortable and she cringed at some of the words put into Teacher's mouth."[9] Some of the words attributed to Annie were indeed cringe-worthy, such as when she says to Michael Anagnos, "Well, what should I say, I'm an ignorant, opinionated girl, and everything I am I owe to you."[10] Nella, however, appears to justify these transgressions as artistic license. "I had a few misgivings on this myself," she wrote McCormick, "but I felt that Teacher was crude when she first went to Alabama and that Mr. Gibson's deviations from the canon were justified for dramatic emphasis."[11]

Polly wasn't the only member of the household with reservations. Before the TV movie aired, a critic asked McCormick what Helen thought of the upcoming production. He revealed that the script had been transcribed into braille for her to read. "Her attitude was not exactly enthusiastic, but Miss Henney's was, and Miss Keller decided that was good enough for her."[12]

On the night the production aired, Nella recorded an entry in her journal that underscored the extent of her anxiety. "The responsibility was mine," she wrote, "for I had overridden H & P's objections and if it had turned into a disaster I hoped, as I told Nancy, that people would think of me as kindly as they could, that I would never be able to forgive myself."[13]

William Gibson ultimately reaped great success following the television special, realizing a lifelong dream when a script he had written—a comedy about a tempestuous affair between a lawyer and a fun-loving woman called *Two for the Seesaw*—was sold to Broadway. The play—starring Henry Fonda and a then unknown actress named Anne Bancroft—was a smash hit, eventually running for more than two years and later adapted into a popular Hollywood film. The success of *Seesaw* turned Gibson into the toast of the theater world, and also made Bancroft an overnight star, earning her a Tony Award for best actress.

Meanwhile, although Gibson had undoubtedly benefited from the critical success of his TV special, Helen received a total of only $500 from the project—designated to the AFB Fund for the Deafblind in her name. She likely assumed at this point that *The Miracle Worker* represented yet another show business venture about her life destined to soon be forgotten, which contributed to her more lackadaisical attitude toward its production. As Nella kept Helen apprised about Gibson's work, she also appeared to take every opportunity to put her own spin on the financial and artistic implications. In August 1958, she wrote Helen about an exciting new development: "Bill Gibson telephoned me the other day. His *Two for the Seesaw* was having a fabulous success, and he proposed to pour a large part of his profits into putting *The Miracle Worker* on the stage…Now that Helen is in the public domain and anyone who wants to can write about her or make a play about her, I feel that we are very fortunate to have Bill to depend upon."[14]

It is particularly noteworthy to watch Nella stress here that *The Story of My Life* had entered into the public domain, suggesting that Helen was not legally entitled to compensation for a dramatization about her life. Nella's words implied, then, that any monies received from the original TV production were being offered out of "goodwill" rather than out of legal obligation. It is unclear whether she had earlier informed Helen that Gibson's original TV movie script would also be based on her own biography of Annie, which was still under copyright, but the records show that Nella received nothing from the TV deal. In March 1957, in fact, she wrote Polly claiming that she would be "very unhappy" if anybody approached Gibson about the idea of paying her royalties.[15] It appears she didn't want to be seen profiting off the project while Helen received a mere pittance.

Over the years since Nella first arrived to work with Helen to help her update her memoirs back in 1923, the two had established an undeniable bond—perhaps facilitated in part because Nella had won the trust of Annie. After Teacher's death, Nella would emerge as one of Helen's most trusted confidantes and friends. And yet while each had long played an important role in the other's life, there are many indications that their relationship was decidedly uneven.

With the exception of her book *Anne Sullivan Macy*, Nella's own publishing career had been mostly undistinguished. For reasons unknown, she quietly left Doubleday in 1938 and shifted from Helen's editor to her "literary counsellor" and occasional agent. For decades afterward, she could frequently be found dining out on her relationship with her famous client, usually at the Harvard Club, where she often lunched with a number of prominent figures connected to Helen, including the celebrated actress Kit Cornell. The association lent her an undeniable cachet. "Nella was not a cozy person," recalled Ken McCormick, who worked with her at Doubleday and later served as editor in chief on a number of Helen's books. "She was a New England type. You would say of her, 'She wore the uniform and knew the drill.' "[16] Noting that she was married to Keith Henney, a scientist, McCormick disparagingly claimed that "he was the brain."[17]

Reviewing their voluminous correspondence and the content of Nella's private journals over the course of the friendship, a pattern emerges that suggests she could never entirely shed the ableist attitudes that prevented some people from appreciating Helen's extraordinary qualities. Like John Macy, in fact, Nella seemed to have the sense that Helen didn't measure up to Teacher. "As Annie Sullivan's biographer," observed Dorothy Herrmann, "she clearly felt that her subject was the more talented and intelligent of the two women and often underestimated Helen, citing what she perceived as her sentimental, pliant nature and penchant for radical or unpopular causes."[18]

Meanwhile, Nella's self-appointed role as Helen's protector was about to face its first serious challenge. In 1957, Polly had suffered a stroke that would cause the AFB to take a more active interest in Helen's affairs—many of which had been routinely handled by her companion for decades. For the most part, this involved the maintenance of Arcan Ridge and paying household bills. This increased involvement in her personal and financial interests continued even as the Foundation also distanced itself from Helen after her radical activities had focused unwanted attention on the AFB during the late 1940s. Any plans to rename the Foundation for Helen had long since been abandoned and it was only a few years earlier that its director, Robert Barnett, had told Nella that he wished Helen would "resign." Shortly after Helen returned from South Africa in 1951, a man named James Adams had been appointed by the AFB to fill a vacancy among the Helen Keller trustees—a group designated to administer her financial and household affairs.[19] It's never been clear how this paternalistic relationship came about, which saw her employer assume the role of guardian over her finances, but there's no record that Helen ever expressed any qualms about the arrangement.

Of all the trustees over the years, Adams—a partner in a prominent New York law firm—is one of the few who had appeared to stand up for Helen's interests, as illustrated by an anecdote later shared by Robert Barnett. "Look Barnett, AFB has been exploiting and gouging Helen Keller for years," Adams told him after his appointment. "It's tragic and you've got to do something about it." Barnett's candid response was revealing: "I intend to exploit her with her consent."[20]

The first signs of trouble surfaced in the spring of 1959 when actress Anne Bancroft appeared on the *Tonight Show* hosted by Jack Paar after *Two for the Seesaw* entered its second year, still drawing enormous audiences. When Bancroft was asked whether she had any other projects on the horizon, she revealed that she was slated to appear in a new Broadway production about Helen Keller and Annie Sullivan in the fall called *The Miracle Worker* and predicted that it would be an even bigger hit than *Seesaw*. According to Nella, it was Bancroft's prediction of financial success that first attracted the attention of James Adams, who had apparently been kept in the dark about plans to bring *The Miracle Worker* to

Broadway. "He realized that he knew little, claimed to know nothing, and came roaring into town, mad as a hornet," Nella recorded in her journal.[21] As Helen's trustee, he may have believed that he should have been informed of the negotiations months earlier, and suspected that Nella had deliberately kept the news from him and the Foundation.

Soon afterward, Adams wrote Nella a letter informing her the trustees had just learned that she had executed a contract for a Broadway production of *The Miracle Worker*. He asked for copies of any contracts along with the power of attorney that Helen had assigned her a decade earlier.[22] Polly was no longer in any condition to review proposals submitted to Helen, he explained, so they had "now assumed the duty of considering and advising upon any important steps taken in Helen Keller's behalf."[23] Nella appeared to recognize this request as a portent of things to come. She was especially suspicious of Adams's motive, as she confided in her journal after receiving his request. "This frightened me. Knowing what an irresponsible liar and egotist he is, I felt that there was nothing he would stop at to place himself in the driver's seat."[24] It's unclear why Nella was so distrustful of Adams—a well-respected lawyer and philanthropist who had always appeared to look out for Helen. "I am proud to think that a man with many far-reaching interests and responsibilities should consider it worth while to watch over my small affairs," Helen wrote him in 1951 when she learned of his appointment.[25] Nella herself had served for many years with Adams as one of Helen's trustees, but had recently been moved onto an advisory committee—a move that she would later characterize as "hanky panky" on the part of the AFB.[26]

The events that followed suggest she had every reason to be frightened. Although she would later claim that she had only used her power of attorney when Helen was in the hospital, the original contract executed between Helen and William Gibson reveals that the signature over Helen's name was not signed in her distinctive block letters, but rather by Nella acting as her power of attorney. This may have raised alarm bells with the trustees when they examined the contracts, yet there's no evidence of any impropriety on Nella's part. On the contrary, the surviving documentation suggests that she tried to do the right thing by her friend and client.

Her correspondence reveals that Nella was keeping Helen fully informed about negotiations around the Broadway production even if she demonstrated an unsophisticated business approach to those negotiations. For reasons unknown, Nella chose to negotiate directly with William Gibson rather than with the producers. She likely still believed—perhaps mistakenly, given the vagaries of entertainment law—that Helen wasn't legally entitled to royalties since *The Story of My Life* was in the public domain. It appears that she attempted to use her cordial relationship with William Gibson to secure a favorable deal for Helen.

As early as October 1958, Nella had written Helen informing her about plans to bring *The Miracle Worker* to Broadway and Gibson's ideas around compensation. "The more he thought about it, the more he felt that you and I ought to have a direct share in the proceeds, since it was based on your book and mine," she wrote. "TMW might bring in a great deal of money, especially if the play is afterwards made into a movie."[27] The result was a supplementary contract that assigned both Nella and Helen 20 percent of any proceeds derived by Gibson.

If a paper trail once existed to explain what happened next, it has been thoroughly excised from the AFB public archives. So, we can only surmise what might have prompted the series of dramatic developments that followed James Adams's request to examine the contracts relating to *The Miracle Worker* in the spring of 1959.[28]

Helen appears to have cut Nella out of her life completely months before the play premiered on Broadway—to enormous critical acclaim—in October 1959. By July of that year, Nella was already describing herself as a "leper" and a "beggar of favors." She kept up with developments in Helen's life from friends but was now cut off from any direct contact with her client.[29] At first, Nella believed that Polly had turned Helen against her. But at some point, she realized that she had in fact been targeted by the Foundation because of events related to *The Miracle Worker* and concluded that it was in fact the AFB, not Polly, that had likely poisoned Helen against her.

The final blow was struck in January 1960 when Helen sent Nella a cold note signed by witnesses:

> Dear Nella: Due to Polly's illness, I have decided that all of my business affairs should be handled by my personal trustees, James S. Adams, Richard H. Migel, and Jansen Noyes, Jr. I therefore desire to cancel the power of attorney granted by me to you in March 1948. I am deeply grateful to you for all you have done to help me with my books and articles.[30]

With the exception of a brief phone call later that year, they would never speak again.[31] Nella did everything she could to get back into Helen's good graces, including offering to fund a Polly Thomson room at the AFB after Helen's companion passed away in March 1960, but her efforts were in vain.

"When Helen dropped someone, she dropped him," observed her old friend Peter Salmon. "Deafblind have a way of dropping people. They have the idea that they are being exploited."[32]

The tempest over *The Miracle Worker* marked a tragic end to a friendship that had spanned almost forty years. Despite the various theories floated by Nella in her journal, why Helen chose to cut her out of her life is a mystery that endures today. Did the AFB turn her against Nella because they genuinely believed she had exploited Helen for her own gain? Or were they motivated by hopes of profiting from Helen's resurgent popularity due to *The Miracle Worker* and the enormous potential payday generated by a hit Broadway play and Hollywood movie? Given the subsequent money trail, and the absence of any genuine impropriety on Nella's part, this appears to most likely have been a factor.

As late as July 1958, Helen had drawn up a last will and testament bequeathing her entire literary estate and all royalties to Nella, though by this time *The Story of My Life* was the only one of her books that still generated any substantial sales and it had entered the public domain, so Helen's royalties were not especially valuable.[33] Only eighteen months later—with *The Miracle Worker* now destined to produce vast sums in future revenues—Helen drew up a new will leaving her entire literary estate to the American Foundation for the Blind.[34]

It is at this point that the mystery deepens. Even though she was now cut out of Helen's will and her life, Nella was still entitled to a 20 percent cut of the proceeds derived from William Gibson's share of *The Miracle Worker*.

And yet in July 1960, only four months after Helen drew up her new will, the Foundation sent Helen a startling letter revealing that there had been a dramatic shift. AFB trustee Jansen Noyes Jr. informed her that a contract had recently been drawn up authorizing a movie version of *The Miracle Worker*. Here, he assures Helen that Nella will not receive any of the income from the film.

"The share that would normally go to you, together with the share that would otherwise go to the Henneys will, under the contracts, go directly to the Foundation," Noyes wrote.[35]

On the same day, Nella confided to her journal that she had indeed agreed to assign the AFB her "direct return" from the movie, while still receiving a percentage from the initial sale of film rights—presumably a much smaller sum, considering the fact that the film would go on to gross millions of dollars at the box office.[36] It is unclear why she agreed to forfeit her substantial share of the lucrative Hollywood production, but a notation in her journal suggests that she wasn't happy about the new arrangement. "I think nearly everyone connected with [Helen] wants something: prestige, glory, money," she lamented. "The AFB wants both."[37]

In all likelihood, Nella had signed the agreement under threat of legal action. She was almost certainly unaware that Helen herself had been persuaded to assign her own share of the film directly to the Foundation even while she was still alive. At the very least, it raises the question of who was exploiting whom.[38]

Despite some of her questionable actions and attitudes over the years, it is difficult to accept that Nella deserved this ignominious fate. There is no question that she cared deeply about Helen and she was genuinely flummoxed at the suggestion that she was acting in anything but her friend's best interests.

Even after they were estranged, however, Nella could not seem to shed the long-held paternalistic attitude that continued to imagine Helen as a victim in need of protection rather than as the strong, capable woman that she obviously was. This attitude surfaced once again in a journal entry after she learned of Polly's death in March 1960, written months after Nella had been cut out of Helen's life for good. Condescending to the end, she wrote, "Who will rehearse her speeches with her and stand beside her on the platform as interpreter? Who to watch her letters to make sure that she is not tricked into support of communism or some other ism?"[39]

After Nella died in 1973, her husband, Keith Henney, claimed that the falling-out with Helen had taken a terrible toll and contributed to her "going downhill."[40]

⠗⠬⠏ ⠯⠓⠄
⠝⠢⠏⠄ ⠐⠱⠄

While the saga over *The Miracle Worker* was unfolding, an important new figure took center stage in Helen's life. After Polly's stroke in 1957, a nurse named Winifred Corbally was hired to step in. When Polly eventually returned from the hospital, it was increasingly evident that her health was too frail for her to carry on the grueling schedule that had seen her and Helen gallivanting around the globe throughout the first half of the decade. Helen's trip to Scandinavia on behalf of the

American Foundation for the Overseas Blind in May 1957 would be her last international tour. With the exception of some minor ailments of age, Helen was as strong as ever, but Polly's health could not stand the rigors of another trip. As a result, most of Helen's days were now spent at Arcan Ridge, where Corbally was kept on as Helen's companion. Having mastered the manual alphabet, she also took on many of Polly's former duties.

"Those were the fun years," Winnie later recalled. "It was the time of her life that she could have fun. Miss Helen was a rogue. They don't talk about that side of her life much. She was a rascal...We had oodles of fun." Among Helen's favorite adventures, she recalled, was an outing to a local hot dog stand. "Polly Thomson would turn in her grave. She would never allow hot dogs in the house, but [Helen] loved it. She'd say, 'Don't forget the mustard.'"[41]

Although Winnie was mostly tight-lipped about her time with Helen, she revealed that Polly was resentful of her presence. "Polly was a very angry woman when I knew her," she told Joseph Lash in an unpublished interview. "She was afraid, afraid that she might be separated from Miss H...[Polly] became very defensive when anyone came who she felt might encroach upon her right to Miss H."[42]

Those closest to Helen had long worried about what would happen when Polly died, but Helen was adamant that she had no desire to move to Alabama to live with her sister, Mildred, and Mildred's husband, Warren Tyson. She had long ago escaped the South and had no wish to return. "There is a great deal of Southern formality in the circles around the Tysons," she politely explained to Winnie shortly before Polly died.[43]

Even as she peacefully lived out her final years, she paid keen attention to world events and lost none of her passion for justice. She was horrified in March 1960 to learn about the Sharpeville Massacre in South Africa, where police fired into a crowd of peaceful demonstrators, gathered to protest the country's racist pass laws, killing or wounding more than 250 protesters. "With tense interest I read of all the events that are now occurring in South Africa," she wrote to Lail Gillies at the South African National Council for the Blind shortly after the massacre. "My heart overflows with sorrow over the ignorance and political incapacity of many of the negroes, but I pray with you that a juster and more liberal government may ultimately be established and teach all the people the essentials of freedom and genuine civilisation."[44]

On her eightieth birthday in June 1960, telegrams arrived from all over the world wishing her a happy birthday. Evelyn Seide, who had been appointed by the AFB as Helen's secretary in 1953, was tasked with reading the greetings to Helen as they poured in, but not all the messages were well received. Among the cables was one from Vice President Richard Nixon, whom Helen had always loathed for his part in the McCarthy witch hunts. Seide recalled that Helen jerked her hand away as soon as she realized who had sent the cable.[45] Although there's no evidence that Helen voted for Nixon's opponent in the 1960 presidential election that November, she happily accepted an invitation to visit the White House in March 1961, two months after the youthful new president was inaugurated. "Give Caroline a kiss for me," she told JFK, the thirteenth president she had met since first visiting Grover Cleveland at the White House when she was seven. It was destined to be her last ever public appearance.

In October that year, Helen suffered her first stroke. A month later, her doctor, Forris B. Chick, broke the news to Evelyn Seide:

> It is my opinion that Miss Keller has reached a stage in her life where she will have to completely retire from public appearances and from here on will have to be cared for with round-the-clock nursing service... We all realize what a great service she has done in the past and now I believe it is time that she be retired. Her condition is static and I cannot offer much hope for further improvement.[46]

A week later, James Adams came to see Helen at Arcan Ridge and reported that "from time to time she seems to feel that she is living back in the period with Teacher and John Macy, but other than this I thought her mind seemed quite clear and normal, although certainly slower than usual."[47]

Helen would live nearly seven years following her retirement, but we know little about her life during this period other than fragments gleaned from the occasional visitor, which suggested that she experienced gradually worsening dementia following her stroke.[48] As a result, there is no record of her thoughts about the many tumultuous events of the 1960s— a decade when America was transforming beyond recognition just outside her door. Given the years that she once spent crusading against the folly of World War I, it is easy to imagine that, had she been healthy, Helen would have thrown herself into the forefront of the battle against another unjust war when America took up arms in Vietnam. Likewise, there is no way of knowing whether she was even aware of the 1965 Selma to Montgomery marches in her home state of Alabama.

Helen died peacefully on the morning of June 1, 1968—less than two months after Martin Luther King Jr. was gunned down by an assassin's bullet. The followers of both towering figures, whose legacies were forged in Alabama, may have been surprised at how much they had in common. Dr. King's widow, Coretta Scott King—still grieving herself—almost certainly knew about Helen's lifelong advocacy against racial discrimination when she took the time to cable her condolences to Helen's loved ones. "My entire family and I send sympathy knowing how you will miss her companionship. We know too how the beauty and power of Helen Keller's spirit will live on to ennoble us all," she wrote.[49] The feeling, however, was unfortunately not necessarily reciprocated among members of Helen's own family. In recent years, her younger brother, Phillips Brooks Keller, had taken it upon himself to share his feelings about the civil rights movement each time he wrote to Winnie Corbally enquiring about his sister's health. Phillips evidently believed he had found a sympathetic ear in Winnie, whose political leanings were very different from those of the two companions who had come before her. In December 1964, she had shared with Phillips her opinion that America was sitting on a "keg of dynamite" and that the country will have very serious problems unless "this integration thing is ironed out."

Referring to J. Edgar Hoover's recent declaration that Dr. King was America's "most notorious liar," she added, "Mr. FBI Hoover surely did tell M.L. King what he thought of him and is not backing down one bit. The best thing this old U.S. can do is make mighty sure they hang on to the FBI and Hoover."[50]

Four months later, shortly after King's Selma-to-Montgomery marches inspired President Lyndon Johnson to introduce voting rights legislation, Phillips wrote to Winnie complaining that King and LBJ had "set back race relations 50 years."[51] Ignoring the fact that King's followers had remained peaceful while the police responded with violence and brutality, he described the marchers as "criminals, perverts, and every sort of bum imaginable."[52] A few months later, he wrote Winnie again suggesting that Dr. King and his followers should be sent "back to Africa for life."[53]

Days after King was gunned down in Memphis, Winnie received another letter from Phillips demonstrating that his hostility toward the civil rights leader had not lessened in the face of tragedy. "I sure will be glad when this Martin Luther King palava is over with," he wrote. "The man not only got himself killed but caused the lives of many others over the country to be lost as well as untold millions of dollars of damages for robbing, looting, stealing and what have you."[54]

Despite the fact that Phillips had never been particularly close with his sister, who had already left Tuscumbia with Annie before he was born, he appears to have designated himself as the family's liaison with the AFB in making arrangements for Helen's funeral long before she died even though Helen was always closer to her sister, Mildred.[55] The correspondence between Phillips and Robert Barnett demonstrates that even in death, her wishes and her lifelong legacy would take a back seat to the image those around her chose to mold. Helen's long-stated desire for a Swedenborgian funeral service in Westport, Connecticut, had quietly been shelved by the AFB after Phillips expressed his objections. Instead, they chose a lavish ceremony at Washington's National Cathedral where her ashes would be interred alongside Annie's. "We never went for the Swedenborgian stuff at all and it was hanging regretfully over our heads," Phillips wrote James Adams in October 1967 when he learned that the AFB had acceded to his request for a Presbyterian service.[56]

Phillips had also arranged to have a former classmate, Alabama senator Lister Hill, deliver the eulogy. It is difficult to believe that Helen would have approved the choice of Lister—one of the most prominent of the Southern Dixiecrats and a longtime opponent of desegregation. Predictably, the senator's sentimental tribute made no mention of Helen's commitment to racial justice nor the myriad other progressive causes she had fought for. Instead, he outlined a long list of her accomplishments from the miracle at the water pump to her mastery of multiple languages and her status as a "citizen of the world" who had worked tirelessly as a "symbol of her own courage and faith to the benefit of millions of her fellow handicapped in America and around the world."[57]

In the end, Helen's request for a Swedenborgian service wasn't her only wish that was ignored. The list of names Helen had drawn up a few years prior to act as "honorary pallbearers" at her funeral had been quietly shelved by Helen's trustees while she was incapacitated. The inclusion of honorary pallbearers was a tradition Helen fondly remembered from Annie's own memorial service a quarter century earlier, and as previously noted, among the names on her list were two prominent friends with disabilities—Peter Salmon, head of the Industrial School for the Blind; and Robert Smithdas, the first deafblind person to receive a graduate degree, with whom Helen had grown closer after Polly's stroke.[58] The inclusion of Smithdas would have undoubtedly delivered a powerful statement to the watching world. And yet neither man ended up being included in the service (although the Perkins School choir, featuring a number of deafblind singers, performed for the assembly of mourners).

In a letter to Nella explaining the decision in October 1966, when Helen's death appeared imminent, Robert Barnett incorrectly claimed that Helen herself had decided against honorary pallbearers at the time of Polly's death, suggesting that it grew out of "the feeling that choosing among so many possible ones would be too difficult a task."[59] In actuality, Helen had forwarded the list with her choices to the Foundation in July 1961, more than a year *after* Polly's death.[60]

On their way to the National Cathedral on the morning of Helen's funeral, more than one mourner took note of the encampments scattered around the nation's capital—an array of three thousand wooden tents erected under the banner of "Resurrection City."[61] Six months earlier, Martin Luther King Jr. had announced his plan to launch a Poor People's Campaign, which he declared would involve "a trek to the nation's capital by suffering and outraged citizens." Dr. King's goals had gradually evolved over the years from his initial call for desegregation and civil rights to a moral crusade against poverty and unemployment. "The curse of poverty has no justification in our age," he wrote in 1967. "It is as socially cruel and blind as the practice of cannibalism at the dawn of civilization."[62] His words echoed Helen's own sentiments, voiced more than a half century before King composed that statement, a powerful symbol of the philosophical alignment of their parallel crusades. In a memorable 1912 speech at the dawn of her own public campaigns against war, racism, and social injustice—billed as the "blindness of society to its problems"—she declared, "Poverty is abominable, unnecessary, a disgrace to our civilization, or rather a denial that we are civilized."[63]

Dr. King never made it to Washington, but the fruition of his final crusade was well underway on the morning when Helen was laid to rest in June 1968, with thousands of his followers camped nearby to carry on his mission. Now, as the mourners inside the cathedral participated in a service that ignored both her wishes and her legacy, there is no doubt that the spirit of Helen Keller was very much outside with the protesters of Resurrection City.

Chapter Twenty-Four

Helen and Teacher

Myriad books were written about Helen over the course of her lifetime—mostly clichéd accounts of her childhood centered around the miracle at the water pump or heartwarming children's books about the bond between Helen and her teacher. With the exception of her 1929 memoir, *Midstream*, few books written before her death focused on Helen's adult life and accomplishments. In 1956, the literary critic Van Wyck Brooks published a volume called *Helen Keller: Sketch for a Portrait*—a breezy reminiscence of his friendship with Helen that endeavored to provide a somewhat more complete picture than the superficial efforts that had come before.[1] Three years later, Peter Salmon contributed to a somewhat pedestrian biography, *The Helen Keller Story*, that briefly discussed her socialist politics and highlighted her foreign travels—concluding with a chapter instructing the reader, "How to Behave with a Deaf, a Blind, or a Deafblind Person."[2] But even a decade after her death, nobody had ever attempted a thorough biography about one of the twentieth century's most celebrated figures.

This would finally change as the centenary of her birth approached. Radcliffe president Martina Horner had recently read a biography of her hero, Eleanor Roosevelt, and concluded that its author, Joseph Lash, would be the ideal candidate to take on a major book about the university's most famous alumna, Helen Keller, for a series it was sponsoring about notable women. When Horner approached him about the project in 1977, Lash was at first reluctant to take it on, as he was busy working on a companion volume to his 1976 book about the wartime partnership between Franklin Roosevelt and Winston Churchill. He began to reconsider, he claimed, after his wife told him it was an "honor" for a women's college to approach a man to write a biography of a woman. He resolved to undertake the project only if he could be convinced that her papers, held at the American Foundation for the Blind, would provide a "fresh portrait." When he examined those papers, he concluded that the prospect of writing about Helen was "irresistible."[3] At the same time, he decided that no biography of Helen would be complete if it didn't also include a portrait of the woman whose life was so intricately connected to hers, and so the book became a dual biography, appropriately titled *Helen and Teacher*.[4]

When the book was released three years later, it seemed a revelation—providing a well-rounded portrait that soared far beyond the hagiography that had emerged over the years. The voluminous biography, spanning nearly nine hundred pages, drew on thousands of previously unexamined letters, journals, and obscure archival documents as well as interviews with surviving members of Helen's inner circle and AFB officials. The book was especially notable for being the first to challenge the narrative around the role of Annie Sullivan—presenting her as a flawed but undeniably important figure in Helen's life. Indeed, Lash was notably the first chronicler to reveal that Annie had lied to cover up her role in the "Frost King" plagiarism incident and that she had also played a role in sabotaging Helen's doomed romance with Peter Fagan.

But for many, the most surprising element of the biography was Lash's lengthy exploration of Helen's radical politics before she went to work for the AFB. Only readers old enough to remember this chapter of her life would have had any idea that Helen had once been a militant socialist extolling the merits of revolution. Other than a compendium of Helen's socialist writings and speeches published by a small Marxist press a year before her death, this chapter of her life had been almost thoroughly whitewashed by the time Lash's biography appeared. The revelation was enough to prompt an article in the *Birmingham News* noting reactions of "horror and dismay" about the news of her radical past, accompanied by complaints from surviving family members in fiercely conservative Alabama. "My reaction is one of horror," Helen's niece Patty Johnson told the paper at the time. "I just hate for people to write things like that. It really is unjust." She probably didn't realize the "consequences" of being a socialist or a Communist, Johnson claimed. "It just wasn't in her nature to be disloyal to America."[5]

As it turned out, Joseph Lash was well qualified to write about Helen's socialist politics. After graduating from City College in 1931 and earning a master's degree from Columbia, he was appointed an officer of the Student League for International Democracy, a socialist youth organization. From 1936 to 1939, he served as executive secretary of the American Student Union, a coalition of left-wing youth groups. When he died in 1987, his *New York Times* obituary discussed this chapter of his past: "Caught up in the political ferment of the 1930's, Mr. Lash recalled that he then considered himself 'a full-time revolutionary,' dedicated to fighting Fascism and achieving the goals of international Socialism."[6]

Given this background, his sympathetic portrayal of Helen's Socialist Party years and early radical politics is not altogether surprising. But it is also his own political history that provides a clue to his decidedly unsympathetic and inaccurate description of Helen's continuing left-wing affiliations during the second half of her life. When the Soviet Union entered into the Nonaggression Pact with Hitler in 1939, Lash later recalled, it brought a "crushing end" to his youthful idealism and his "growing affinity for the Communist Party."[7] As someone who had dedicated years to warning of the dangers of Nazism, he was stunned to discover that he was now required to follow the new party line and refrain from any criticism of Hitler. Unlike the majority of his former comrades and Helen Keller herself, he appeared to immediately recognize the apparent hypocrisy of this stand.

As one of a minority of party followers who quit the movement after the Hitler-Stalin Pact,[8] Lash would have been uniquely placed to recognize that Helen's initial stand against American intervention in the European war and subsequent flip-flop after the invasion of the Soviet Union indicated that she had come under the orbit of the Communist Party as a Fellow Traveler. Instead, he chooses to disingenuously echo the description used by the *New York Times*, which concluded at the time that she was merely a "convinced pacifist." Subsequent chroniclers less familiar with the murky political currents of the period simply took Lash's cue and accepted as gospel this misleading characterization of her initial opposition to US intervention.

Following his disillusionment with left-wing politics, Lash would eventually go on to found the anti-Communist organization Americans for Democratic Action with Eleanor Roosevelt, whom he had first met on a train in 1939. He would become Eleanor's lifelong friend, biographer, and confidant. Before his death, a series of declassified FBI files revealed that he may have also been her lover, though he always denied the relationship.[9]

Lash's rightward turn may explain the condescending tone he takes in explaining Helen's leadership in the 1940 anti-fascist mission to rescue Loyalist refugees who had fought Franco during the Spanish Civil War. In *Helen and Teacher*, he writes that she had been "duped by the Communists in the Spanish refugee ship affair."[10] His descriptions of the various political controversies that dogged Helen during the McCarthy era largely continue along this same theme, though he does acknowledge that she retained some of her "radical" beliefs well into the 1940s.

Still, all biographers bring their own biases when writing about their subjects and these lapses don't necessarily mar what is still considered by many to be the definitive Helen Keller biography. On the surface, Lash possessed the bona fides to write about Helen, and his book was generally well received when it was released.

Four decades after *Helen and Teacher* was first published, however, new information has surfaced that casts doubt about Lash's motivations and raises concern about how his book has influenced Helen's continuing legacy.

⠗⠲⠄⠃ ⠴⠓⠄
⠗⠄⠃⠄ ⠐⠊⠄

In the acknowledgments section of the 1980 edition, Lash writes that the American Foundation for the Blind, the repository for Helen Keller's papers, "offered me its co-operation without any restrictions on what I could write."[11] As it turns out, there was considerably more to the relationship that Lash failed to acknowledge.

His primary contact at the AFB was a woman named Marguerite Levine, the AFB's chief archivist, who he describes in his acknowledgment as a "cultivated Frenchwoman." Born in France, Levine had come to work at the AFB in 1960 after seven years spent working in records management at the March of Dimes. Although she worked with Helen for less than a year, she would later reveal the awe that she felt in her presence, describing Helen as a "secular saint, almost a religion to herself."[12] A notation she left on a newspaper clipping about Helen's seventy-fifth birthday party in 1955 suggests how fiercely protective Levine was of preserving that saintly image. In the article, the reporter writes about an exchange she witnessed at the party between Helen and Polly after Helen asked for a beer. When Polly told her "Not yet," Helen snuck one anyway. "Helen does like beer," Polly said, laughing. Presumably finding this an unseemly portrait when she came across it in the archives, Levine added a personal notation to the clipping, which she scrawled in pencil: "Horrible."[13]

In an exit interview that she conducted upon her retirement from the AFB in 1985, Levine noted that the Foundation had "contracted" with Joseph Lash to write a biography of Helen Keller. Appearing to realize her slipup, she quickly corrects herself and states that the Foundation had "made available the Helen Keller collection" to Lash.[14] Her slip of the tongue led to a search of the archives to determine what she may have been concealing. Those files include a trove of documentation revealing that the Foundation had in fact signed a contract with Lash—an arrangement that neither he nor the AFB ever formally acknowledged when the book was released.

It wasn't the first time that the AFB had contracted a writer to tell its story. To commemorate its fiftieth anniversary in 1971, the Foundation commissioned a woman named Frances Koestler to chronicle the history of the AFB, which was published under the title *The Unseen Minority*. The book—billed as a "social history of blindness in the United States" but focusing primarily on the history of the Foundation—discussed at length Helen's work with the AFB. The author was granted unrestricted access to many people who had known her for decades. Although Koestler always claimed that she had "complete freedom" and that her book was never censored, the Foundation's former director Robert Barnett would later confess that he had been forced to intervene to prevent Koestler from turning the book into an "exposé" of Helen.[15] Nevertheless, the Foundation did at least acknowledge their formal arrangement with Koestler when the book was published in 1976.

From the time that Lash signed on with the AFB, the pace of his research and writing was astonishing and could have only been accomplished with the assistance of Levine, who had applied for a $10,000 grant to build an office so that Lash could work with her in close collaboration. The original contract is missing from the archives, so we don't know the exact terms of his agreement, or whether he also had a financial arrangement with Radcliffe, but there is enough available documentation to piece together the key provisions, including evidence that the contract called for the Foundation to receive 25 percent of any TV or movie rights derived from the book.[16] It also gave him exclusive access to the contents of the Helen Keller Archives, as William Gibson discovered when he was denied permission to use the archives while he was researching his follow-up to *The Miracle Worker* in 1981—a

Broadway play called *Monday after the Miracle*. And while the AFB did publicly acknowledge Lash's "exclusive access" to the archives, few knew the true extent of this arrangement. A full year after the publication of *Helen and Teacher*, Lash himself personally wrote to Gibson explaining that he was reluctantly barring him from accessing the Keller papers. "Unfortunately, we are in the midst of negotiations for the television and movie rights to *HELEN AND TEACHER*," Lash wrote. "I do not wish to cheapen these rights and risk legal challenges on the basis that I gave permission to another writer to go through the Helen Keller materials."[17]

Although it's uncertain whether the original agreement gave the AFB the right to make changes to his manuscript, there is evidence that Lash was sending regular updates to Patricia Smith, director of the AFB information department. Moreover, he was also sending her his chapters to "critique" as the book progressed, despite the fact that Helen had frequently found herself at odds with her longtime employer. Why, then, was Lash giving the Foundation the opportunity to shape the narrative?[18]

In light of this apparent conflict of interest, it is worth delving into Lash's papers to determine what he may have deliberately left out of his biography. The FDR Presidential Library in Hyde Park, New York, houses the unpublished transcripts of interviews Lash conducted in 1977 and 1978 with a number of friends and associates close to Helen. Most notably, Lash spoke at length with former AFB director Robert Barnett, who provided valuable candid insights about his years at the helm of the American Foundation for the Blind. Among the most surprising revelations, he confided to Lash the unusual financial arrangement that he discovered upon replacing Bob Irwin as director in 1949. Barnett revealed that Helen's compensation had previously been handled in the books by a "revolving door entry" that saw the Foundation covering all the significant maintenance and upkeep expenses for both Helen's car and her home in Easton, Connecticut. "None of this ever showed up on (Helen's) IRS tax return," Barnett confessed. Needless to say, Barnett's revelation is found nowhere in Lash's book, nor anything else that reflected poorly on the AFB.

He also interviewed Nancy Hamilton, director of the Oscar-winning 1954 documentary about Helen's life, *The Unconquered*. Among the many memories Hamilton shares with the biographer is an important anecdote about her friend's evolving political beliefs. She reveals that when she once found Helen reading a book about a female Russian revolutionary, Helen told her that "the Communism of Russia was the Communism of Christ."[19] This revelation from one of Helen's closest friends is certainly significant in establishing her complex attitudes toward Communism during the latter part of her life as well as establishing a convincing link between her radical political philosophy and her religious beliefs. Yet, Lash omits the quote from his book—perhaps because it contradicts his thesis that she had been "duped" by the Communists and had long since abandoned her Communist sympathies by the 1950s when she was close with Hamilton.

The most striking theme that emerges during these interviews is the question of Helen's sexuality—a subject that Lash returns to again and again as he probes Helen's former friends and associates. During the course of his research, in fact, two of his interview subjects expressed their belief that Helen and Annie may have had a sexual relationship. One of these interviewees, Frances Koestler, had never actually met Helen, but had been given significant access to her friends and associates while writing her own book about the history of the AFB a few years earlier. The other was Ken McCormick, editor in chief at Doubleday, who had known Helen for more than thirty years and also expressed his belief that she and Annie were romantically or sexually involved.

Others interviewed, however, firmly denied any such insinuation. "Heavens no," protested Helen's last companion, Winnie Corbally, when Lash broached the subject. Robert Barnett told him he thought Helen was "sexless" while Eric Boulter caged his opinion. "Were they lesbians?" Lash asked him in November 1978. "I am prepared to believe it was just a very close friendship," Boulter responded. Neither of the interview subjects who raised questions about Helen's sexuality presented any credible evidence. Moreover, Lash himself wrote movingly about Helen's thwarted relationship with Peter Fagan, so it's certainly possible that he chose not to write about these rumors because he had dismissed them as baseless gossip. But he did address the subject in a letter he wrote to AFB public information director Patricia Smith while his book was in progress, making it clear that he had been sharing his suspicions all along about a subject that would have almost certainly been controversial within the conservative corridors of the AFB. "My own working hypothesis is that whatever lesbian tendencies Helen had were sublimated in good works," he assured Smith in 1978.[20]

It's not the only potentially dicey issue that he raised with Smith. In the same letter, he shares his suspicion that both Helen and Annie may have been "fudging" the facts about the chronology of Helen's conversion to socialism—another detail that he failed to share with his readers. Considering how thoroughly he documented almost every other aspect of her life, it is also notable that he fails to include a word about Helen's flirtation with eugenics and her intervention in the Bollinger baby case. Although his book certainly presents Annie as a flawed figure, Lash repeatedly goes out of his way to dismiss or ignore anything that might have tainted *Helen's* image. Would a biography that revealed Helen was a longtime Communist sympathizer have commanded a substantial film contract in 1980, a decade before glasnost finally helped extinguish the Cold War for good? In the end, Lash would sell the rights to 20th Century Fox, which produced a network TV movie called *The Miracle Continues* in 1984.[21]

Considering that Lash's book is still believed by many to be the definitive Helen Keller biography, it is worth at least considering how much his undisclosed arrangement with the AFB and his own political biases may have clouded the treatment of his subject.

For nearly two decades, *Helen and Teacher* remained the only notable Keller biography until 1998, when Dorothy Herrmann published *Helen Keller: A Life*. Though highly readable and less dense than Lash's encyclopedic treatment, Herrmann's book offered few new revelations and borrowed liberally from Lash's biography while offering a somewhat dubious psychosexual analysis of Annie's relationship with the men in her and Helen's lives.

In more recent years, an academic named Kim Nielsen has filled an important void in the scholarship around both Helen and Annie Sullivan. A professor of women's studies and disability history at the University of Toledo, Nielsen published a short academic analysis of Helen's political activities in 2004 titled *The Radical Lives of Helen Keller*. The book covered much of the same political ground as Lash, although it was the first book about Helen Keller to explore her involvement in the Bollinger baby case and her brief, controversial embrace of eugenics. As the first researcher to ever access the State Department materials around Helen's foreign travels in the 1950s, Nielsen also provides important new information about her international work during the last decade of her public career and the State Department's attempt to exploit her image for propaganda purposes. At the same time, however, she comes to the questionable conclusion that by this period, Helen had transformed into a "Cold War liberal" in the service of American interests abroad. This ignores compelling evidence from friends and associates demonstrating that Helen had, in fact, maintained her socialist beliefs until the end while reluctantly and disingenuously disassociating herself from radical politics during the McCarthy era as a result of pressure from Nella Henney and the AFB. Still, Nielsen is a credible and objective observer without the political biases that mar some of Lash's own dubious assertions.

The most notable aspect of her analysis is her withering critique of Helen's attitudes around disability. "For most of her life, the disability politics she adopted were frequently conservative, consistently patronizing, and occasionally repugnant," Nielsen writes, arguing that Helen considered people with disabilities "inherently damaged."[22] In many ways, this reflects the sentiment of a segment of the present-day academic establishment and even elements of the wider disability community where opinions on Helen and her legacy remain very much divided. Considering that Nielsen is one of the few academics familiar with Helen's wide-ranging political beliefs, it is somewhat surprising that she doesn't offer a more balanced perspective on those politics. By today's standards, Helen's attitudes—especially her language around disability—come off as undeniably patronizing. Her brief flirtation with eugenics before the First World War is still a stain on her legacy even if she did eventually reverse herself and later helped alert the world to the monstrous eugenic policies of the Nazi regime. None of these aspects of her life should be glossed over or ignored as Joseph Lash chose to do when he purported to present the first warts-and-all portrait.

That said, Nielsen fails to acknowledge that in many ways, Helen's disability politics were also decades ahead of their time and might be considered progressive in any era. She was the first prominent disability activist to masterfully call out the media for its ableist coverage. Time and again, she used a combination of sarcasm and scorn to put her critics in their place. In addition, she explicitly linked the roots of disability to capitalism and offered a far-reaching analysis tying disability politics to race, gender, and class—a critique that was often conspicuously absent even in the curriculum of disability studies programs early on. For decades, she extolled the importance of economic empowerment and self-determination for people with disabilities and traveled the world calling for the eradication of systemic poverty that she claimed led to blindness. She also repeatedly called out her own employer when she sensed that the AFB's philanthropic efforts were geared toward the affluent rather than the most vulnerable. Similarly, while some of Helen's language and attitudes around her own disability came off as questionable—often allowing herself to be presented as a superwoman—she made it clear that she was very conscious of and often frustrated by her "limitations," but that she hesitated to complain because she understood that her privilege meant that she was far better off than many other people with disabilities. "No one knows—no one can know—the bitter denials of limitation better than I do," she wrote in 1957. "I am not deceived about my situation. It is not true that I am not sad or rebellious; but long ago I determined not to complain."[23]

Even as Nielsen and other academics have turned a more critical lens on Helen in recent years, Annie Sullivan has largely escaped the "savior" reckoning that has become common in deflating narratives around heroic figures who "rescue" members of marginalized groups. In 2009, Nielsen published the second major biography of Annie, titled *Beyond the Miracle Worker*, that provides a considerably more nuanced portrait than Nella Braddy Henney's 1933 effort or Helen's 1955 tribute. The book is especially notable for its acknowledgment of the impact of Annie's own visual impairment on her life and its startling conclusion that Annie's struggle with chronic illness and depression was "far more debilitating than Helen's deafblindness."[24] And yet, Nielsen mostly spares Annie from some of the withering criticism that she had previously leveled against her famous pupil while leaving the narrative around Annie's outsize role in Helen's education mostly intact.

In the absence of a truly balanced perspective of her legacy, then, it is hardly a surprise that Helen Keller has been transformed in recent years from a once-admired icon in the disability community to a divisive figure whose life and work, some believe, are best forgotten.

Epilogue

In December 2020, with the world mired in a deadly pandemic and Donald Trump recently defeated in a presidential election, Helen Keller became embroiled in a political controversy for the first time in decades. The catalyst was an interview given to *Time* magazine by an African American disability rights advocate named Anita Cameron, who reflected on Helen's legacy as an activist. "Helen Keller is not radical at all," Cameron told the newsweekly. "Just another, despite disabilities, privileged white person, and yet another example of history telling the story of privileged white Americans."[1]

The backlash was immediate, led by Republican senator Ted Cruz, who tweeted, "This is INSANE. Woke Lefties are now attacking Helen Keller? There are many adjectives one can use to describe the extraordinary Helen Keller. 'Privileged' is not one of them."[2]

Donald Trump Jr. took time out from his attempt at overturning the recent election to express his own outrage, tweeting, "Holy shit… they're now canceling Helen Keller for being white. You can't make this crap up anymore. You can never be woke enough."[3]

Not long before America witnessed the unlikely spectacle of the country's most notorious right-wing senator unwittingly defending a radical socialist, a video went viral on the social media platform TikTok, claiming that Helen Keller was a "fraud who didn't exist." Its creator argued that no deafblind person could possibly have written books, flown an airplane, or accomplished all the things attributed to her. The thread also served to revive a disturbing trend that had first emerged during the

1960s—a series of deeply offensive Helen Keller jokes that once circulated widely in junior high schoolyards mocking her disabilities.

It's hard not to conclude that these incidents are all rooted in the same phenomenon—the tendency to reduce the story of Helen Keller to the cliché of a six-year-old girl and a miraculous teacher. In the absence of an acknowledgment of her extraordinary adult life, such trivial ephemera serve to fill the void.

Anita Cameron's scornful dismissal underscores the fact that even within the disability community, many people have understandably come to question the inflated role that Helen has assumed in representing the image of people with disabilities. Much of this reckoning tends to center around a word that has been used to describe her almost from the moment that news circulated of the so-called miracle at the water pump—the description of Helen and her life as an "inspiration."

For many disability activists, Helen Keller's mainstream image has come to embody the epitome of a phenomenon known as "inspiration porn"—a term coined by the late disability advocate Stella Young in a 2014 TedX Talk to describe the practice of objectifying people with disabilities to make nondisabled people feel uplifted. "They are there so that you can look at them and think that things aren't so bad for you, to put your worries into perspective," she declared.[4]

In 2021, after a Hollywood studio announced it was planning a new biopic based on Helen's Radcliffe years, a deafblind advocate named Cristina Hartmann shared her feelings about the shadow that Helen has cast over people like herself. "I did well enough at school but was no prodigy," she wrote in an essay for the Disability Visibility Project. "She was in a different league intellectually yet had little control over her life and faced persistent skepticism about her abilities. Instead of feeling inspired, I was terrified. Our society had reduced this brilliant and complicated woman into an inspirational parable and jokes. If America could trivialize someone like Keller, what would become of me?" Hartmann believes that it's time for Hollywood and popular culture to stop idealizing Helen's life. "It is time to give her a rest. Not because anything is wrong with her—she was a remarkable woman who touched many lives—but she has been in the public eye for over a century. She has yet to get a break from the scrutiny, even decades after her death." Instead of idealizing Helen, she argues, it is time to turn attention on figures who have never been recognized. "What we all need are extraordinary stories about ordinary deafblind people falling in love, picking fights, tangling with midlife crises, and having torrid affairs with traveling photojournalists. We are not so different, so neither should our stories be. With these stories, children like me can imagine a future outside of Helen Keller's shadow."[5]

It is a sentiment shared by an increasing segment of the disability community, including those like Anita Cameron who believe focusing on Helen to the exclusion of others extols stories of privilege. More recently, there has even been a call to remove her name from the Helen Keller National Center for DeafBlind Youths and Adults—one of a number of organizations working to further her legacy. "We need to do this in order to challenge and overthrow the dominant ableist, racist tradition that anointed Helen Keller in the first place," argued Marc Safman, a board member of the American Association of the DeafBlind, in 2022.[6]

Despite this rising chorus of criticism, not everybody believes it's time to simply cast Helen and her legacy aside. More than a century after Helen received her diploma from Radcliffe, a woman named Haben Girma became the first deafblind person to earn a Harvard Law degree. After the publication of her 2019 memoir, *Haben: The Deafblind Woman Who Conquered Harvard Law*, Girma was widely acclaimed as "a millennial Helen Keller." It is a description reminiscent of the designation bestowed on a variety of accomplished deafblind people over the years just as Helen was once called the "second Laura Bridgman." For figures such as Robert Smithdas, the comparison was meant to signify someone who had accomplished great things *despite* their disability. But for Haben Girma, the comparison has taken on a very different meaning.

In many ways, she has carried on Helen's legacy as a passionate political crusader—a history that many have preferred to ignore in favor of a saccharine narrative that bears little resemblance to the reality of her message.

Born in Oakland to an Ethiopian father and an Eritrean mother, Girma lost her sight and hearing in early childhood. Since graduating from law school in 2013, she has become a high-profile advocate—working to increase access to technology for people with disabilities and using her considerable platform to spotlight a wide variety of social issues. She has consistently battled ableist attitudes while speaking out against racism and police violence, and is a longtime advocate for refugee rights. In 2013, President Barack Obama designated her as a "Champion of Change."

In her years as an advocate, Girma has frequently acknowledged the importance of Helen Keller within the realm of disability history. But unlike many who came before, she also understands Helen as more than a symbol. Nor does she necessarily believe, like some of her contemporaries, that Helen's image serves only as a hindrance. When the state of Texas moved to strike Helen Keller from the school curriculum in 2018, Girma wrote a powerful op-ed arguing that students need to learn about Helen's life. "Deleting Keller from the curriculum," she wrote, "can mean deleting disability from the curriculum. Of course, relying on a single story to represent the disability community is itself a problem. The disability community is diverse, full of rich stories of talented people improving their communities."[7] In fact, Girma has also used the continued fascination with Helen Keller to highlight the accomplishments of an array of deafblind people and to amplify underrepresented voices. Among these are Geraldine Lawhorn—the first African American deafblind person to earn a college degree—who had an accomplished career as a performer and teacher; and Conchita Hernandez, a blind Latina activist who analyzes disability through an anti-oppression perspective.

Girma has also gone out of her way to draw attention to Helen's long-ignored political crusades. She frequently uses her enormous social media following to highlight often-overlooked aspects of her life. "She was a white woman who recognized white privilege and worked to help end all the racism that exists in this country," she declared in a video on the 140th anniversary of Helen's birth in 2020. "If Helen Keller was alive today, I am confident that she would support Black Lives Matter."[8] Despite this recognition, however, she is also troubled by the nature of the recent resurgence of popular culture interest. "If Helen Keller were alive today, she would lecture filmmakers for failing to raise their gaze from that one Alabama water pump," she stated after the announcement of the Hollywood biopic. Girma herself withdrew from participating in a 2021 PBS documentary, *Becoming Helen Keller*, because of what she believed were troubling issues with its narrative.[9]

To its credit, the American Foundation for the Blind recently enlisted Girma as an "Ambassador," despite her often outspoken and controversial political convictions—the same kind of convictions that the Foundation once suppressed when they convinced Helen to downplay her own deep-seated political beliefs to avoid hurting their fundraising efforts all those years ago. The AFB has also recently developed a number of comprehensive lesson plans that acknowledge some of Helen's progressive political analysis, especially around gender, class, and race. Notwithstanding the efforts of a small handful of advocates like Girma, however, much of the Helen Keller establishment—which includes dozens of schools and organizations named after her around the world—have chosen to downplay her history as a militant activist while occasionally offering generic platitudes about her support of "social causes."

How would Helen react to the modern-day portrayal of her life and legacy or the criticism leveled against her in recent years? "I like frank debate and I do not object to harsh criticism so long as I am treated like a human being with a mind of her own," she once wrote.[10] In fact, she would almost certainly be more comfortable with the well-meaning criticism directed at her life's work than with those who dishonestly twist her legacy to serve their own agenda. One can easily imagine how she would have responded to the news that she had been defended by Ted Cruz—a politician who arguably stands for everything that she opposed in her lifetime. She may have even applied the same epithet—"dung-beetle"— to Cruz that she once leveled at Westbrook Pegler after he attacked her radical politics in his column.

Helen herself had mixed feelings at the idea of being presented as a symbol of overcoming adversity or discussing disability issues without acknowledging the deeper social context of class and privilege. There is little doubt that she would be elated at the efforts of a new generation of progressive disability activists—including her critics—who are building on her legacy, learning from her mistakes, and paving new paths in a field that was once considered hers alone.

And while others take up that mantle, perhaps history will one day recall the image of a flawed but feisty woman who enjoyed a beer and a ribald joke, instead of the secular saint frozen in time as a six-year-old girl at the water pump.

Acknowledgments

This book would not have been possible without my own team of miracle workers. First, thanks to my amazing editor, Haley Weaver, at Grand Central, for believing in the book all the way through and for her guidance and patience in helping bring it to fruition and for unscrambling my words and ideas. Thanks to Rachael Kelly at Grand Central for helping bring it over the finish line with a fresh perspective and valuable improvements; and to Deborah Wiseman for a superb and meticulous copyedit; and Luria Rittenberg, Hachette's ever-creative production editor. Thanks also to my agents, John Pearce and Chris Casuccio at Westwood Creative Artists, for once again giving me the kick in the pants to emerge from complacency and plow full steam ahead into yet another book project. I am deeply grateful for the loving support of my partner, Morag York, and son, Dashiell. I owe so much to my late aunt Ruth, the first blind person I ever knew, who taught me early on that society is not always eager to accommodate people with disabilities or to treat them with dignity.

It seems impossible that I managed to finish this book in the midst of a worldwide pandemic. It would not have been possible without the extraordinary efforts of the dedicated librarians and archivists who went above and beyond the call of duty to dig up obscure documents for me at a time when I couldn't travel and do the digging myself. Like a generation of Helen Keller researchers, I owe a huge debt to Helen Selsdon. As the former archivist at the American Foundation for the Blind, she was also instrumental in nudging the once conservative AFB to acknowledge and incorporate the progressive legacy of Helen Keller in their lesson plans and advocacy efforts. Her successor, Justin Gardner, had enormous shoes to fill when he took over the collection for the American Printing House for the Blind, and I am truly grateful to Justin for going the extra mile time and time again even as he was simultaneously navigating his daunting new position and sorting through boxes uncovering hidden nuggets. Enormous thanks also to Jennifer Arnott, Jennifer Hale, and Susanna Coit at the Perkins School Archives for their valuable assistance during a time when Perkins was closed to the general public and I was forced to stumble through the maze of archival materials from a distance. Thanks also to Chris Belena at the FDR Presidential Library for scanning a trove of valuable materials at a time when the library and archives were still closed to the public. And finally, special thanks to Lee Freeman, local historian at the Florence Lauderdale Public Library, for helping me sort out the Keller family's antebellum and postbellum history, along with crucial nineteenth-century census data, and for helping me track down the real identity of the girl whom Helen Keller mistakenly referred to as "Martha Washington" in her memoir.

Thanks to the intrepid Mark Twain scholars Matt Seybold, Kevin MacDonnell, and Brent Colley, who helped direct me to resources around Helen's relationship with Mark Twain and to sort out the provenance of the best-known Twain quotes—real and apocryphal—about his friend.

I am deeply indebted to the deafblind educator and activist Paul Richard McGann—my first ever deafblind friend—for his advice and input throughout my research and for his candid revelations about his mentor and "second father," Robert Smithdas. Rich also helped me navigate the modern-day deafblind community and made invaluable introductions.

It was a great privilege to speak to Ela Gandhi and Arun Gandhi, who both shared their memories of Helen Keller's 1951 tour of South Africa and of their grandfather Mohandas Gandhi.

In the forty years that I have known MIT Professor Noam Chomsky,

I have never had the opportunity until now to discuss the subject for which he is best known, linguistics. When I finally had occasion to pose a question related to his specialty, I was thrilled to discover that he was familiar with the contentious issue of Annie Sullivan's role in Helen Keller's acquisition of language and generously offered his expert take around a question that will likely never be satisfactorily settled.

In my long career as a writer, I have accessed dozens of archives on five continents and witnessed the slow and costly transition from analog to digital that has been indispensable to historians. But I am truly flabbergasted by the extraordinary efforts of Laurie Block and her team in compiling the archive and exhibits of the Disability History Museum—one of the most valuable resources on the planet for learning about the history of disability and the historical experience of people with disabilities and their communities.

I am truly grateful to Elizabeth Emerson, who so generously shared with me family materials about her great-great-grandfather Joseph Edgar Chamberlin and his long friendship with Helen Keller. Likewise, deep thanks to Hilary Nelson Jacobs—granddaughter of Helen Keller's close friends Stuart and Sandra Grummon—who shared her family archives and connected me with a cousin who spent time with Helen and Polly.

As the world finally began to open up, I was privileged to spend time with Helen Keller's great-grandniece, Keller Johnson-Thompson, who generously spent part of Christmas Eve 2021, along with her sons, Johnson and Griffin, sharing family stories and filling in some of the gaps about Helen's relationship with Peter Fagan and other family lore passed on by her grandmother Katherine Tyson.

Thanks to Dashiell York for his pivotal political research. Thanks also to Candida Hadley for reading the manuscript and offering valuable suggestions and input. Any ableist language or attitudes in the book are mine alone.

Thanks also to Jeremiah Wall, Emma Wallace, Geoffrey York, Katie Booth, Ellen Meister, Marion Meade, M. Leona Godin, Noam

Chomsky, Ela Gandhi, Arun Gandhi, Frank Vito Mondelli, Susan Crutchfield, Laura Rocchio, Dr. Sanja Gulati, Sue Ruzenski, John Fox, Prof. Harvey Klehr, Prof. Jason Roberts, Prof. Andrew Hartman, Dave Swift, Prof. Nicholas Cox, Frieda Wishinsky, Steve Simon, Willa Marcus, Paul Schroeder, Mike Hudson, Sarah Latha-Elliott, Joe Jacobs, Helen Armstrong, Margaret van Nooten, Gizmo, Blue and Poly, Jacquie Charlton, Tony Rapoport, Ethan Nelson, Teresa Simon, Steve Simon, Seema and Richard Marcus, Maxine Hermolin, Ian Halperin, Hope Wallace, Myles Lipton, Sue Pilkington, Antonio Michael Downing, David Nanasi, Barbara Davidson, Haben Girma, Edwin Black, Joyce MacPhee, Chris Fitzgerald, Eric Scott, Alysa Touati, Shaheen Touati, Chris Dempniak, Lynn Lubitz, Ian York, Lee Charlton Sunol, Charna Gord, Diana Ballon, Elinor Mahoney, Robert Fleming, Hope Wallace, Megan Hutton, Ester Reiter, Eva Belikova, Judy Bailey, Pam and Alan Marjerrison, Mari Drexler, Lisa Ross, Julien Feldman, Shalini Roy, Anneke van Nooten, Jamel Touati, Peter Asswad, Jennifer Feinberg, Evan Beloff, Esther Delisle, Todd Shapiro, Paula David, Barb Linds, Hannah Blazer, Robin Vogl, Marilyn Tate, Adam Chaleff-Freudenthaler, Harriet and Andy Lyons, and the United Jewish People's Order.

Primary Sources

AAS—American Antiquarian Society

AFB—American Foundation for the Blind Archives

APH—American Printing House for the Blind

AVA—American Vaudeville Museum Archive, University of Arizona Special Collections

CFA—Chamberlin Family Archives courtesy of Elizabeth Emerson

CHS—Connecticut Historical Society

CPUSA—Communist Party of the USA and Workers Party of America Archive via Marxists Internet Archive

DHM—Disability History Museum virtual archive

FDRL—Franklin Delano Roosevelt Presidential Library, Hyde Park, New York
   Joseph Lash Papers
   Eleanor Roosevelt Papers

FLPL—Florence Lauderdale Public Library

GFA—Grummon Family Archives courtesy Hilary Nelson Jacobs

GUA—Gallaudet University Archives

HFM—Henry Ford Museum, Greenfield Village Archives, Dearborn, Michigan

HKA—Helen Keller Archives, American Foundation for the Blind

HKS—Helen Keller Services

HL—Houghton Library, Harvard University

HW—Henry Wallace Papers

IDL—Iowa Digital Library
   Henry Wallace Papers

IWW—Historical Archive, Industrial Workers of the World

JWA—Jewish Women's Archive

LOC—Library of Congress
   Alexander Graham Bell Family Papers
   Jo Davidson Papers
   Theodore Roosevelt Papers
   Henry Wallace Papers
   Woodrow Wilson Papers

MHS—Massachusetts Historical Society

MIA—Marxists Internet Archive
NARA—National Archives and Research Administration, Washington, DC
NBH—Nella Braddy Henney
NBHC—Nella Braddy Henney Collection, held at the Perkins School for the Blind
    Archives via the Internet Archive
NH—Nancy Hamilton Papers, Smith College
PSB—Perkins School for the Blind Archives
SP—Mark Twain Stormfield Project (1908–2012)
THM—Mark Twain House and Museum, Hartford, Connecticut
TIA—Tuskegee Institute Archives
USHMM—United States Holocaust Memorial Museum Archives
WHS—Wisconsin Historical Society
    John Reed Papers
WLA—Wagner Labor Archives, New York University
WWPL—Woodrow Wilson Presidential Library

FBI Files

Lucille Ball
Earl Browder
Albert Einstein
Will Geer
Elizabeth Gurley Flynn
Helen Keller
Joseph Lash
Jean Muir
Dorothy Parker
Harold Urey

Author Interviews

Joanna Brunso
Allison Burrows, Helen Keller National Center for DeafBlind Youths and Adults
Professor Noam Chomsky, MIT
Brent Colley, Stormfield Project
Professor Nicholas Cox, Houston Community College System
Professor Susan Crutchfield, University of Wisconsin
Elizabeth Emerson
Professor Susan Fillippeli, Auburn University
John Fox, FBI
Lee Freeman, Local historian, Florence-Lauderdale Public Library
Arun Gandhi, M.K. Gandhi Institute for Nonviolence
Ela Gandhi, Gandhi Development Trust
Professor Alan Gribben, Auburn University
Dr. Sanjay Gulati, Harvard Medical School
Professor Andrew Hartman, Illinois State University
Professor John E. Haynes, Library of Congress
Mallory Howard, Mark Twain House and Museum
Hilary Nelson Jacobs
Keller Johnson-Thompson, great-grandniece of Helen Keller
Professor Harvey Klehr, Emory University
Haley Linville, American Foundation for the Blind
Paul Richard McGann, Western Pennsylvania Association of the Deafblind
Keith McGregor, Leader Dogs for the Blind
Frank Mondelli, UC Davis
Sue Pilkington, Helen Keller Birthplace Museum
Professor Jason Roberts, Quincy College
Laura Rocchio, Helen Keller National Center for DeafBlind Youths and Adults
Sue Ruzenski, Helen Keller National Center for DeafBlind Youths and Adults
Professor Matthew Seybold, Center for Mark Twain Studies
Roz Usiskin, United Jewish People's Order

Notes

Chapter One: Before the Miracle

1. Elisabeth Gitter, *The Imprisoned Guest* (New York: Farrar, Straus and Giroux, 2001), p. 13.
2. Ibid., p. 15.
3. Samuel Gridley Howe, *The Letters and Journals of Samuel Gridley Howe*, vol. 1 (Boston: D. Estes, 1906), pp. 54, 209.
4. Gitter, *Imprisoned Guest*, p. 23.
5. Perri Meldon, "Disability History: Early and Shifting Attitudes of Treatment," Telling All Americans' Stories, US National Park Service, 2017.
6. Mary Klages, *Woeful Afflictions: Disability and Sentimentality in Victorian America* (Philadelphia: University of Pennsylvania Press, 1999).
7. "Address of the Trustees of the New England Institution for the Education of the Blind to the Public," 1833, DHM.
8. Ernest Freeberg, *The Education of Laura Bridgman* (Cambridge: Harvard University Press, 2001), p. 11.
9. Ibid., p. 12.
10. Ibid., p. 15.
11. Ibid.
12. Ibid., p. 11.
13. Maud Howe and Florence Howe Hall, *Laura Bridgman: Dr. Howe's Famous Pupil and What He Taught Her* (Boston: Little, Brown, 1903), p. 11.
14. "Perkins' Milestones," PSB.
15. Samuel G. Howe, *Ninth Annual Report of the Trustees of the Perkins Institution and Massachusetts Asylum for the Blind* (Boston: John H. Eastburn, 1841), appendix A, pp. 34–35, PSB.
16. Ibid.
17. Clifford Olstrom, *Undaunted by Blindness*, 2nd ed. (Perkins School for the Blind, 2012), eBookit.com.
18. Lydia Sigourney, "The Deaf, Dumb and Blind Girl," *Juvenile Miscellany* 4, no. 2 (May 1828), pp. 127–41.
19. Samuel Gridley Howe to Lydia Sigourney, Sept. 3, 1841, Hoadley Collection, CHS.

20. Jan Seymour Ford, "Laura Dewey Bridgman: 1829–1889; Laura's Early Life," Dec. 2002, PSB.

21. S. G. Howe, *An Account of Laura Bridgman, of Boston, Massachusetts: A Blind, Deaf and Dumb Girl, with Brief Notices of Three Other Blind Mutes in the Same Institution* (London: John Wright, 1843), p. 6.

22. Ibid., p. 6.

23. Howe and Hall, *Laura Bridgman*, p. 50.

24. Howe, *Account of Laura Bridgman*, p. 8.

25. Freeberg, *Education of Laura Bridgman*, pp. 37–38.

26. Howe, *Account of Laura Bridgman*, p. 10.

27. Gitter, *Imprisoned Guest*, p. 87.

28. Ibid., pp. 13–14.

29. Ibid., p. 11.

30. Ibid., p. 3.

31. Samuel G. Howe, *Sixth Annual Report of the Trustees of the New-England Institution for the Education of the Blind, to the Corporation* (Boston: Henry Lewis, 1838), pp. 9–12, PSB.

32. Freeberg, *Education of Laura Bridgman*, p. 9.

33. Howe and Hall, *Laura Bridgman*, p. 269.

34. Mary Swift Lamson, *Life and Education of Laura Bridgman, the Deaf, Dumb and Blind Girl* (London: Trubner, 1878), pp. 46–47.

35. Ibid.

36. Gitter, *Imprisoned Guest*, p. 36.

37. Lamson, *Life and Education of Laura Bridgman*, pp. 322–23.

38. Freeberg, *Education of Laura Bridgman*, p. 56.

39. Rosemary Mahoney, *For the Benefit of Those Who See: Dispatches from the World of the Blind* (New York: Little, Brown, 2014), p. 127.

40. "When Charles Dickens Fell Out with America," BBC News, Feb. 14, 2012.

41. Charles Dickens, *American Notes for General Circulation* (New York: Appleton, 1868), p. 41.

Chapter Two: Teacher

1. Nella Braddy Henney, *Anne Sullivan Macy: The Story behind Helen Keller* (New York: Doubleday, Doran, 1933), p. 15. This book is hereafter cited as *ASM*.

2. "Anne Sullivan," PSB website.

3. Henney, *ASM*, p.15.

4. Ibid., p. 6.

5. Ibid., p. 7.

6. Annie Sullivan Notes, PSB.

7. Henney, *ASM*, p. 14.

8. Ibid., p. 15.

9. Ibid.

10. Ralph Waldo Emerson, "Man the Reformer," in *The Portable Emerson*, ed. Mark Van Doren (New York: Viking, 1946), p. 70.

11. Ibid., p. 77.

12. Michael B. Katz, *In the Shadow of the Poorhouse: A Social History of Welfare in America* (New York: Basic Books, 1986), p. 61.

13. David Wagner, *The Poorhouse: America's Forgotten Institution* (Lanham, MD: Rowman and Littlefield, 2005), p. 41.

14. David Wagner, "Poor Relief and the Almshouse," VCU Social History Project.

15. Henney, *ASM*, p. 19.

16. "Anne Sullivan's Admission to Tewksbury State Almshouse," DHM.

17. Henney, *ASM*, p. 20.

18. Ibid., p. 22.

19. "Anne's Formative Years (1866–1886); The Death of Her Brother Jimmie," AFB website.

20. Ibid.

21. Kim E. Nielsen, *Beyond the Miracle Worker: The Remarkable Life of Anne Sullivan Macy and Her Extraordinary Friendship with Helen Keller* (Boston: Beacon Press, 2009), p. 29. This book is hereafter cited as *BTMW*.

22. Henney, *ASM*, p. 32.

23. Ibid., p. 31.

24. Ibid., p. 38.

25. Henney, *ASM*, pp. 51–54.

26. "Revolting Revelations," *St. Louis Post Democrat*, Mar. 23, 1876, p. 2.

27. Henney, *ASM*, p. 59.

28. "Speech given by Frank B. Sanborn at a memorial service for Michael Anagnos entitled 'Successors to Success,'" Oct. 24, 1906, HKA.

29. Henney, *ASM*, pp. 61–62.

30. Gitter, *Imprisoned Guest*, p. 277.

31. Ibid., p. 174.

32. Henney, *ASM*, p. 75.

33. Ibid.

34. Ibid., p. 67.

35. The second operation took place in 1882. "Anne's Education," AFB website.

36. "Valedictory speech given by Anne Sullivan at the Perkins Institution's commencement ceremony," 1886, HKA.

Chapter Three: "The Second Laura Bridgman"

1. *56th Annual Report of the Perkins Institution and the Massachusetts School for the Blind for the Year Ending September 30, 1887*, pp. 74–75, PSB.

2. Ibid.

3. Ibid.

4. Ibid.

5. Joseph P. Lash, *Helen and Teacher: The Story of Helen Keller and Anne Sullivan Macy* (New York: Delacorte, 1980), p. 56. This book is hereafter cited as *HAT*.

6. In *The Story of My Life* (New York: Doubleday, Page, 1903; this book is hereafter cited as *SOML*), Helen writes that she accompanied her father to an appointment with a Baltimore

oculist, Dr. Julian Chisholm, who told them he could do nothing to "cure" her condition but advised they consult Bell. This is the account that has been repeated by most chroniclers. Yet the initial correspondence between Arthur Keller and Michael Anagnos suggests that Arthur was on his way to consult a Baltimore oculist, presumably Chisholm, long after they had visited Bell. Helen may have mixed up the chronology in her account.

7. Brian H. Greenwald, "Alexander Graham Bell and His Role in Oral Education," DHM.

8. M. Yeager to Helen Keller, June 25, 1965, HKA.

9. Keller, *SOML*, p. 9.

10. Ibid., p. 19.

11. Ibid.

12. Michael Anagnos to Arthur Keller, Aug. 16, 1886, PSB.

13. *56th Annual Report of the Perkins Institution and the Massachusetts School for the Blind for the Year Ending September 30, 1887*, PSB.

14. Michael Anagnos to Annie Sullivan, Aug. 26, 1886, PSB.

15. *56th Annual Report of the Perkins Institution and the Massachusetts School for the Blind for the Year Ending September 30, 1887*, PSB.

16. Michael Anagnos to Arthur Keller, Jan. 21, 1887, PSB.

17. Carroll Davidson Wright, "Prices by Wages and Decade—1880–1889," in *The Working Girls of Boston* (Boston: Massachusetts Bureau of Statistics of Labor, 1889).

18. Keller, *SOML*, p. 4.

19. Henney, *ASM*, p. 101.

20. Arthur Keller to Michael Anagnos, Jan. 28, 1887, PSB.

21. Annie Sullivan to Michael Anagnos, Mar. 4, 1888, HKA.

22. Keller, *SOML*, p. 22.

23. Annie Sullivan to Michael Anagnos, Mar. 13, 1887, PSB.

24. Annie Sullivan to Sophia Hopkins, Mar. 4, 1888, HKA. In the AFB's Helen Keller Archives, the recipient of this letter is incorrectly described as Michael Anagnos.

25. "Helen Keller," *American Annals of the Deaf*, vol. 33, p. 108.

26. Annie Sullivan to Michael Anagnos, Mar. 13, 1887, PSB.

27. Michael Anagnos, *Helen Keller: A Second Laura Bridgman*, reprinted from the *56th Annual Report of the Perkins Institution and the Massachusetts School for the Blind for the Year Ending September 30, 1887*, PSB.

28. Keller, *SOML*, Annie Sullivan to Sophia C. Hopkins, Mar. 11, 1887, p. 308.

29. Henney, *ASM*, p. 130.

30. Keller, *SOML*, Annie Sullivan to Sophia C. Hopkins, Mar. 11, 1887, p. 309.

31. Ibid.

32. Ibid., Annie Sullivan to Sophia C. Hopkins, Mar. 20, 1887, pp. 311–12.

33. Dorothy Herrmann, *Helen Keller: A Life* (New York: Alfred A. Knopf, 1998), p. 44.

34. Keller, *SOML*, Annie Sullivan to Sophia C. Hopkins, Mar. 11, 1887, pp. 264–65.

35. Helen Keller, *Teacher: Anne Sullivan Macy* (New York: Doubleday, 1955), p. 49.

36. Ibid., p. 49.

37. Adam Politzer, *A Text-Book of the Diseases of the Ear and Adjacent Organs* (London: Henry C. Leah's Son, 1833), p. 238.

38. Keller, *Teacher*, p. 68.

39. Manuscript by Anne Sullivan Macy titled "Foolish Remarks of a Foolish Woman," HKA.

40. Keller, *SOML*, Annie Sullivan to Sophia C. Hopkins, Apr. 5, 1887, pp. 315–16.

41. Henney, *ASM*, p. 126.

42. Keller, *SOML*, p. 25.

43. Ibid., p. 25.

Chapter Four: *"A Bold Plagiarism"*

1. *56th Annual Report of the Perkins Institution and the Massachusetts School for the Blind for the Year Ending September 30, 1887*, p. 83, PSB.

2. Keller, *SOML*, Annie Sullivan to Sophia C. Hopkins, June 2, 1887, pp. 264–65.

3. Keller, *SOML*, p. 37.

4. Ibid., p. 43.

5. "A Deaf Mute's Evolution," *New York Sun*, July 11, 1887, p. 3.

6. Lash, *HAT*, p. 97.

7. Keller, *SOML*, Helen Keller to Alexander Graham Bell, Nov. 1887, p. 148.

8. Ibid., Annie Sullivan to Sophia C. Hopkins, Apr. 10, 1887, p. 299.

9. Ibid.

10. "A Deaf Mute's Evolution," *New York Sun*, July 11, 1887.

11. *56th Annual Report of the Perkins Institution and the Massachusetts School for the Blind for the Year Ending September 30, 1887*, p. 96, PSB.

12. Keller, *SOML*, Annie Sullivan to Sophia C. Hopkins, Jan. 9, 1888, p. 344.

13. Annie Sullivan to Michael Anagnos, quoted by Franklin Sanborn in a letter to the Perkins School Trustees, Oct. 24, 1906, HKA.

14. Keller, *SOML*, Annie Sullivan to Sophia C. Hopkins, June 2, 1887, p. 323.

15. *57th Annual Report of the Trustees, Perkins Institution and the Massachusetts School for the Blind for the Year Ending September 30, 1888* (Boston: 1889), PSB.

16. "Helen Keller, a Second Laura Bridgman," *Boston Evening Transcript*, Mar. 27, 1888, p. 6.

17. Keller, *SOML*, Annie Sullivan to Sophia C. Hopkins, June 2, 1887, p. 324.

18. Ibid., Sullivan to Hopkins, June 2, 1887, p. 325.

19. *57th Annual Report of the Trustees, Perkins Institution and the Massachusetts School for the Blind for the Year Ending September 30, 1888* (Boston: 1889), p. 123, PSB.

20. Keller, *SOML*, p. 44.

21. Helen Keller, *Midstream: My Later Life* (New York: Doubleday, Doran, 1929), pp. 245–46.

22. Keller, *Midstream*, p. 246.

23. *57th Annual Report of the Trustees, Perkins Institution and the Massachusetts School for the Blind for the Year Ending September 30, 1888* (Boston: 1889), pp. 83–84, PSB.

24. "Esperanto as World Hope," press clipping, 1948, HKA. This article reports Helen telling Dr. A. Einihovici, an executive member of the Perth Esperanto League, that she had studied Esperanto for "many years." In a 1953 letter, she thanked a man named Franz Kruse for helping her obtain Esperanto books from the UK National Institute of the Blind and tells him it is encouraging to note the "growing unity between the

blind living in distant parts of the world" through a "world auxiliary language." In the same letter, she expresses her regret that she is unable to skillfully write in Esperanto.

25. Annie Sullivan Macy to Michael Anagnos, Feb. 1, 1889, HKA.

26. Michael Anagnos to Anne Sullivan, Mar. 5, 1889, HKA.

27. Lash, *HAT*, p. 136.

28. Ibid.

29. Oliver Wendell Holmes to Helen Keller, Aug. 1, 1890, HKA.

30. John Whittier to Helen Keller, Aug. 5, 1890, HKA.

31. Alexander Graham Bell, "The Method of Instruction Pursued with Helen Keller: A Valuable Study for Teachers of the Deaf," *The Silent Educator*, Alexander Graham Bell Family Papers, LOC.

32. Author interview with Professor Noam Chomsky, Dec. 13, 2021. Chomsky originally argued that all babies are born with what he called a "Universal Grammar" and while in recent years, many linguists have challenged this theory, there is a broader consensus that babies are indeed born with what psycholinguist Evan Kidd calls a "cognitive tool kit." Kidd argues that children in the womb "start to learn aspects of their language from the time the auditory cortex becomes mature."

33. Keller, *SOML*, p. 25.

34. Author interview with Dr. Sanjay Gulati, Sept. 18, 2022.

35. "Helen Keller's Marvellous New Accomplishment," *Boston Daily Journal*, May 17, 1890, p. 10. Despite Annie's claim that Helen's father paid her salary, Helen would later admit to her sister, Mildred, that Arthur had not paid Annie after she and Teacher left for Perkins in June 1888.

36. Frank B. Sanborn to the Board of Trustees of the Perkins School for the Blind, Oct. 24, 1906, HKA.

37. Anne Sullivan to the Board of Trustees of the Perkins Institution, June 17, 1890, PSB.

38. *60th Annual Report of the Trustees of the Perkins Institution and Massachusetts Asylum for the Blind*, Sept. 1891, PSB.

39. Annie Sullivan to Michael Anagnos, Nov. 4, 1891, HKA.

40. Scrapbook titled "Scrapbook of Helen Keller and The Blind. Book VIII," image 13, HKA.

41. "Miss Sullivan's Methods: A Comparison between Her Reports to the Perkins Institution and the Statements Made in the Volume Entitled *The Story of My Life* by Helen Keller," author and year unknown (possibly David Prescott Hall), PSB.

42. Annie Sullivan to Michael Anagnos, Apr. 2, 1888, HKA.

43. "A Statement," *American Annals of the Deaf*, vol. 36, no. 2 (Apr. 1892), p. 154.

44. Keller, *SOML*, p. 71.

45. Helen Keller to Michael Anagnos, Oct. 17, 1892, HKA.

46. Keller, *SOML*, p. 73.

47. Henney, *ASM*, p. 161.

48. Nielsen, *BTMW*, p. 95.

49. Annie Sullivan to Michael Anagnos, Aug. 17, 1892, HKA.

50. Nielsen, *BTMW*, p. 123.

51. Keller, *SOML*, pp. 78–79.

Chapter Five: The Story of My Life

1. Helen Keller, "How I Succeeded in Overcoming the Difficulties Confronting a Blind Girl and Passed the Entrance Examination for Harvard," *American Magazine*, Oct. 22, 1899.
2. Keller, *SOML*, p. 100.
3. John Albert Macy, "Helen Keller at Radcliffe College," *The Youth's Companion*, vol. 78, no. 22 (June 2, 1904), p. 341.
4. Lash, *HAT*, p. 332.
5. Ibid., p. 340.
6. Henney, *ASM*, pp. 198–99.
7. Ibid.
8. John A. Macy to Charles Scribner's Sons, NYC, Feb. 18, 1902, HKA.
9. Henney, *ASM*, 200.
10. "Helen Keller Tells the Remarkable Story of Her Life," *San Francisco Call*, Apr. 19, 1903, p. 24.
11. "The Story of My Life" (review), *Brooklyn Citizen*, Apr. 12, 1903, p. 21.
12. William Wade, *The Blind-Deaf: A Monograph, Being a Reprint of The Deaf-Blind* (Indianapolis, IN: Hecker Brothers, 1904), p. 65.
13. Frances Koestler, *The Unseen Minority: A Social History of Blindness in the United States* (New York: American Foundation for the Blind, 2004), p. 506.
14. Ibid.
15. Henney, *ASM*, p. 201.
16. Wade, *Blind-Deaf*. The 1903 edition had a slightly different title, the *Blind-Deaf*, compared to the original 1901 edition, the *Deaf-Blind*.
17. Ibid., p. 8.
18. Ibid., p. 6.
19. Keller, *SOML*, p. 317.
20. Wade, *Blind-Deaf*, p. 65.
21. William Wade to John Macy, Aug. 31, 1903, HKA.
22. Ibid.
23. Wade, *Blind-Deaf*, p. 4.
24. Keller, *Midstream*, p. 247.
25. Keller, *SOML*, p. 72.
26. Ibid., p. 65.
27. NBH, Book 10, Mark Twain to Helen Keller, Mar. 17, 1903, NBHC.
28. Lash, *HAT*, p. 134.
29. Lash, *HAT*, p. 176.
30. Helen Keller to Mildred Keller Tyson, June 9, 1933, HKA.
31. Keller, *SOML*, p. 3.

Chapter Six: "Mr. Clemens"

1. Albert Bigelow Paine, *Mark Twain* (New York: Chelsea House, 1980), p. 1273.
2. Article by Helen Keller entitled "The Hundredth Anniversary of Mark Twain's Birth," Nov. 13, 1935, HKA.

3. Keller, *Midstream*, p. 104.

4. Helen Keller to Mildred Keller Tyson, June 9, 1933, HKA. Helen had written in *The Story of My Life* that Arthur Keller was not well off before he died. After Mildred admonished her for besmirching their father's name, Helen set the record straight: "You know it is a fact, Mildred, that Teacher never received a dollar of salary after she and mother and I went to Boston in June 1888."

5. Samuel L. Clemens to Mrs. H. H. Rogers. (In the Helen Keller Archives, this undated letter is annotated as sent in 1896, but it was almost certainly sent closer to 1900, the year Helen entered Radcliffe.)

6. Keller, "Hundredth Anniversary," HKA.

7. Keller, *SOML*, "A Supplementary Account of Helen Keller's Life and Education," p. 286.

8. "Speech given by Anne Sullivan Macy at the University of Glasgow when Helen Keller was given an honorary degree," HKA. Sullivan claimed that Twain made this remark on the occasion of Helen's Radcliffe graduation, but in fact the first part of the quote had appeared in *The Story of My Life*, published in 1903, a year before Helen graduated with honors from Radcliffe. Although the quote is found nowhere in Twain's writings or in his surviving correspondence with Helen, it is likely that the original quote is authentic while, like many quotations attributed to the author, the second part is apocryphal.

9. Paine, *Mark Twain*, p. 1490; "Excerpt from Mark Twain's autobiography, with reprint of letter from Helen Keller to Mr. Twain," vol. 2, pp. 295–303, HKA.

10. Mark Twain, *Autobiography of Mark Twain*, vol. 2, ed. Benjamin Griffin and Harriet Elinor Smith (Berkeley: University of California Press, 2010), p. 374.

11. Ibid., journal entry, Jan. 17, 1901.

12. Quoted in the Mark Twain Stormfield Project, 1908–2012, compiled by Twain scholar Brent Colley.

13. Keller, *Midstream*, p. 50.

14. Paine, *Mark Twain*, p. 1375.

15. Keller, *Midstream*, p. 48.

16. Mark Twain speech to the New York Woman's Press Club, Oct. 27, 1900.

17. Keller, *Midstream*, p. 48.

18. Ibid., p. 54.

19. Helen Keller to Samuel Clemens, Dec. 8, 1905, HKA.

20. Keller, *Midstream*, p. 66.

21. Ibid, p. 49.

22. "Writing by Helen Keller for the *Brooklyn Eagle*, including a letter in response to a critic," 1916, HKA.

23. Mark Twain, *The Autobiography of Mark Twain*, ed. Charles Neider (New York: Harper & Brothers, 1959), p. 7.

24. Mark Twain, *The Complete Essays of Mark Twain: Now Collected for the First Time* (New York: Doubleday, 1963), p. 679.

25. Mark Twain, *Mark Twain: The Complete Interviews*, ed. Gary Scharnhorst (Tuscaloosa: University of Alabama Press, 2006), p. 542.

26. Keller, *Midstream*, p. 49.

27. Ibid., p. 66.

28. Ibid., p. 52.

29. Ibid., pp. 58–59.

30. Photographic full-length portrait of Samuel L. Clemens (Mark Twain), Jan.11, 1909, HKA.

31. Booker T. Washington, "A Tribute to Mark Twain," *North American Review*, vol. 191 (June 1910).

32. Author interview, Brent Colley, Sept. 28, 2020.

Chapter Seven: Political Epiphany

1. "How I Became a Socialist," *New York Call*, Nov. 3, 1912.

2. H. G. Wells, *New Worlds for Old: A Plain Account of Modern Socialism* (London: Constable, 1908), p. 354.

3. Henney, *ASM*, p. 211.

4. Ibid, p. 212.

5. Ibid.

6. Nielsen, *BTMW*, p. 187.

7. Ibid.

8. Ibid., p. 186.

9. Dumas Malone, ed., *Dictionary of American Biography*, vol. 6 (New York: Scribner's, 1932), pp. 177–78.

10. Elizabeth Emerson, *Letters from Red Farm* (Amherst: Bright Leaf, an imprint of Massachusetts University Press, 2021), p. 40.

11. Helen Keller to J. E. Chamberlin, Feb. 2, 1934, HKA.

12. Lorena A. Hickok, *The Story of Helen Keller* (New York: Scholastic, 1958), p. 77.

13. It would become known as the National Congress of American Indians in 1944.

14. Lash, *HAT*, p. 267.

15. Arthur Gilman to Kate Keller, Dec. 1897, HKA.

16. Keller, *Teacher*, p. 81.

17. J. E. Chamberlin to Nella Braddy Henney, Dec. 6, 1933, HKA.

18. Kate Keller to John Hitz, Dec. 28, 1897, HKA.

19. "Chamberlin Timeline: With Helen Keller and Annie Sullivan History," chronology prepared by Elizabeth Emerson, great-great-granddaughter of J. E. Chamberlin, CFA; "Letter from Helen Keller to John Hitz about Her Education in Wrentham," Feb. 9, 1898, HKA.

20. Joseph Edgar Chamberlin, "Helen Keller as She Really Is," *American Annals of the Deaf*, vol. 44, no. 4 (1899), p. 300.

21. Helen Keller, "Joseph Edgar Chamberlin," *American Magazine*, vol. 73 (1912), pp. 421–22.

22. "Helen Keller's journals from 1897–1899 in which she records daily life, education, beliefs," journal entry, Aug. 8, 1898, HKA.

23. Lash, *HAT*, p. 756.

24. "Anne's Final Years (1930–36) and Her legacy: 'Foolish Remarks of a Foolish Woman,'" HKA.

25. *60th Annual Report of the Trustees*, 1891, PSB.

26. Henney, *ASM*, pp. 149–50.

27. Ibid.

28. Helen Keller, *My Religion* (New York: Swedenborg Foundation, 1956), p. 48.

29. Lord's New Church, "Who Is Emanuel Swedenborg?"

30. Lash, *HAT*, p. 781.

31. When a 1914 media report claimed that Helen had converted to the Baha'i faith, she wrote a letter to the president of the New Church denying the report and affirming her faith in Swedenborgianism. "As you know since I was 16 years old, I have been a strong believer in the doctrines of Emanuel Swedenborg," she wrote. Joseph Lash (*HAT*, p. 927) claimed that she didn't become a formal member of any church, "including the New Church," until the early thirties.

32. "Speech by Helen Keller on the New Church and Its Relevance in the Twentieth Century," 1919, HKA.

33. Charles Arthur Hawley, "Swedenborgianism and the Frontier," *Church History*, vol. 6, no. 3 (1937), pp. 203–22.

34. Peter D'Alroy Jones, *Christian Socialist Revival, 1877–1914* (Princeton: Princeton University Press, 2015), p. 355.

35. "Helen Keller's speech regarding the welfare of the poor and blind children of Atlanta," HKA.

36. "Helen Keller Socialist and Suffragist," *Des Moines Register*, Jan. 30, 1914, p. 7.

37. Annie Sullivan Macy to Michael Anagnos, July 7, 1890, HKA.

38. "Helen Keller—A Wonderful Girl," *Demorest's Family Magazine*, Oct. 1896.

39. "From Helen Keller," *Fall River Daily Evening News*, Mar. 1, 1906, p. 6.

40. "Helen Keller Honored by Governor Guild," *St. Louis Globe Democrat*, July 7, 1906.

41. Keller, *Midstream*, p. 75.

42. Keller, *Teacher*, p. 150.

43. Helen Keller, "I Must Speak: A Plea to the American Woman," *Ladies' Home Journal*, vol. 26, no. 2 (Jan. 1909).

44. "Writing by Helen Keller—The World I Live In; Legal—Royalties," HKA.

45. Helen Keller, *The World I Live In* (New York: Century, 1908), pp. xi–xii.

46. Keller, *Midstream*, p. 22.

47. Helen Keller, "Manuscript about the Death of Eugene V. Debs," Oct. 20, 1926, HKA.

48. The Socialist Party of America was formed as a result of the merger of two existing parties, the Social Democratic Party of America and a breakaway faction of the Socialist Labor Party of America.

49. "Mission of the Socialist Party," speech by Eugene Debs, Coliseum Hall Arena, Denver, May 26, 1902.

50. Socialist Party of America Membership 1903–1932, WHS.

51. *Helen Keller: Her Socialist Years*, ed. Philip S. Foner (New York: Internationalist Publishers, 1967), pp. 10, 12. Foner wrote that Helen "joined the Socialist party in Massachusetts" in 1909, implying that she had joined a local chapter. The first documentation of her formal involvement in the national Socialist Party, however, is a copy of a membership card dated 1912. Contemporary accounts suggest that she definitely considered herself a socialist before 1912 so it's possible that she had joined a state chapter as early as 1909. Foner unfortunately fails to provide a citation for his assertion.

52. Lash, *HAT*, p. 431.

53. Malone, *Dictionary of American Biography*, pp. 177–78.

54. Henney, *ASM*, p. 223.

55. "Marxian Club Socialist," *Ogden Standard*, Oct. 22, 1910, p. 12.

56. "The Gathering Storm," *Appeal to Reason*, Dec. 31, 1910, p. 1.

57. "Helen Keller Writes," *Appeal to Reason*, Dec. 24, 1910.

58. "The Dumb Girl Speaks," *Appeal to Reason*, Jan. 14, 1911, p. 2.

59. "How I Became a Socialist," *New York Call*, Nov. 3, 1912.

60. "Let the Blind See," *Boston Evening Transcript*, Feb. 15, 1911, p. 28.

61. Kenneth E. Hendrickson, "George R. Lunn and the Socialist Era in Schenectady, New York, 1909–1916," *New York History*, vol. 47, no. 1 (1966), pp. 22–40.

62. "Why a Harvard Man Should Be a Socialist," *Boston Evening Transcript*, Nov. 29, 1911.

63. "The Suffragettes," *Boston Globe*, Mar. 3, 1912, p. 80.

64. Upon Macy's appointment as secretary to Mayor Lunn, he would tell a reporter that he was a member of the Intercollegiate Socialist Society.

65. The party was formally known as Sozialdemokratische Partei Deutschlands, which translates as the "Social Democratic Party of Germany," but in 1912, the party was considered the country's socialist party.

66. "German Socialists and the Blind," *Derby Daily Telegraph*, Jan. 9, 1912, p. 4.

67. Joseph Lash to Patricia Smith, Aug. 2, 1978, HKA. In the same letter, Lash writes that he is sure that Macy joined the party in 1909 but he is dubious about the date of Helen's conversion. Yet in his subsequent biography, he fails to provide any footnote citing the source documenting Macy's 1909 membership. We can be reasonably sure that no such source exists.

68. There were no footnotes in Lash's book *Helen and Teacher* when it was published in 1980. However, Lash donated an annotated copy to the AFB and Perkins School archives with detailed handwritten citations and footnotes.

69. Hendrickson, "George R. Lunn," p. 31.

70. "Noted Blind Girl Coming with Macy," *Knickerbocker Press*, Apr. 18, 1912.

71. Ibid.

72. Ibid.

73. "Helen Keller Will Take Up New Work Soon," *Montgomery Times*, June 19, 1912, p. 6.

Chapter Eight: "Industrial Blindness and Social Deafness"

1. "Article praising Helen Keller's Socialism, and criticizing those who fail to see Socialism as she does," 1912, HKA.

2. Helen Keller, "How Helen Keller Would Try to Make Schenectady Better," *Knickerbocker Press*, July 7, 1912.

3. Ibid.

4. "Writing by Helen Keller for the *Brooklyn Eagle*, including a letter in response to a critic," 1916, HKA.

5. Ibid.

6. Keller, "I Must Speak."

7. Foner, *Helen Keller*, p. 13.

8. Alleyne Ireland, "Helen Keller Enters Politics to Cure Social Blindness," *St. Louis Post-Dispatch*, Sept. 15, 1912, p. 1.

9. Ibid.

10. Ibid.

11. Ibid.

12. Ibid.

13. Henney, *ASM*, p. 231.

14. Helen Keller to Kate Keller, Aug. 15, 1912, HKA.

15. "Helen Keller Will Not Aid Socialists," *Knickerbocker Press*, Sept. 21, 1912.

16. "How I Became a Socialist," *New York Call*, Nov. 3, 1912.

17. "Exploiting Helen Keller," *Common Cause* (New York: Social Reform Press, 1912), p. 204. *Common Cause*—published by a Jesuit priest, Father Terence Shealy, and his Social Reform Press—appeared only three times between 1912 and 1913.

18. Ibid.

19. "How I Became a Socialist," *New York Call*, Nov. 3, 1912.

20. Ibid.

21. Ibid.

22. Ibid.

23. "The Contemptible Red Flag," *New York Times*, Sept. 21, 1912, p. 10.

24. "How I Became a Socialist," *New York Call*, Nov. 3, 1912.

25. Ibid.

26. Ibid.

27. Ibid.

28. *New York Call*, May 4, 1913.

29. Ibid., p. 274.

30. Lash, *HAT*, p. 371.

31. Helen Keller to Annie Sullivan, Oct. 14, 1912, HKA.

32. Helen Keller to Annie Sullivan, Oct. 7, 1912, HKA.

33. Helen Keller to Annie Sullivan, Oct. 14, 1912, HKA.

34. Ibid.

35. Helen Keller to John Macy, Oct. 9, 1912, HKA.

36. Ibid.

37. James Oppenheim, "Bread and Roses," *The American Magazine*, Dec. 1911.

38. "A Letter by Helen Keller," *Franklin Evening News*, Nov. 23, 1912, p. 4.

39. Ibid.

40. Keller, *Midstream*, p. 269.

41. Andrew Carnegie, "The Gospel of Wealth," *North American Review*, vol. 183 (1906), pp. 526–37.

42. Lucy D. Fuller to Helen Keller, Dec. 17, 1910, HKA.

43. Keller, *Midstream*, p. 41.

Chapter Nine: Radical Shift

1. June Hannam, "Suffragette," *International Encyclopedia of Women's Suffrage* (Santa Barbara, CA: ABC-CLIO, 2000), p. 287.

2. Mrs. Grindon to Helen Keller, Oct. 4, 1909, HKA.

3. "Letter from Helen Keller to Mrs. Grindon about women's suffrage," Mar. 3, 1911.

4. "Blind Girl Believes Suffrage Will Lead to Socialism," *New York Times*, May 6, 1913.
5. Keller, *Teacher*, p. 105.
6. "Moving Tale of Guiding the Young Woman," *Boston Globe*, Mar. 25, 1913, p. 10.
7. Ibid.
8. "Helen Keller," *Asheville Citizen-Times*, Oct. 12, 1913, p. 4.
9. "Helen Keller Lectures," *Nebraska State Journal*, May 4, 1913, p. 24.
10. "Helen Keller Likes Criticism. For It Helps Her 'See Better,'" *Ohio State Journal*, Nov. 10, 1913.
11. Winifred A. Corbally to Lotta Dempsey, Toronto *Daily Star*, June 8, 1967, HKA.
12. Helen Keller to Mildred Keller Tyson, Sept. 23, 1914, HKA.
13. Helen Keller to John A. Macy, Jan. 25, 1914, HKA.
14. Lash, *HAT*, p. 464.
15. Helen Keller to John A. Macy, Jan. 25, 1914, HKA.
16. Helen Keller to John A. Macy, Apr. 4, 1914, HKA.
17. Helen Keller to John A. Macy, Feb. 8, 1914, HKA.
18. Keller, *Teacher*, p. 128.
19. Ibid.
20. "The manuscript of Helen Keller's book *Teacher*," HKA.
21. Keller, *Teacher*, p. 12.
22. Helen Keller to M. C. Migel, Nov. 1, 1935, HKA.
23. Helen Keller to John A. Macy, Feb. 8, 1914, HKA.
24. Ibid.
25. Helen Keller to John A. Macy, Mar. 14, 1914, HKA.
26. "Draft of letter from Helen Keller correcting Mildred Keller about their family life," June 9, 1933, HKA.
27. Keller, *Teacher*, p. 126.
28. Henney, *ASM*, p. 239.
29. Helen Keller, "Why Men Need Woman Suffrage," *New York Call*, Oct. 17, 1913.
30. Helen Keller to I. Graham, Aug. 29, 1911, HKA.
31. Ibid.
32. Ibid.
33. Helen Keller to the editor of the *New York Call*, Apr. 6, 1916, HKA.
34. "Article from the *New York Herald* arguing Helen Keller's radical Socialist beliefs have ended her career," Nov. 4, 1923, HKA.

Chapter Ten: "A Defective Race"

1. "Baby Doomed, Autopsy Shows," *Boston Globe*, Nov. 19, 1915.
2. "Mother Love," *Chicago Tribune*, Nov. 17, 1915, p. 1.
3. "Mother Approves Refusal to Prolong the Life of Deformed Infant," *Chicago Daily Tribune*, Nov. 17, 1915, DHM.
4. Keller, *SOML*, dedication.
5. Alexander Graham Bell, "Memoir Upon the Formation of a Deaf Variety of the Human Race," a paper presented to the National Academy of Sciences, New Haven, Nov. 13, 1883.

6. Ibid.

7. Brian H. Greenwald, "Taking Stock: Alexander Graham Bell and Eugenics, 1883–1922," in *The Deaf History Reader*, ed. John Vickrey Van Cleve (Washington, DC: Gallaudet University Press, 2007).

8. Alexander Graham Bell, "A Few Thoughts Concerning Eugenics," *Annual Report of the American Genetic Association—Breeding*, vol. 4, 1908.

9. P. R. Reilly, "Involuntary Sterilization in the United States: A Surgical Solution," *Quarterly Review of Biology* (June 1987), pp. 153–70.

10. "Facts about Children and Hearing Loss," Dallas Hearing Foundation. The foundation reports that "two deaf parents with unknown genetic information have a 10% chance of having a deaf child."

11. Douglas C. Baynton, *Forbidden Signs: American Culture and the Campaign against Sign Language* (Chicago: University of Chicago Press, 1996), p. 31.

12. Keller, *Midstream*, p. 107.

13. Annie Sullivan, "How Helen Keller Acquired Language," *American Annals of the Deaf*, vol. 37, no. 2 (Apr. 1892), p. 132.

14. Sullivan, "How Helen Keller Acquired Language," pp. 127–28.

15. Ibid.

16. In her earliest accounts, including a passage that Anagnos cited in the 1891 Perkins annual report, Annie claimed that Helen's first words were "I am not dumb now," but later began to tell audiences that the actual words were "I am no longer dumb." "Throng Thrilled as Famous Blind Woman Appears," *Morning Post* (Camden, NJ), Jan. 20, 1926, p. 3.

17. Keller, *Midstream*, 98. 1955 Video: *Helen Keller Speaks Out*. In this video, Helen speaks but her words are mostly unintelligible, so Polly translates her words as she and Annie often did when Helen delivered a lecture in front of a live audience.

18. See Edwin Black's landmark work, *War against the Weak*, for an important analysis of how the American eugenics movement inspired Hitler's program.

19. Katie Booth, *The Invention of Miracles* (New York: Simon & Schuster, 2021), p. 513.

20. Diane Paul. "Eugenics and the Left," *Journal of the History of Ideas*, vol. 45, no. 4, Oct.–Dec. 1984, pp. 567–590.

21. Jonathan Freedland, "Eugenics and the Master Race of the Left," *Guardian*, Aug. 30, 1997.

22. "Deformed Baby Dies," *Philadelphia Inquirer*, Nov. 18, 1915, p. 7.

23. "Helen Keller, Blind, Deaf and Dumb Genius, Writes on Defective Baby Case," *Pittsburgh Press*, Nov. 28, 1915, p. 14.

24. "The Sins of the Parents Shall Not Be Visited," *Washington Herald*, Dec. 5, 1915, p. 35.

25. "Helen Keller, Blind, Deaf and Dumb Genius, Writes on Defective Baby Case," *Pittsburgh Press*, Nov. 28, 1915.

26. Nathalie Oveyssi, "The Short Life and Eugenic Death of Baby John Bollinger," *Psychology Today*, Oct. 12, 2015.

27. "Jury Clears, Yet Condemns, Dr. Haiselden," *Chicago Tribune*, Nov. 20, 1915, p. 8.

28. Nathalie Oveyssi, "The Short Life and Eugenic Death of Baby John Bollinger," *Psychology Today*, Oct. 12, 2015.

29. Helen Keller, "Physicians' Juries for Defective Babies," *New Republic*, Dec. 18, 1915.

Chapter Eleven: Helen vs. Jim Crow

1. United States Census, 1880, "Population by Race, Sex, and Nativity." The 1880 census recorded the demographic makeup of Colbert County, where Tuscumbia is located, as 9,203 whites vs. 6,950 "colored," but Joseph Lash (*HAT*, p. 54) claims that Black people made up "more than half" of Tuscumbia's population in 1880.

2. United States Federal Census, 1830, fifth census of the United States, microfilm M19, Record Group 29, NARA; author interview with Sue Pilkington, June 14, 2022.

3. United States Federal Census, 1850, Slave Schedule, M432, NARA.

4. "Helen Keller to Mildred Keller Tyson," June 9, 1933, HKA. In 1947, a woman named Mary White Vinson wrote to Helen (Mary Vinson to Helen Keller, Oct. 1, 1947, HKA) claiming that her mother, Jessie Hart, worked as the Keller family cook in the 1880s and that Mary often played with Helen. The 1880 federal census records confirm that "Jessy Hart" worked as a servant for Arthur and Kate Keller, which would appear to give credibility to Mary's claim. In 1971, the Helen Keller estate wrote to Mary asking for any correspondence she may have exchanged with Helen, but she had passed away in 1969. Years later, an African American man from Russellville, Alabama, named Thomas McKnight claimed that he had traced his genealogy and discovered that "Martha Washington" was in fact Mariah Watkins, the niece of his great-grandmother, Sophia Napier Watkins, who he claims was the cook at Ivy Green when Helen was growing up. McKnight, however, failed to supply any evidence to back up his assertion. Sophia Napier Watkins is listed in the 1880 federal census as "keeping house" and there's no known record listing her as a Keller family cook. McKnight failed to return several calls and emails requesting an interview to elaborate on any additional evidence he had to back up his claim.

5. Keller, *SOML*, p. 25.

6. Ibid, p. 300.

7. "Captain Arthur H. Keller," Civil War Soldier Service Records, Confederate Army, Fold 3.

8. Lash, *HAT*, p. 53.

9. "The Ku Klux Klan," *North Alabamian*, Jan. 4, 1906, p. 1. This is the only known reference to Arthur's membership in the Klan and, according to local historian Lee Freeman, it may be "anecdotal."

10. "Tuscumbia," *Nashville Republican Banner*, Sept. 22, 1868, p. 1. The paper reported that "three Negroes"—Fort Simpson, Jake Bell, and Ben Cooper—were dragged by a "body of Ku Klux" from the local jail where they were confined for suspicion of burning down the Tuscumbia Seminary. They were "hung by a bridge." The following day, the *Nashville Tennessean* (p. 4) reported that a placard had been found on the back of one of the hanged men announcing that the "Ku Klux Klan was upon them." Author interview with Lee Freeman, local historian at the Florence Lauderdale Public Library, July 7, 2022.

11. Eugene Debs, "The Negro in the Class Struggle," *International Socialist Review*, vol. 4, no. 5 (November 1903).

12. Ray Ginger, *The Bending Cross* (Chicago: Haymarket Books, 1947), p. 260.

13. Richard Iton, *Solidarity Blues: Race, Culture, and the American Left* (Chapel Hill: University of North Carolina Press, 2003), p. 103.

14. Henney, *ASM*, p. 89.

15. Keller, *SOML*, p. 272.

16. Ibid., p. 272.

17. Lash, *HAT*, p. 335.

18. W. E. B. Du Bois, in *Double Blossoms*, ed. Edna Porter (New York: Lewis Copeland, 1931), p. 64.

19. Helen Keller to Van Wyck Brooks, Jan. 28, 1957, HKA.

20. NAACP, "Our History."

21. "Notes and Excerpts from 'The North Alabamian,' A. H. Keller, Editor and Prop'r," HKA.

22. Oswald Garrison Villard, "Socialism and Syndicalism," *The Nation*, May 30, 1912.

23. Helen Keller to Oswald Garrison Villard, Feb. 3, 1916, HKA.

24. Keller, *Midstream*, p. 220.

25. Day 2, 1901 Proceedings, Constitutional Convention of Alabama.

26. "Villard and Letter from Helen Keller," *Selma Journal*.

27. "The Bourbons and Helen Keller," *The Crisis*, June 1916, p. 70.

28. Author interview with Professor Susan Fillippeli, Jan. 19, 2022.

29. "Lynchings: By State and Race, 1882–1968," TIA.

30. "Helen Keller Indicates Her Attitude anent the Advertisement in Local Paper of Recent Date," *Selma Times*, Apr. 8, 1916.

31. Van Wyck Brooks, *Helen Keller: Sketch for a Portrait* (New York: Dutton, 1956), p. 138.

32. Du Bois, in Porter, *Double Blossoms*, p. 64.

Chapter Twelve: "A Little Island of Joy"

1. Keller, *Midstream*, p. 134.

2. Ibid.

3. Ibid., p. 135.

4. "All Should Wed," *Sisseton Weekly Standard*, July 7, 1916.

5. Helen Keller to John A. Macy, Mar. 4, 1914, HKA.

6. "How Helen Keller First Sensed Love," *Boston Post*, Nov. 26, 1916, p. 45.

7. Keller, *Midstream*, p. 178.

8. "Helen Keller Says All Women Should Marry," *Chicago Daily Tribune*, June 9, 1916.

9. Ibid., p. 179.

10. Ibid.

11. Author interview with Keller Johnson-Thompson, Helen Keller's great-grandniece, Dec. 24, 2021.

12. "Rumor Helen Keller to Wed," *Boston Globe*, Nov. 18, 1916, p. 1.

13. "Love Affair Is Ended by Duty," *Tacoma Daily Ledger*, Jan. 7, 1917, p. 37.

14. "Obstacles to Helen Keller's Marrying," *Boston Globe*, Nov. 18, 1916, p. 8.

15. "Helen Keller's Romance Fades," *Boston Post*, Nov. 19, 1916, pp. 1, 13.

16. Keller, *Midstream*, p. 180.

17. "Unalloyed Rot. Says Peter Fagan," *Boston Globe*, Nov. 23, 1916, p. 2.

18. "Mrs. Macy Has Left Her Pupil," *Boston Post*, Nov. 21, 1916, p. 1.

19. Ibid.

20. "Miss Keller Not to Marry," *Selma Times*, Dec. 1, 1916, p. 4.

21. "Helen Keller's Romance Fades," *New York Herald Tribune*, Nov. 19, 1916, p. 1.

22. Kim E. Nielsen, *The Radical Lives of Helen Keller* (New York: New York University Press, 2004), p. 40.

23. Author interview with Keller Johnson-Thompson, Dec. 24, 2021.

24. Lash, *HAT*, p. 224.

25. "Love and Socialism on the Front Porch," *San Francisco Chronicle*, May 11, 1984.

26. Interview with Ann Fagan Ginger, in *The Real Helen Keller*, produced by Liz Crow and Ann Pugh, Roaring Girl Productions, 2000.

27. Interview with Bill Johnson, in ibid.

28. Ann Fagan Ginger to Helen Keller, Feb. 4, 1960, HKA.

29. "Correspondence between Fred Elder and Anne Sullivan Macy searching for a mutual acquaintance in Kansas City," Sept. 20, 1922, HKA.

30. Keller, *Midstream*, p. 182.

31. Ibid., p. 181.

Chapter Thirteen: Helen vs. Teddy Roosevelt

1. Helen Keller to Anne Sullivan Macy, Mar. 26, 1917, HKA.

2. Ibid.

3. Anne Sullivan Macy to Helen Keller, 1917, HKA.

4. "Helen Keller Helps the Blind in Germany," *Twin-City Daily Sentinel*, Jan. 10, 1917, p. 10.

5. Helen Keller to Kate Keller, Oct. 9, 1914, HKA.

6. "Helen Keller's speech 'America against Wars' delivered on the Midland Chautauqua Circuit," 1916, HKA.

7. Ibid.

8. M. J. Stevenson to Polly Thomson, May 5, 1916, HKA.

9. "Haywood's Expulsion," *South Bend Tribune*, March 5, 1913, p. 8. In a party-wide plebiscite, Haywood was expelled from the Socialist party National Executive Committee by a nearly 2–1 margin for calling for "direct action" and "sabotage." He left the Party soon afterward.

10. "Helen Keller Would Be IWW's Joan of Arc," *New York Herald Tribune*, Jan. 16, 1916, p. 41.

11. Ibid.

12. Helen Keller to Woodrow Wilson, Nov. 16, 1915, vol. 35, Woodrow Wilson Presidential Papers, Oct. 1, 1915–Jan. 27, 1916, LOC.

13. Wilson to Helen Keller, Nov. 17, 1915, Woodrow Wilson Presidential Papers, vol. 35, Oct. 1, 1915–Jan. 27, 1916, LOC.

14. "Transcript for telegram from Helen Keller to Governor William Spry of Utah asking for a stay of execution for Joe Hill," Nov. 1915, HKA.

15. "Helen Keller Speech at Carnegie Hall," Jan. 5, 1916, HKA; "War-Mad Men and Women to Blame for Europe's Cataclysm," *Buffalo Evening Times*, Jan. 10, 1916, p. 2.

16. "Miss Keller on the War," *Outlook*, Dec. 29, 1915.
17. Helen Keller to Sister Mary Joseph, May 5, 1902, HKA.
18. "War-Mad Men and Women to Blame for Europe's Cataclysm," *Buffalo Evening Times*, Jan. 10, 1916, p. 2.
19. Anne Terry White, *Eugene Debs: American Socialist* (New York: Hill, 1974), p. 93.
20. Helen Keller to Annie Sullivan, Mar. 1, 1917, HKA.
21. "Note from Helen Keller about her letter to Henry Ford and his work for peace," Nov. 30, 1915, HKA.
22. Helen Keller, "The Ford Peace Plan Is Doomed to Failure," *New York Call*, Dec. 16, 1915.
23. "War-Mad Men and Women to Blame for Europe's Cataclysm—Helen Keller," *Buffalo Evening Times*, Jan. 7, 1916.
24. Emma Goldman to Helen Keller, Feb. 8, 1916, HKA.
25. Annie Sullivan to Helen Keller, 1917, HKA.
26. Ibid.
27. "Doing Her Bit," *Lincoln Journal Star*, Oct. 31, 1918, p. 12.
28. "Raids on I.W.W. Show Germans Back of Plots," *Brooklyn Times Union*, Sept. 6, 1917.
29. "America Calls," *New York Herald Tribune*, Nov. 2, 1917, p. 8.
30. "Letter to Morris Hillquit," *New York Call*, Nov. 5, 1917, p. 3.
31. Ibid.
32. Ibid.
33. Foner, p. 125.
34. Helen Keller to Woodrow Wilson, Dec. 12, 1917, HKA.
35. Ibid.

Chapter Fourteen: "The Human Wonder"

1. Advertisement, B.F. Keith's, Philadelphia *Evening Ledger*, May 8, 1920, p. 12.
2. Annie Sullivan to Eleanor Hutton, Mar. 22, 1905, HKA.
3. Helen Keller to Horace Traubel, Sept. 25, 1918, Box 152, Folder 22: Communist Party of the United States, "Helen Keller Correspondence," WLA.
4. "Film script by Francis T. Miller, for movie *Deliverance* about Helen Keller," HKA.
5. Keller, *Teacher*, p. 147.
6. Keller, *Midstream*, p. 194.
7. "Helen Keller Cheers Actors' Strike Pickets," *Illustrated Daily News*, Aug. 21, 1919.
8. Helen Keller to Judge Nieman, Aug. 13, 1919, HKA.
9. "Stagehands Quit, 3 More Shows Hit; Film Strike, Too?" *Brooklyn Daily Eagle*, Aug. 17, 1919, p. 5.
10. Keller, *Midstream*, p. 208.
11. "Eugene V. Debs on the Three L's," *Labor Action*, vol. 13, no. 5 (Feb. 1919).
12. *Debs v. the United States*, 249 U.S. 211 (1919).
13. "To Eugene V. Debs," *New York Call*, Apr. 29, 1919.
14. "Letter from the American Civil Liberties Bureau, NYC to Helen Keller, Forest Hills, NYC regarding the restructuring of the Bureau," Dec. 30, 1919, HKA.

15. "Documents relating to Helen Keller and Anne Sullivan's income and investments, including lists of assets and letters," HKA.

16. "1920 Statistics of Income," United States Treasury Department, Internal Revenue. Washington Government Printing Office, 1922. The average income of an American family in 1920 was $3,269.40.

17. Helen Keller, *The Story of My Life: The Restored Edition* (New York: Random House, 2003). Very little is known about Myla, who reputedly had a daughter with John during the early '20s and died five years later, leaving him a single parent.

18. Annie Sullivan to Eleanor Hutton, Mar. 22, 1905, HKA.

19. Helen Keller to Kate Keller, July 7, 1920, HKA.

20. Helen Keller to Mildred Keller Tyson, June 9, 1933.

21. "Helen Keller Buys Forest Hills Home," *Brooklyn Daily Eagle*, Sept. 7, 1917.

22. John A. Macy to Helen Keller, Jan. 4, 1918, HKA.

23. John A. Macy to Helen Keller, Jan. 2, 1918, HKA.

24. Ibid.

25. John A. Macy to Helen Keller, Feb. 1, 1918, HKA.

26. John A. Macy to Helen Keller, Jan. 4, 1918, HKA.

27. Keller, *Midstream*, p. 209.

28. Keller, *Teacher*, p. 154.

29. "Script for Helen Keller and Anne Sullivan Macy's Vaudeville Performances," HKA.

30. "Helen Keller Tells of Her Novel Sensations on Stage," *New York Sun and Herald*, Feb. 29, 1920, p. 4.

31. "Helen Keller, as Vaudeville Star, Wins Audience by Her Personality," *Sandusky Star Journal*, Mar. 6, 1920, p. 2.

32. "Receipt from Andrew J. Lloyd Company Opticians, Boston, MA for an artificial eye for Helen Keller," Sept. 1911, HKA.

33. "Helen Keller Tells of Her Novel Sensations on Stage," p. 43.

34. In his 1988 memoir *Lilly* (New York: Morrow, 1988), about his lifelong friendship with Lillian Hellman, Peter Feibleman writes (p. 102) about a party for Helen given by Polly. Both Hellman and her friend Dorothy Parker were invited, but Parker declined the invitation. Later, Hellman came back from the party and told her friend that she was disgusted by all the pious chatter. To this, Parker is alleged to have said, "It's your own fault, dear. Didn't I tell you she was a con woman and a dyke?" Although some interpret this as a reference to Helen, it is more likely that it referred to Katharine ("Kit") Cornell, since the party he refers to was Helen's eighty-first birthday party hosted by Cornell at her Martha's Vineyard home, Chip Chop, in July 1961. Although she was married to Guthrie McClintic, it was an open secret that Cornell was a lesbian, the longtime lover of Helen's friend Nancy Hamilton. Feibleman himself wasn't present at the party, so he could have only heard the anecdote secondhand.

35. "Helen Keller: The Unconquerable," *Coronet*, Mar. 1949, p. 132.

36. Helen and Annie had prepared for the vaudeville tour by anticipating some of the questions and preparing answers in advance, so it's likely that not all of Helen's responses were as quick-witted as they might have appeared.

37. "List of questions asked to Helen Keller by her Vaudeville audiences," HKA.

38. Ibid.

39. Keller, *Midstream*, p. 210.

40. Ibid., p. 209.

41. Susan Crutchfield, "'Playing Her Part Correctly': Helen Keller as Vaudevillian Freak," *Disability Studies Quarterly*, vol. 25, no. 3 (Summer 2005).

42. Ibid.

43. Helen Keller to Yvonne Pitrois, undated, HKA.

44. Ibid.

45. Ibid.

46. Helen Keller to Daisy Sharpe, Dec. 19, 1923, HKA.

Chapter Fifteen: The Foundation

1. Helen Keller to Mildred Keller Tyson, Dec. 1, 1922, HKA.

2. Helen Keller to Mildred Keller Tyson, Dec. 17, 1923, HKA.

3. Ibid.

4. Koestler, *Unseen Minority*, pp. 15–16.

5. M. C. Migel to Charles F. F. Campbell, Nov. 27, 1923, HKA.

6. Charles F. F. Campbell to M. C. Migel, Nov. 30, 1923, HKA.

7. F. F. Campbell to M. C. Migel, Nov. 30, 1923, HKA.

8. M. C. Migel to Charles F. F. Campbell, Apr. 18, 1924, HKA.

9. Annie Sullivan to M. C. Migel, Nov. 10, 1924, HKA.

10. Annie Sullivan to M. C. Migel, Aug. 6, 1924, HKA.

11. Koestler, *Unseen Minority*, p. 69.

12. Ibid., p. 64.

13. S. Stanwood Menken to M. C. Migel, Feb. 6, 1924, HKA. Note: Menken's name is misspelled as Meuken in the AFB digital archives.

14. C. W. Toth, "Samuel Gompers, Communism, and the Pan American Federation of Labor," *Americas*, vol. 23, no. 3 (1967), pp. 273–78.

15. "Letter from Helen Keller with a donation to the Friends of Soviet Russia to benefit Russian children," Feb. 8, 1923, HKA.

16. Helen Keller to Iva Ettor, Nov. 17, 1923, HKA.

17. Helen Keller to Robert La Follette, July 27, 1924, HKA.

18. Ibid.

19. Helen Keller's speech in Washington, D.C. advocating for the AFB, 1925, HKA.

20. "Average Hours and Earnings by Sex and City, 1926 & 1928, New York, 1926, Bulletin of the Bureau of United States Labor Statistics (US Government Printing Office, 1929), p. 810.

21. Helen Keller to Herbert H. White, July 6, 1926, HKA.

22. Ibid.

23. Helen Keller to Nella Braddy Henney, Sept. 18, 1944, HKA.

24. Keller, *Midstream*, pp. 151–52.

25. "Lecture given by Anne Sullivan Macy about the education of Helen Keller," 1914, HKA.

26. "Monument of Shame to John D, Her Suggestion," *New Castle News*, Sept. 24, 1914.
27. John Louis Recchiuti, *Civic Engagement: Social Science and Progressive-Era Reform in New York City* (Philadelphia: University of Pennsylvania Press, 2007), p. 117.
28. Koestler, *Unseen Minority*, pp. 98–99.
29. Helen Keller to Olin H. Burritt, Oct. 17, 1926, HKA.

Chapter Sixteen: Helen vs. the Führer

1. "Nazi Book Burning Fails to Stir Berlin," *New York Times*, May 11, 1933, pp. 1, 12.
2. Ibid.
3. Ibid.
4. Although "How I Became a Socialist" was the title of an essay Helen wrote for the *New York Call* and later reprinted in her 1913 book, *Out of the Dark*, her socialist writings were translated into German and published in book form under that title (*Wie ich Sozialistin Wurde*) in 1914.
5. "1933 Book Burnings," USHMM.
6. "Germany Burns Blacklisted Books Tonight," *Herald-News*, May 10, 1933.
7. See my book *The American Axis: Henry Ford, Charles Lindbergh, and the Rise of the Third Reich* (New York: St. Martin's Press, 2003), p. 12.
8. "Protocols of the Elders of Zion," *Holocaust Encyclopedia*, USHMM.
9. "Article from *The Jewish Advocate* with letter from Helen Keller to editor denouncing anti-Semitic comments in the *Dearborn Independent*," Dec. 30, 1920, HKA.
10. Max Wallace, *The American Axis* (New York: St. Martin's Press, 2003), p. 2.
11. "Letter from Helen Keller to Adolf Hitler/German students expressing anger over Hitler's policies," May 9, 1933, HKA; "Helen Keller Warns Germany's Students," *New York Times*, May 10, 1933, p. 10.
12. Ibid.
13. Helen Keller to Governor Franklin D. Roosevelt, Feb. 1929, HKA.
14. "Helen Keller Wins Achievement Prize," *New York Times*, Oct. 19, 1932.
15. Helen Keller to Eleanor Roosevelt, Feb. 19, 1933, HKA.
16. "Letter to Helen Keller regarding employment opportunities for the blind in Washington, D.C. and asking her to write to President Franklin D. Roosevelt in thanks for his assistance," May 21, 1933, HKA; Koestler, *Unseen Minority*, p. 196.
17. In her book *The Radical Lives of Helen Keller*, Kim Nielsen has described the work programs Helen promoted as "sheltered workshops" that were later condemned by disability activists as "exploitative and segregated," though it's unclear what she is referring to.
18. "Annual Report of the President," Dec. 5, 1935, AFB.
19. Koestler, *Unseen Minority*, p. 144.
20. Telegram from Helen Keller to M. C. Migel, Sept. 2, 1933, HKA.
21. "Writing by Helen Keller for the *Brooklyn Eagle*, including a letter in response to a critic," 1916, HKA.
22. "Speech given by Helen Keller," Mar. 27, 1930, HKA.
23. Koestler, *Unseen Minority*, p. 153.

24. "Correspondence between Robert Irwin, NYC and Helen Keller, Westport, CT regarding tax bill H. R. 3687 on income taxes on the employed blind," Dec. 8, 1943, HKA. The recipient of this letter is incorrectly identified as Robert Barnett in the AFB's digital Helen Keller Archives.

25. "An Epic of Courage: 'Seen' by Helen Keller," *New York Times Magazine*, Jan. 6, 1946, p. 5.

26. Helen Keller to John H. Finley, Oct. 29, 1935, HKA.

27. Ibid., p. 224.

28. Telegram from Polly Thomson to Lenore Smith, Oct. 15, 1936, HKA.

29. Keller, *Teacher*, pp. 225–26.

30. Haas would later go to work for Helen and Polly as their chauffeur, gardener, and handyman, often described as their "general factotum."

31. Keller, *Teacher*, pp. 226–27.

32. "Funeral Service for Mrs. A. S. Macy," *New York Times*, Oct. 23, 1936.

33. Herrmann, *Helen Keller*, p. 5.

34. Lash, *HAT*, p. 746.

35. Ibid.

36. Ibid., p. 489.

37. Helen Keller to M. C. Migel, Oct. 26, 1932, HKA.

38. Lash, *HAT*, p. 227.

39. Helen Keller, *Helen Keller's Journal* (New York: Doubleday, 1938), journal entry, Jan. 24, 1937, p. 137.

40. Ibid.

41. "Copy of *The Hour* news bulletin reporting Helen Keller's remarks after Nazi Germany bans her book," Aug. 30, 1939, HKA.

42. Ibid.

43. Helen Keller, *American Viewpoints on Nazi Aggression* (American Council against Nazi Propaganda, 1939).

44. "Article reporting on case of baby with eye tumor for whom Helen Keller advocated surgery rather than death," 1938, HKA.

45. "Blind Can Be Happy, Helen Keller Writes," *Des Moines Register*, May 9, 1938, p. 1.

46. Helen Keller to John H. Finley, Dec. 2, 1938, HKA.

47. Keller, *Journal*, journal entry, Apr. 9, 1937.

48. "Helen Keller Expresses Admiration for the Negro," *The Call* (Kansas City), Dec. 30, 1938.

49. "Helen Keller's letter to James Sun Eagle of the Pawnee Tribe and remarks to the Stoney Indians," July 21, 1939, HKA.

50. Helen Keller to M. C. Migel, Oct. 26, 1932, HKA.

Chapter Seventeen: "The Spirit of Revolt"

1. Helen Keller to Eleanor Roosevelt, Jan. 30, 1939, HKA.

2. "Uncorrected proof copy of Helen Keller's Journal, published in 1938," HKA.

3. "The Painful Past of Spanish Civil War Refugees in France, 80 Years On," *France 24*, Sept. 2, 2019.

4. Helen Keller to Eleanor Roosevelt, Dec. 1, 1940, HKA.

5. Koestler, *Unseen Minority*, p. 162.

6. "My Day," *Pittsburgh Press*, Dec. 12, 1940, p. 12.

7. "First Lady Disowns Spanish Aid Drive," *New York Times*, Jan. 7, 1941, p. 1.

8. Ibid.

9. Ibid.

10. Polly Thomson to Nella Braddy Henney, 1941, HKA.

11. Art Young to Helen Keller, Jan. 9, 1941, HKA.

12. "Miss Keller Studies Charges," *New York Times*, Jan. 9, 1941, p. 23.

13. Nella Braddy Henney to Polly Thomson, Jan. 28, 1941.

14. Ibid.

15. Ibid.

16. Ibid.

17. Ibid.

18. Eugene P. Link, *Labor-Religion Prophet: The Times and Life of Harry F. Ward* (Boulder, CO: Westview Press, 1984), p. 148.

19. Lash, *HAT*, p. 832.

20. Ibid., p. 621.

21. "Helen Keller's Liberal Leanings Often Forgotten," *Birmingham News*, May 16, 2005.

22. Foner, *Helen Keller*.

23. Emma Goldman to Helen Keller, 1918, HKA.

24. Speech by Vladimir Lenin, Second All-Russia Congress of Soviets of Workers' and Soldiers' Deputies, Oct. 25, 1917.

25. Ginger, *Bending Cross*, p. 394.

26. Ibid.

27. "Emma Goldman in Exile," Emma Goldman Papers, Berkeley Library, University of California.

28. Scrapbook entitled "Anne Sullivan Macy's Scrapbook #1—Vaudeville," HKA.

29. "Affidavits affirming Helen Keller's interest in Communism, accompanied by an envelope for the documents," Feb. 1926, HKA.

30. In 1919, Citlow had been charged with criminal anarchy by the state of New York for publishing a manifesto calling for revolution. He was convicted and given a sentence of five to ten years in prison. He was pardoned by New York governor Al Smith in 1925.

31. Ibid.

32. Keller, *Midstream*, p. 334.

33. Ibid., pp. 334–35.

34. Helen Keller to J. E. Chamberlin, Feb. 2, 1934, HKA.

35. Keller, *Journal*, journal entry, Dec. 29, 1937, p. 87.

36. Otto Schramm to Helen Keller, Dec. 3, 1936, HKA.

37. Keller, *Journal*, journal entry, Dec. 29, 1936, p. 87.

38. Ibid.

39. Ibid., journal entry, Jan. 23. 1937, p. 136.

40. Ibid., journal entry, Jan. 26, 1937, p. 149.

41. Ibid.
42. Ibid., journal entry, Feb. 10, 1937, p. 191.
43. Ibid., pp. 145–46.
44. "Americans Who Died in Spain Honored," *New York Times*, Feb. 23, 1939, p. 12.
45. Helen Keller FBI file.
46. Ibid.
47. Keller, *Journal*, journal entry, Jan. 23, 1937, pp. 134–35.

Chapter Eighteen: Fellow Traveler

1. John Earl Haynes, *Red Scare or Red Menace?* (Chicago: Ivan R. Dee, 1996).
2. "Whose War Is It," speech by Earl Browder, Town Hall, Philadelphia, Sept. 29, 1939.
3. Author interview with Roz Usiskin, president of the United Jewish People's Order (Winnipeg), Apr. 9, 2018. Usiskin, who was a Red Diaper baby, remembers her bemusement as a nine-year-old child when the pact was announced and being told by her Communist relatives that Stalin was being strategic and needed time to build up Russia's military machine.
4. Bernard Bellush and Jewell Bellush, "A Radical Response to the Roosevelt Presidency: The Communist Party (1933–1945)," *Presidential Studies Quarterly*, vol. 10, no. 4 (1980), p. 654.
5. Ibid., p. 655.
6. Helen Keller to Phillips Keller, Feb. 6, 1940, HKA.
7. "Helen Keller Pities the Real Unseeing," *New York Times*, June 23, 1940.
8. "Helen Keller on Visit Here, Holds Faith in the Future," *Tallahassee Daily Democrat*, Apr. 22, 1941.
9. Harvey Klehr, *The American Communist Movement* (Woodbridge, CT: Twayne, 1992), p. 96.
10. "Helen Keller Calls Upon America to Stem Barbarism with Faith," *Dallas Times Herald*, Nov. 14, 1941.
11. "Miracle Woman Visits Denver," *Rocky Mountain News*, Nov. 9, 1941.
12. In August 1940, a woman named Elizabeth Bonbright wrote Helen a letter taking issue with her stand against American intervention a few weeks after she read the *New York Times* profile calling Helen a "convinced pacifist." She questioned how Helen could maintain that stand in light of Nazi aggression. In the digital archives of the AFB, her letter is printed alongside an undated response by Helen in which she acknowledges Bonbright's concerns and states that she had reevaluated her anti-intervention and had "now come to a decision." It is better, she declares, for "all of us who uphold freedom, though often sinned against, to be impoverished together by war" than to submit to doctrines that impose dictatorship, "murder the soul and destroy human rights, liberty, happinesss," and "independent thinking." These two letters are understandably placed together in the archives, suggesting that Helen's response was written in the summer of 1940. But her continuing publicly stated stance against American intervention until after the German invasion of the Soviet Union a year later suggests that Helen in fact waited until 1941 to respond to Bonbright's letter. Helen's letter to Bonbright is undated.

13. Author interview with John Haynes, Nov. 15, 2021.
14. Bellush and Bellush, "Radical Response to the Roosevelt Presidency," p. 656.
15. Helen Keller to Nella Braddy Henney, Sept. 18, 1944, HKA.
16. Author interview with Harvey Klehr, Nov. 15, 2021.
17. Harvey Klehr, John Earl Haynes, and Kyrill M. Anderson, *The Soviet World of American Communism* (New Haven, CT: Yale University Press, 1998), p. 1.
18. Helen Keller to Walter G. Holmes, Dec. 19, 1941, HKA.
19. "Miss Keller Lauds Russia," *New York Times*, Jan. 7, 1942, p. 2.
20. "What the Negro Means to the War," *New Masses*, Oct. 20, 1942, pp. 23–24.
21. Fred Ho and Bill V. Mullen, eds., *Afro Asia: Revolutionary Political and Cultural Connections between African Americans and Asian Americans* (Durham, NC: Duke University Press, 2008), p. 167.
22. Randolph Boehm, ed., "Papers of the U.S. Commission on Wartime Relocation and Internment of Civilians, Part 1: Numerical File Archives" (Frederick, MD: University Publications of America, 1984).
23. Jonathan van Harmelen, "Finding Sunshine among Shadows: The Unknown History of Wartime Disabled Japanese Americans," www.discovernikkei.org, Nov. 2, 2020.
24. Helen Keller to Hannah Takagi, Aug. 2, 1943, HKA.
25. "Helen Keller," *Soviet Russia Today*, Mar. 1943, p. 11.
26. Helen Keller to Clare Heineman, Apr. 28, 1943, HKA.
27. "Blind Awards in Americas," *New York World Telegram*, Sept. 20, 1944.
28. Roosevelt sent a message to Congress in June 1934 promising a social insurance plan, but the final act was only passed in August 1935 after a special committee developed its key provisions.
29. Helen Keller's testimony to a subcommittee of the Committee on Labor (House of Representatives) to investigate Aid to the Physically Handicapped, Oct. 2, 1944.
30. Ibid.
31. Ibid.
32. "Jo Davidson Heads Unit for Roosevelt," *New York Times*, Aug. 24, 1944, p. 32.
33. Bellush and Bellush, "Radical Response to the Roosevelt Presidency," p. 658.
34. Helen Keller to Nella Braddy Henney, Sept. 18, 1944, HKA.

Chapter Nineteen: Gathering Storm

1. Richard Gergel, "An Account of the Blinding of Sgt. Isaac Woodard by the Police Officer, Lynwood Shull," *Literary Hub*, Jan. 22, 2019.
2. Many accounts claim that the incident happened in Batesburg, but, according to Woodard's deposition, the bus driver waited until Aiken to summon police.
3. Olivia B. Waxman, "How a 1946 Case of Police Brutality against a Black WWII Veteran Shaped the Fight for Civil Rights," *Time*, Mar. 30, 2021.
4. Isaac Woodard deposition, April 23, 1946.
5. "Police Chief Freed in Negro Beating," *New York Ttimes*, Nov. 6, 1946, p. 36.
6. "1946 Orson Welles Commentaries," July 28, 1946; "Aiken Is Angered at Welles Charge," *New York Times*, Aug. 9, 1946, p. 15.

7. NBH, Box 11, NBH journal entry, Nov. 26, 1951.

8. Helen Keller to Nella Braddy Henney, Sept. 22, 1946, HKA.

9. Ibid.

10. Nielsen, *Radical Lives*, p. 11.

11. Jo Davidson, *Between Sittings* (New York: Dial Press, 1951), p. 333.

12. Ibid., p. 178.

13. Louis Budenz, *Men without Faces: The Communist Conspiracy in the USA* (New York: Harper Brothers, 1948), p. 221.

14. Jean Muir FBI file, p. 10.

15. Jo Davidson to Henry Wallace, Aug. 1, 1944, HW.

16. Helen Keller to Henry Wallace, Oct. 30, 1944, HKA.

17. Henry A. Wallace to Helen Keller, Nov. 7, 1944, HKA.

18. A. L. Hamby, "Henry A. Wallace, the Liberals, and Soviet-American Relations," *Review of Politics*, vol. 30, no. 2 (1968), p. 158.

19. Helen Keller to Nella Braddy Henney, Sept. 22, 1946, HKA.

20. Ibid.

Chapter Twenty: Red Scare

1. "McKellar Will Fight Lilienthal Appointment," *Nashville Banner*, Jan. 2, 1946, p. 1; "Senator McKellar," *Nashville Banner*, Jan. 27, 1946, p. 2.

2. "Naming of Mr. Lilienthal Urged," Helen Keller to the editor, *New York Times*, Feb. 25, 1947, p. 24.

3. Testimony of Walter S. Steele regarding Communist activities in the United States. Hearings before the Committee on Un-American Activities, House of Representatives, Eightieth Congress, first session, on H. R. 1884 and H. R. 2122, bills to curb or outlaw the Communist Party in the United States. Public law 601, section 121, subsection Q (2) July 21, 1947.

4. Ibid.

5. Ibid.

6. "Reagan, Communism Met in Hollywood," Associated Press, Nov. 13, 1985.

7. Helen Keller FBI file, p. 10.

8. Ibid.

9. Helen Keller. "We Are Judged by What We Do to Them," *Soviet Russia Today*, Nov. 1946, pp. 21–22.

10. Helen Keller to Eric T. Boulter, Feb. 10, 1947.

11. NBH, Box 11, NBH journal entry, Mar. 21, 1947.

12. Helen Keller to Van Wyck Brooks, Nov. 12, 1940.

13. Dorothy Parker FBI file.

14. NBH, Box 11, NBH journal entry, Nov. 29, 1947, NBHC.

15. "Correspondence concerning H. Keller's invitation to an American-Soviet Friendship event," Nov. 17, 1947, HKA.

16. Transcript of Proceedings, Un-American Activities Committee, Second Report, Un-American Activities in Washington State, 1948.

17. Helen Keller FBI file.

18. Westbrook Pegler, "As I See it," *Charlotte Observer*, Dec. 9, 1947, p. 14.

19. Ibid.

20. "Winning the Battle but Losing the War Over the Blacklist," *New York Times*, Jan. 25, 1998.

21. Lucille Ball FBI file.

22. Ibid., "Memo to the Director re: Lucille Ball; Desi Arnaz."

23. "Apparently the FBI Did Not Love Lucy," *Washington Post*, Dec. 7, 1989.

24. Lucille Ball FBI file, Memo to the Director, Dec. 16, 1953.

25. Lucille Ball FBI file, "Memo to the Director," Oct. 21, 1954.

26. Joyce Millman, "The Good, the Bad, the Lucy," *New York Times*, Oct. 14, 2001, p. 30.

27. Author interview with John Fox, Nov. 19, 2021.

28. NBH, book 11, journal entry, Dec. 17, 1947, NBHC.

29. "Correspondence between Robert B. Irwin, William Ziegler, Jr., and Mrs. Walter Fosnot regarding Helen Keller's Communist sympathies," Feb. 3, 1948, HKA. Note: The letter is incorrectly labeled as "February 3, 1947" in the AFB digital archives.

30. Ibid.

31. "Thomas Group Plans New Quiz on Ways to Curb Communism," *Boston Globe*, Jan. 19, 1948, p. 2.

32. Helen Keller FBI file.

33. "Wallace Advocates Program of 'Progressive Capitalism,'" *Richmond Times Dispatch*, Feb. 29, 1948, p. 20.

34. Osler L. Peterson, "Henry Wallace: A Divided Mind," *Atlantic*, Aug. 1948.

35. Helen Keller, "Albert Einstein," *Home Magazine*, Apr. 1931, p. 6.

36. Nella Braddy Henney to Polly Thomson, March 3, 1948, HKA.

37. NBH, Box 11, journal entry, Feb. 26, 1948, NBHC.

38. Ibid.

39. Helen Keller to Jo Davidson, undated, HKA.

40. Mary D. Blankenhorn to M. R. Barnett, Nov. 24, 1950, HKA.

41. NBH, Box 11, NBH journal entry, Nov. 26, 1950, NBHC.

42. NBH, Box 11, NBH journal entry, Nov. 29, 1950, NBHC.

43. M. R. Barnett to Robert Irwin, Nov. 17, 1949, HKA.

44. Joseph Barry, "At 70, 'New Spirit, New Freedom,'" *New York Times Magazine*, June 25, 1950, p. 157.

45. Ibid.

Chapter Twenty-One: Helen vs. Apartheid

1. M. C. Migel to Charles A. Thomson, Nov. 19, 1941, HKA.

2. Helen Keller to Nella Braddy Henney, Oct. 14, 1948, HKA.

3. Ken McCormick to Helen Keller, Oct. 1954, HKA.

4. "Helen Keller Operates a Plane," *Philadelphia Inquirer*, Nov. 20, 1946, p. 3.

5. Helen Keller Speech on the Prevention of Blindness, 1951.

6. Chizuru Saeki, "Helen Keller's Civil Diplomacy in Japan in 1937 and 1948," *Japan Review*, no. 27, 2014, pp. 201–20.

7. Lash, *HAT*, p. 553.
8. Nielsen, *Radical Lives*, p. 111.
9. Ibid., p. 112.
10. Helen Keller to Nella Braddy Henney, July 2, 1952, HKA.
11. O Chimere-Dan, "Apartheid and Demography in South Africa," *Etude de la Population Africaine*, Apr. 1992.
12. "Essay by Helen Keller entitled 'An Unforgettable Tour' about her trip to South Africa," Nov. 4, 1951, HKA.
13. Helen Keller to Alexander Graham Bell, Mar. 9, 1900, HKA.
14. Helen Keller, "An Unforgettable Tour," *Journal of Visual Impairment and Blindness*, vol. 46, no. 1, 1952.
15. Helen Keller to Rev. Arthur W. Blaxall, Oct. 26, 1950, HKA.
16. "Helen Keller Pays UN Visit, Meets Dr. Bunche," *Montgomery Advertiser*, Nov. 25, 1949, p. 18.
17. Helen Keller to Jo Davidson, Jan. 24, 1951, HKA.
18. John Wilson to Helen Keller, Feb. 27, 1951, HKA.
19. Helen Keller to John F. Wilson, Mar. 13, 1951, HKA.
20. "Article from the *Cape Argus* reporting Helen Keller's criticism of Cape Town's segregation and failure to provide resources to blind Natives," Mar. 30, 1951, HKA.
21. NBH, Box 11, NBH journal entries, July 13–15, 1951, and Nov. 29, 1950, NBHC.
22. Helen Keller to Jo and Florence Davidson, 1951, HKA.
23. Ibid.
24. Ibid.
25. Arthur William Blaxall, *Helen Keller Under the Southern Cross* (Capetown, South Africa: Juta, 1952), p. 51.
26. NBH, Box 11, NBH journal entry, July 1951, NBHC.
27. "Article from *The Friend* announcing Helen Keller has arrived in Bloemfontein, South Africa," Apr. 24, 1951, HKA.
28. Ibid.
29. "Article from the *Cape Argus* reporting on Helen Keller's impression of South Africa upon her departure," May 22, 1951, HKA.
30. Helen Keller to Victor Maxwell, Sept. 7, 1951, HKA.
31. Helen Keller to Takeo Iwahashi, Aug. 8, 1951, HKA.
32. Rajmohan Gandhi, *Gandhi: The Man, His People, and the Empire* (Berkeley: University of California Press, 2008), p. 172.
33. Keller, *Journal*, journal entry, Dec. 30, 1936, p. 93.
34. "A Lesson in Courage and Determination," *Graphic*, vol. 1, no. 10 (May 1951); "Helen Keller's speech to the Indian Society for the Blind in South Africa urging education for the blind," 1951, HKA.
35. "Keller Aroused Conscience of Many on SA Visit," *Saturday Star*, May 5, 2018.
36. Author interview with Ela Gandhi, Nov. 12, 2021.
37. Ibid.
38. Author interview with Arun Gandhi, Nov. 18, 2021.

39. Ibid.

40. Manilal Gandhi to Helen Keller, Apr. 26, 1951, HKA.

41. B. K. Murray,. "Wits as an 'Open' University 1939–1959: Black Admissions to the University of the Witwatersrand," *Journal of Southern African Studies*, vol. 16, no. 4 (1990), pp. 649–76.

42. "Essay draft by Helen Keller entitled 'An Unforgettable Tour' about her trip to South Africa," Nov. 4, 1951, HKA.

43. Blaxall, *Helen Keller under the Southern Cross*, p. 51.

44. Helen Keller to Takeo Iwahashi, Aug. 5, 1951, HKA.

45. "Essay draft by Helen Keller entitled 'An Unforgettable Tour' about her trip to South Africa," Nov. 4, 1951, HKA.

46. Keller, *Midstream*, pp. 81–82.

47. Transcript of unpublished Joseph Lash interview with Robert Barnett, Mar. 11, 1978, Joseph Lash Papers, Box 53—Interviews, FDRL.

48. Author interview with Dr. Frank Vito Mondelli, post-doc fellow at UC Davis. Mondelli has chronicled a number of visits that Helen made to Japanese schools for the deaf on her tours of Japan in 1937 and 1948, despite the fact that AFB press releases about those visits focused exclusively around her work for the blind community. In contrast, the itinerary of her 1948 Australia tour didn't include visits to any schools for the deaf community other than one serving the "Blind, Deaf and Dumb."

49. Keller, *Journal*, journal entry, Jan. 18, 1937, p. 126.

50. Ibid., journal entry, Jan. 18, 1937, pp. 125–26.

51. Ibid.

52. Jo Davidson to Helen Keller, Oct. 9, 1951, HKA.

53. Helen Keller to Jo and Florence Davidson, 1951, HKA.

54. Helen Keller to Polly Thomson, Feb. 14, 1952, HKA

55. NBH, Box 11, NBH journal entry, Jan. 10, 1952, NBHC.

56. "Essay by Helen Keller 'My Work in the Near East' about her travels to the Middle East," HKA.

57. Helen Keller to Nella Braddy Henney, July 2, 1952, HKA.

58. Ibid.

59. Ibid.

60. Ibid.

61. Helen Keller, "My Work in the Near East," 1953.

62. "Israelis Stirred by Helen Keller," *New York Times*, May 27, 1952, p. 12; "Essay by Helen Keller 'My Work in the Near East' about her travels to the Middle East," HKA.

Chapter Twenty-Two: Helen vs. Joe McCarthy

1. "McCarthy as a Symbol," *New York Times*, Aug. 24, 1952, p. 129.

2. "McCarthy Issue Discussed," letter to the editor from Helen Keller, *New York Times*, Aug. 28, 1952, p. 22.

3. Helen Keller FBI file.

4. "Letters, press clippings, and a publication about Senator Joseph McCarthy, Communism, and Helen Keller's letter to the *NY Times* criticizing Senator McCarthy," Aug. 28, 1952, HKA.

5. Ibid.

6. Günter Wernicke, "The Race to Tip the Scales: Nuclear Paradox for the Eastern Bloc," *Journal of Peace Research*, vol. 40, no. 4 (2003), pp. 457–77.

7. "Telegram, Helen Keller to World Council for Peace," Nov. 10, 1952, HKA.

8. "Interoffice memorandum denouncing the World Council of Peace by the US Government and encouraging Helen Keller to distance herself from this 'Communist' organization," undated, AFB.

9. Telegram from Helen Keller to Frédéric Joliot-Curie, Nov. 21, 1952, HKA.

10. "Helen Keller Duped into Giving Endorsement," *Asheville Citizen,* Nov. 29, 1952, p. 3.

11. "Statement read by M.R. Barnett broadcast over 'Voice of America' regarding Rude Pravo's misrepresentation of Helen Keller and the World Council of Peace, asking for a reprint of their statement to correctly represent Helen's opinion," Dec. 9, 1952, HKA.

12. NBH, Box 11, NBH journal entry, Dec. 11, 1952, NBHC. Nella writes that the six statements were "from Helen," but it's almost certain from the context that Helen had in fact forwarded her the statements supplied to her by the AFB.

13. Ibid., Nov. 24, 1953.

14. NBH, Box 11, NBH journal entry, Dec. 11, 1952, NBHC.

15. "Helen Keller's essay 'We Meet a King' about her meeting with King Alexander I of Yugoslavia," July 1931, HKA.

16. Jo Davidson to Helen Keller, Nov. 10, 1949, HKA.

17. NBH, Box 11, NBH journal entry, Feb. 20, 1953, NBHC.

18. Ibid.

19. Helen Keller to William Ziegler Jr., undated, HKA.

20. "Who We Are—Our History," Helen Keller International, www.hki.org.

21. "National Register of Historic Places," NPS Form 10-900, National Park Service.

22. NBH, Box 11, NBH journal entry, Nov. 11, 1951.

23. Ibid.

24. Guthrie McClintic and Katharine Cornell, GLBTQ Encyclopedia Project.

25. "Document entitled 'Memo by Nella Braddy Henney on Dramatic Production of the Helen Keller Story,' outlining various aspects and legal issues surrounding Helen Keller's autobiography and dramatization of her life," undated, HKA.

26. A slightly revised version was shown on television the following year renamed *Helen Keller: Her Life Story*.

27. Kory Rothman, "Somewhere There's Music: Nancy Hamilton, the Old Girls' Network, and the American Musical Theatre of the 1930s and 1940s" (PhD diss., University of Maryland, 2005).

28. "Photograph of Joseph Lash, Helen Keller, Eleanor Roosevelt, Katharine Cornell, Polly Thomson and others at Cornell's home, Massachusetts," 1954, HKA.

29. NBH, Box 11, NBH journal entry, Jan. 1, 1947, NBHC.

30. Transcript of unpublished Lash interview with Winifred Corbally, Apr. 25, 1978, Joseph Lash Papers, Box 53—Interviews, FDRL.

31. Unpublished Joseph Lash interview with Robert Barnett, Mar. 11, 1978, Joseph Lash Papers, Box 53—Interviews, FDRL.

32. Ruth Gordon, "Devotedly, Your Friend, Helen Keller," *New York Times*, Aug. 10, 1969.

33. Nielsen, *Radical Lives*, p. 10.

34. "History: Helen Keller Services Historical Timeline," HKS.

35. Transcript of unpublished Joseph Lash interview with Robert Barnett, Mar. 11, 1978, Joseph Lash Papers, Box 53—Interviews, FDRL.

36. "Correspondence regarding the work and graduation of Robert J. Smithdas," May 21, 1953, HKA.

37. Author interview with Paul Richard McGann, October 3, 6, and 23, 2021; and Feb. 10, 2022. McGann is the founder of the Western Pennsylvania Association of the Deafblind and was Smithdas's longtime protégé.

38. Ibid.

39. Unpublished Joseph Lash interview with Robert Barnett, Mar. 11, 1978, Joseph Lash Papers, Box 53—Interviews, FDRL.

40. Paul Richard McGann claims that Smithdas told him about this conversation with Helen, but it's unclear exactly what she believed Bell had "lied" to her about.

41. "Printed negatives from the 80th birthday celebration for Helen Keller including Robert J. Smithdas and Anne Bancroft," June 1960, HKA.

42. Evelyn D. Seide to James S. Adams, July 19, 1961, HKA.

43. "Copy of Helen Keller's Will," Mar. 12, 1960, HKA.

44. Transcript of unpublished Lash interview with Robert Barnett, Mar. 11, 1978. In his book *Helen and Teacher*, Lash uses this quote from Barnett but conspicuously omits the qualifier—"to their own aggrandizement." Joseph Lash Papers, Box 53—Interviews, FDRL.

45. Robert Barnett to Gordon Browning, July 16, 1952, HKA.

46. Unpublished transcript of Lash interview with Frances Koestler, Oct. 31, 1978, Joseph Lash Papers, Box 53—Interviews, FDRL.

47. NBH, Box 11, NBH journal entry, Jan. 6, 1954, NBHC.

48. Keller, *World I Live In*, p. 74.

49. Author interview with Keith McGregor, manager of Canine Quality Assurance, at Leader Dogs for the Blind, who began training deafblind clients to use guide dogs in the 1980s, Aug. 23, 2002.

50. Transcript of unpublished Lash interview with Winifred Corbally, Apr. 25, 1978, Joseph Lash Papers, Box 53—Interviews, FDRL.

51. Joseph Lash to Marguerite Levine, June 1979, AFB.

52. "Helen Keller Pays Tribute to Her Devoted Teacher," *Kansas City Star*, Oct. 15, 1955, p. 9.

53. NBH, Box 11, NBH journal entry, Mar. 11, 1954, NBHC.

54. Nella Braddy Henney to Polly Thomson, Oct. 23, 1955, HKA.

55. Leslie A. Weary to Helen Keller, May 2, 1956, HKA.

56. Ibid.

57. Muriel I. Symington to Helen Keller, July 7, 1955, HKA.

58. "Birthday wishes to Elizabeth Gurley Flynn from Helen Keller," Box 1, Folder 200, WLA.

59. "Publication denouncing Communism entitled *The New Counterattack*, with a paragraph to write to Helen Keller denouncing her support of Elizabeth Gurley Flynn," vol. 9, no. 34, Aug. 26, 1955, HKA.

60. Nella Braddy Henney to Polly Thomson, Sept. 7, 1955, HKA.

61. Ibid.

62. Helen Keller to Lucy McNaught, Sept. 20, 1955, HKA.

63. Helen Keller, *The Open Door* (New York: Doubleday, 1957), p. 5.

64. Unpublished transcript of Lash interview with Ken McCormick, Nov. 8, 1977, Joseph Lash Papers, Box 53—Interviews, FDRL.

65. Helen Keller to Robert La Follette, July 27, 1924, HKA.

66. NBH, Box 11, NBH journal entry, Dec. 19, 1956, NBHC.

67. Marvel Scholl, "Why FBI Hounded Socialist Helen Keller," New York *Militant*, Sept. 9, 1977.

68. Brooks, *Helen Keller*, p. 87.

69. Unpublished transcript of Lash interview with Eric Boulter, Nov. 9, 1978, Joseph Lash Papers, Box 53—Interviews, FDRL.

70. NBH, Box 11, NBH journal entry, Nov. 14–Dec. 12, 1956, NBHC.

71. P. F. van Mekarh to Helen Keller, Mar. 1951, HKA.

72. Helen Keller to P. F. van Mekarh, date unknown, HKA.

73. "The Freedom Charter," adopted at the Congress of the People at Kliptown, Johannesburg, June 25–26, 1955.

74. Helen's original comment was issued in a letter to Arthur Blaxall in 1957 but was not printed in the bulletin until October 1958. "Miss Helen Keller from the United States," *Treason Trial Bulletin*, no. 4 (Oct. 1958), p. 9; Helen Keller to Arthur Blaxall, Nov. 8, 1957, HKA.

75. George M. House[r] to Helen Keller, Apr. 13, 1959, HKA.

Chapter Twenty-Three: The Miracle Worker

1. "Oral history interview with Margaret Brenman-Gibson," 1983, Harvard University Collections, Joint Committee on the Status of Women, HL.

2. Ibid.

3. Clifford Odets testimony before the House Un-American Activities Committee, May 19–20, 1952. In his testimony, Odets claimed that he was a member of the Communist Party for only eight months in 1934 and 1935.

4. Ken McCormick to Nella Braddy Henney, Oct. 3, 1956, HKA.

5. NBH, Box 11, NBH journal entry, Dec. 22, 1956, NBHC.

6. Ibid.

7. "Press release from CBS News, NYC, *Miracle Worker* Wins Praise of American Foundation for Blind Upcoming *Playhouse 90* Drama of Helen Keller's Childhood," Jan. 29, 1957, HKA.

8. "Document entitled 'Memo by Nella Braddy Henney on Dramatic Production of the Helen Keller Story,' outlining various aspect and legal issues surrounding Helen Keller's autobiography and dramatization of her life," undated, HKA.

9. Nella Braddy Henney to Ken McCormick, Oct. 15, 1956, HKA.

10. "Script of television broadcast from the program *Playhouse 90* entitled *The Miracle Worker* about Helen Keller and Anne Sullivan Macy, by William Gibson," HKA.

11. Nella Braddy Henney to Ken McCormick, Oct. 15, 1956, HKA.

12. "The Lively Arts," *Berkshire Eagle*, Aug. 22, 1957, p. 14.

13. NBH, Box 11, NBH journal entry, Feb. 7, 1957, NBHC.

14. Nella Braddy Henney to Helen Keller, Aug. 5, 1958, HKA.

15. Nella Braddy Henney to Helen Keller, Mar. 15, 1957, HKA.

16. Unpublished transcript of Lash interview with Ken McCormick, Nov. 8, 1977, Joseph Lash Papers, Box 53—Interviews, FDRL.

17. Henney is often described as a photographer, editor, and writer, but he was also a respected specialist in radio engineering and electronics, which may be why McCormick described him as a "scientist."

18. Herrmann, *Helen Keller*, p. 270.

19. Helen Keller to James S. Adams, 1951, HKA.

20. Unpublished transcript of Lash interview with Robert Barnett, Mar. 11, 1978, Joseph Lash Papers, Box 53—Interviews, FDRL.

21. NBH, Box 11, NBH journal entry, July 4, 1959. Although Nella discussed this in her journal for the first time on July 4, Bancroft's *Tonight Show* appearance took place on Apr. 9, 1959.

22. "Letter from James S. Adams to Nella Braddy Henney, Garden City, NY," Apr. 23, 1959, HKA.

23. Ibid.

24. Ibid.

25. Helen Keller to James Adams, July 9, 1951, HKA.

26. NBH, Box 11, NBH journal entry, July 4, 1959, NBHC.

27. Nella Braddy Henney to Helen Keller, Oct. 16, 1958, HKA.

28. Ibid.

29. NBH, Box 11, NBH journal entry, July 4, 1959, NBHC.

30. "Letter from Helen Keller, Westport, CT to Nella Braddy Henney, Garden City, NY cancelling her power of attorney," Jan. 15, 1960, HKA.

31. NBH, Box 11, NBH journal entry, Sept. 6, 1960. Nella claimed in her journal that Kit Cornell asked Helen whether it would be okay to invite Nella to Helen's eightieth birthday party in June 1960. Helen allegedly gave permission but Nella claims she decided not to go for fear of risking "public repudiation." Nella wrote Helen frequently during the final years but never received a response. Years later, on her way to New Hampshire, she dropped by Arcan Ridge one day for an unannounced visit but claimed Helen didn't recognize her.

32. Transcript of Lash interview with Peter Salmon, Joseph Lash Papers, Box 53—Interviews, FDRL.

33. "Note and letter from Helen Keller to Nella Braddy Henney, James S. Adams, M.C. Migel, and Jansen Noyes, Jr., regarding the incorporation of a clause in her will bequeathing all royalties from her writings to Nella Braddy Henney and assigning her as her literary agent," July 21, 1958, HKA.
34. James S. Adams to Jansen Noyes Jr., Mar. 17, 1960, HKA.
35. Jansen Noyes Jr. to Helen Keller, July 29, 1960, HKA.
36. "*The Miracle Worker*," IMDB Pro Box Office stats.
37. NBH, Box 11, NBH journal entry, Sept. 18, 1960, NBHC.
38. I submitted a request to the AFB asking how much the Foundation has received from *The Miracle Worker* over the years and whether the AFB still receives royalties. Haley Linville, business service manager at the AFB, responded that she could "not find records of any royalties received by AFB for *The Miracle Worker*."
39. NBH, Box 11, NBH journal entry, Apr. 4, 1960, NBHC.
40. Transcript of unpublished Lash interview with Keith Henney, Nov. 29, 1977, Joseph Lash Papers, Box 53—Interviews, FDRL.
41. Transcript of unpublished Lash interview with Winifred Corbally, Apr. 25, 1978, Joseph Lash Papers, Box 53—Interviews, FDRL.
42. Ibid.
43. Ibid.
44. Helen Keller to Lail Gillies, Aug. 22, 1960, HKA.
45. NBH, Box 11, journal entry, July 2, 1960, NBHC. Nella was not present to witness this incident, but she had been checking in regularly with Seide and Winnie Corbally to keep tabs on her old friend.
46. Dr. Forris B. Chick to Evelyn Seide, Nov. 6, 1961, HKA.
47. "Correspondence between Evelyn D. Seide, Dr. Forris B. Chick, Jansen Noyes, Jr., and James S. Adams regarding the health of Helen Keller, including the course of action after her stroke," Nov. 6, 1961, HKA.
48. Author interview with Paul Richard McGann, Sept. 24, 2021. He recalls that Robert Smithdas believed Helen had "dementia or Alzheimer's disease" in her final years.
49. Coretta Scott King to Winifred Corbally, June 3, 1968, HKA.
50. Winifred A. Corbally to Phillips and Ravia Keller, Dec. 9, 1964, HKA.
51. Phillips Keller to Winifred A. Corbally, Apr. 7, 1965, HKA.
52. Ibid.
53. Phillips Keller to Winifred Corbally, Sept. 20, 1965, HKA.
54. Phillips Keller to Winifred Corbally, Apr. 9, 1968, HKA.
55. Phillips was eleven years younger than Helen. She did spend one summer with her brother and his equally conservative wife, Ravia, at their Dallas home, but the experience was not a pleasant one, according to Polly, who told Nella that Helen had no desire to live with Phillips.
56. Phillips Keller to Winifred A. Corbally and James S. Adams, Oct. 21, 1967, HKA.
57. "Copy of eulogy given by Senator Lister Hill at Helen Keller's funeral," HKA.
58. "Letter from E. Seide forwarding Helen Keller's final wishes regarding funeral services," July 19, 1961, HKA.

59. M. R. Barnett to Nella Braddy Henney, Oct. 6, 1966, HKA.

60. "Letter from E. Seide forwarding Helen Keller's final wishes regarding funeral services," July 19, 1961, HKA.

61. Describing the service to Joseph Lash, Winnie Corbally mentioned "the poor people's march with tents in the capital."

62. Dr. Martin Luther King Jr., *Where Do We Go from Here: Chaos or Community?* (Boston: Beacon Press, 1967), p. 165.

63. "Speech written by Helen Keller about the blindness of society to its problems," 1912, HKA.

Chapter Twenty-Four: Helen and Teacher

1. Van Wyck Brooks, *Helen Keller, Sketch for a Portrait* (New York: Dutton, 1956).

2. Catherine Owens Peare, *The Helen Keller Story* (New York: Thomas Y. Crowell, 1959).

3. Jansen Noyes Jr. to Garfield Merner, undated, HKA.

4. Joseph Lash, *Helen and Teacher* (New York: Delacorte, 1980).

5. "Horror Expressed Following Report," *Birmingham News*, July 23, 1981; "Let the Dead Rest Is Reaction to Story on Helen Keller Politics," *Birmingham News*, July 12, 1981.

6. "Joseph Lash Is Dead," *New York Times*, Aug. 23, 1987, p. 40.

7. Ibid.

8. In their 1998 study, *The Soviet World of American Communism*, historians John Haynes, Harvey Klehr, and Kyrill M. Anderson document a loss of approximately 13 percent of party members after the pact, contradicting the dubious claim of Jeffrey Burds in a book review of *The American History of Communism* published in the *American Historical Review* (vol. 124, no. 2 [Apr. 2019], pp. 595–99) that "more than three quarters of American Communists (including most Jews) would abruptly resign from the Communist Party after the Pact." Haynes and Klehr document CPUSA membership at a peak of 66,000 in January 1939, falling to 50,000 members by January 1941, though the party had dropped from its rolls 7,500 immigrants who weren't US citizens, which accounts for approximately 50 percent of that loss. A number of other historians have concurred that Burds's claim is vastly inflated. It is impossible, of course, to estimate how many Fellow Travelers distanced themselves from the party after August 1939.

9. "Secret Hoover Files Show Misuse of FBI," *Washington Post*, Dec. 12, 1983. In 1983, a cache of declassified FBI files revealed that an FBI agent named G. C. Burton had written a memo in 1943 revealing that two colonels had told him the army counterintelligence corps had brought FDR tapes that purported to capture Eleanor Roosevelt having sex in a hotel room with Lash, who was a thirty-three-year-old Army Air Corps sergeant at the time and allegedly under surveillance for suspected involvement with leftist groups. Lash later vehemently denied the affair.

10. Lash, *HAT*, p. 704.

11. Ibid., p. 14.

12. "Biographical interview, article, and letters of congratulations regarding the retirement of archivist Marguerite Levine from the Helen Keller Archive at the American Foundation for the Blind," Apr. 1985, AFB.

13. "Helen Likes Beer," blog post by Justin Gardner, June 1, 2021, APH.

14. "Biographical interview, article, and letters of congratulations regarding the retirement of archivist Marguerite Levine from the Helen Keller Archive at the American Foundation for the Blind," Apr. 1985, AFB.

15. Unpublished transcript of Joseph Lash interview with Robert Barnett, Mar. 11, 1978, Joseph Lash Papers, Box 53—Interviews, FDRL.

16. Joseph Lash to Marguerite Levine, Dec. 26, 1981, AFB.

17. Joseph Lash to William Gibson, Feb. 21, 1981, AFB.

18. Patricia Smith to Joseph Lash, Apr. 7, 1978, AFB.

19. Transcript of unpublished Lash interview with Nancy Hamilton, Joseph Lash Papers, Box 53—Interviews, FDRL.

20. Joseph Lash to Patricia Smith, Aug. 2, 1978, AFB.

21. Joseph Lash to Marguerite Levine, Dec. 26, 1981, AFB.

22. Nielsen, *Radical Lives*, 9; Nielsen, *Helen Keller: Selected Writings*, 235.

23. Keller, *Open Door*, p. 134.

24. Nielsen, *BTMW*, introduction.

Epilogue

1. Olivia B. Waxman, "Co-Founding the ACLU, Fighting for Labor Rights and Other Helen Keller Accomplishments Students Don't Learn in School," *Time*, Dec. 15, 2020.

2. Ted Cruz tweet, Dec. 17, 2020.

3. Donald Trump Jr. tweet, Dec. 17, 2020.

4. Stella Young TedX Talk, Sydney, Australia, 2014.

5. Cristina Hartmann, "Helen Keller's Shadow: Why We Need to Stop Making Movies about Helen Keller," *Disability Visibility Project*, Nov. 15, 2021.

6. Email from Marc Safman to Paul Richard McGann, Feb. 15, 2022.

7. Haben Girma, "Texas, Keep Helen Keller in Your Schools," *Santa Fe New Mexican*, Sept. 24, 2018.

8. Haben Girma Facebook post, June 24, 2020.

9. Author interview with a producer of *Becoming Helen Keller*, Jan. 25, 2022.

10. Keller, *Midstream*, p. 173.

Index

About the Author

Max Wallace is a *New York Times* bestselling author, historian, and disability advocate. His books include *The American Axis*, about the Nazi collaboration of two American icons, Charles Lindbergh and Henry Ford; and *Muhammad Ali's Greatest Fight*, about Ali's battle against the US government over the Vietnam War, which was later adapted into a Hollywood movie directed by Stephen Frears. In 2018, his book *In the Name of Humanity* won the Canadian Jewish Literature Award for Holocaust history. For more than a decade, Wallace has written video description for AMI-TV, the world's first television network for blind and visually impaired people.